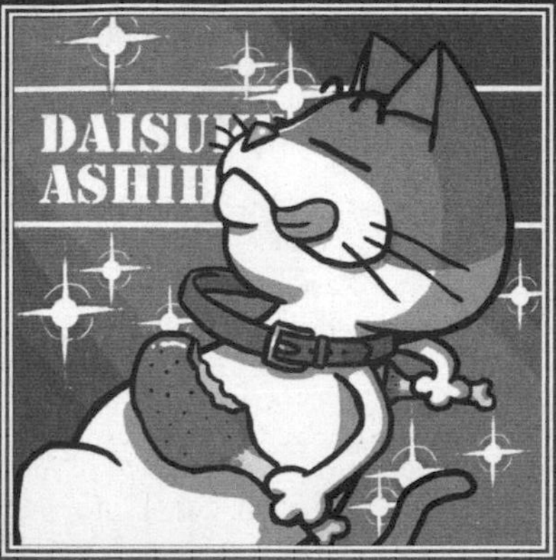
DAISU
ASHIH

At this very moment, all over the world, Daisuke Ashihara is getting fatter at the speed of one person every fifteen minutes. Here's ***World Trigger*** 5.

—**Daisuke Ashihara, 2014**

Daisuke Ashihara began his manga career at the age of 27 when his manga ***Room 303*** won second place in the 75th Tezuka Awards. His first series, ***Super Dog Rilienthal***, began serialization in ***Weekly Shonen Jump*** in 2009. ***World Trigger*** is his second serialized work in ***Weekly Shonen Jump***. He is also the author of several shorter works, including the one-shots ***Super Dog Rilienthal***, ***Trigger Keeper*** and ***Elite Agent Jin***.

WORLD TRIGGER VOL. 5
SHONEN JUMP Manga Edition

STORY AND ART BY DAISUKE ASHIHARA

Translation/Lillian Olsen
Touch-Up Art & Lettering/Annaliese Christman
Design/Sam Elzway
Editor/Hope Donovan

Printed in the U.S.A.

Published by VIZ Media, LLC
P.O. Box 77010
San Francisco, CA 94107

10 9 8 7 6 5 4 3 2 1
First printing, April 2015

SHONEN JUMP MANGA EDITION

5

WORLD TRIGGER

DAISUKE ASHIHARA

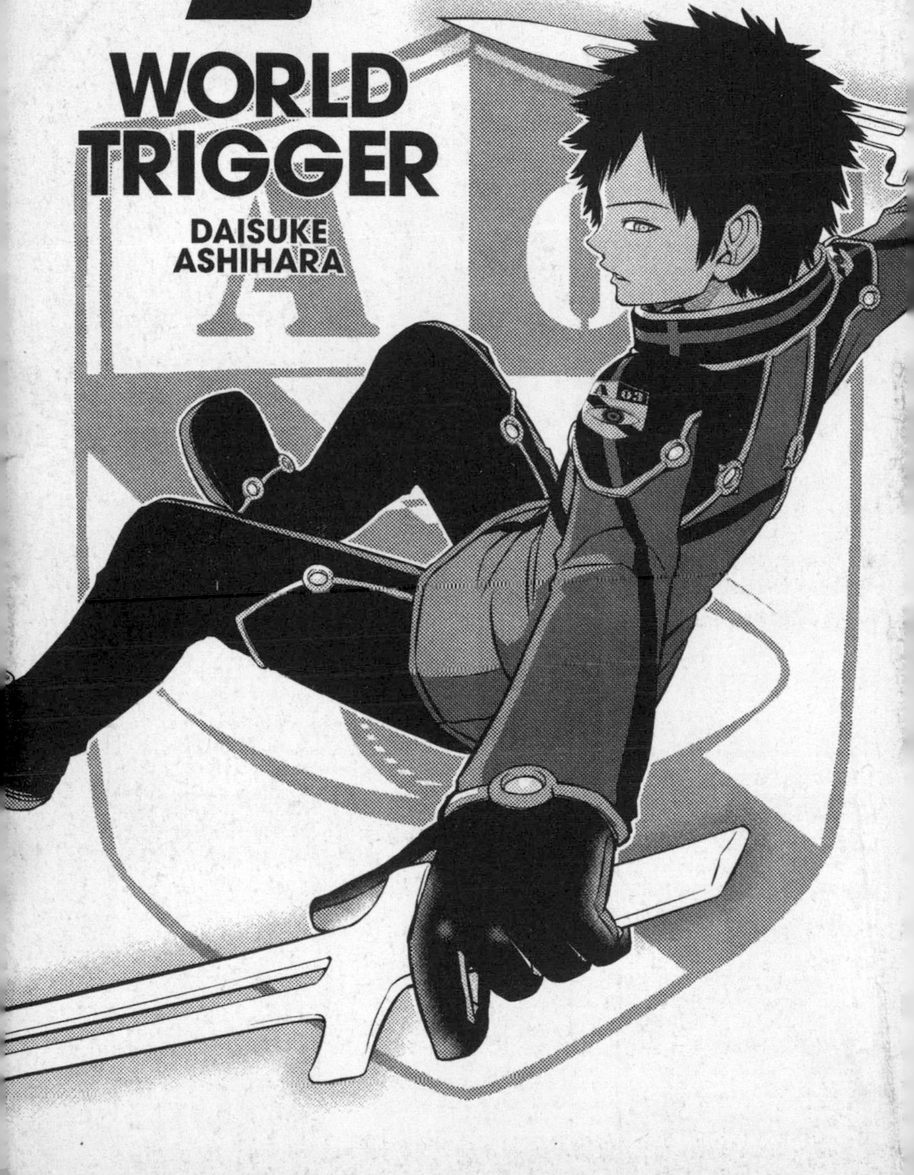

WORLD TRIGGER DATA BASE

NEIGHBOR

Invaders from another dimension that enter Mikado City through Gates. Most "Neighbors" here are Trion soldiers built for war. The Neighbors who actually live on the other side of the Gates are human, like Yuma.

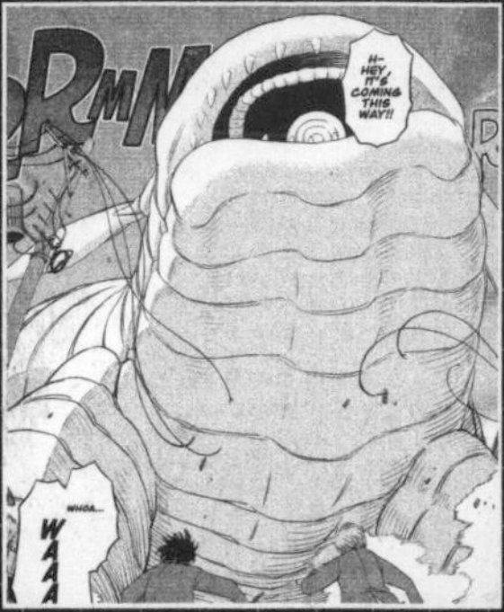
H-HEY, IT'S COMING THIS WAY!!
WHOA...

Trion solider built for war. ▶

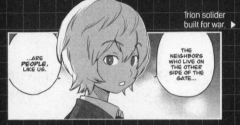

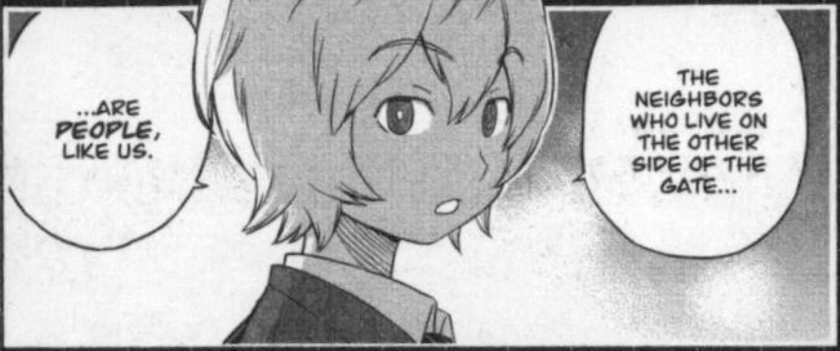
THE NEIGHBORS WHO LIVE ON THE OTHER SIDE OF THE GATE...
...ARE PEOPLE, LIKE US.

Invasion ▽ BORDER △ Resistance

An agency that protects the city from Neighbors. Agents are classified as follows: C-Rank for trainees, B-Rank for main forces and A-Rank for elites and S-rank for those with Black Triggers. Osamu's squad is trying to make A-Rank, so they can go on away missions to the Neighborhood.

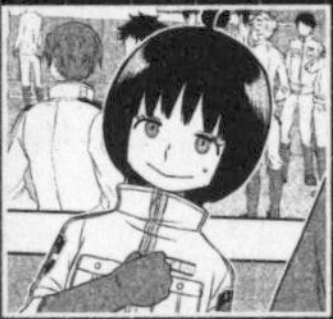

C-Rank: Chika

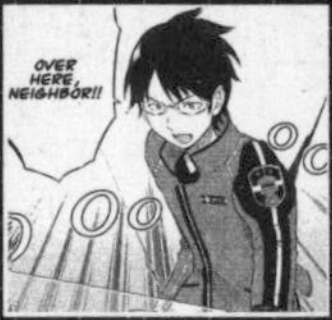
OVER HERE, NEIGHBOR!!

B-Rank: Osamu

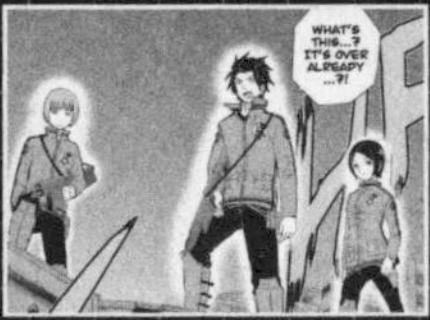
WHAT'S THIS...? IT'S OVER ALREADY...?!

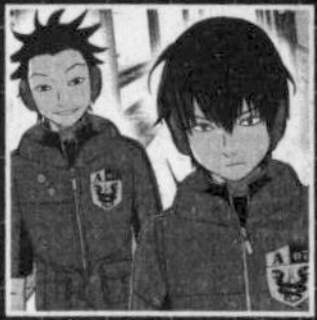

A-Rank: Arashiyama Squad, Miwa Squad

Trigger

A technology created by Neighbors to manipulate Trion. Used mainly as weapons, Triggers come in various types. Border classifies them into three groups: Attacker, Gunner and Sniper.

▶ Attacker Trigger

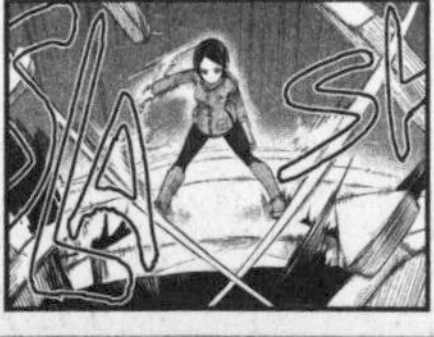

▶ Gunner Trigger

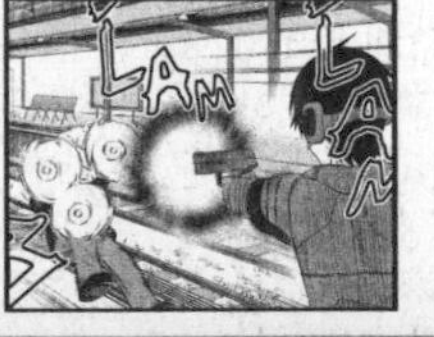

▶ Sniper Trigger

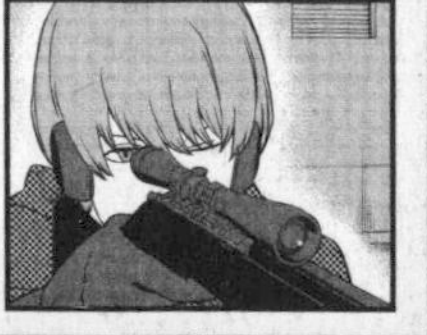

Black Trigger

A special Trigger created when a skilled user pours their entire life force and Trion into a Trigger. Outperforms regular Triggers, but the user must be compatible with the personality of the creator, meaning only a few people can use any given Black Trigger.

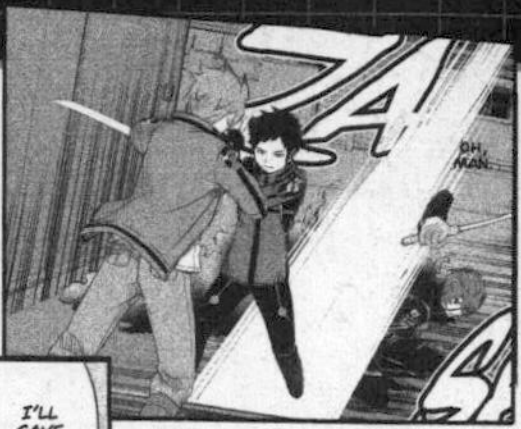
OH, MAN.

▲ The Black Trigger Fujin can transmit a slashing attack through objects within sight.

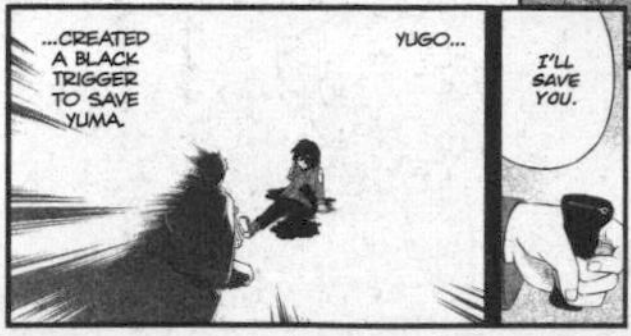
I'LL SAVE YOU.
YUGO...
...CREATED A BLACK TRIGGER TO SAVE YUMA.

▶ Yuma's father Yugo sacrificed his life to create a Black Trigger and save Yuma.

Trion

Energy supply for Triggers. Everyone has a Trion gland, but there is individual variation. Two people using the same Trigger may get different results.

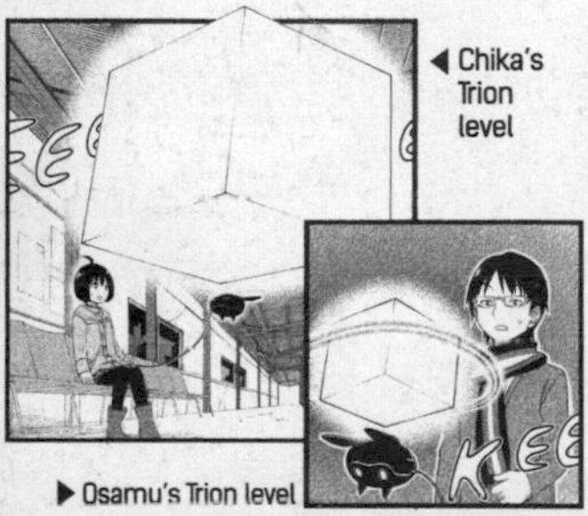

◀ Chika's Trion level

▶ Osamu's Trion level

Side Effect

Term for extrasensory perception abilities manifested by rare individuals with high Trion levels. A Side Effect is not a supernatural ability; rather, it is an extension of a human ability.

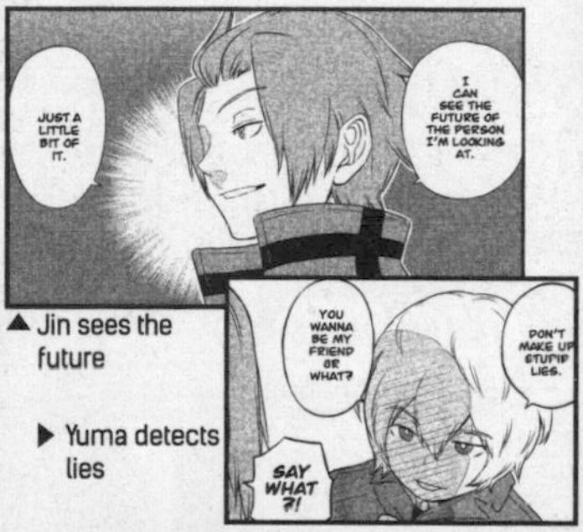
I CAN SEE THE FUTURE OF THE PERSON I'M LOOKING AT.
JUST A LITTLE BIT OF IT.
DON'T MAKE UP STUPID LIES.
YOU WANNA BE MY FRIEND OR WHAT?
SAY WHAT?!

▲ Jin sees the future

▶ Yuma detects lies

STORY

About four years ago, a Gate connecting to another dimension opened in Mikado City, leading to the appearance of invaders called Neighbors. After the establishment of the Border Defense Agency, people were able to return to their normal lives.

Osamu Mikumo is a junior high student who meets Yuma Kuga, a Neighbor. Yuma is friendly, but Border HQ orders his capture! S-Rank agent Yuichi Jin is appointed to the task, but recruits Yuma to Border instead. Osamu, Yuma and Chika decide to work together toward making A-Rank as agents from the Tamakoma branch. Meanwhile, Jin and Arashiyama Squad stop the top squads from HQ who come after Yuma's Black Trigger. Jin gets permission for Yuma to join Border in exchange for his Black Trigger, and enlistment day safely arrives. Yuma and Chika stand out with their extraordinary skills, but Osamu is the one who A-Rank agent Kazama challenges to a duel!

WORLD TRIGGER CHARACTERS

TAMAKOMA BRANCH

Understanding toward Neighbors. Considered divergent from Border's main philosophy.

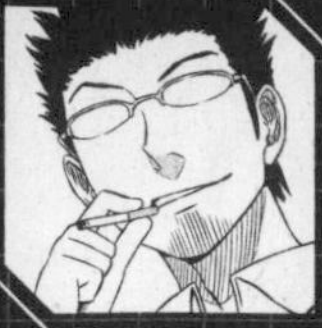

TAKUMI RINDO

Tamakoma Branch Director

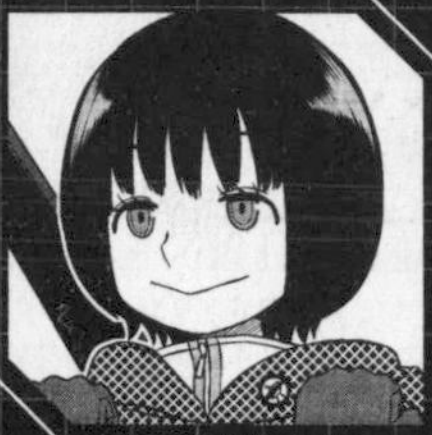

CHIKA AMATORI

Targeted by Neighbors because of her high Trion levels.

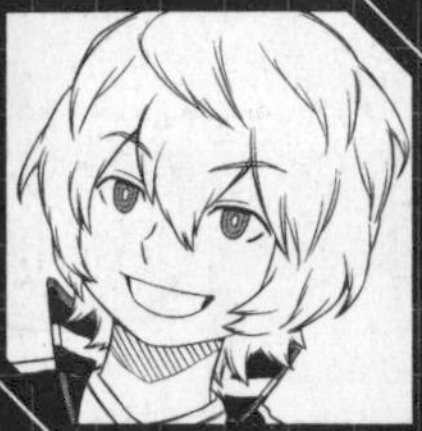

YUMA KUGA

Since he's a Neighbor, he lacks common sense. Has a Black Trigger.

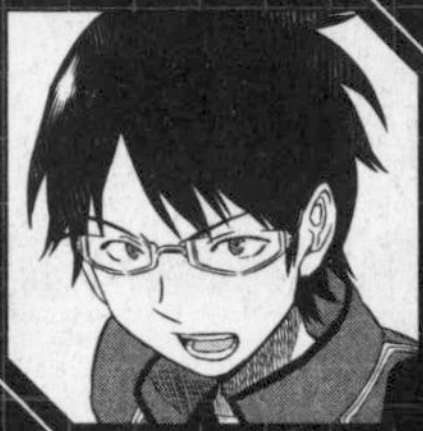

OSAMU MIKUMO

Ninth-grader who's compelled to help those in trouble. Border agent.

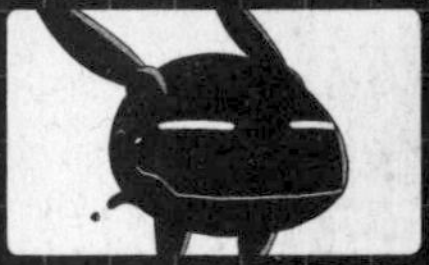

REPLICA

Yuma's chaperone.

TAMAKOMA-1

Tamakoma's A-Rank squad.

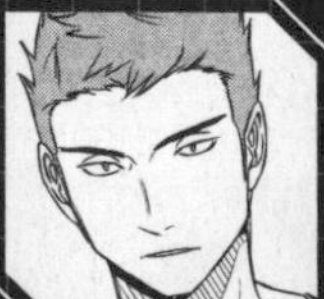

REIJI KIZAKI

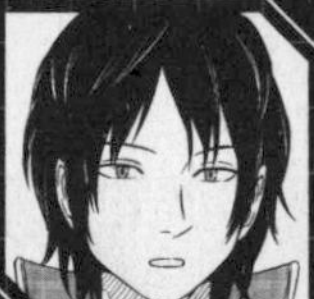

KYOSUKE KARASUMA

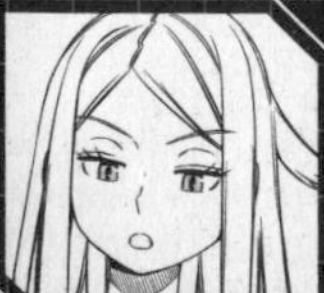

KIRIE KONAMI

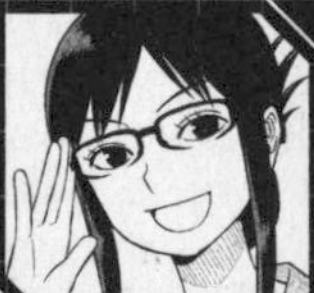

SHIORI USAMI

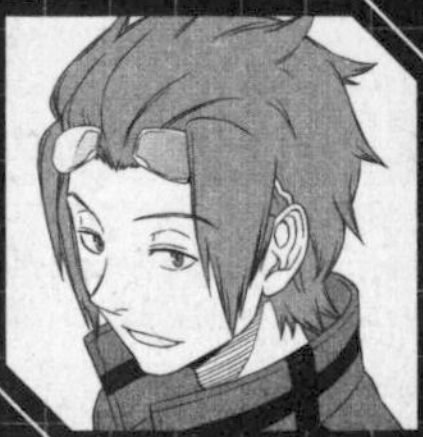

YUICHI JIN

Former S-Rank Black Trigger user. His Side Effect lets him see the future.

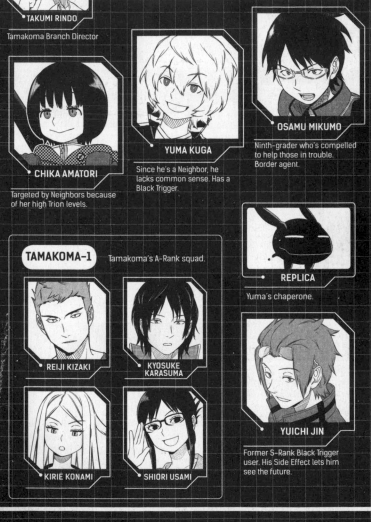

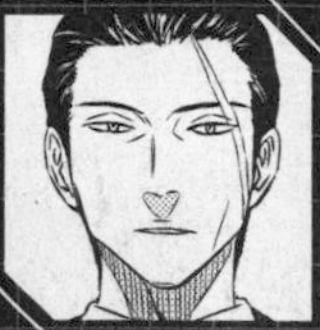

MASAMUNE KIDO

HQ Commander

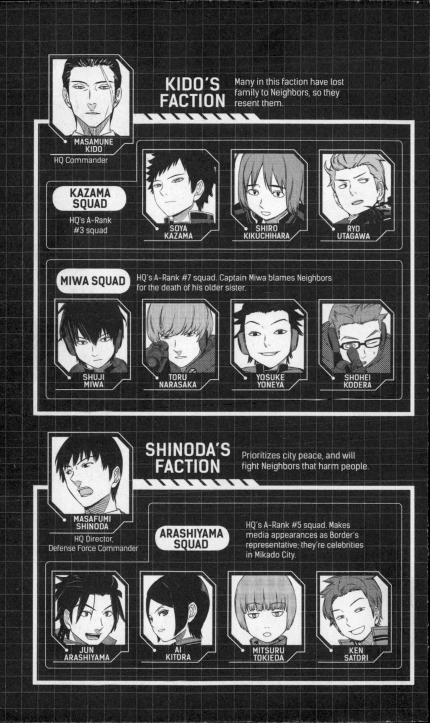

KIDO'S FACTION

Many in this faction have lost family to Neighbors, so they resent them.

KAZAMA SQUAD

HQ's A-Rank #3 squad

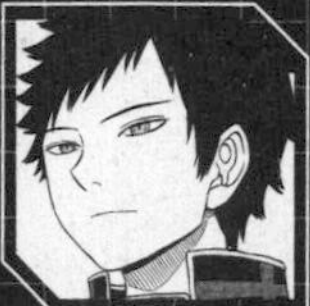

SOYA KAZAMA

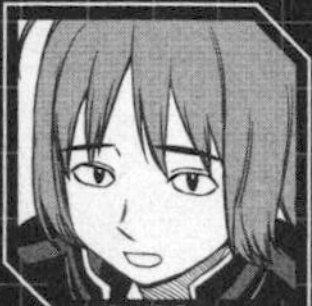

SHIRO KIKUCHIHARA

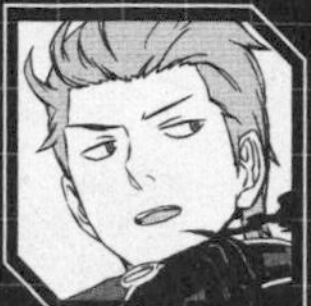

RYO UTAGAWA

MIWA SQUAD

HQ's A-Rank #7 squad. Captain Miwa blames Neighbors for the death of his older sister.

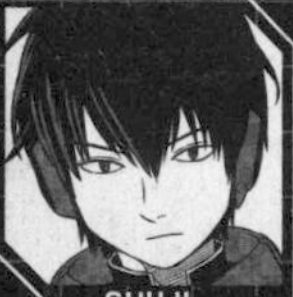

SHUJI MIWA

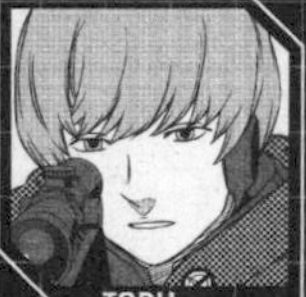

TORU NARASAKA

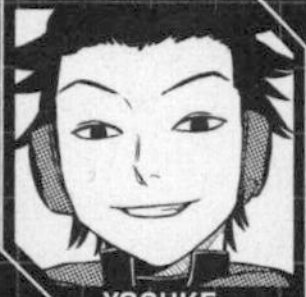

YOSUKE YONEYA

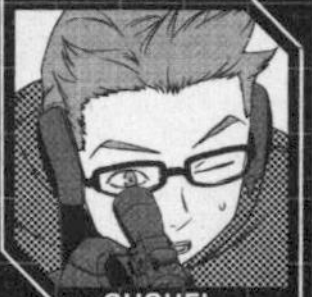

SHOHEI KODERA

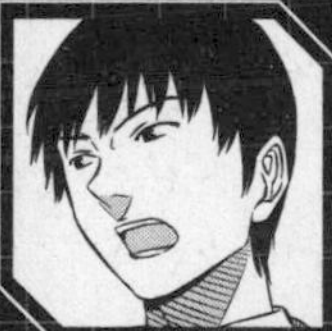

MASAFUMI SHINODA

HQ Director, Defense Force Commander

SHINODA'S FACTION

Prioritizes city peace, and will fight Neighbors that harm people.

ARASHIYAMA SQUAD

HQ's A-Rank #5 squad. Makes media appearances as Border's representative; they're celebrities in Mikado City.

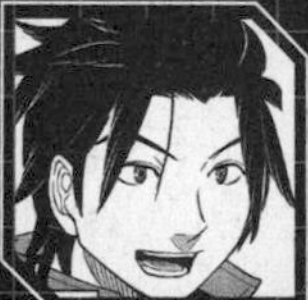

JUN ARASHIYAMA

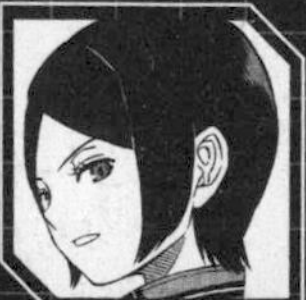

AI KITORA

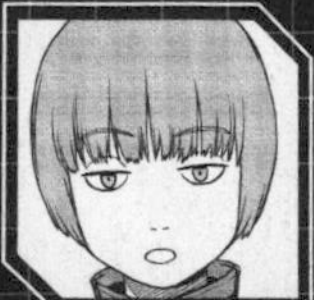

MITSURU TOKIEDA

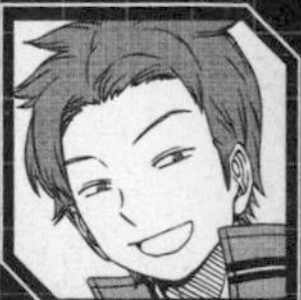

KEN SATORI

WORLD TRIGGER

CONTENTS

5

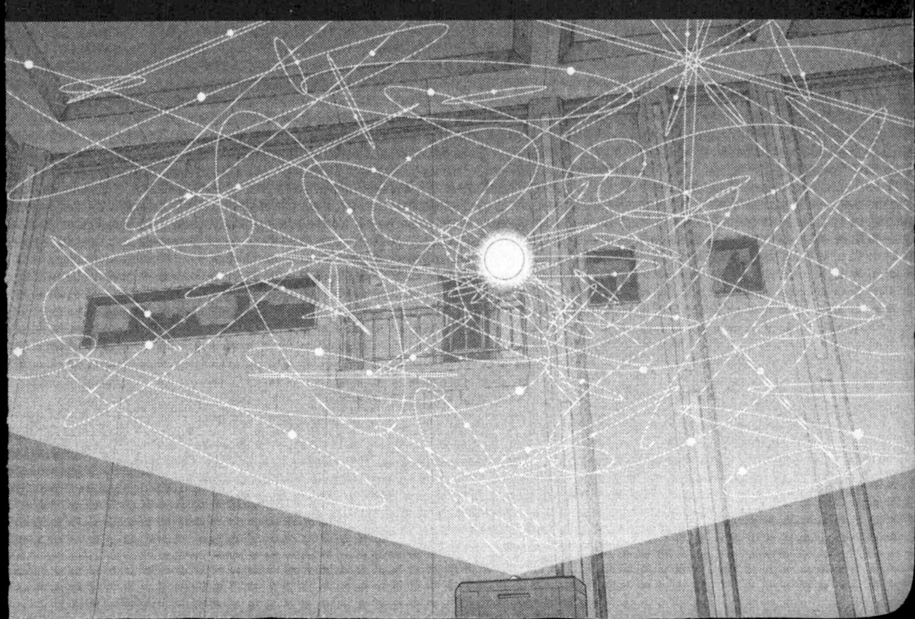

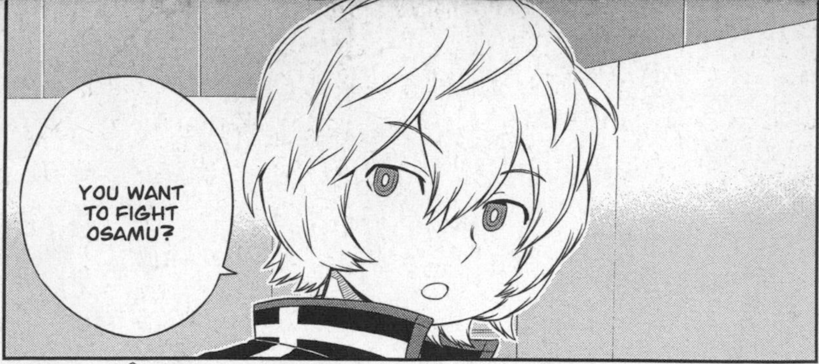
YOU WANT TO FIGHT OSAMU?

Chapter 35 Osamu Mikumo: Part 4

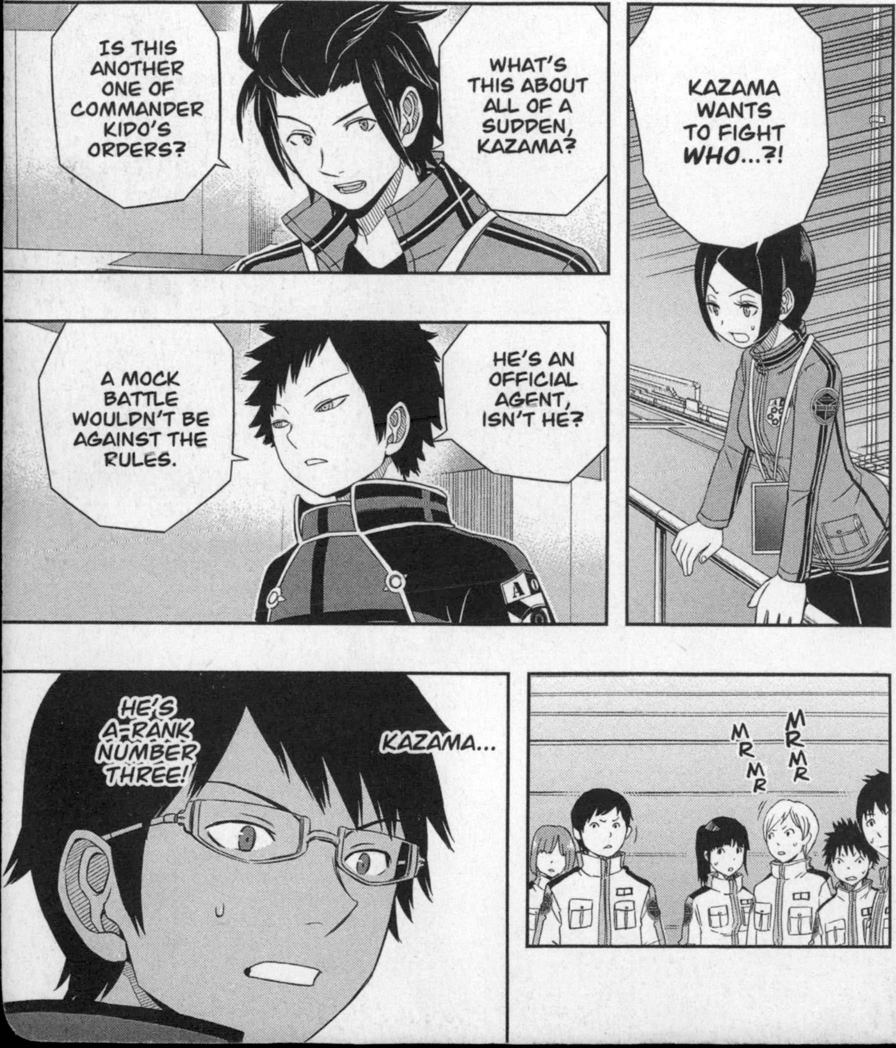
KAZAMA WANTS TO FIGHT WHO...?!
WHAT'S THIS ABOUT ALL OF A SUDDEN, KAZAMA?
IS THIS ANOTHER ONE OF COMMANDER KIDO'S ORDERS?
HE'S AN OFFICIAL AGENT, ISN'T HE?
A MOCK BATTLE WOULDN'T BE AGAINST THE RULES.
MRMR
MRMR
KAZAMA...
HE'S A-RANK NUMBER THREE!

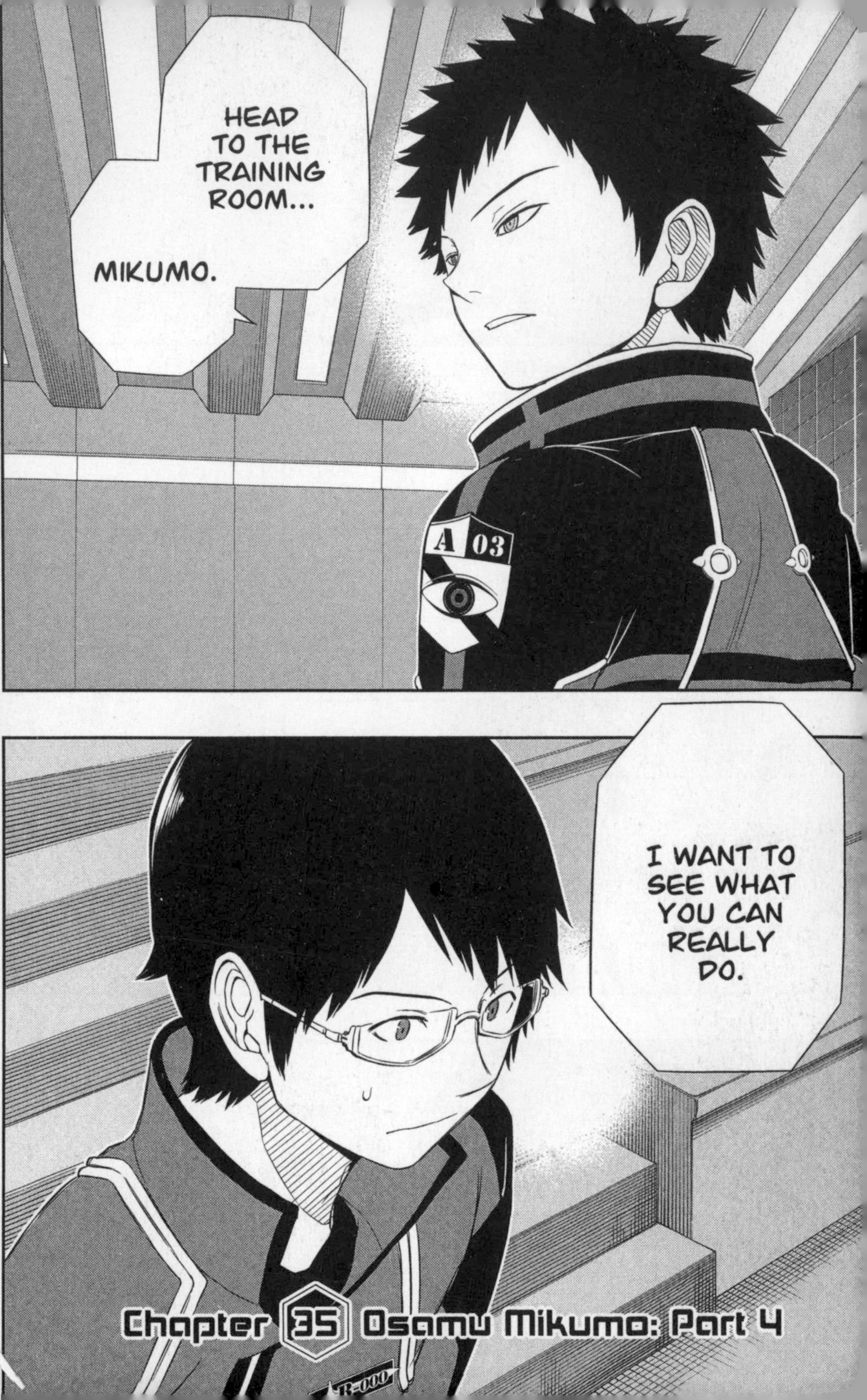
HEAD TO THE TRAINING ROOM... MIKUMO.
I WANT TO SEE WHAT YOU CAN REALLY DO.
A 03
Chapter 35 Osamu Mikumo: Part 4

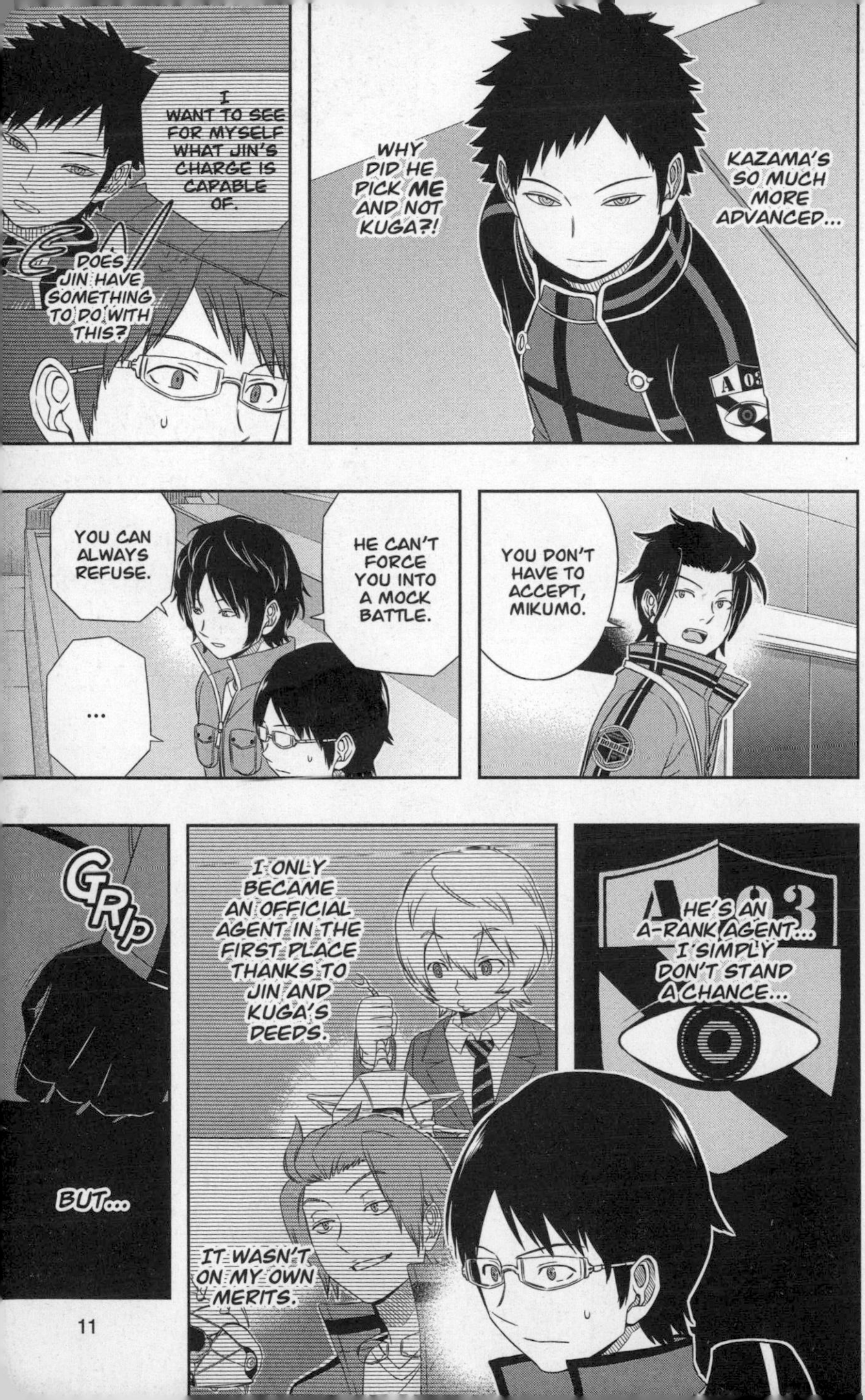
KAZAMA'S SO MUCH MORE ADVANCED...
WHY DID HE PICK ME AND NOT KUGA?!
I WANT TO SEE FOR MYSELF WHAT JIN'S CHARGE IS CAPABLE OF.
DOES JIN HAVE SOMETHING TO DO WITH THIS?
YOU DON'T HAVE TO ACCEPT, MIKUMO.
HE CAN'T FORCE YOU INTO A MOCK BATTLE.
YOU CAN ALWAYS REFUSE.
...
HE'S AN A-RANK AGENT... I SIMPLY DON'T STAND A CHANCE...
I ONLY BECAME AN OFFICIAL AGENT IN THE FIRST PLACE THANKS TO JIN AND KUGA'S DEEDS.
IT WASN'T ON MY OWN MERITS.
GRIP
BUT...

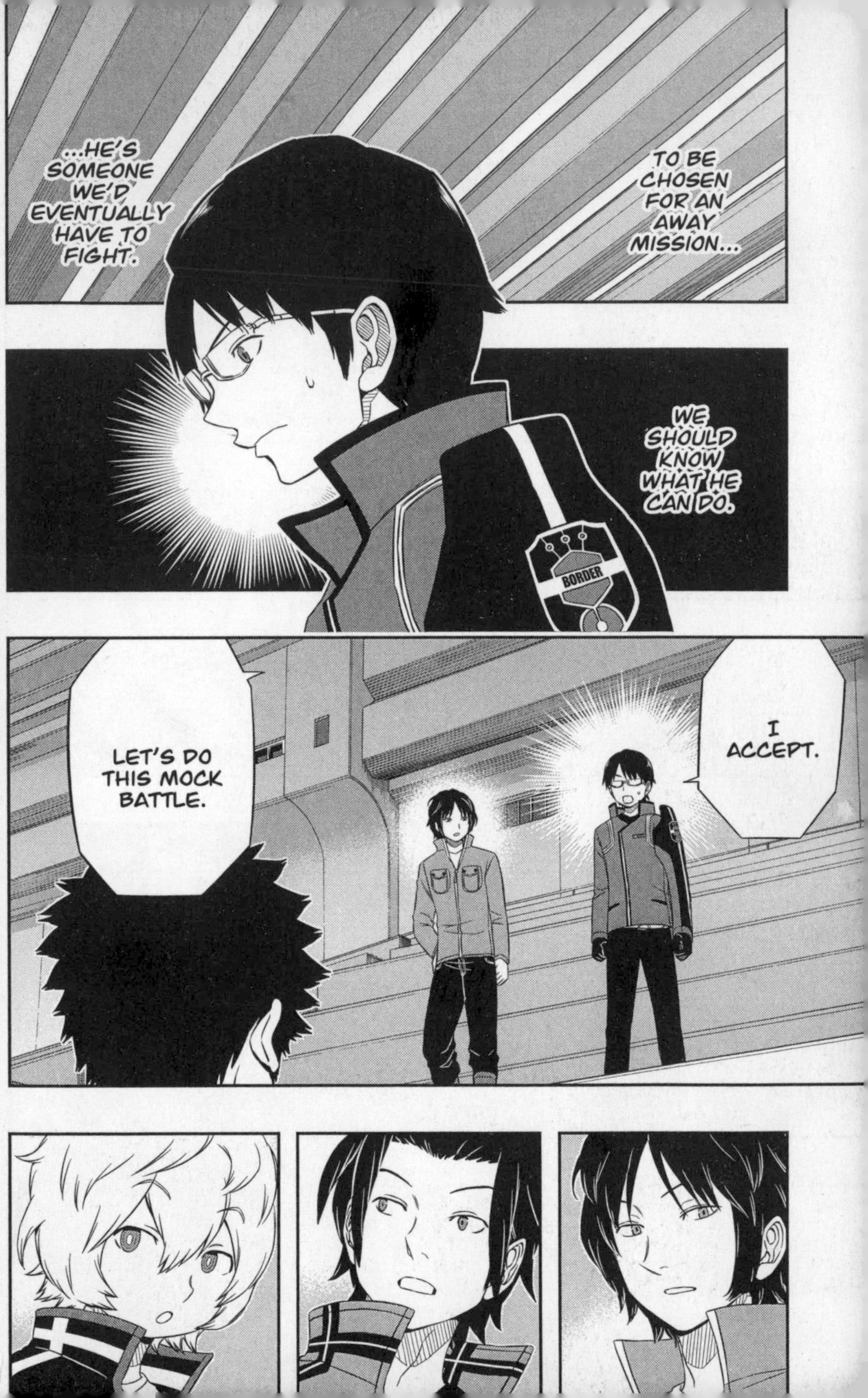

TO BE CHOSEN FOR AN AWAY MISSION...
...HE'S SOMEONE WE'D EVENTUALLY HAVE TO FIGHT.
WE SHOULD KNOW WHAT HE CAN DO.
BORDER
I ACCEPT.
LET'S DO THIS MOCK BATTLE.

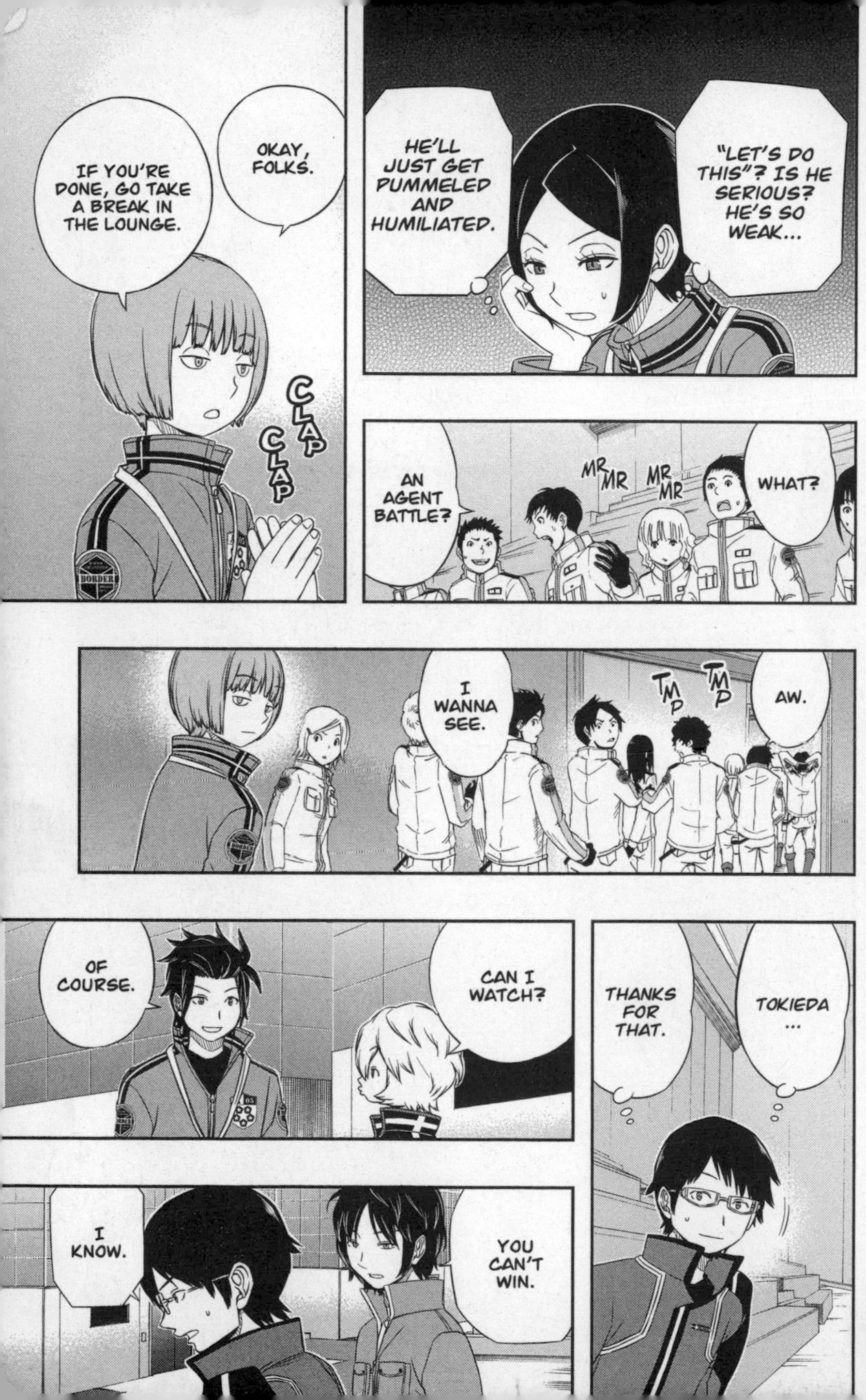
"LET'S DO THIS"? IS HE SERIOUS? HE'S SO WEAK...
HE'LL JUST GET PUMMELED AND HUMILIATED.
WHAT?
MR MR
MR MR
AN AGENT BATTLE?
OKAY, FOLKS.
IF YOU'RE DONE, GO TAKE A BREAK IN THE LOUNGE.
CLAP
CLAP
AW.
TMP
TMP
I WANNA SEE.
TOKIEDA...
THANKS FOR THAT.
CAN I WATCH?
OF COURSE.
YOU CAN'T WIN.
I KNOW.

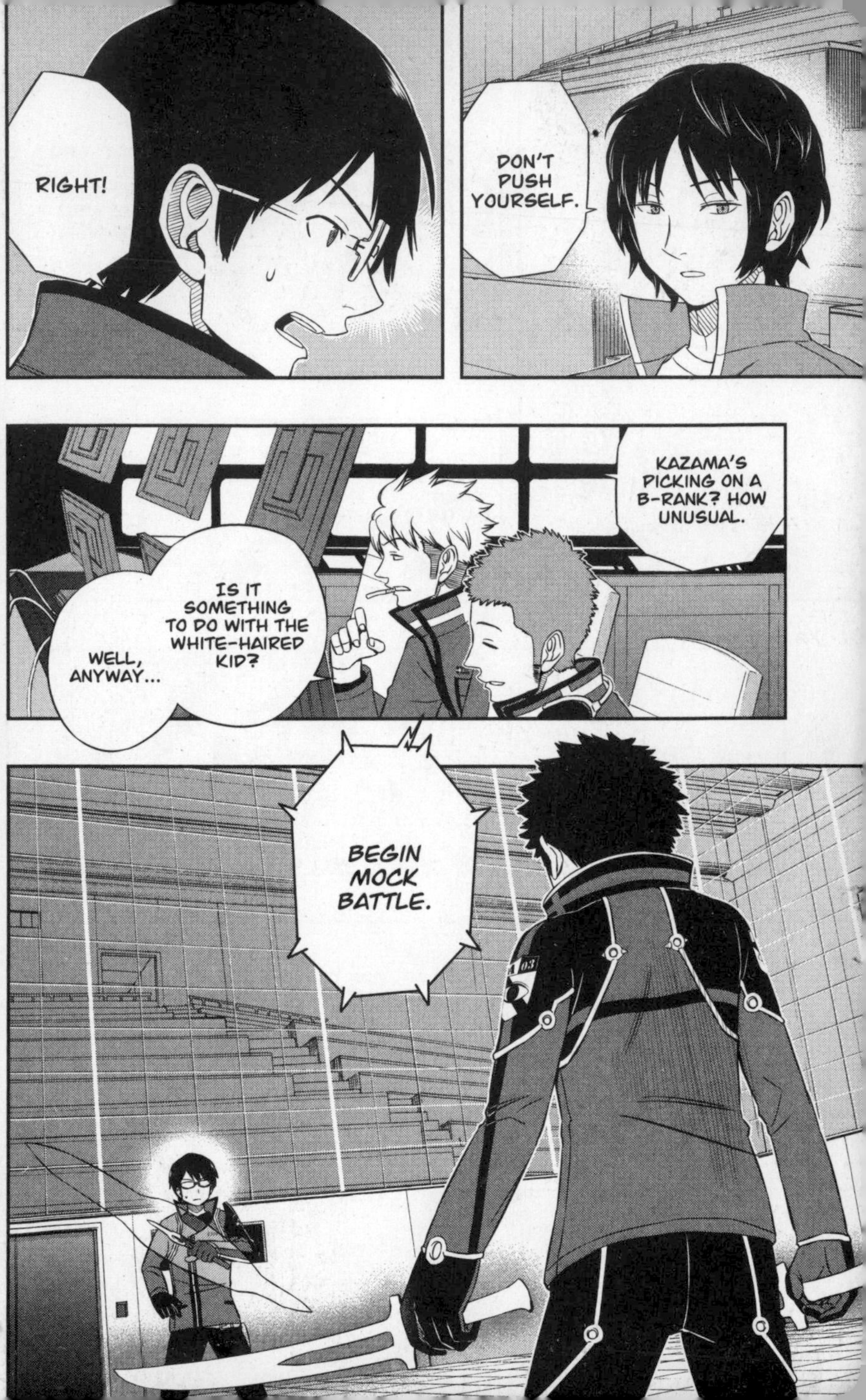
DON'T PUSH YOURSELF.
RIGHT!
KAZAMA'S PICKING ON A B-RANK? HOW UNUSUAL.
IS IT SOMETHING TO DO WITH THE WHITE-HAIRED KID?
WELL, ANYWAY...
BEGIN MOCK BATTLE.

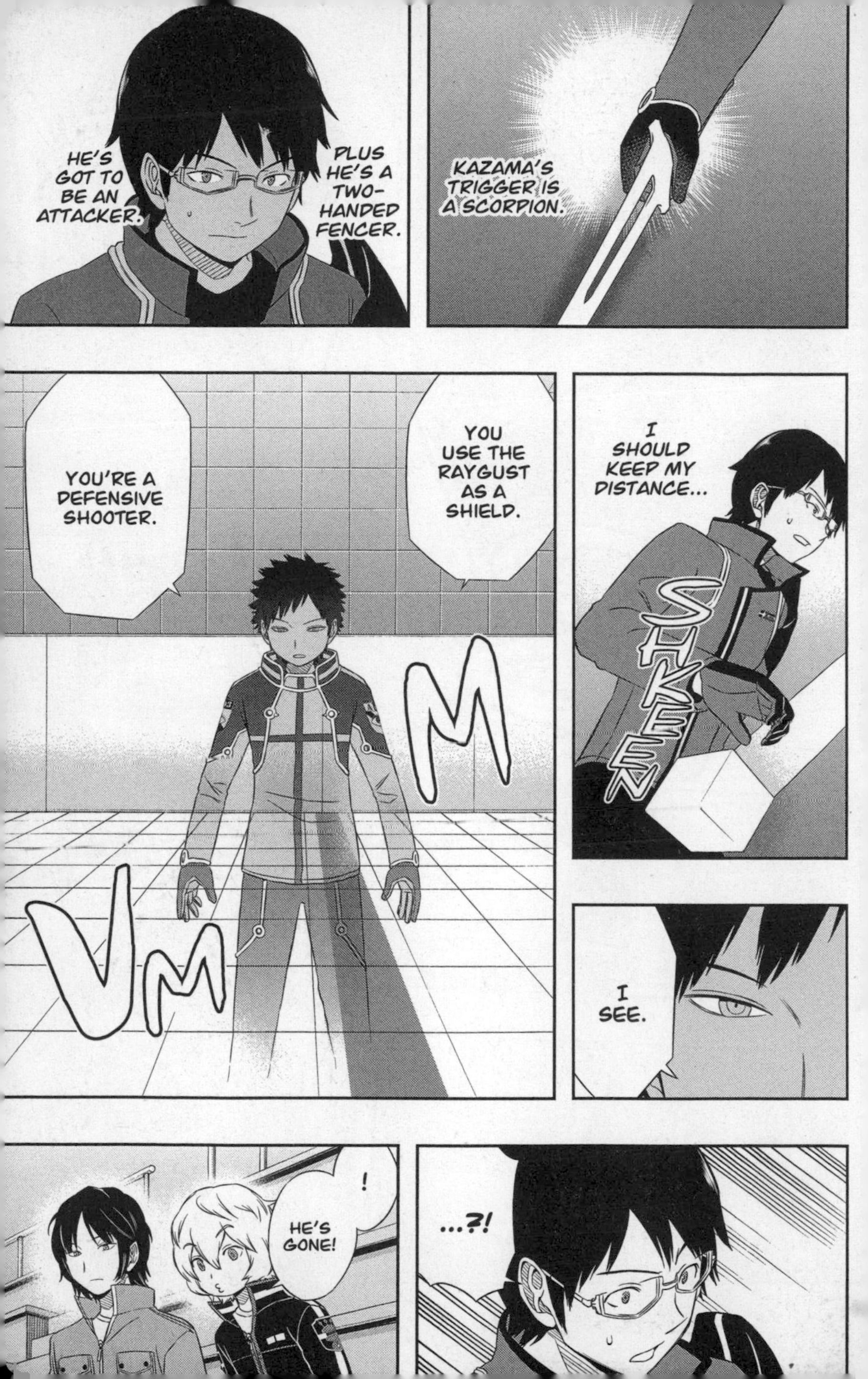
KAZAMA'S TRIGGER IS A SCORPION.
PLUS HE'S A TWO-HANDED FENCER.
HE'S GOT TO BE AN ATTACKER.
I SHOULD KEEP MY DISTANCE...
SHKEEN
I SEE.
YOU USE THE RAYGUST AS A SHIELD.
YOU'RE A DEFENSIVE SHOOTER.
VMM
...?!
!
HE'S GONE!

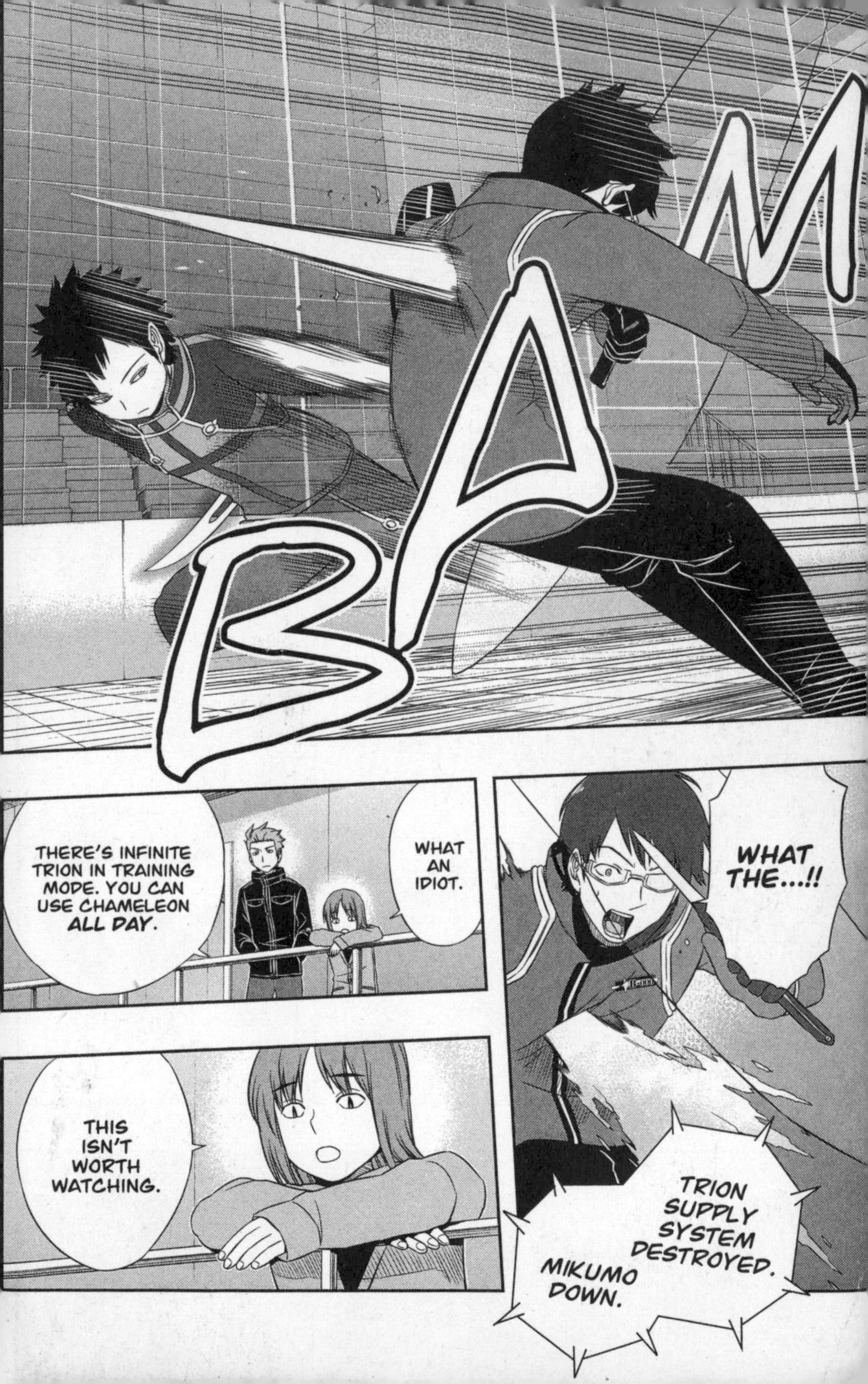
BAM
WHAT THE...!!
TRION SUPPLY SYSTEM DESTROYED.
MIKUMO DOWN.
WHAT AN IDIOT.
THERE'S INFINITE TRION IN TRAINING MODE. YOU CAN USE CHAMELEON ALL DAY.
THIS ISN'T WORTH WATCHING.

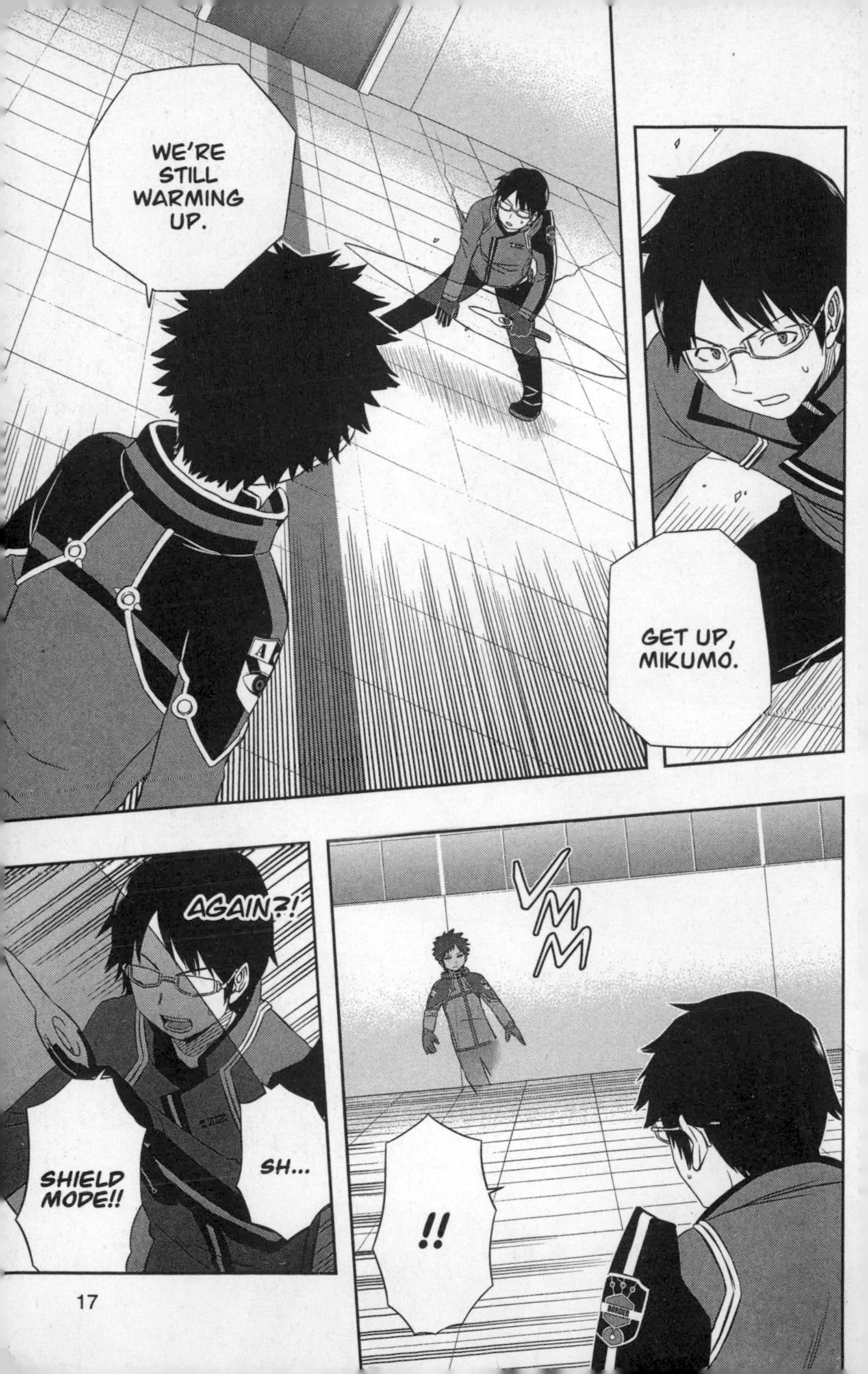

GET UP, MIKUMO.
WE'RE STILL WARMING UP.
VMM
!!
AGAIN?!
SH...
SHIELD MODE!!

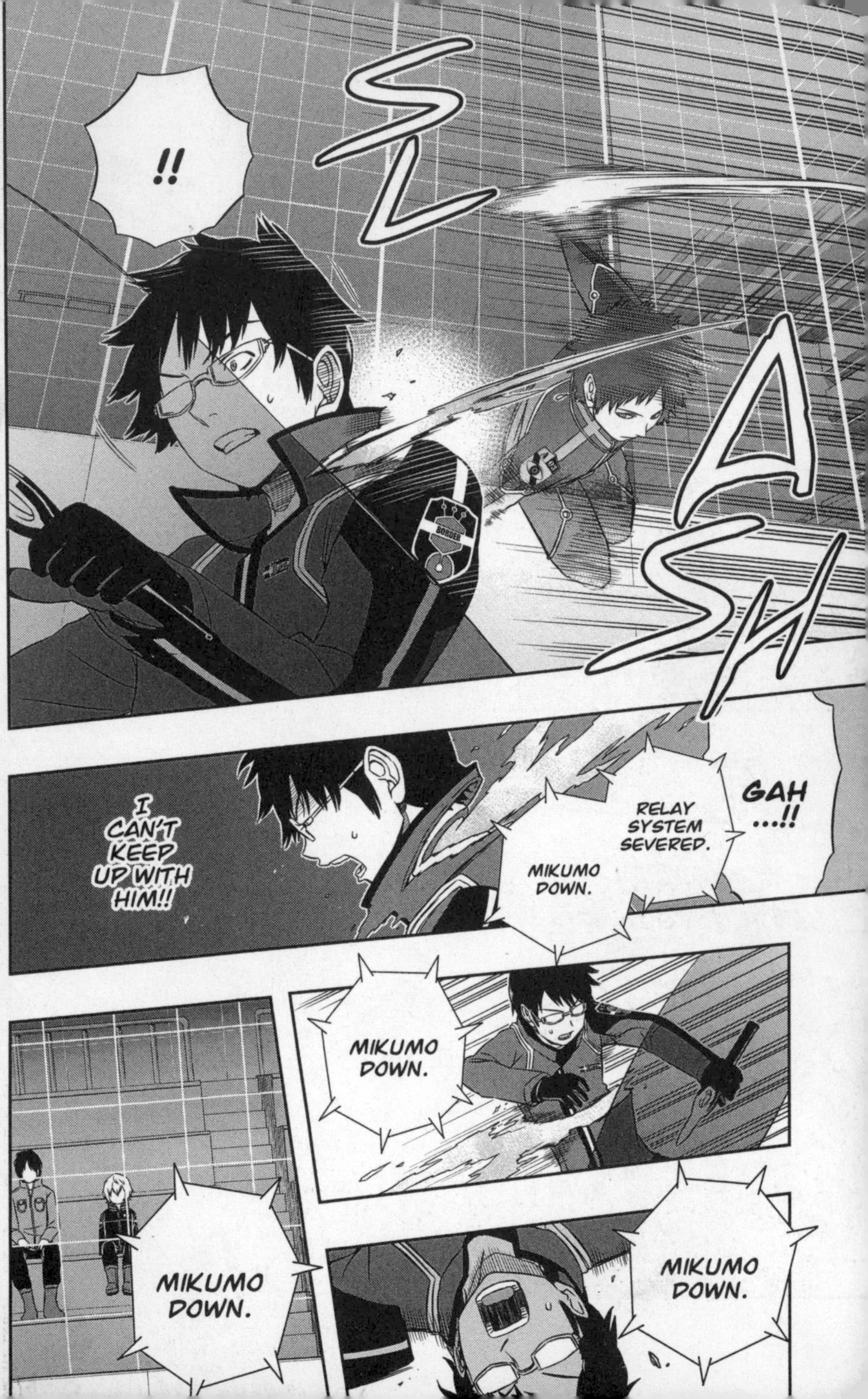
SLASH
!!
GAH ...!!
RELAY SYSTEM SEVERED.
MIKUMO DOWN.
I CAN'T KEEP UP WITH HIM!!
MIKUMO DOWN.
MIKUMO DOWN.
MIKUMO DOWN.

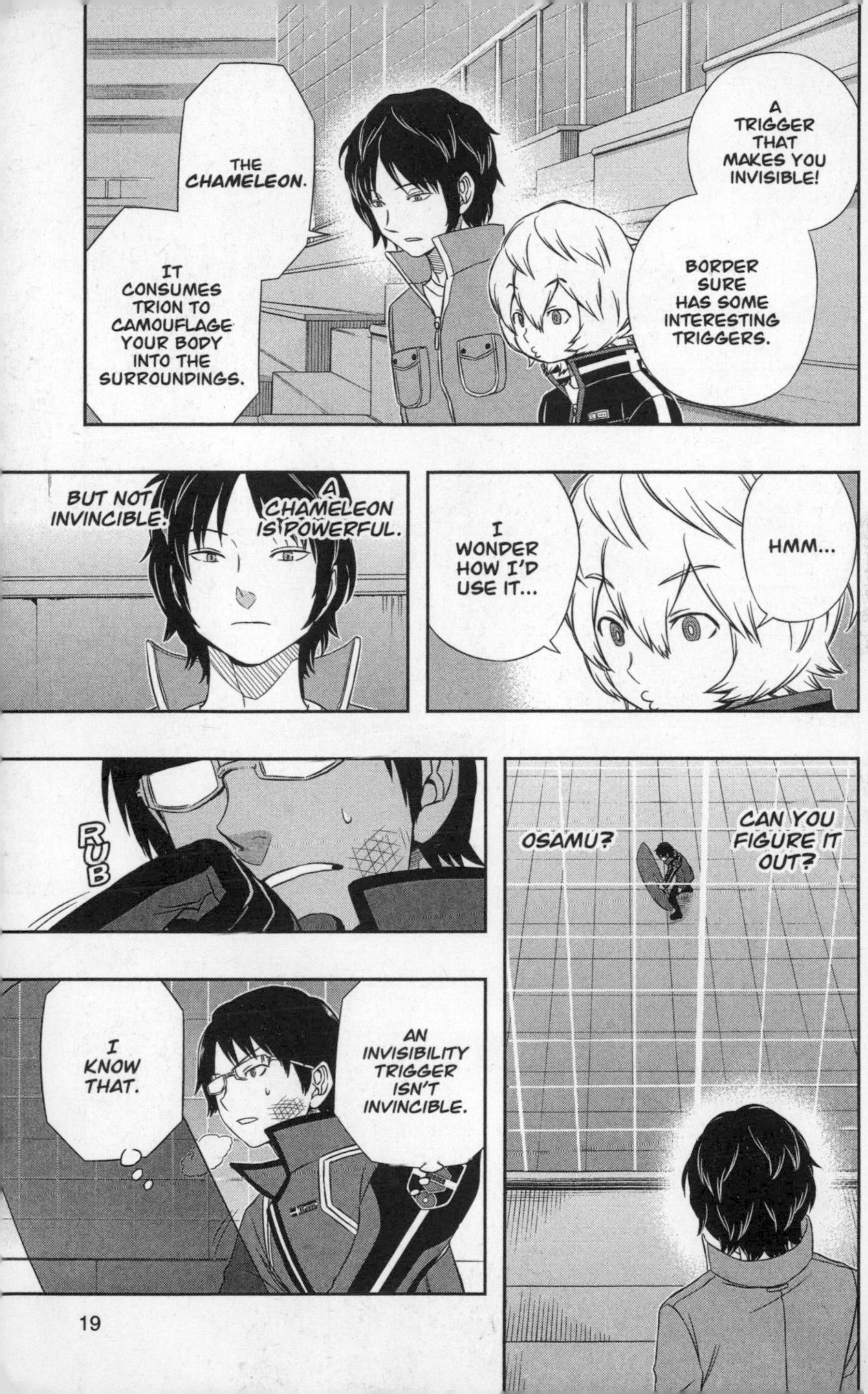
A TRIGGER THAT MAKES YOU INVISIBLE!
THE CHAMELEON.
IT CONSUMES TRION TO CAMOUFLAGE YOUR BODY INTO THE SURROUNDINGS.
BORDER SURE HAS SOME INTERESTING TRIGGERS.
HMM...
I WONDER HOW I'D USE IT...
A CHAMELEON IS POWERFUL.
BUT NOT INVINCIBLE.
CAN YOU FIGURE IT OUT?
OSAMU?
RUB
AN INVISIBILITY TRIGGER ISN'T INVINCIBLE.
I KNOW THAT.

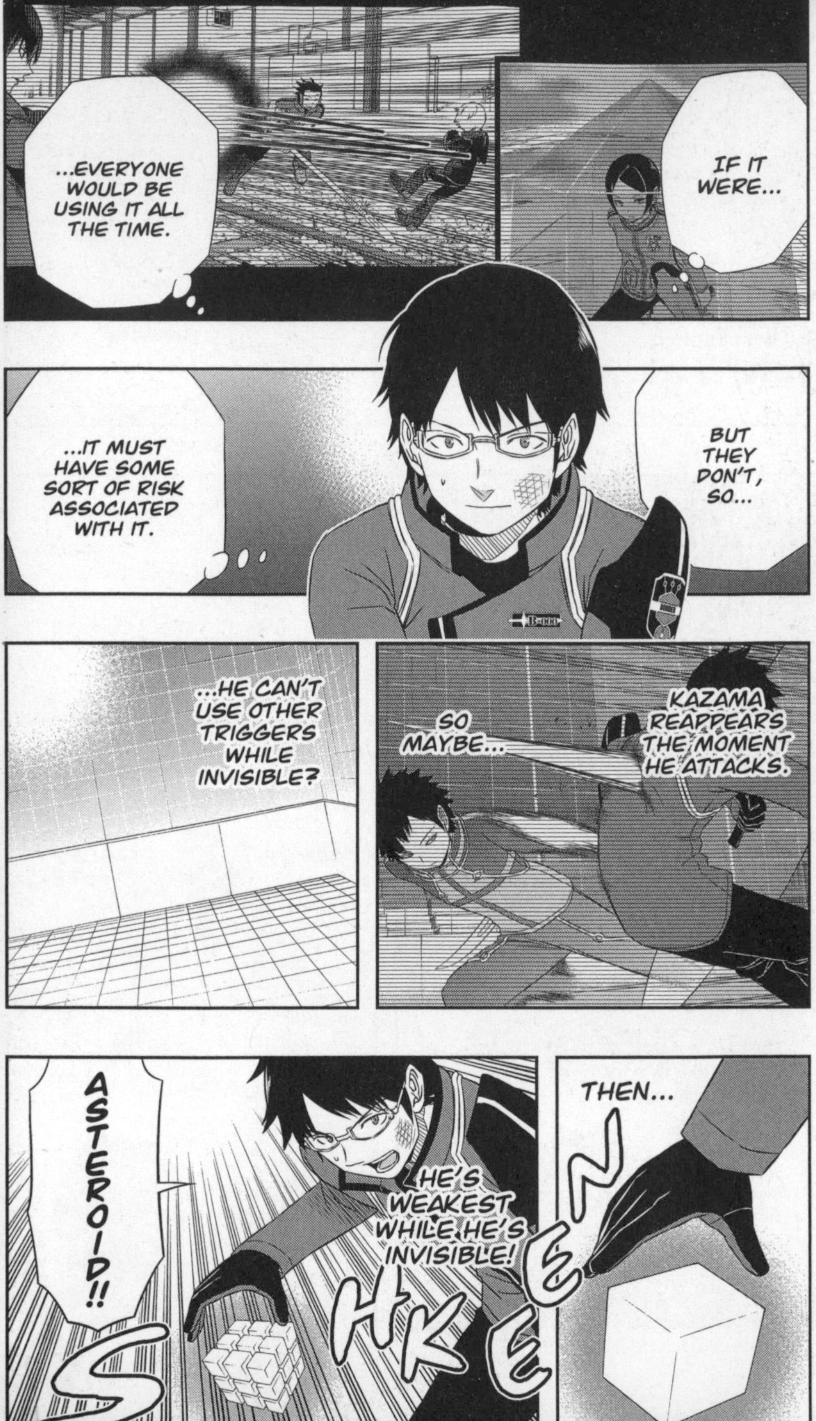
IF IT WERE...
...EVERYONE WOULD BE USING IT ALL THE TIME.
BUT THEY DON'T, SO...
...IT MUST HAVE SOME SORT OF RISK ASSOCIATED WITH IT.
KAZAMA REAPPEARS THE MOMENT HE ATTACKS.
SO MAYBE...
...HE CAN'T USE OTHER TRIGGERS WHILE INVISIBLE?
THEN...
HE'S WEAKEST WHILE HE'S INVISIBLE!
ASTEROID!!
SHKEEN

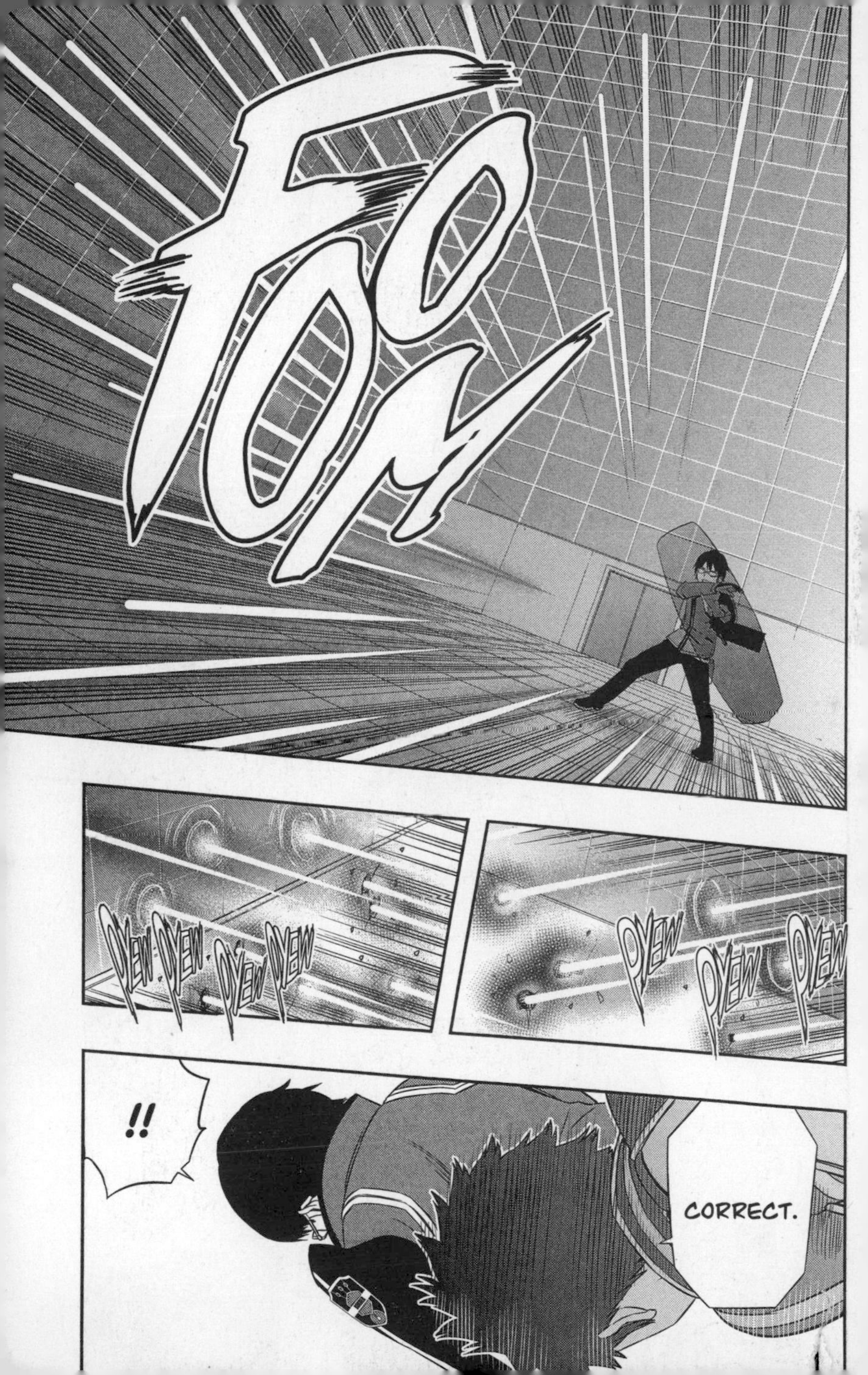
PYEW
PYEW
PYEW
PYEW
PYEW
PYEW
PYEW
CORRECT.
!!

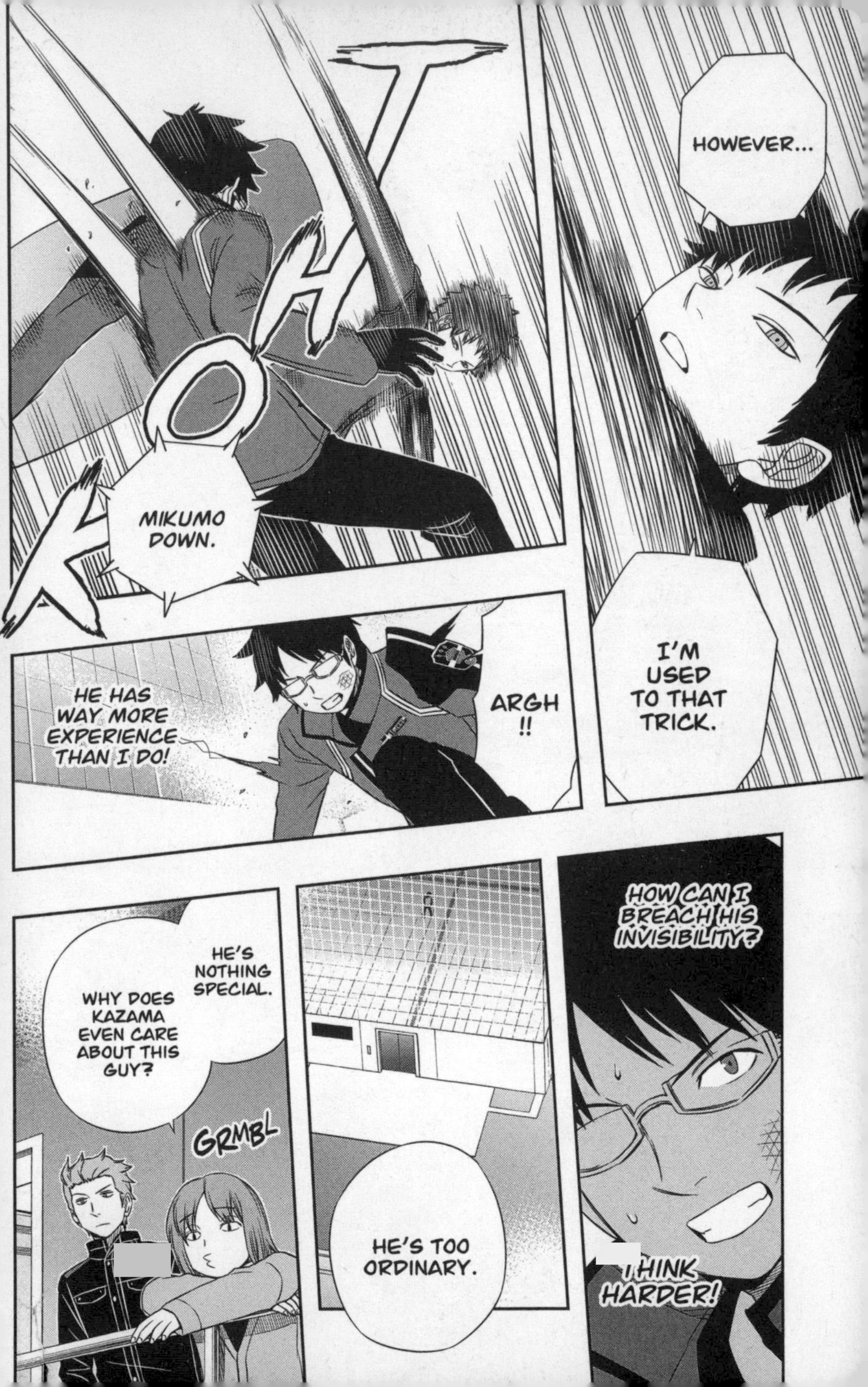
HOWEVER...
I'M USED TO THAT TRICK.
MIKUMO DOWN.
ARGH!!
HE HAS WAY MORE EXPERIENCE THAN I DO!
HOW CAN I BREACH HIS INVISIBILITY?
THINK HARDER!
HE'S TOO ORDINARY.
HE'S NOTHING SPECIAL.
WHY DOES KAZAMA EVEN CARE ABOUT THIS GUY?
GRMBL

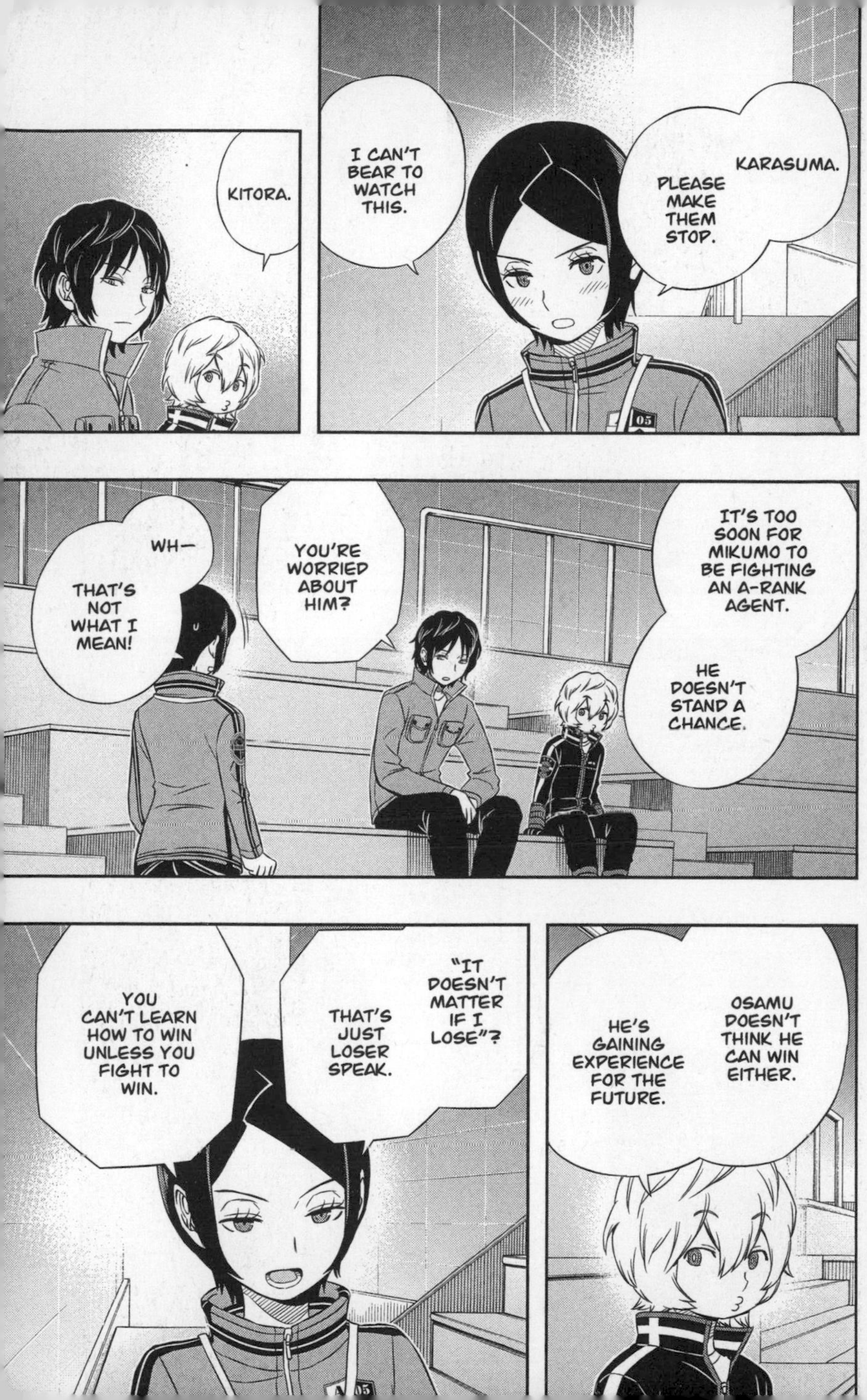
KARASUMA.
PLEASE MAKE THEM STOP.
I CAN'T BEAR TO WATCH THIS.
KITORA.
IT'S TOO SOON FOR MIKUMO TO BE FIGHTING AN A-RANK AGENT.
HE DOESN'T STAND A CHANCE.
YOU'RE WORRIED ABOUT HIM?
WH—
THAT'S NOT WHAT I MEAN!
OSAMU DOESN'T THINK HE CAN WIN EITHER.
HE'S GAINING EXPERIENCE FOR THE FUTURE.
"IT DOESN'T MATTER IF I LOSE"?
THAT'S JUST LOSER SPEAK.
YOU CAN'T LEARN HOW TO WIN UNLESS YOU FIGHT TO WIN.

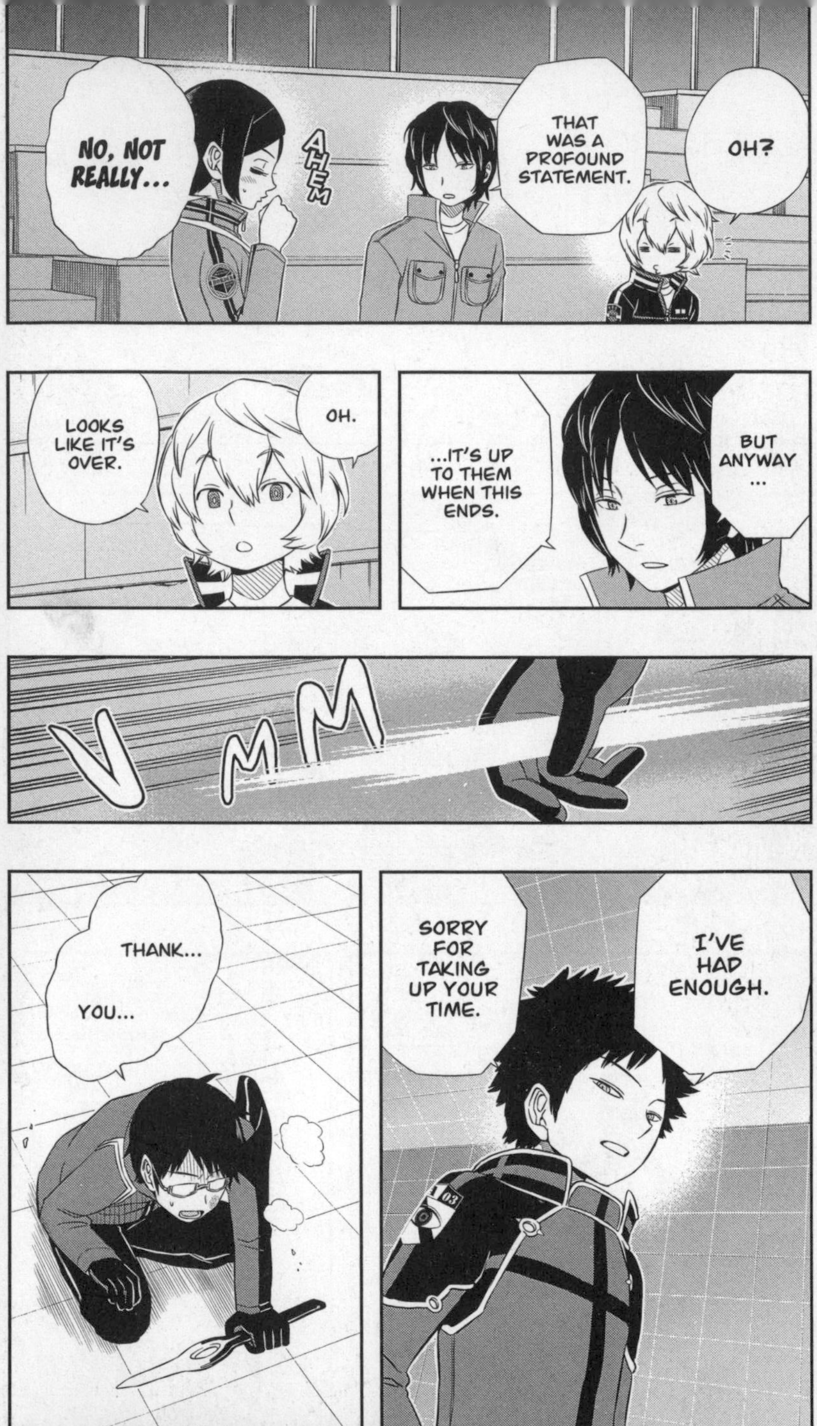
OH?
THAT WAS A PROFOUND STATEMENT.
AHEM
NO, NOT REALLY...
BUT ANYWAY ...
...IT'S UP TO THEM WHEN THIS ENDS.
OH.
LOOKS LIKE IT'S OVER.
VMMM
I'VE HAD ENOUGH.
SORRY FOR TAKING UP YOUR TIME.
THANK...
YOU...

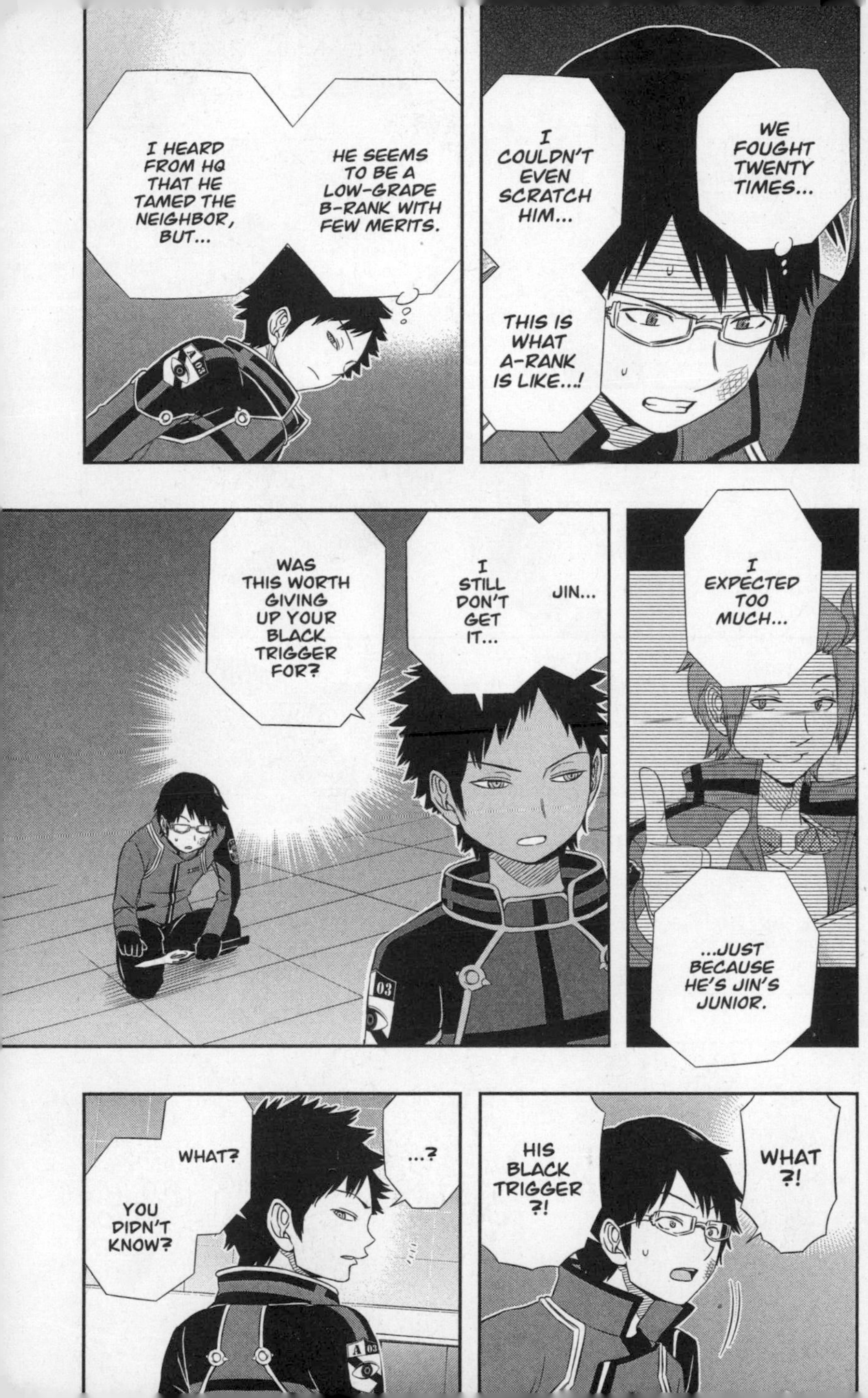
WE FOUGHT TWENTY TIMES...
I COULDN'T EVEN SCRATCH HIM...
THIS IS WHAT A-RANK IS LIKE...!
HE SEEMS TO BE A LOW-GRADE B-RANK WITH FEW MERITS.
I HEARD FROM HQ THAT HE TAMED THE NEIGHBOR, BUT...
I EXPECTED TOO MUCH...
...JUST BECAUSE HE'S JIN'S JUNIOR.
JIN...
I STILL DON'T GET IT...
WAS THIS WORTH GIVING UP YOUR BLACK TRIGGER FOR?
WHAT ?!
HIS BLACK TRIGGER ?!
...?
WHAT?
YOU DIDN'T KNOW?

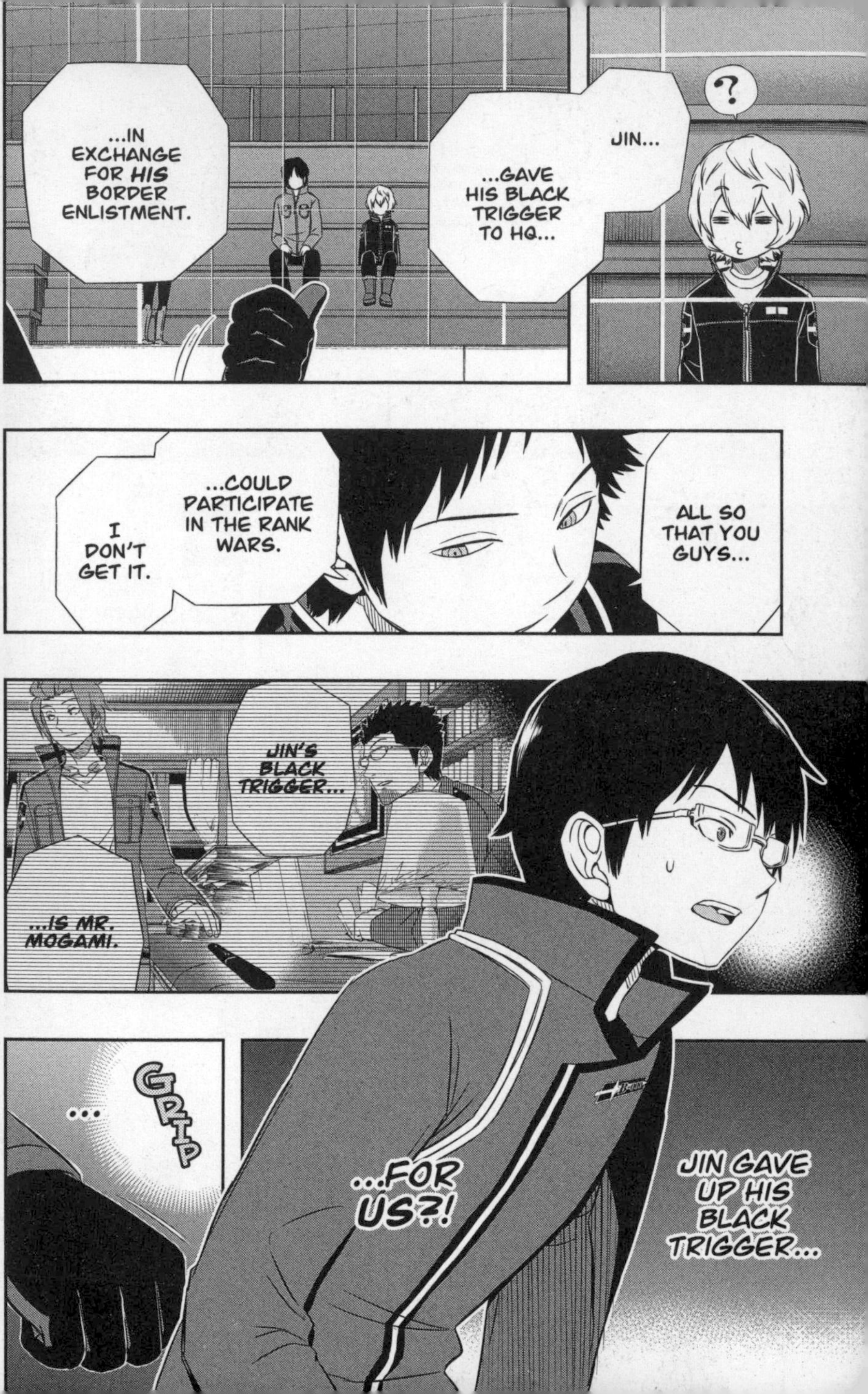
?
JIN...
...GAVE HIS BLACK TRIGGER TO HQ...
...IN EXCHANGE FOR HIS BORDER ENLISTMENT.
ALL SO THAT YOU GUYS...
...COULD PARTICIPATE IN THE RANK WARS.
I DON'T GET IT.
JIN'S BLACK TRIGGER...
...IS MR. MOGAMI.
JIN GAVE UP HIS BLACK TRIGGER...
...FOR US?!
GRIP
...

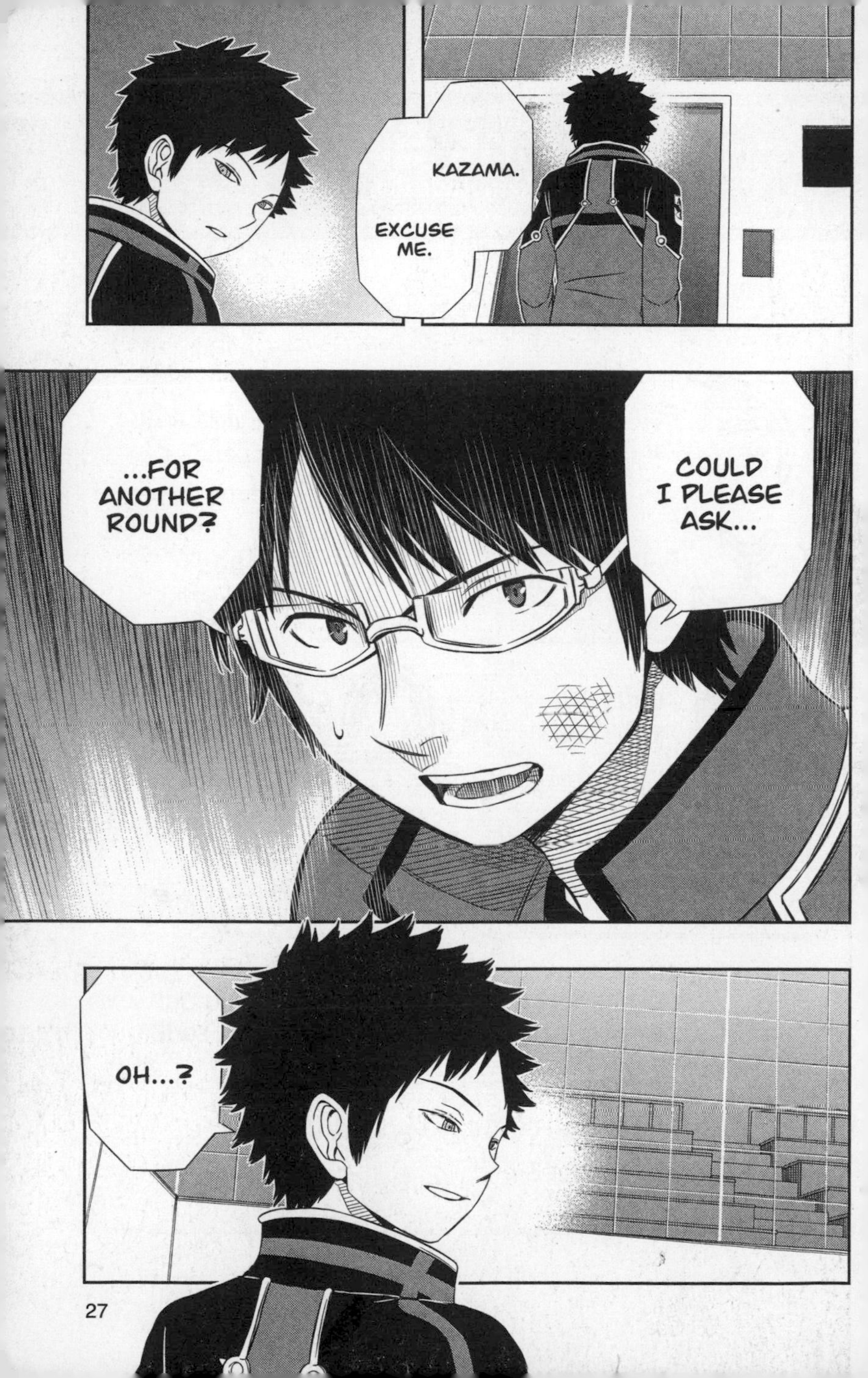
KAZAMA.
EXCUSE ME.
COULD I PLEASE ASK...
...FOR ANOTHER ROUND?
OH...?

Zodiac Signs

I forgot to include this earlier.

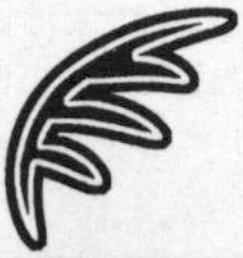

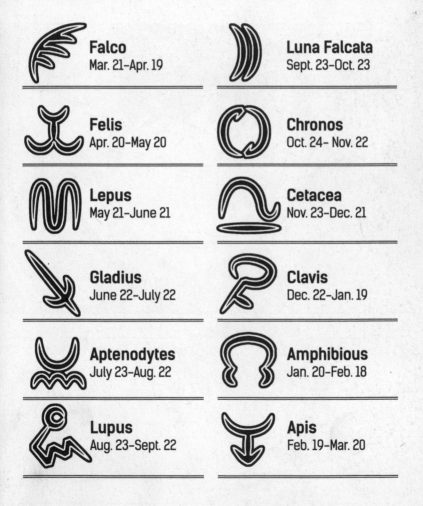

Falco
Mar. 21–Apr. 19

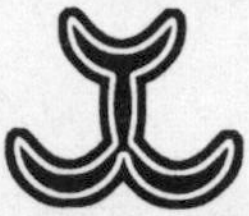

Felis
Apr. 20–May 20

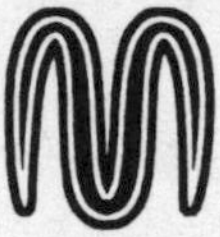

Lepus
May 21–June 21

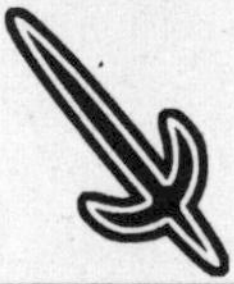

Gladius
June 22–July 22

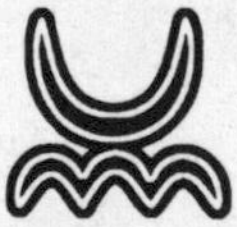

Aptenodytes
July 23–Aug. 22

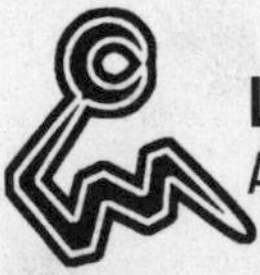

Lupus
Aug. 23–Sept. 22

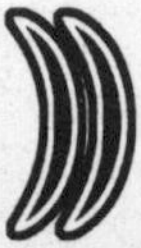

Luna Falcata
Sept. 23–Oct. 23

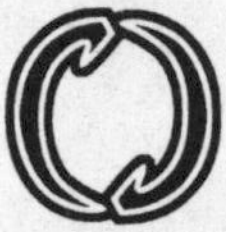

Chronos
Oct. 24– Nov. 22

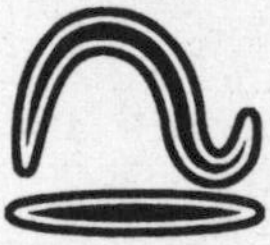

Cetacea
Nov. 23–Dec. 21

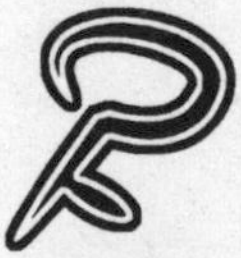

Clavis
Dec. 22–Jan. 19

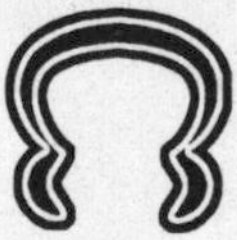

Amphibious
Jan. 20–Feb. 18

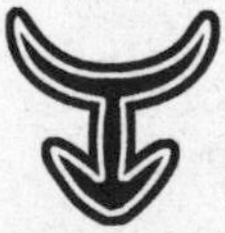

Apis
Feb. 19–Mar. 20

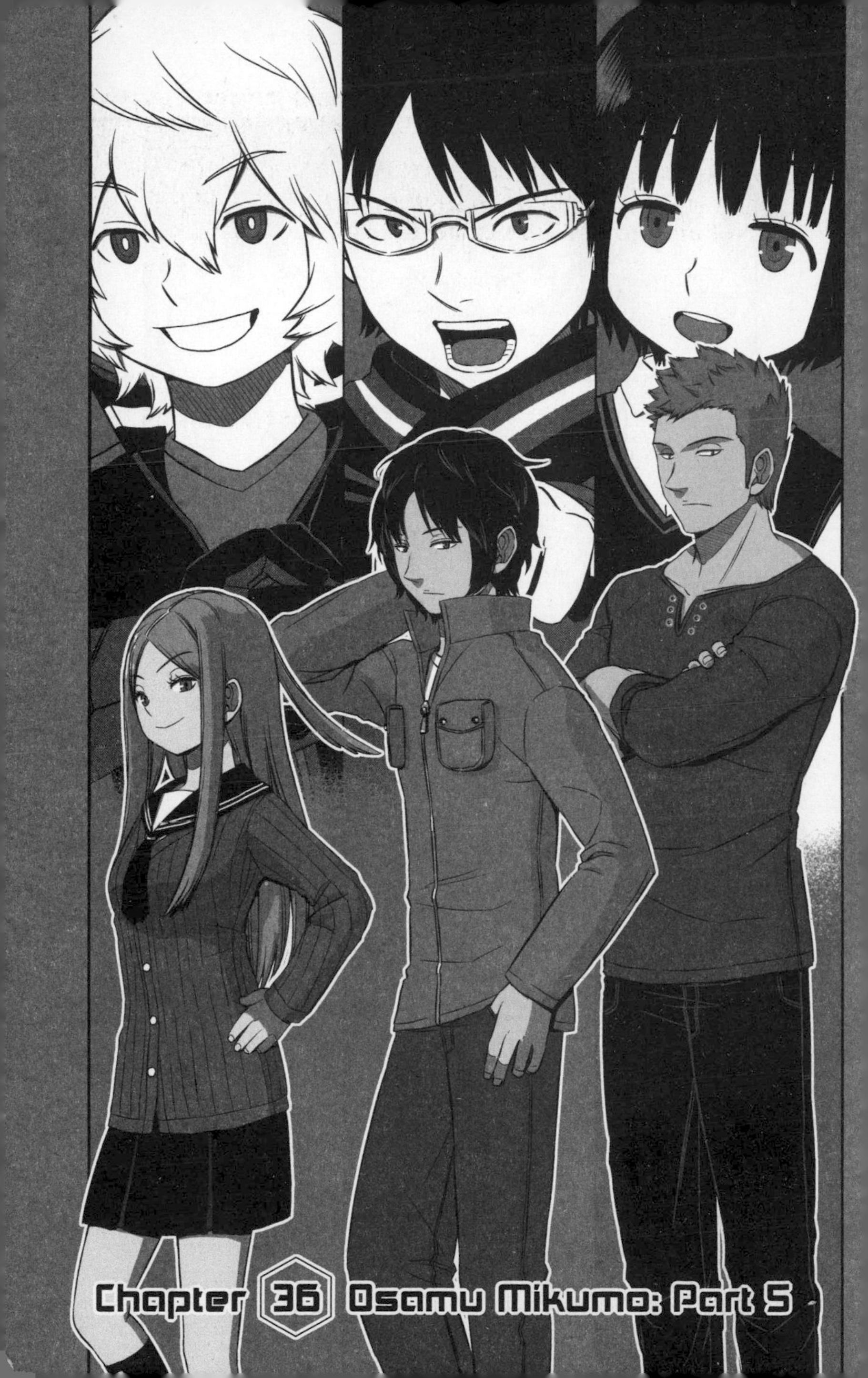
Chapter 36 Osamu Mikumo: Part 5

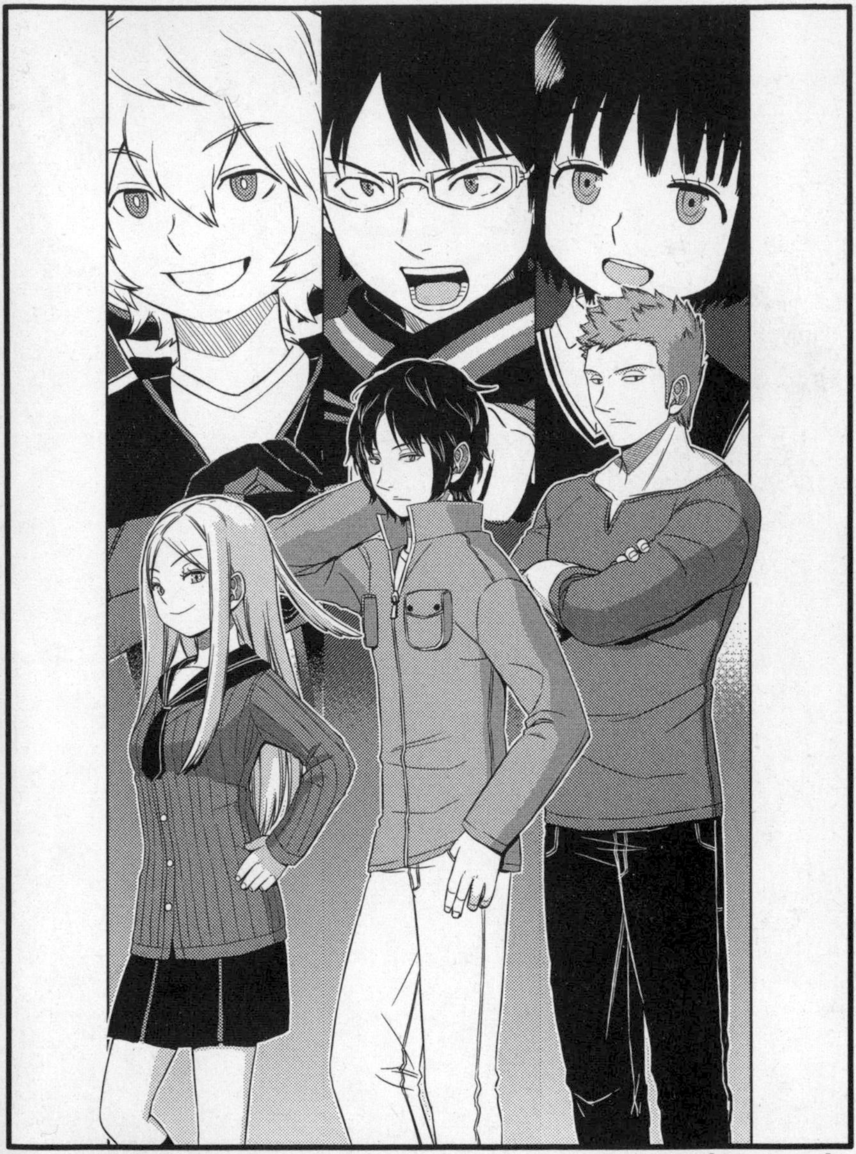

■ 2013 *Weekly Shonen Jump* issue 48, center color page (sixth one)
Relationships like master and apprentice, which are established later in life, have a different passion than blood relations, established at birth. I really liked the color scheme here, so it's too bad it can't be printed in color.

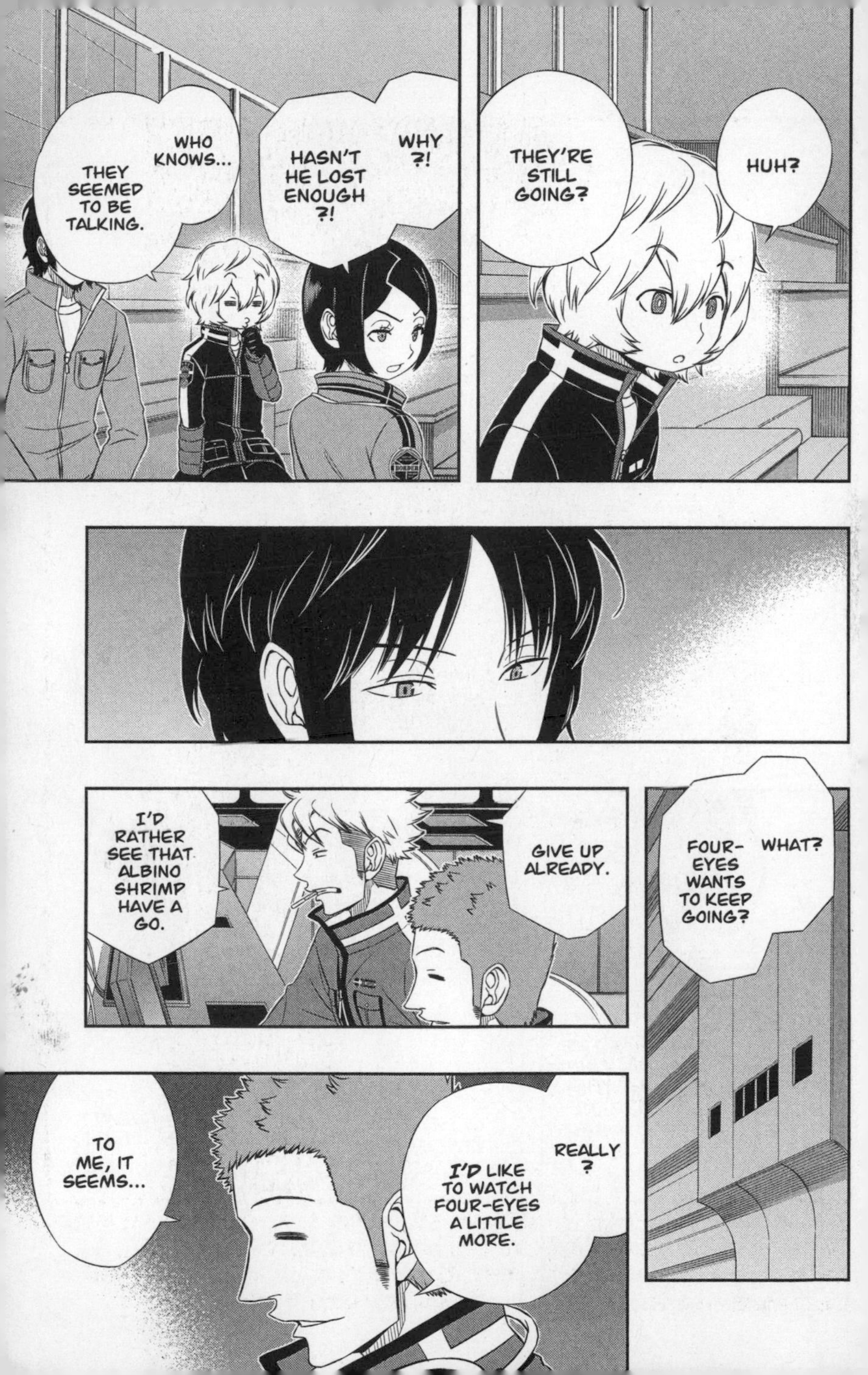
HUH?
THEY'RE STILL GOING?
WHY?!
HASN'T HE LOST ENOUGH?!
WHO KNOWS...
THEY SEEMED TO BE TALKING.
WHAT?
FOUR-EYES WANTS TO KEEP GOING?
GIVE UP ALREADY.
I'D RATHER SEE THAT ALBINO SHRIMP HAVE A GO.
REALLY?
I'D LIKE TO WATCH FOUR-EYES A LITTLE MORE.
TO ME, IT SEEMS...

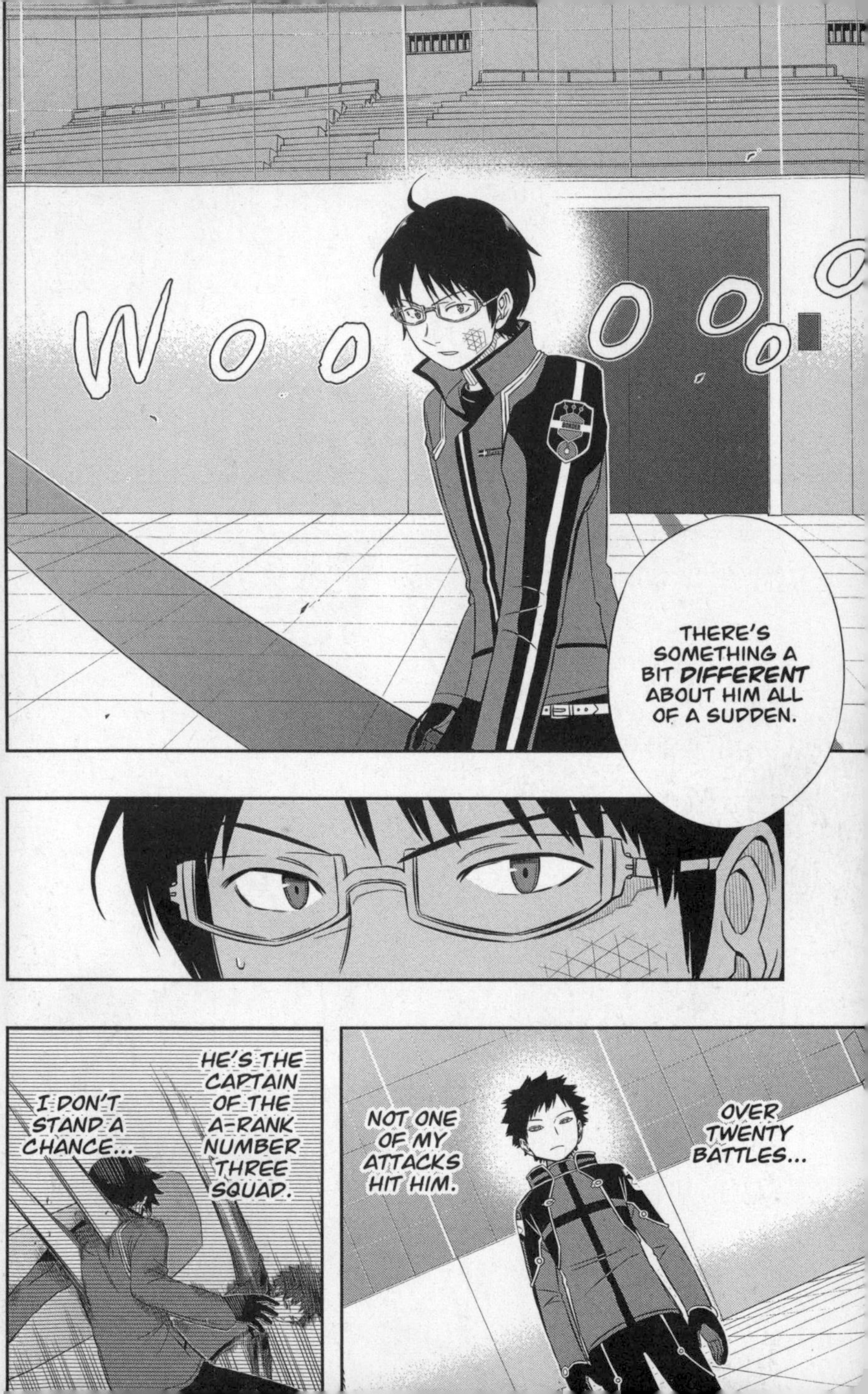
WOOOOOOO
THERE'S SOMETHING A BIT **DIFFERENT** ABOUT HIM ALL OF A SUDDEN.
OVER TWENTY BATTLES...
NOT ONE OF MY ATTACKS HIT HIM.
HE'S THE CAPTAIN OF THE A-RANK NUMBER THREE SQUAD.
I DON'T STAND A CHANCE...

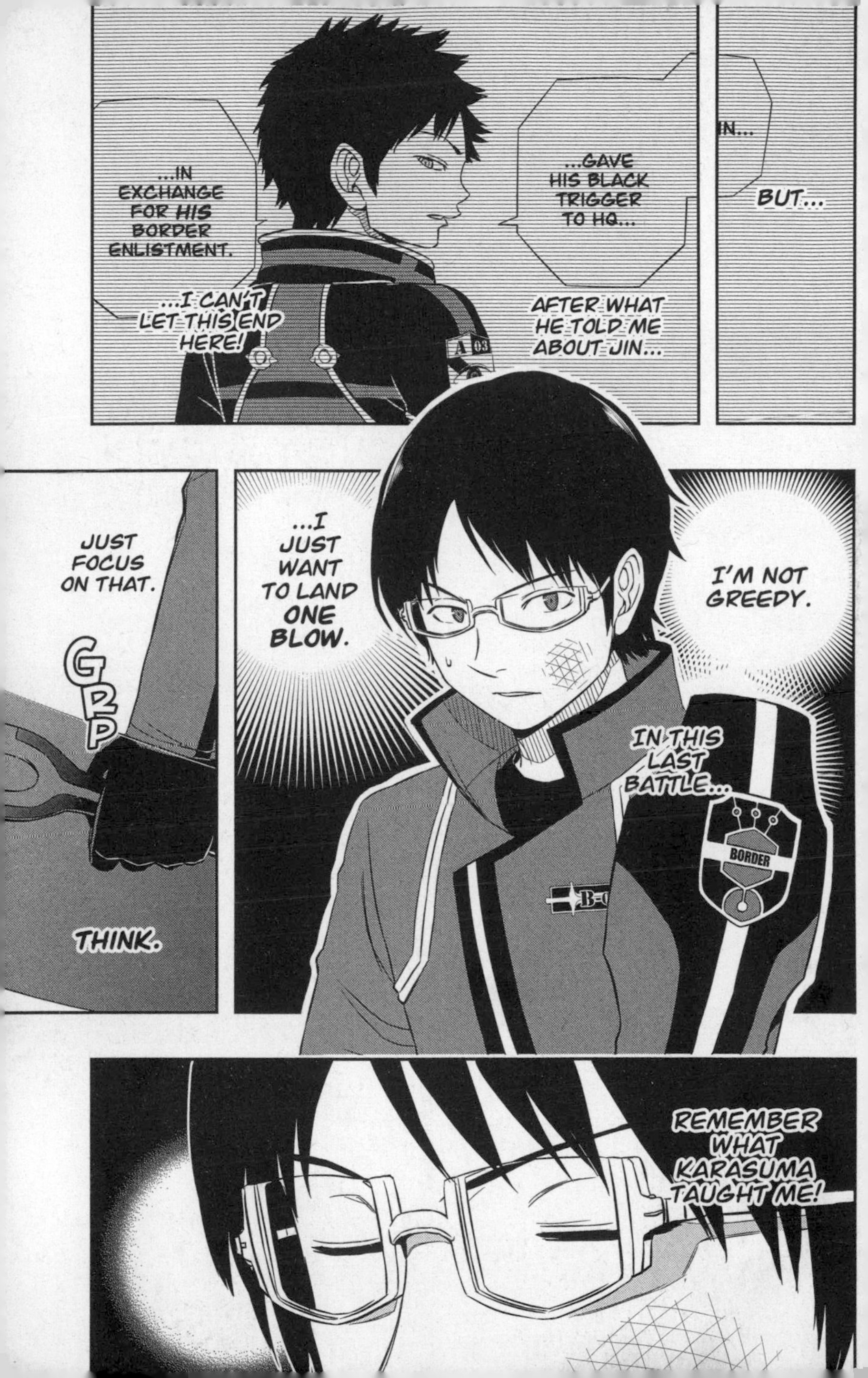
BUT...
IN...
...GAVE HIS BLACK TRIGGER TO HQ...
...IN EXCHANGE FOR HIS BORDER ENLISTMENT.
AFTER WHAT HE TOLD ME ABOUT JIN...
...I CAN'T LET THIS END HERE!
I'M NOT GREEDY.
...I JUST WANT TO LAND ONE BLOW.
IN THIS LAST BATTLE...
BORDER
JUST FOCUS ON THAT.
GRP
THINK.
REMEMBER WHAT KARASUMA TAUGHT ME!

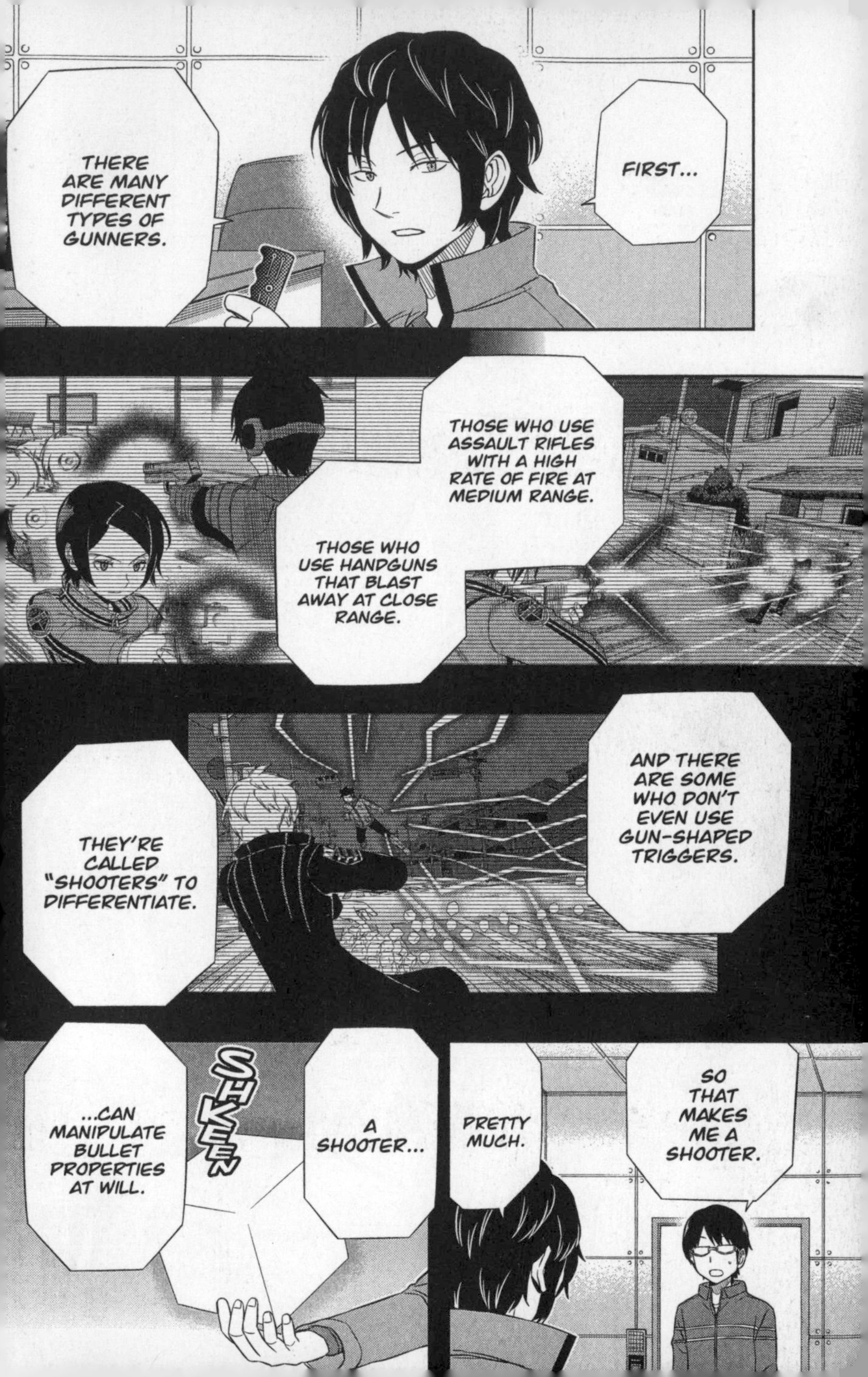
FIRST...
THERE ARE MANY DIFFERENT TYPES OF GUNNERS.
THOSE WHO USE ASSAULT RIFLES WITH A HIGH RATE OF FIRE AT MEDIUM RANGE.
THOSE WHO USE HANDGUNS THAT BLAST AWAY AT CLOSE RANGE.
AND THERE ARE SOME WHO DON'T EVEN USE GUN-SHAPED TRIGGERS.
THEY'RE CALLED "SHOOTERS" TO DIFFERENTIATE.
SO THAT MAKES ME A SHOOTER.
PRETTY MUCH.
A SHOOTER...
SHKEEN
...CAN MANIPULATE BULLET PROPERTIES AT WILL.

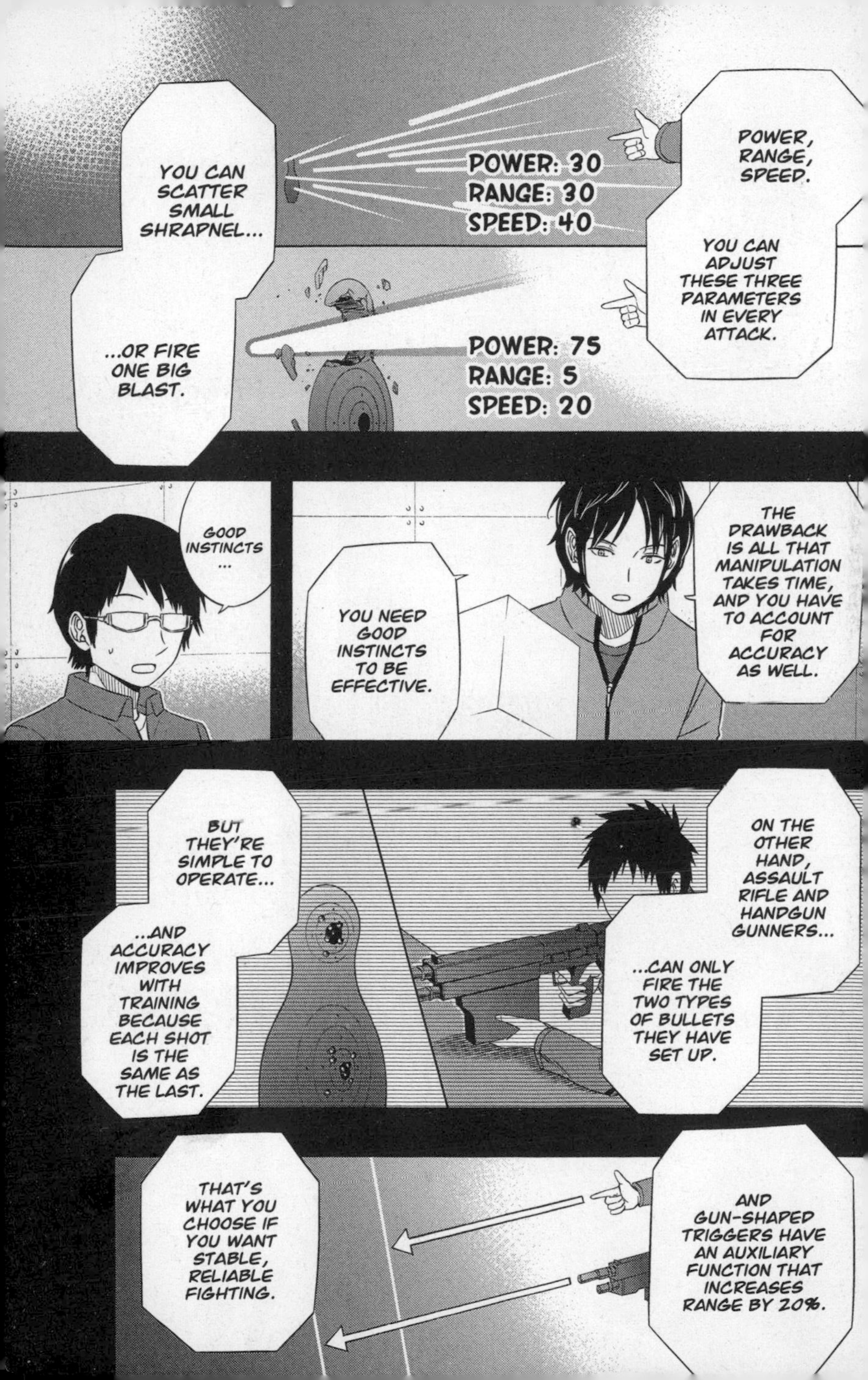
POWER, RANGE, SPEED.
YOU CAN ADJUST THESE THREE PARAMETERS IN EVERY ATTACK.
POWER: 30
RANGE: 30
SPEED: 40
YOU CAN SCATTER SMALL SHRAPNEL...
POWER: 75
RANGE: 5
SPEED: 20
...OR FIRE ONE BIG BLAST.
THE DRAWBACK IS ALL THAT MANIPULATION TAKES TIME, AND YOU HAVE TO ACCOUNT FOR ACCURACY AS WELL.
YOU NEED GOOD INSTINCTS TO BE EFFECTIVE.
GOOD INSTINCTS ...
ON THE OTHER HAND, ASSAULT RIFLE AND HANDGUN GUNNERS...
...CAN ONLY FIRE THE TWO TYPES OF BULLETS THEY HAVE SET UP.
BUT THEY'RE SIMPLE TO OPERATE...
...AND ACCURACY IMPROVES WITH TRAINING BECAUSE EACH SHOT IS THE SAME AS THE LAST.
AND GUN-SHAPED TRIGGERS HAVE AN AUXILIARY FUNCTION THAT INCREASES RANGE BY 20%.
THAT'S WHAT YOU CHOOSE IF YOU WANT STABLE, RELIABLE FIGHTING.

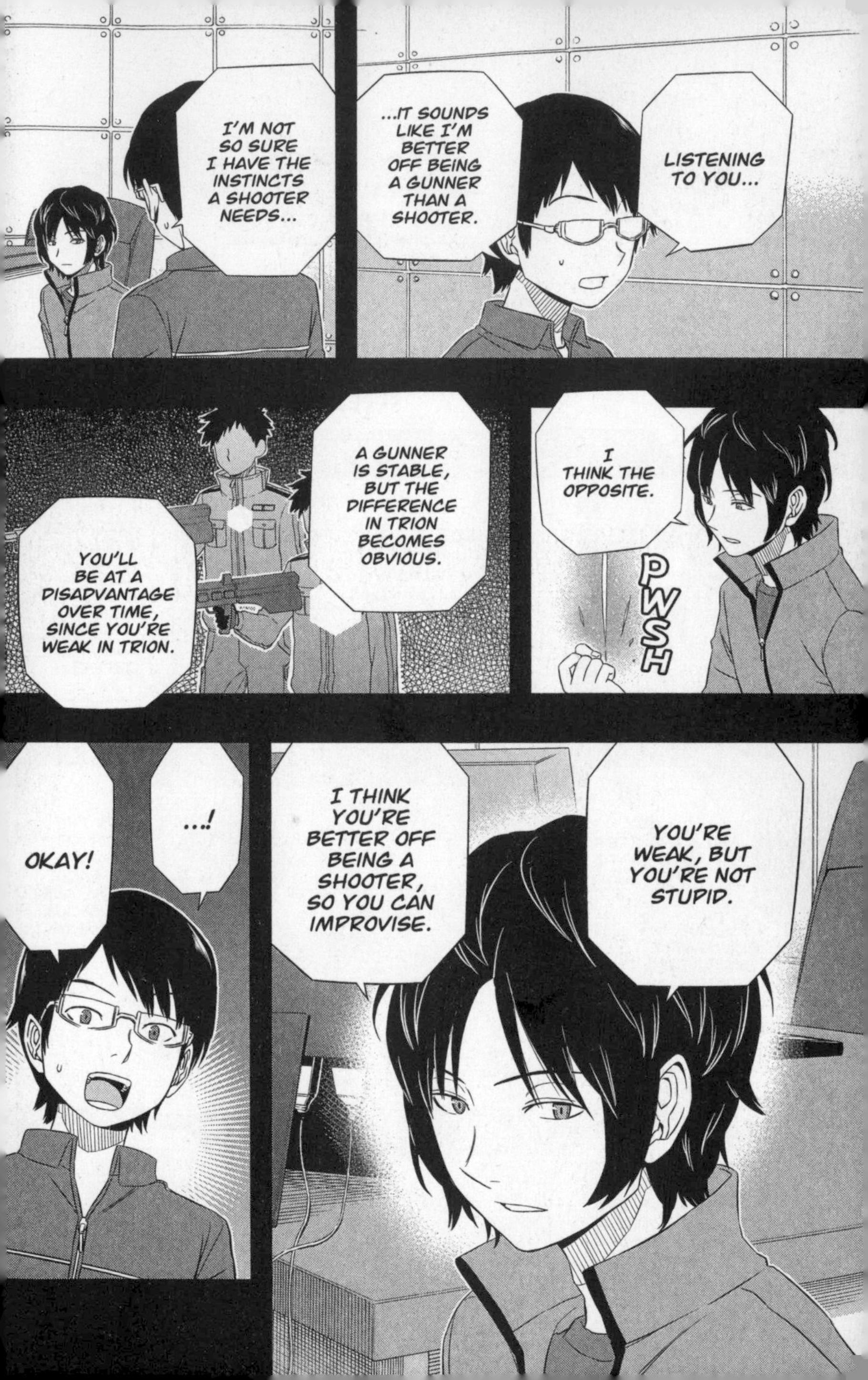
LISTENING TO YOU...
...IT SOUNDS LIKE I'M BETTER OFF BEING A GUNNER THAN A SHOOTER.
I'M NOT SO SURE I HAVE THE INSTINCTS A SHOOTER NEEDS...
I THINK THE OPPOSITE.
PWSH
A GUNNER IS STABLE, BUT THE DIFFERENCE IN TRION BECOMES OBVIOUS.
YOU'LL BE AT A DISADVANTAGE OVER TIME, SINCE YOU'RE WEAK IN TRION.
YOU'RE WEAK, BUT YOU'RE NOT STUPID.
I THINK YOU'RE BETTER OFF BEING A SHOOTER, SO YOU CAN IMPROVISE.
...!
OKAY!

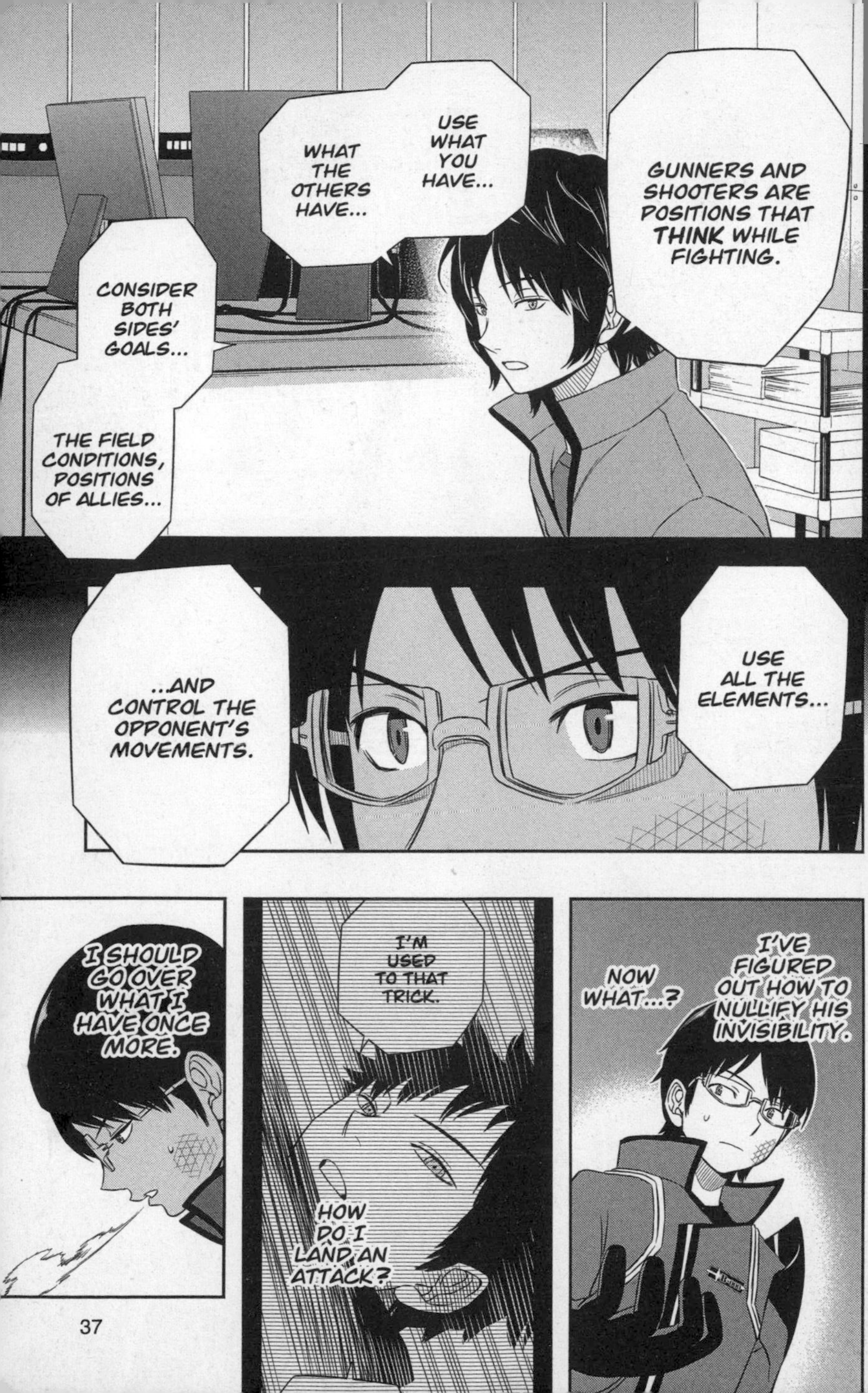
GUNNERS AND SHOOTERS ARE POSITIONS THAT THINK WHILE FIGHTING.
USE WHAT YOU HAVE...
WHAT THE OTHERS HAVE...
CONSIDER BOTH SIDES' GOALS...
THE FIELD CONDITIONS, POSITIONS OF ALLIES...
USE ALL THE ELEMENTS...
...AND CONTROL THE OPPONENT'S MOVEMENTS.
I'VE FIGURED OUT HOW TO NULLIFY HIS INVISIBILITY.
NOW WHAT...?
I'M USED TO THAT TRICK.
HOW DO I LAND AN ATTACK?
I SHOULD GO OVER WHAT I HAVE ONCE MORE.

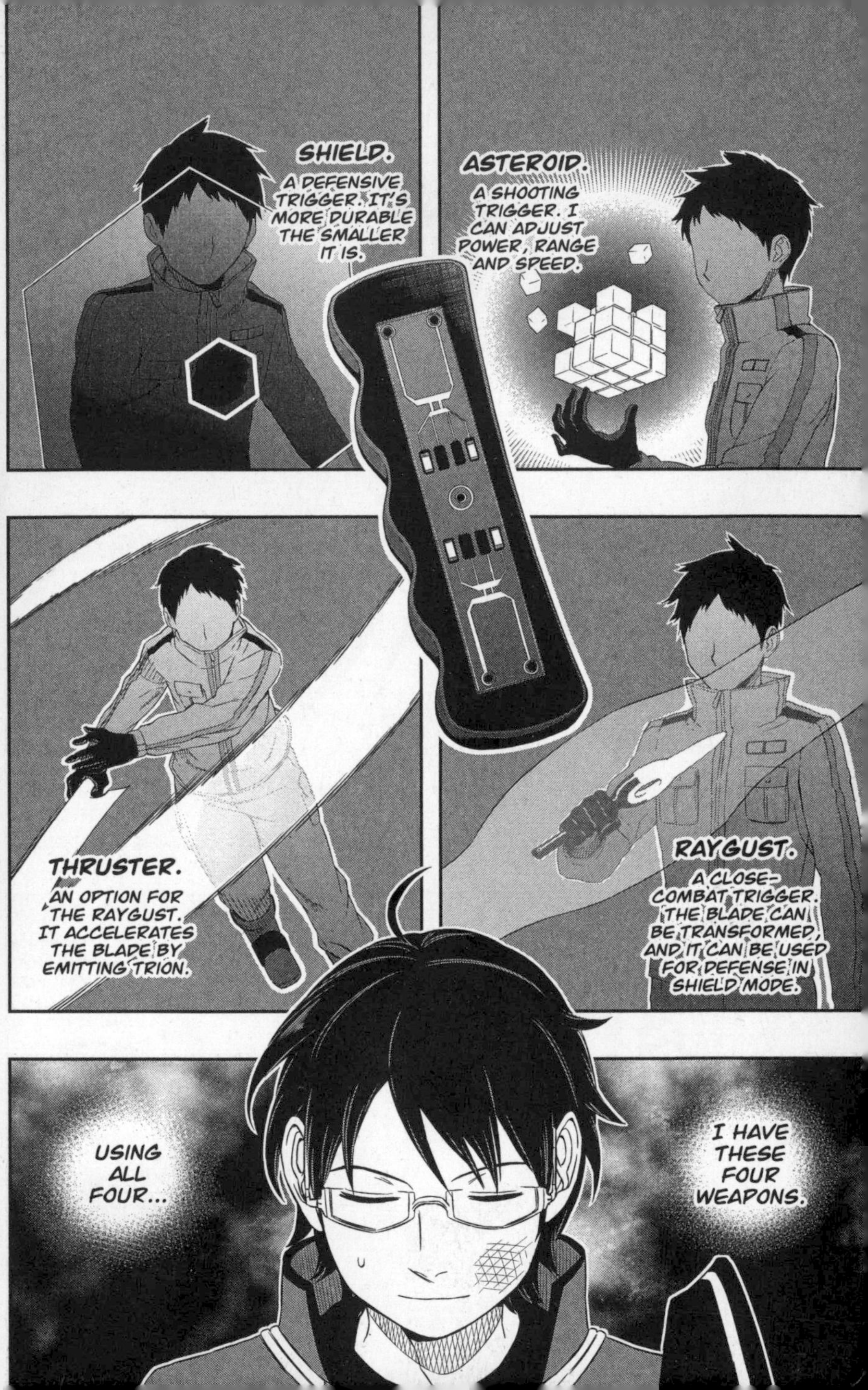
ASTEROID.
A SHOOTING TRIGGER. I CAN ADJUST POWER, RANGE AND SPEED.
SHIELD.
A DEFENSIVE TRIGGER. IT'S MORE DURABLE THE SMALLER IT IS.
RAYGUST.
A CLOSE-COMBAT TRIGGER. THE BLADE CAN BE TRANSFORMED, AND IT CAN BE USED FOR DEFENSE IN SHIELD MODE.
THRUSTER.
AN OPTION FOR THE RAYGUST. IT ACCELERATES THE BLADE BY EMITTING TRION.
I HAVE THESE FOUR WEAPONS.
USING ALL FOUR...

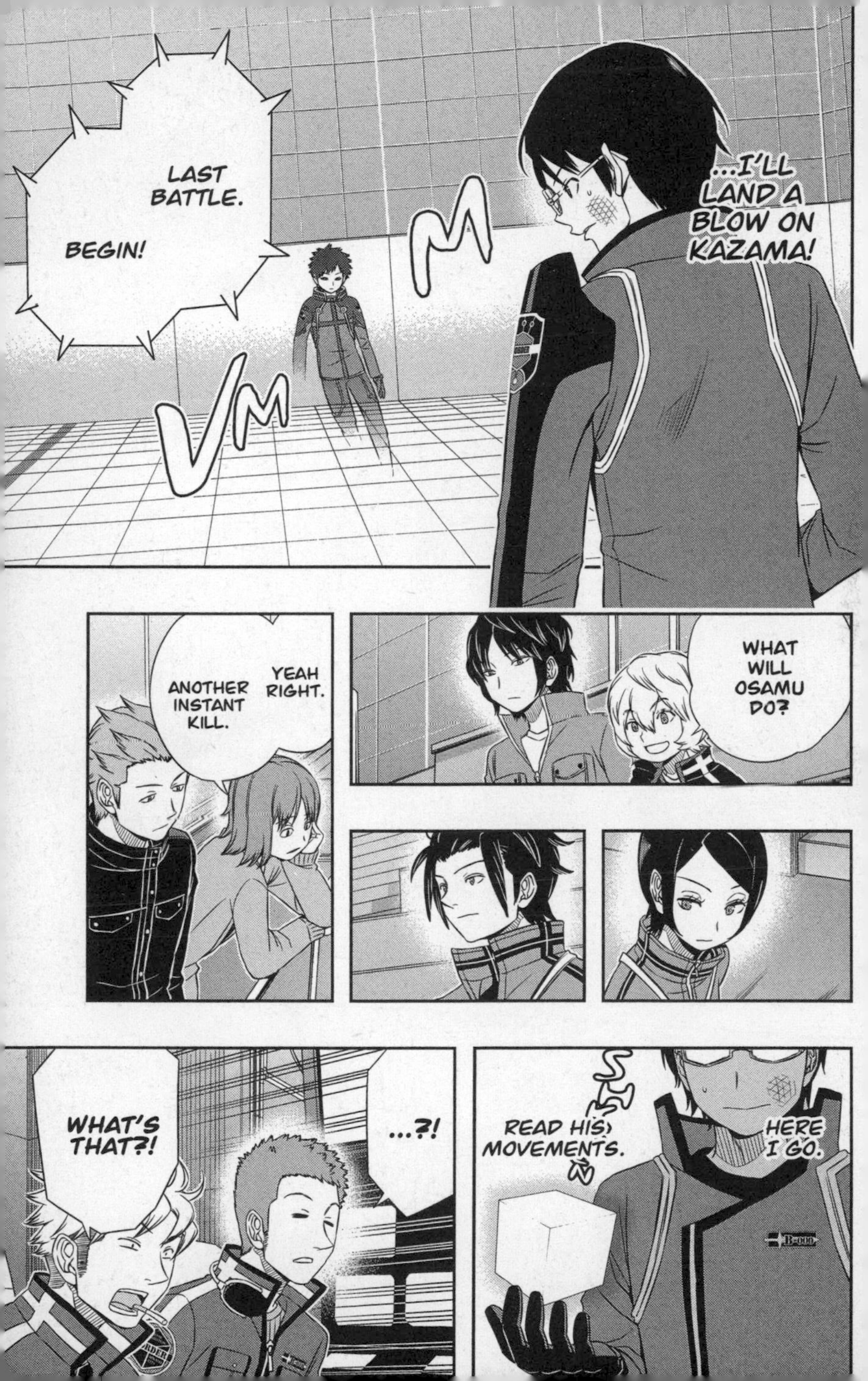
...I'LL LAND A BLOW ON KAZAMA!
LAST BATTLE.
BEGIN!
VMM
WHAT WILL OSAMU DO?
YEAH RIGHT.
ANOTHER INSTANT KILL.
HERE I GO.
READ HIS MOVEMENTS.
...?!
WHAT'S THAT?!

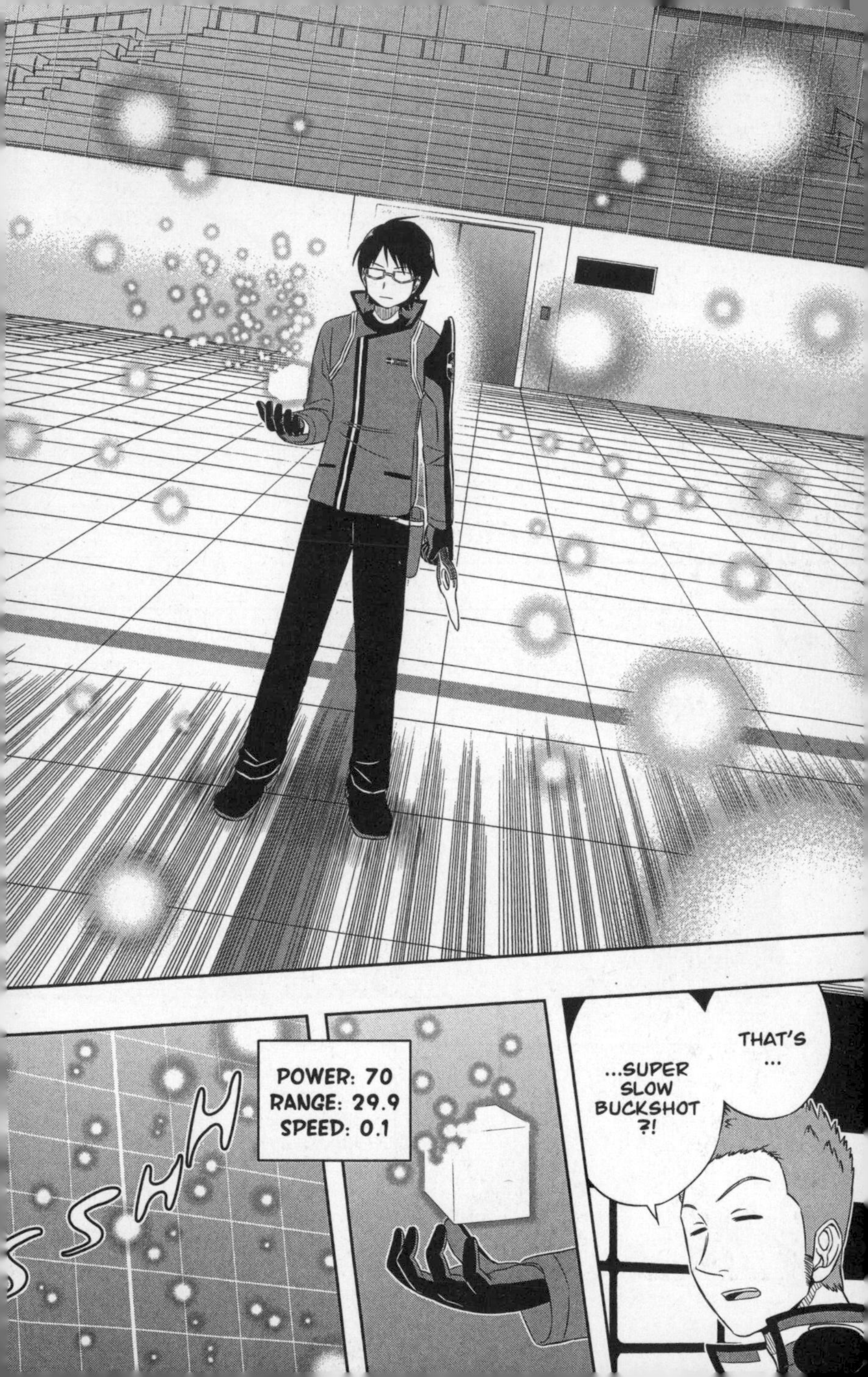

THAT'S ...
...SUPER SLOW BUCKSHOT ?!
POWER: 70
RANGE: 29.9
SPEED: 0.1
SSHH

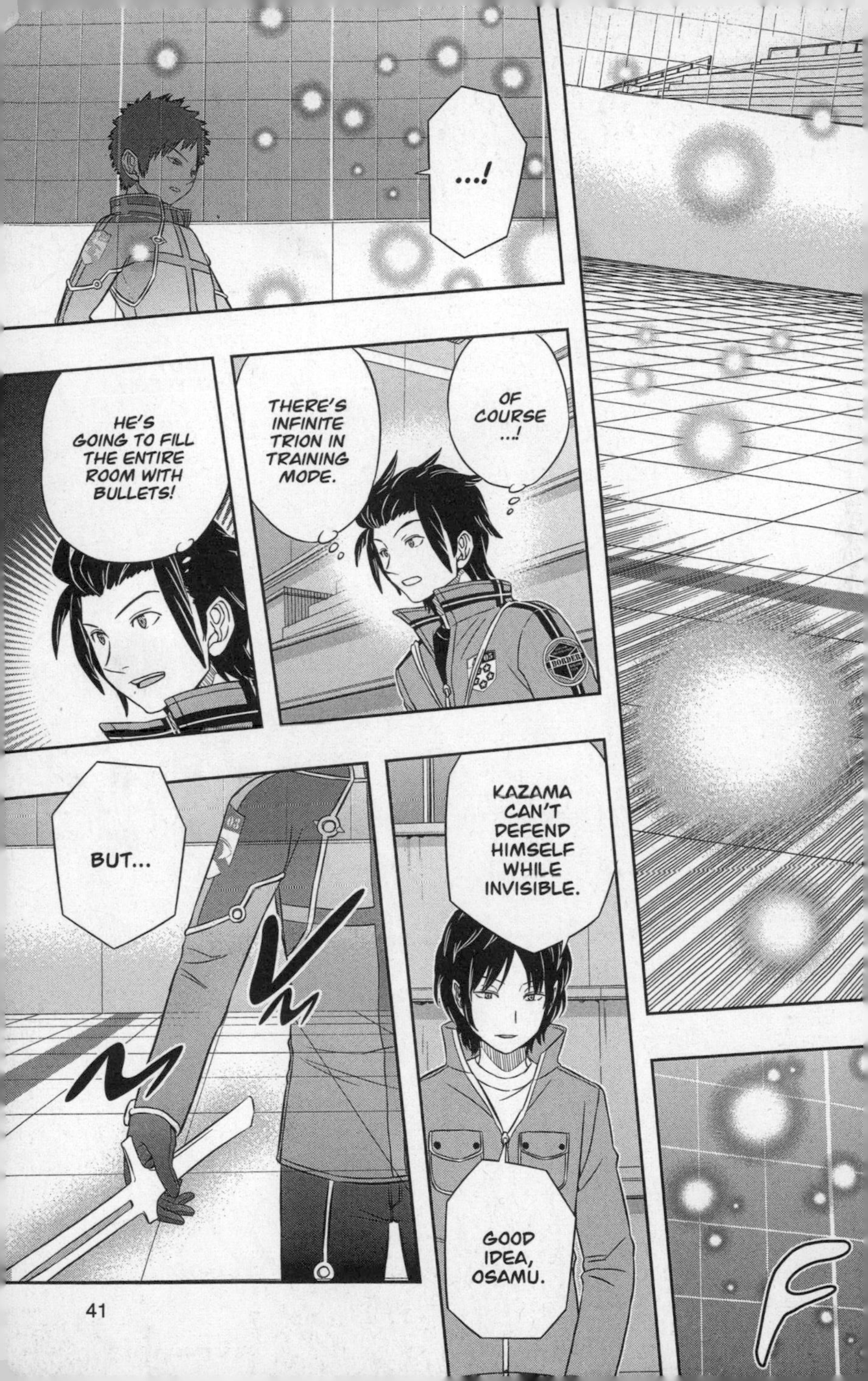
...!
OF COURSE ...!
THERE'S INFINITE TRION IN TRAINING MODE.
HE'S GOING TO FILL THE ENTIRE ROOM WITH BULLETS!
F
KAZAMA CAN'T DEFEND HIMSELF WHILE INVISIBLE.
GOOD IDEA, OSAMU.
BUT...

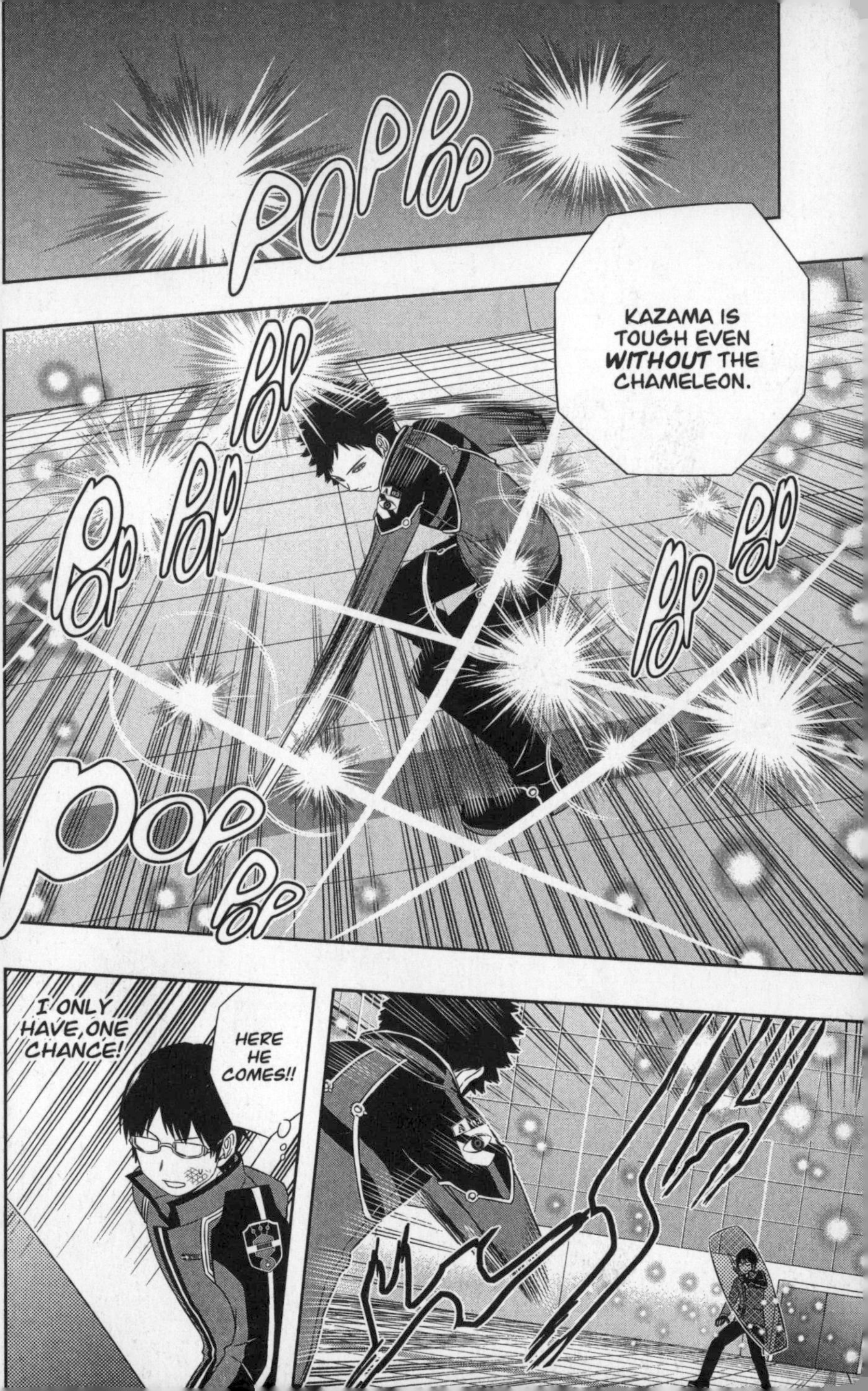
POP POP POP
KAZAMA IS TOUGH EVEN WITHOUT THE CHAMELEON.
POP POP
POP POP
POP POP
POP POP
POP POP
HERE HE COMES!!
I ONLY HAVE, ONE CHANCE!

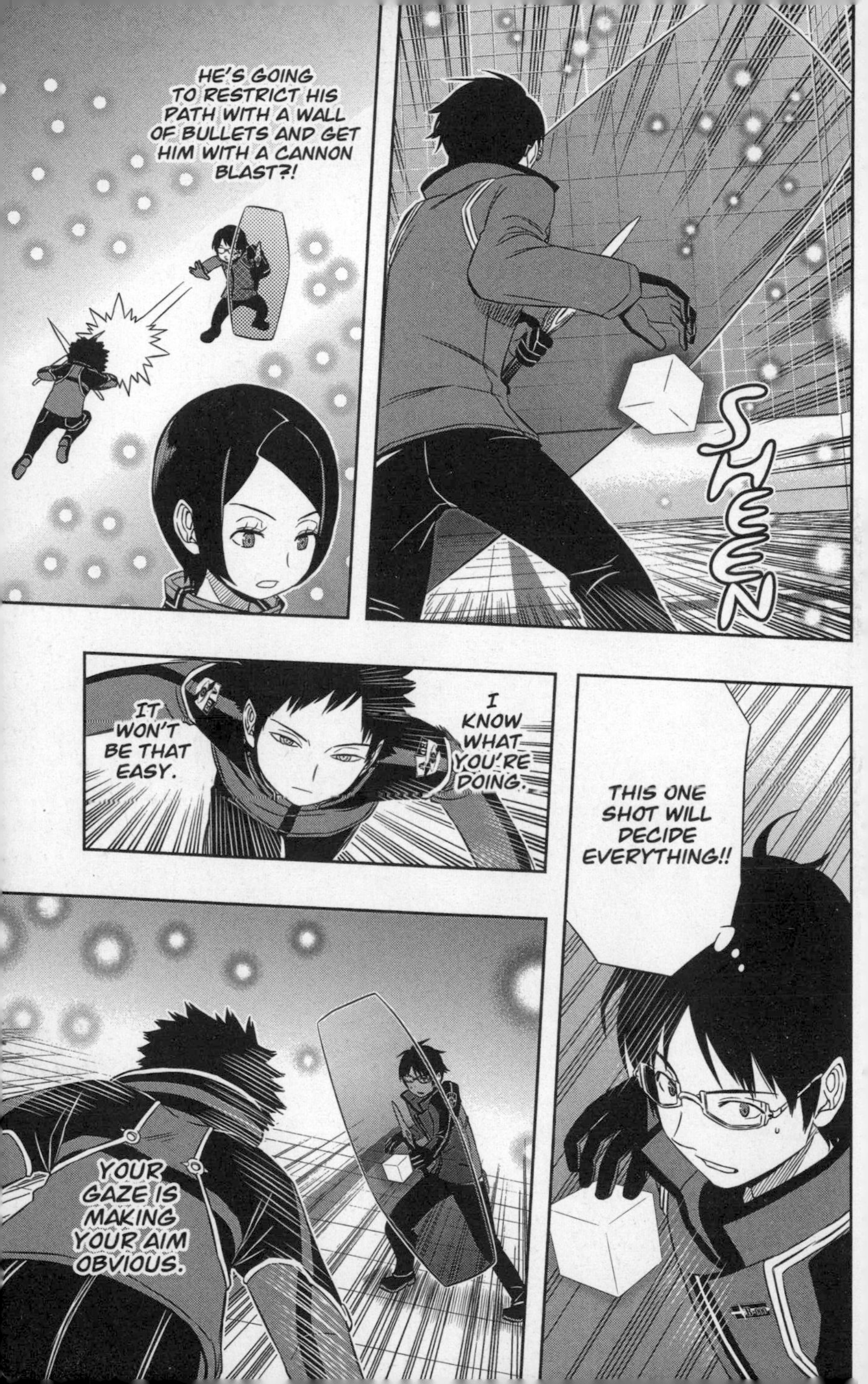
SHEEN
HE'S GOING TO RESTRICT HIS PATH WITH A WALL OF BULLETS AND GET HIM WITH A CANNON BLAST?!
THIS ONE SHOT WILL DECIDE EVERYTHING!!
I KNOW WHAT YOU'RE DOING.
IT WON'T BE THAT EASY.
YOUR GAZE IS MAKING YOUR AIM OBVIOUS.

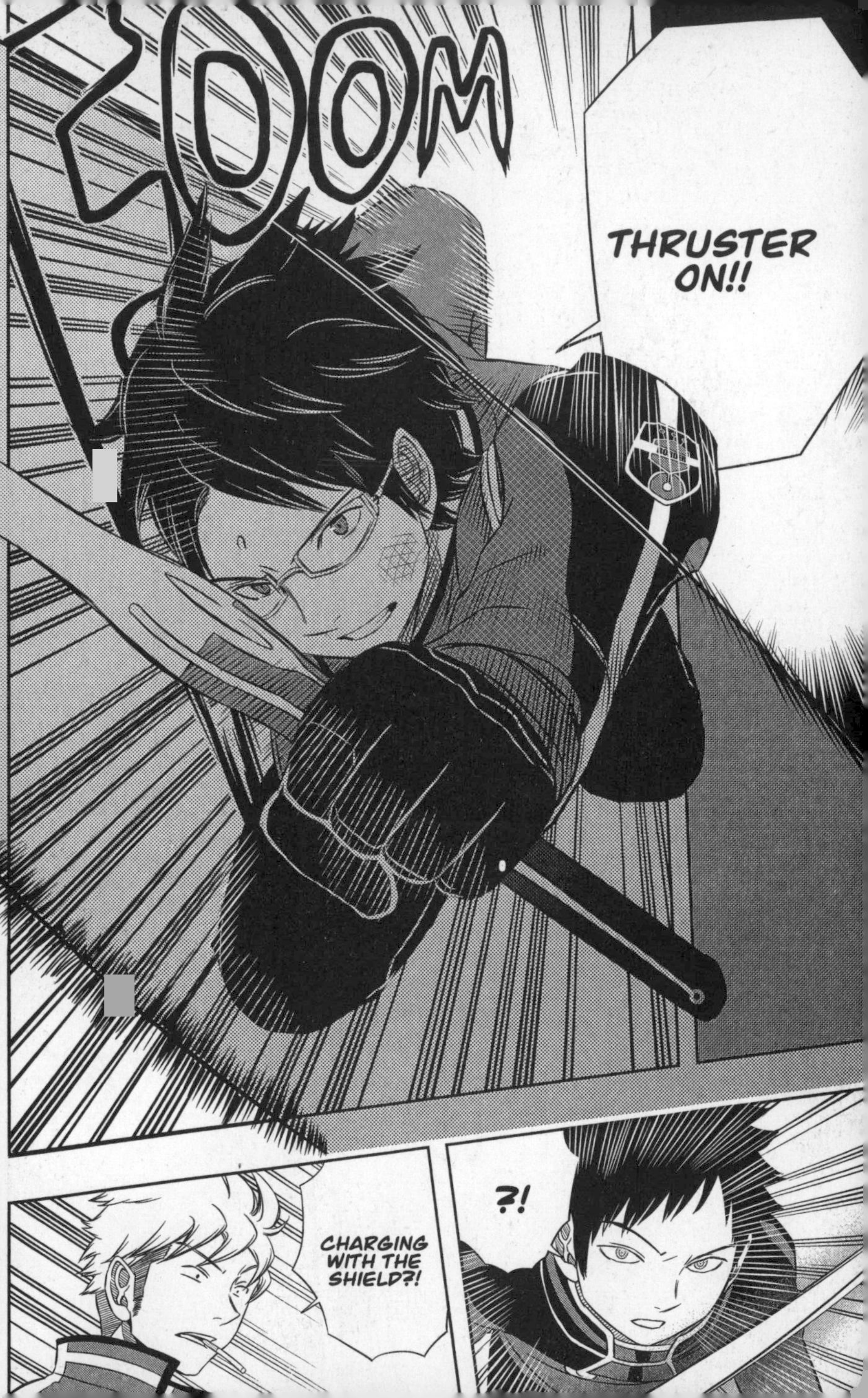
ZOOM
THRUSTER ON!!
?!
CHARGING WITH THE SHIELD?!

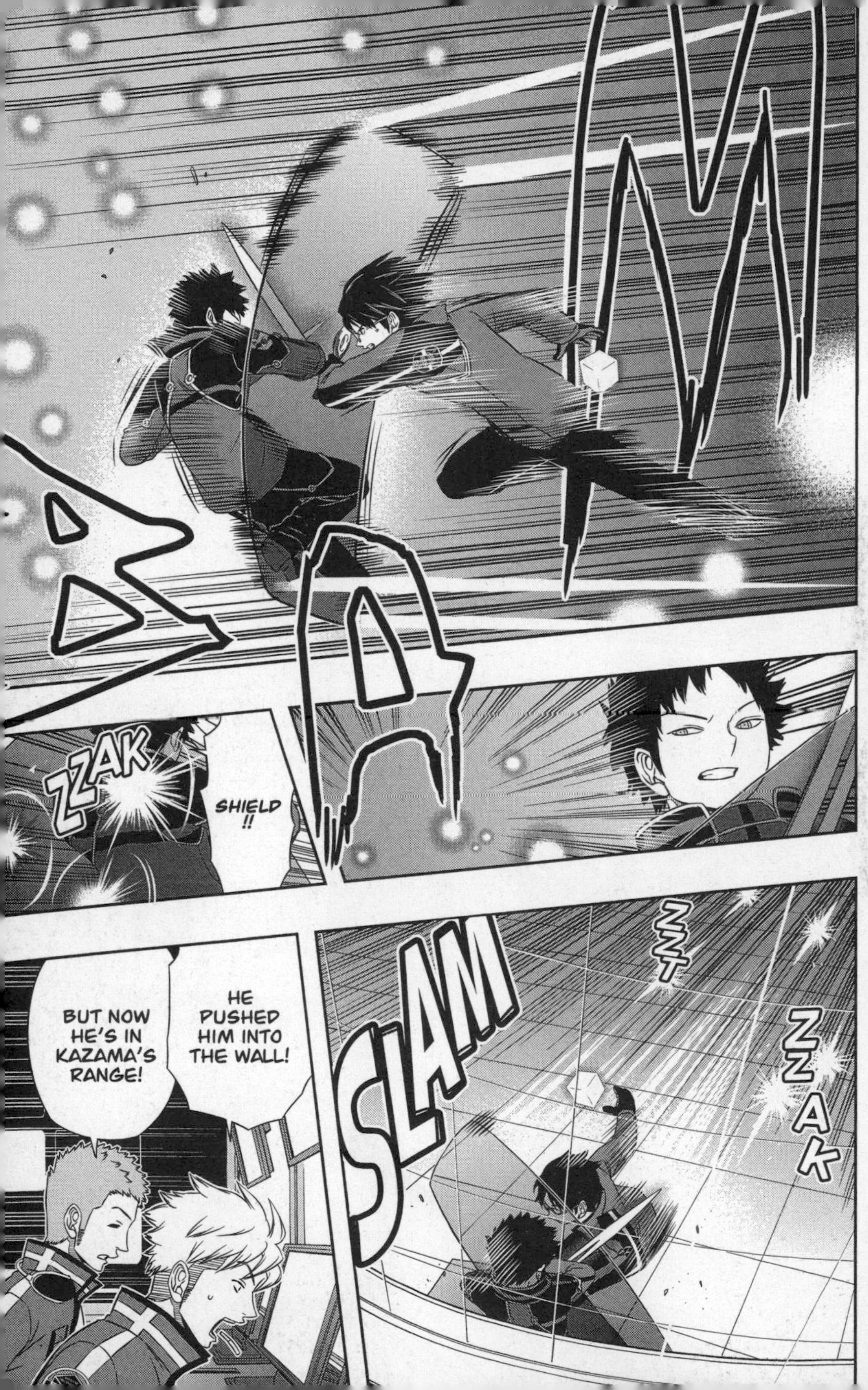
ZZAK
SHIELD!!
ZZZT
ZZAK
SLAM
HE PUSHED HIM INTO THE WALL!
BUT NOW HE'S IN KAZAMA'S RANGE!

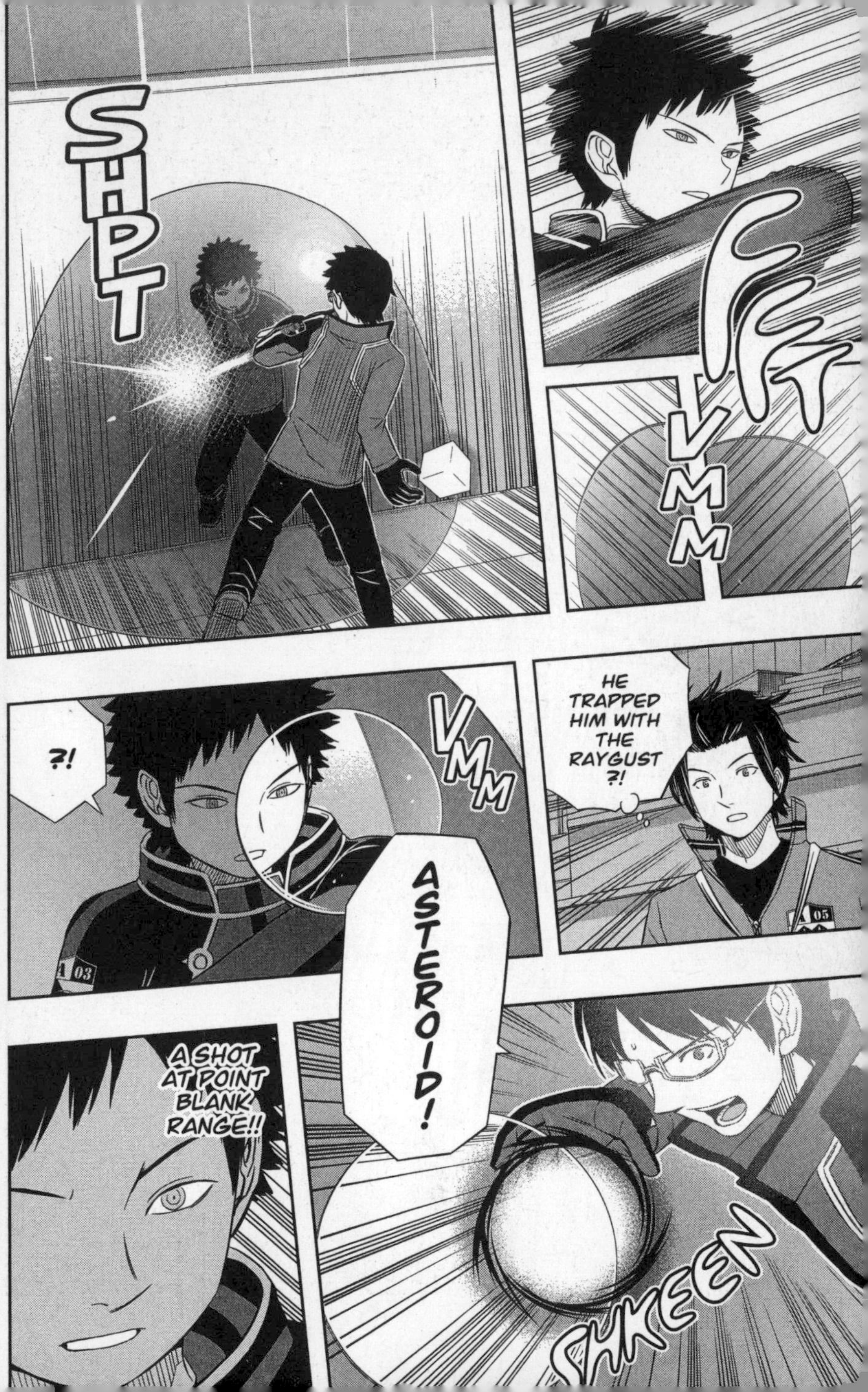
FFFT
VMMM
SHPT
HE TRAPPED HIM WITH THE RAYGUST ?!
?!
VMM
ASTEROID!
SHKEEN
A SHOT AT POINT BLANK RANGE!!

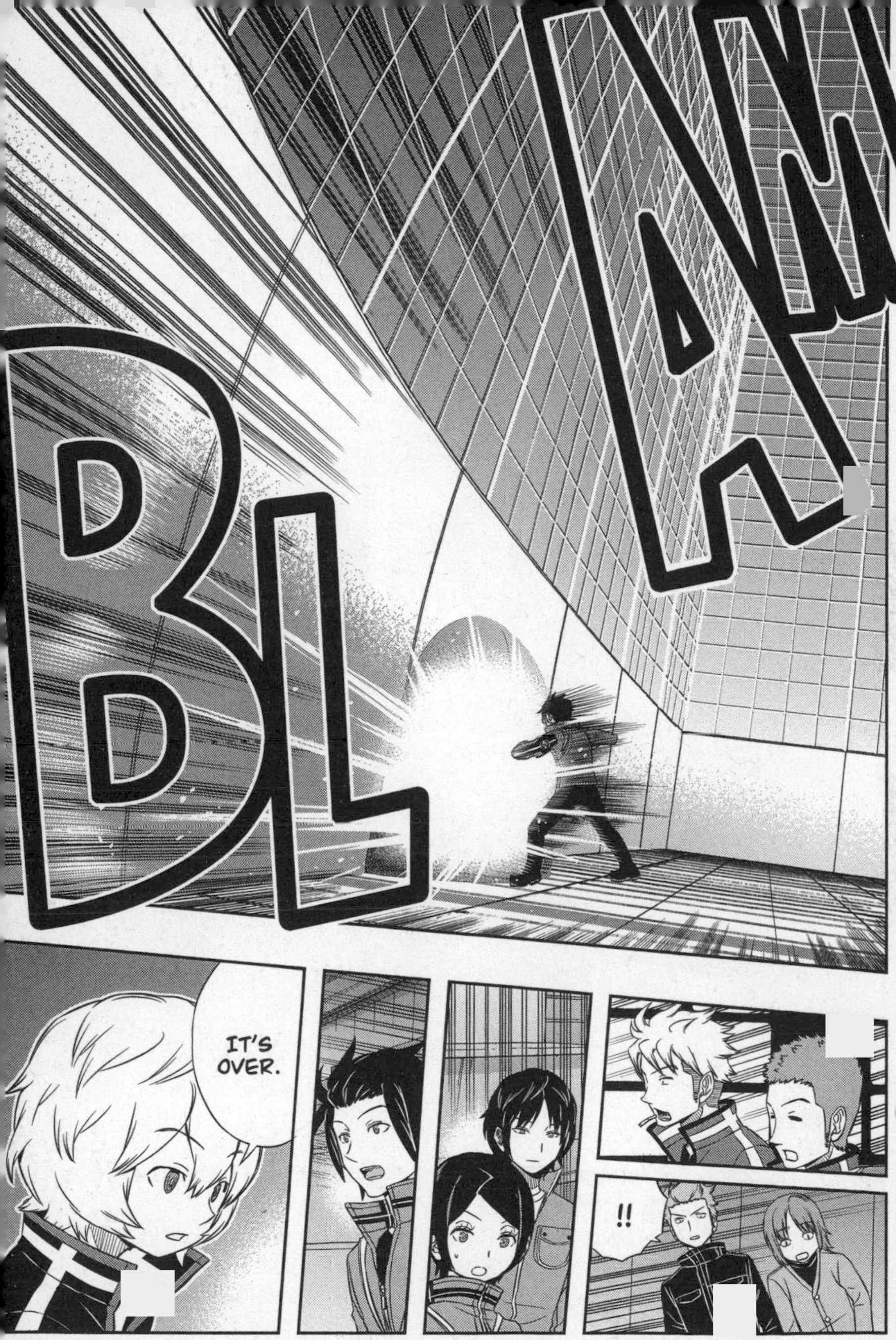
BLAM
!!
IT'S OVER.

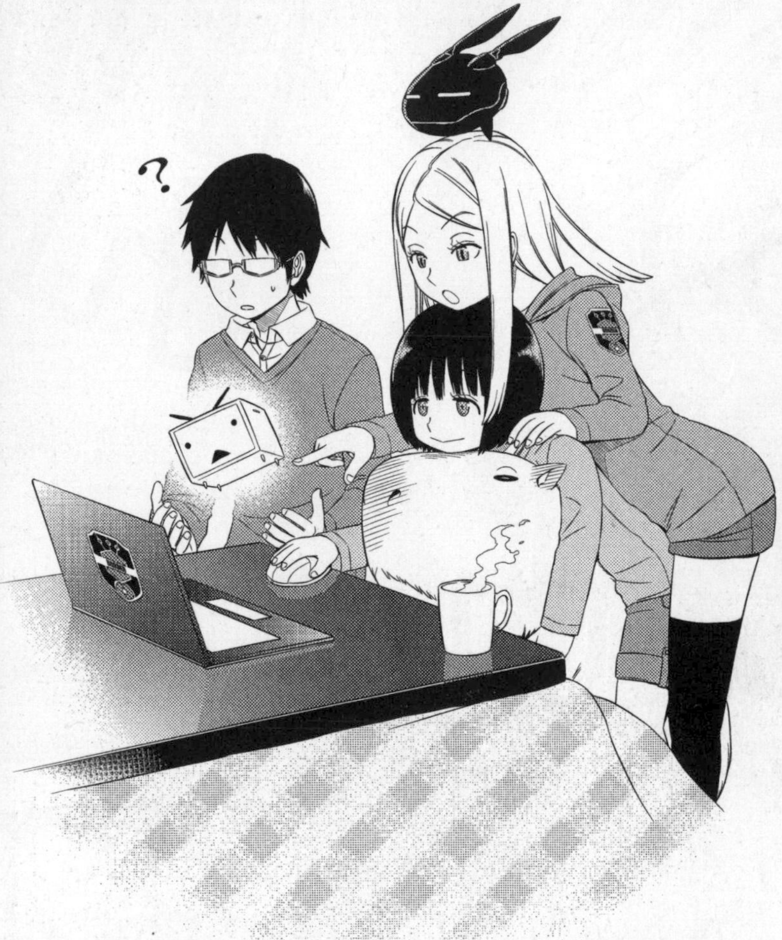

■ **2014 Niconico Still Image MAD contest, Participation Award illustration (actual image was in color)**

Now that I think about it, Yuma probably would've been more interested in online videos, but I figured girls (and animals) are more suited for Niconico. I like it because they look like they're having fun, and it shows Raijin-maru's relative size.

Chapter 37 Osamu Mikumo: Part 6

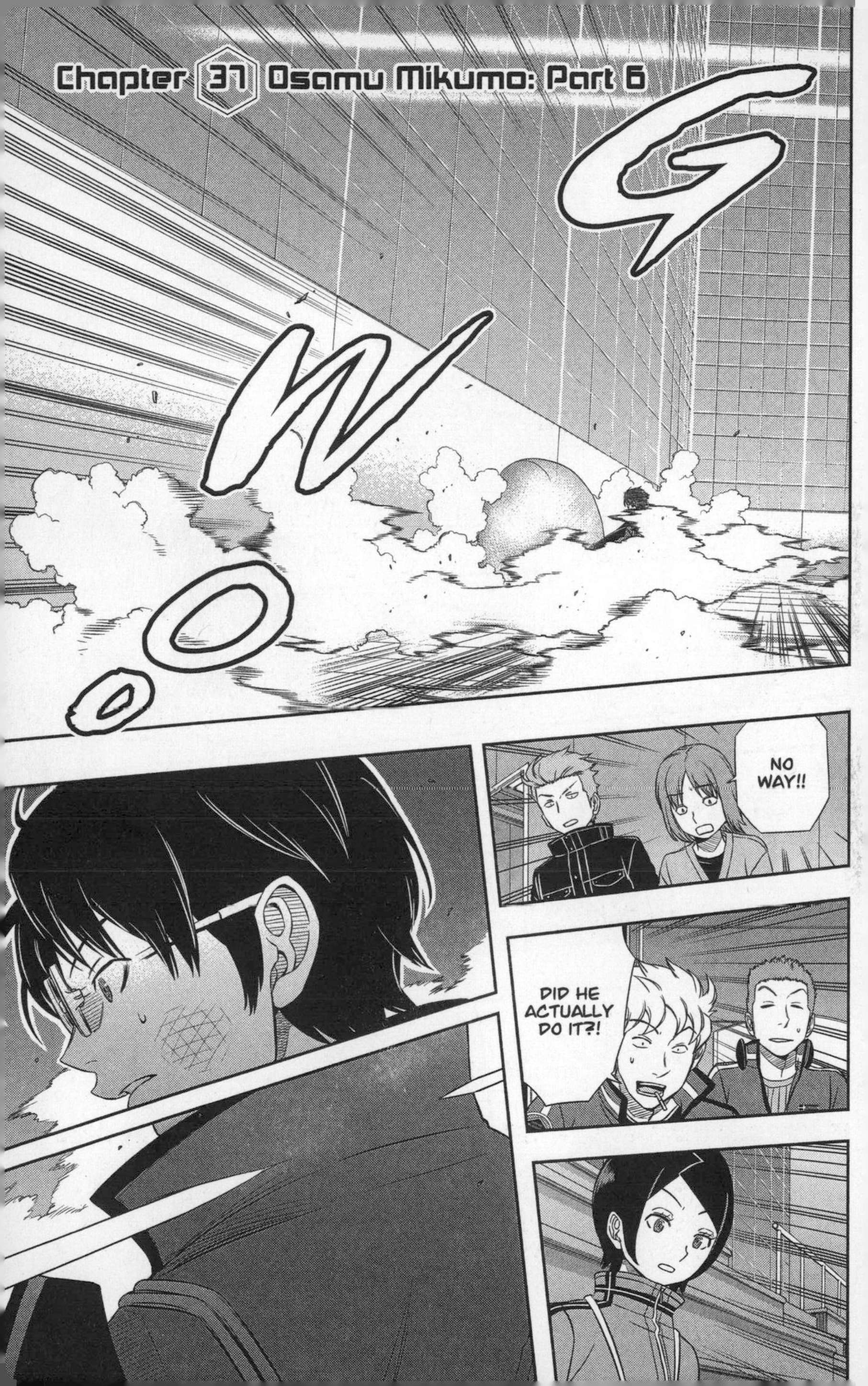

GWOOO
NO WAY!!
DID HE ACTUALLY DO IT?!

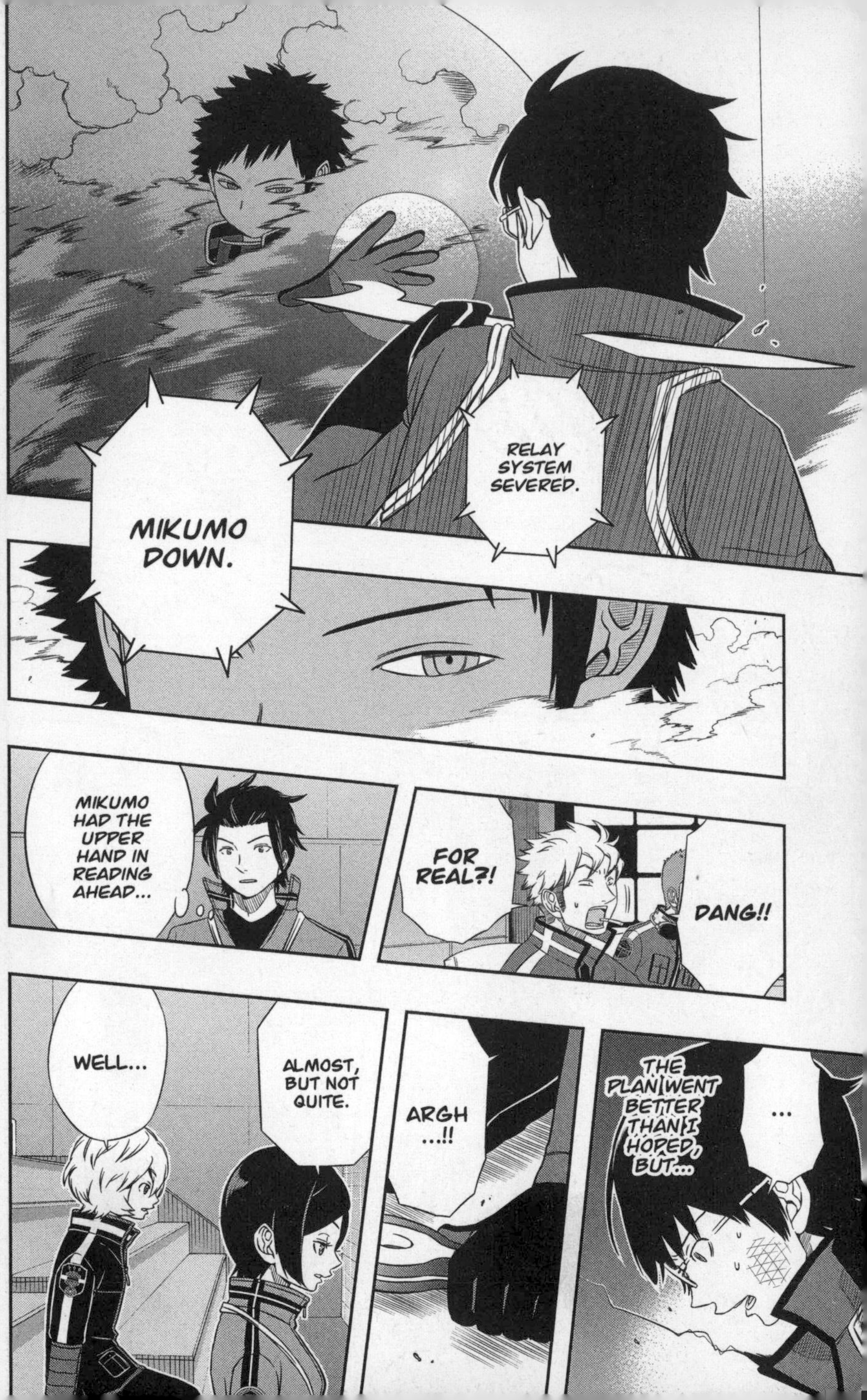
RELAY SYSTEM SEVERED.
MIKUMO DOWN.
DANG!!
FOR REAL?!
MIKUMO HAD THE UPPER HAND IN READING AHEAD...
...
THE PLAN WENT BETTER THAN I HOPED, BUT...
ARGH ...!!
ALMOST, BUT NOT QUITE.
WELL...

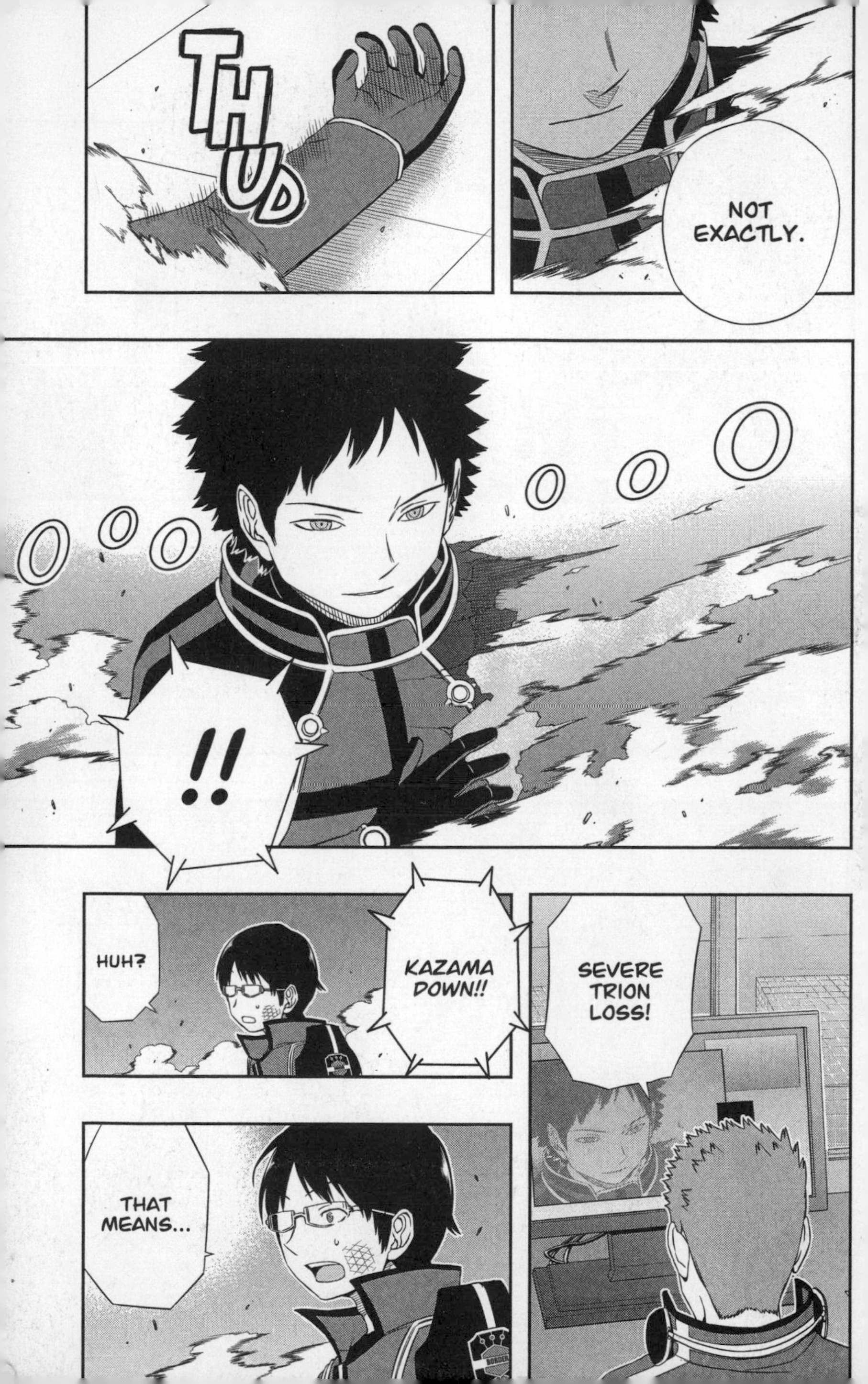
NOT EXACTLY.
THUD
OOOOOO
!!
SEVERE TRION LOSS!
KAZAMA DOWN!!
HUH?
THAT MEANS...

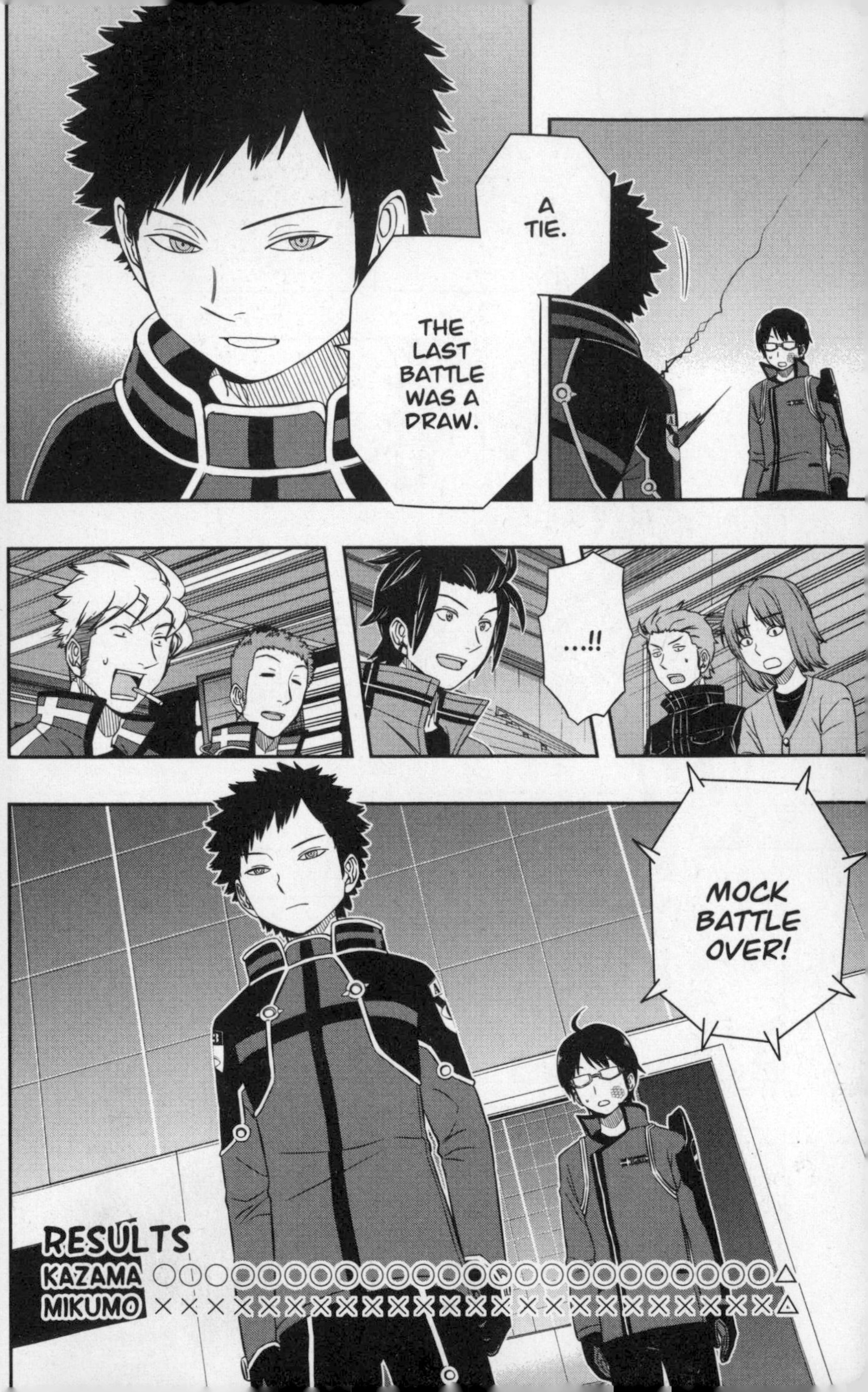
A TIE.
THE LAST BATTLE WAS A DRAW.
...!!
MOCK BATTLE OVER!
RESULTS
KAZAMA ○○○○○○○○○○○○○○○○○○○○○○○○△
MIKUMO ××××××××××××××××××××××××△

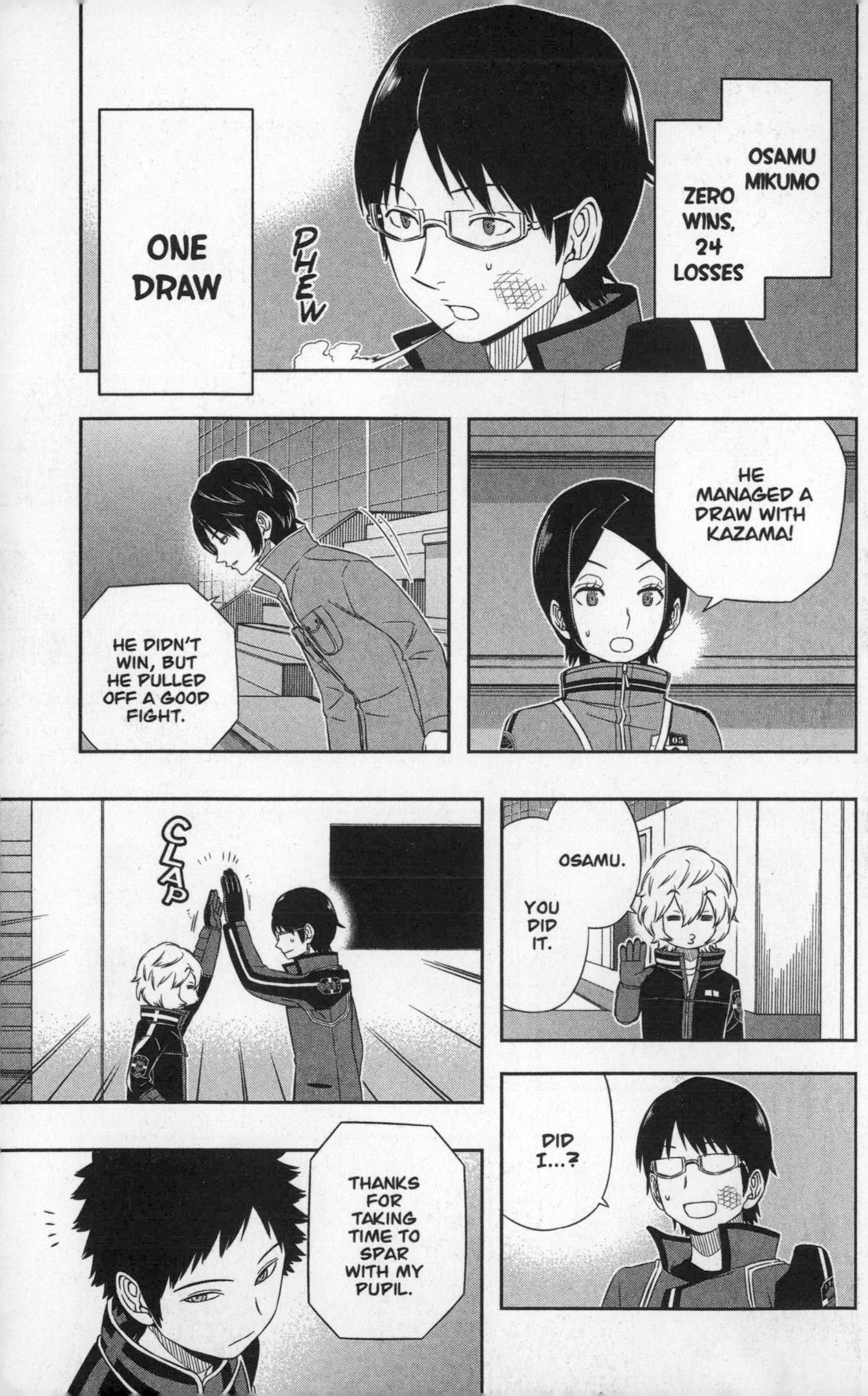
OSAMU MIKUMO
ZERO WINS, 24 LOSSES
PHEW
ONE DRAW
HE MANAGED A DRAW WITH KAZAMA!
HE DIDN'T WIN, BUT HE PULLED OFF A GOOD FIGHT.
OSAMU.
YOU DID IT.
CLAP
DID I...?
THANKS FOR TAKING TIME TO SPAR WITH MY PUPIL.

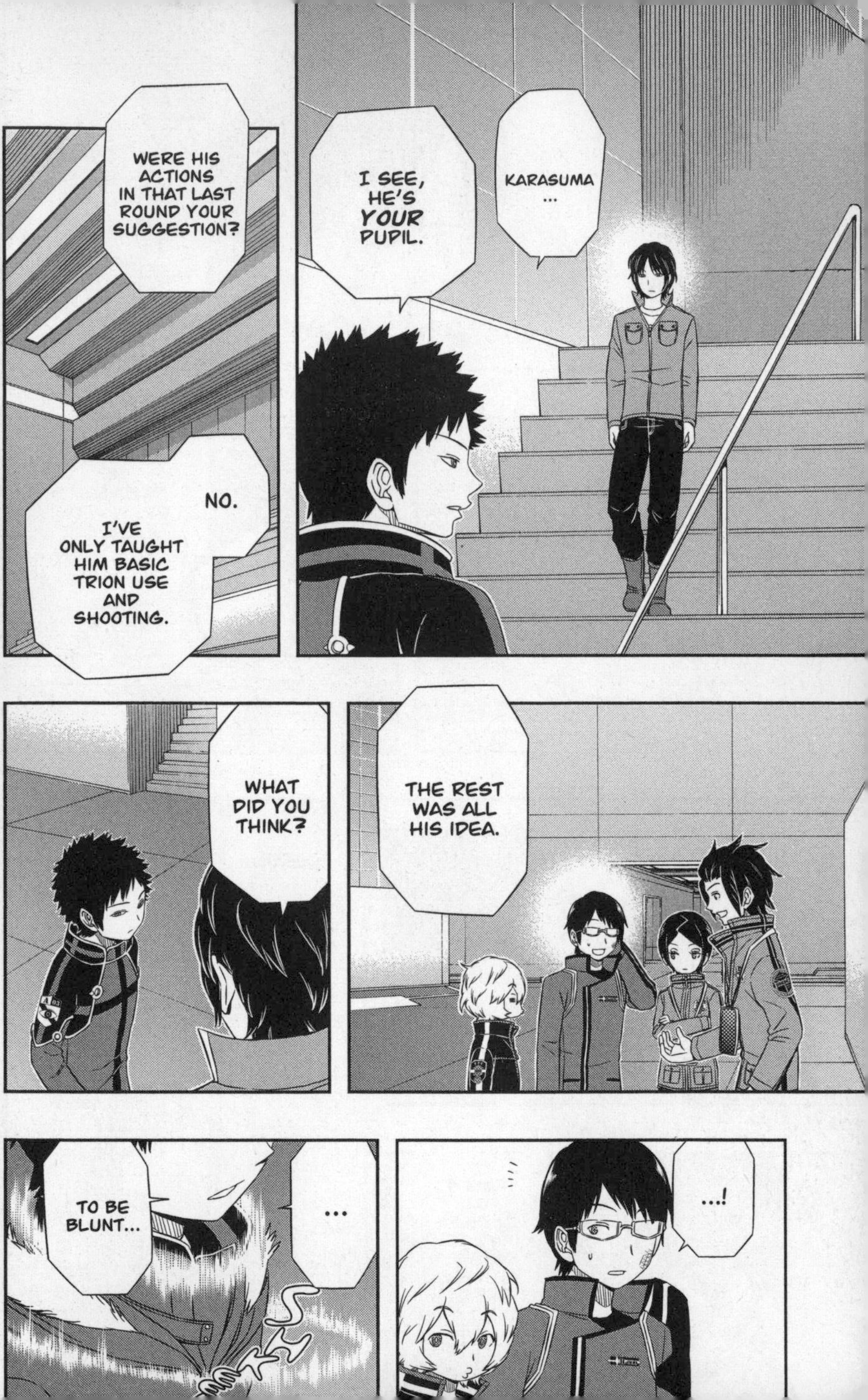

KARASUMA ...
I SEE, HE'S YOUR PUPIL.
WERE HIS ACTIONS IN THAT LAST ROUND YOUR SUGGESTION?
NO.
I'VE ONLY TAUGHT HIM BASIC TRION USE AND SHOOTING.
THE REST WAS ALL HIS IDEA.
WHAT DID YOU THINK?
...!
...
TO BE BLUNT...

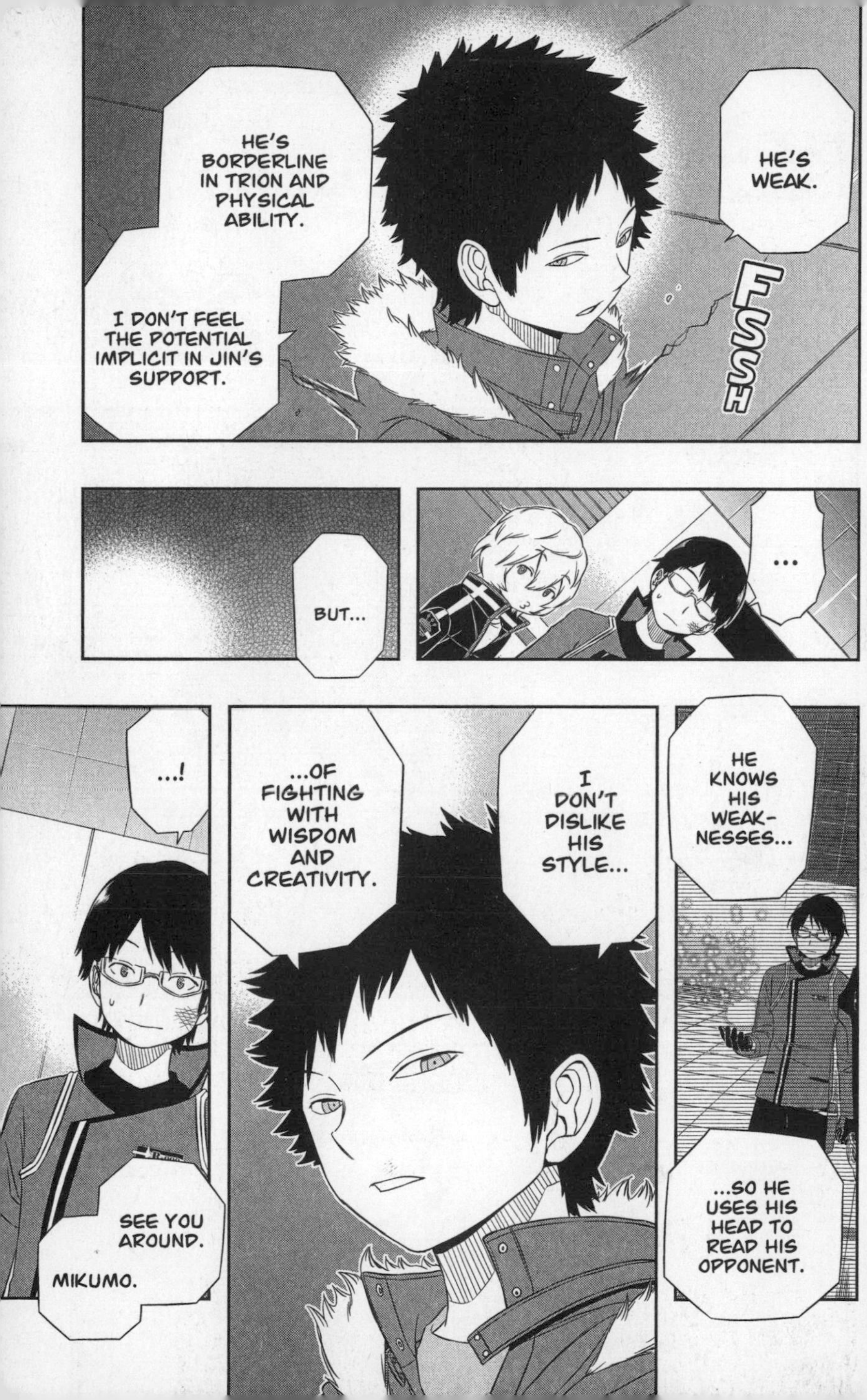
HE'S WEAK.
FSSH
HE'S BORDERLINE IN TRION AND PHYSICAL ABILITY.
I DON'T FEEL THE POTENTIAL IMPLICIT IN JIN'S SUPPORT.
...
BUT...
HE KNOWS HIS WEAK-NESSES...
...SO HE USES HIS HEAD TO READ HIS OPPONENT.
I DON'T DISLIKE HIS STYLE...
...OF FIGHTING WITH WISDOM AND CREATIVITY.
...!
SEE YOU AROUND.
MIKUMO.

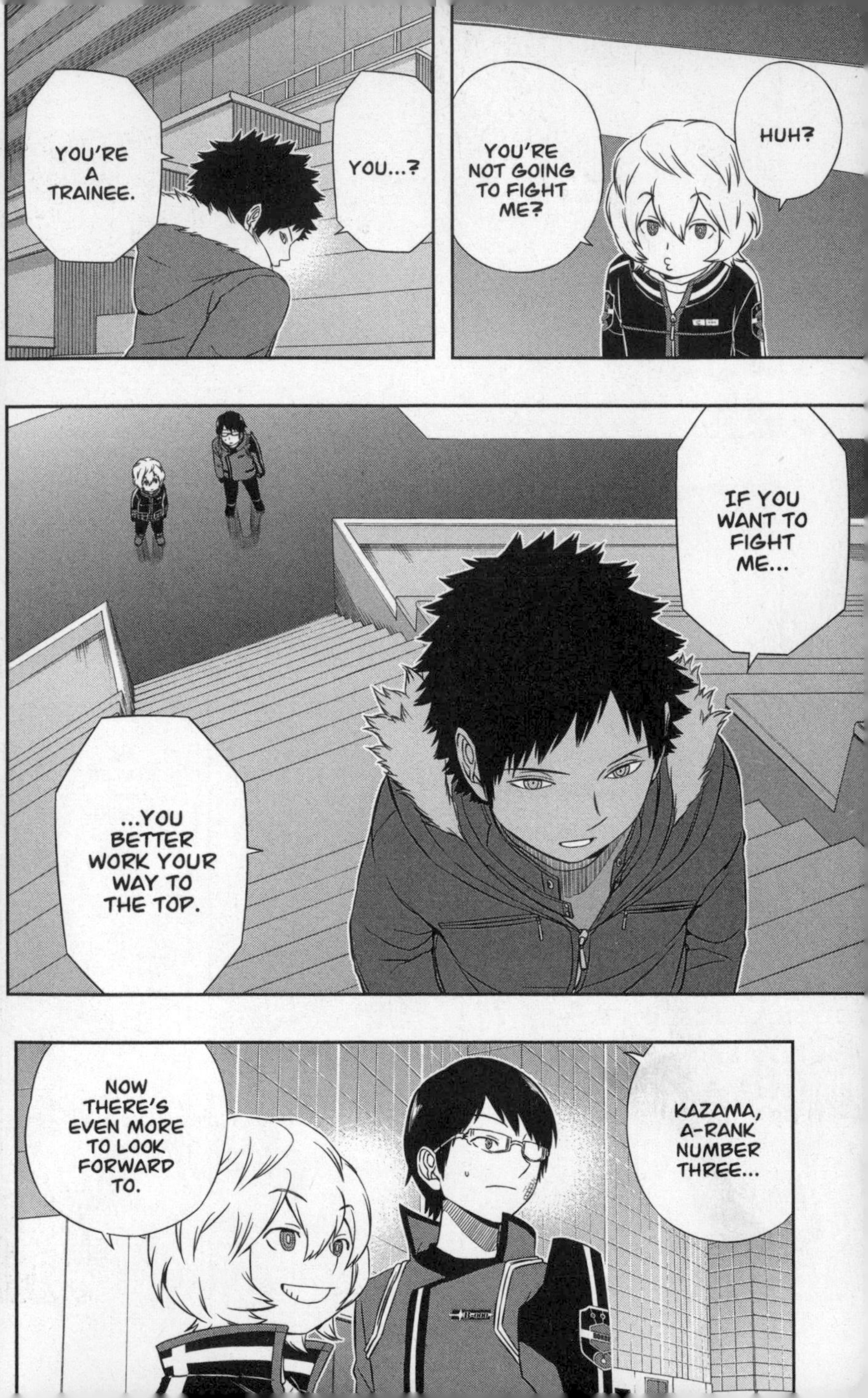
HUH?
YOU'RE NOT GOING TO FIGHT ME?
YOU...?
YOU'RE A TRAINEE.
IF YOU WANT TO FIGHT ME...
...YOU BETTER WORK YOUR WAY TO THE TOP.
KAZAMA, A-RANK NUMBER THREE...
NOW THERE'S EVEN MORE TO LOOK FORWARD TO.

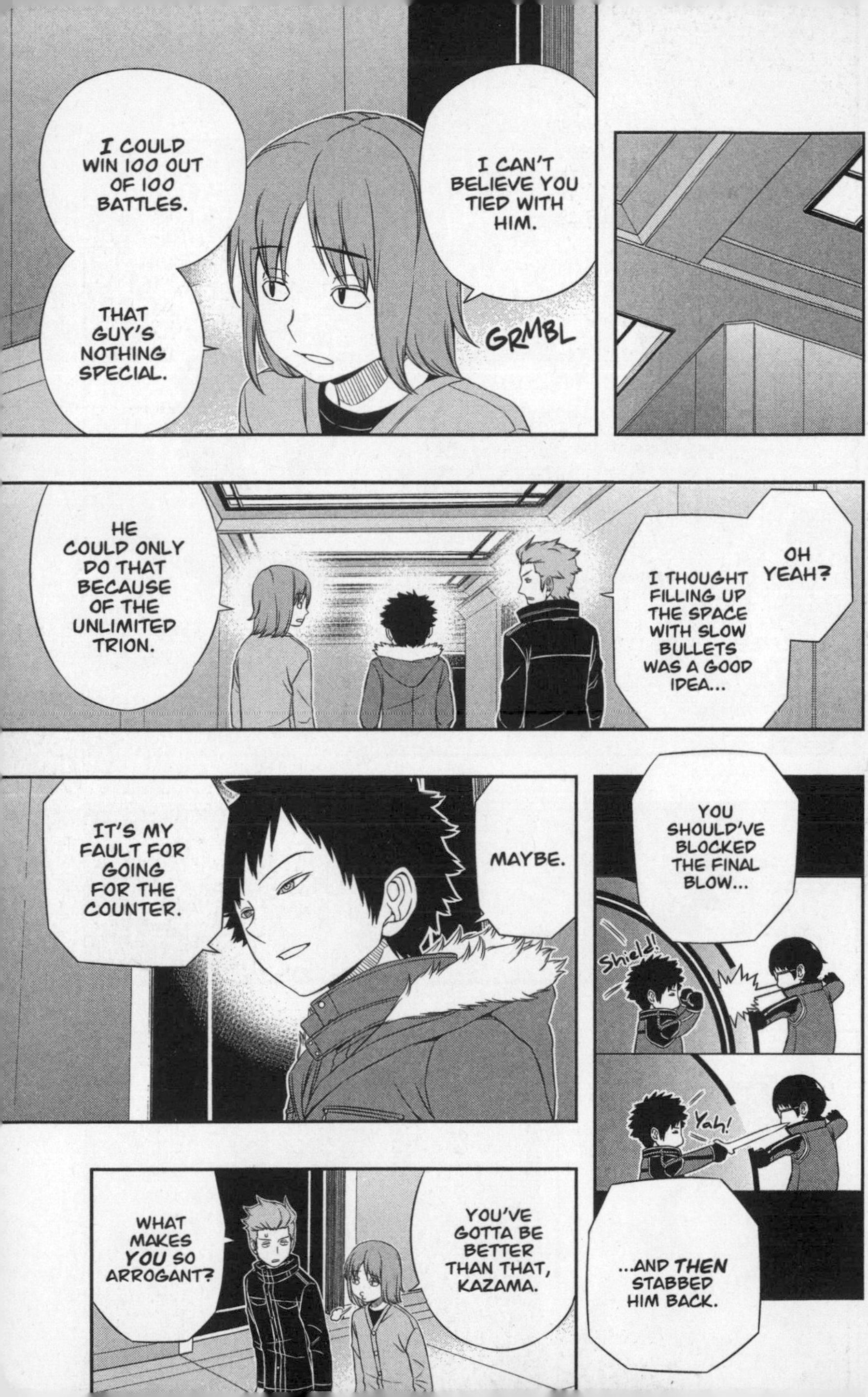
I CAN'T BELIEVE YOU TIED WITH HIM.
GRMBL
I COULD WIN 100 OUT OF 100 BATTLES.
THAT GUY'S NOTHING SPECIAL.
OH YEAH?
I THOUGHT FILLING UP THE SPACE WITH SLOW BULLETS WAS A GOOD IDEA...
HE COULD ONLY DO THAT BECAUSE OF THE UNLIMITED TRION.
YOU SHOULD'VE BLOCKED THE FINAL BLOW...
Shield!
Yah!
...AND THEN STABBED HIM BACK.
MAYBE.
IT'S MY FAULT FOR GOING FOR THE COUNTER.
YOU'VE GOTTA BE BETTER THAN THAT, KAZAMA.
WHAT MAKES YOU SO ARROGANT?

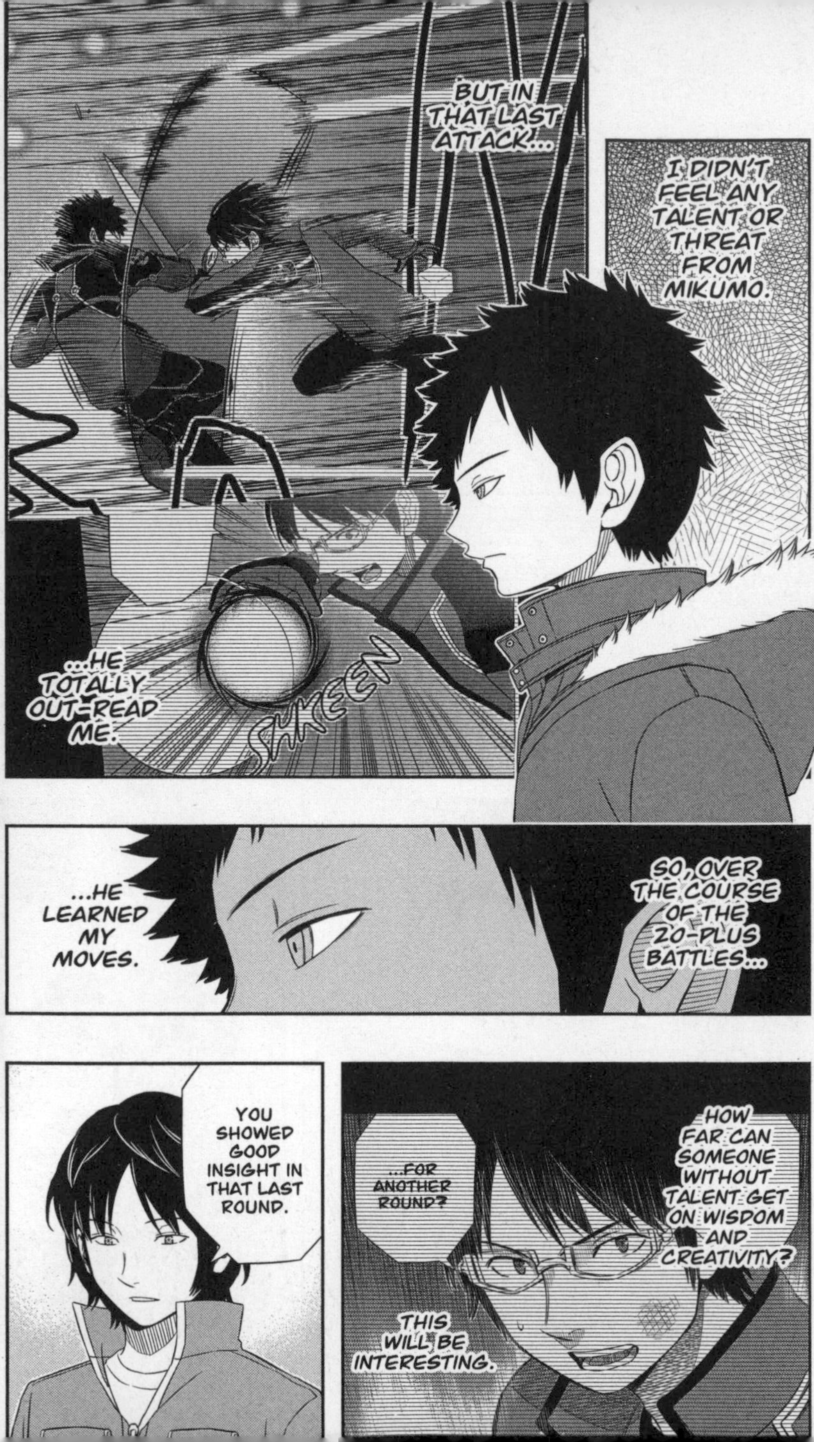
I DIDN'T FEEL ANY TALENT OR THREAT FROM MIKUMO.
BUT IN THAT LAST ATTACK...
...HE TOTALLY OUT-READ ME.
SHKEEN
SO, OVER THE COURSE OF THE 20-PLUS BATTLES...
...HE LEARNED MY MOVES.
HOW FAR CAN SOMEONE WITHOUT TALENT GET ON WISDOM AND CREATIVITY?
...FOR ANOTHER ROUND?
THIS WILL BE INTERESTING.
YOU SHOWED GOOD INSIGHT IN THAT LAST ROUND.

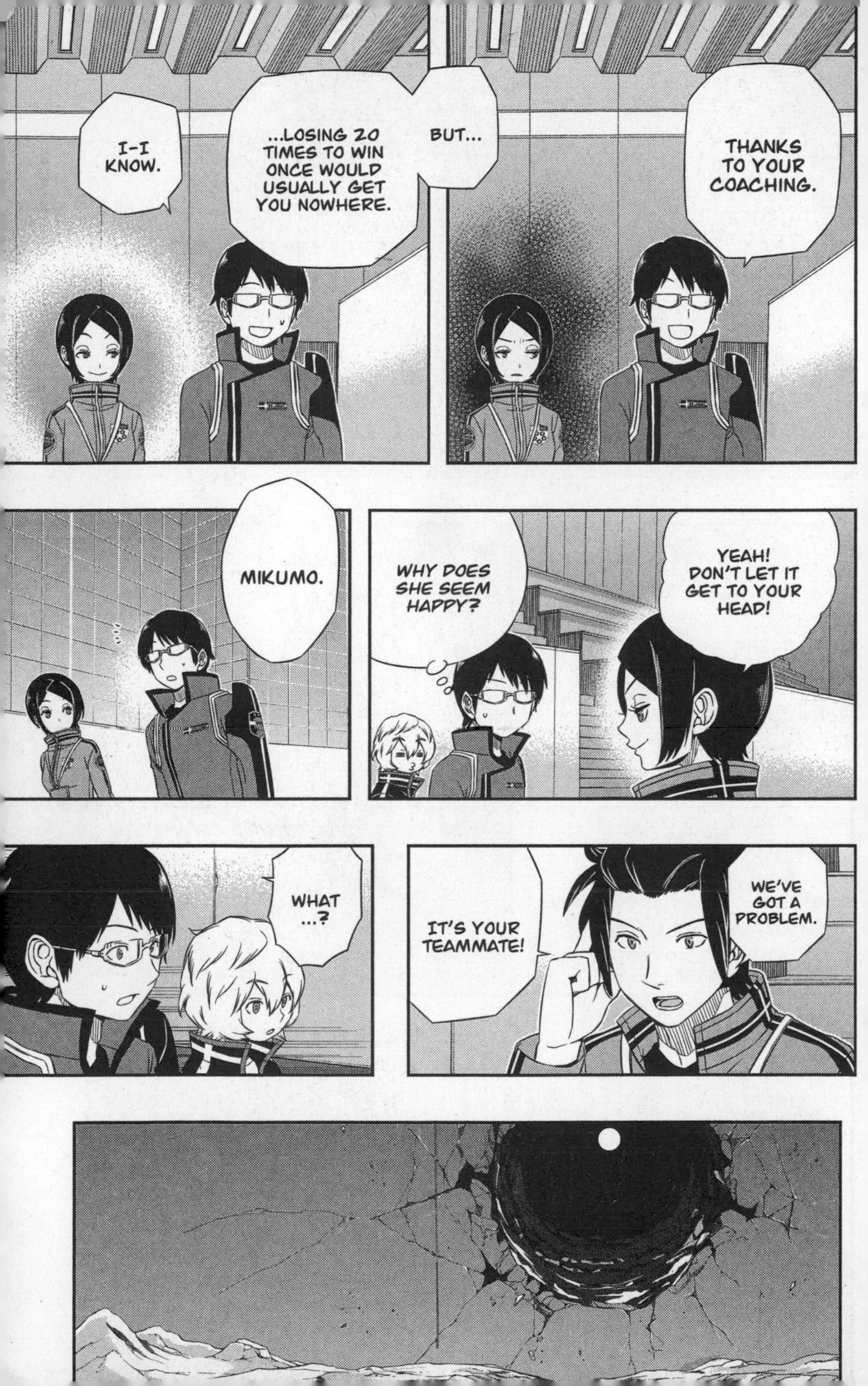
THANKS TO YOUR COACHING.
BUT...
...LOSING 20 TIMES TO WIN ONCE WOULD USUALLY GET YOU NOWHERE.
I-I KNOW.
YEAH! DON'T LET IT GET TO YOUR HEAD!
WHY DOES SHE SEEM HAPPY?
MIKUMO.
WE'VE GOT A PROBLEM.
IT'S YOUR TEAMMATE!
WHAT ...?

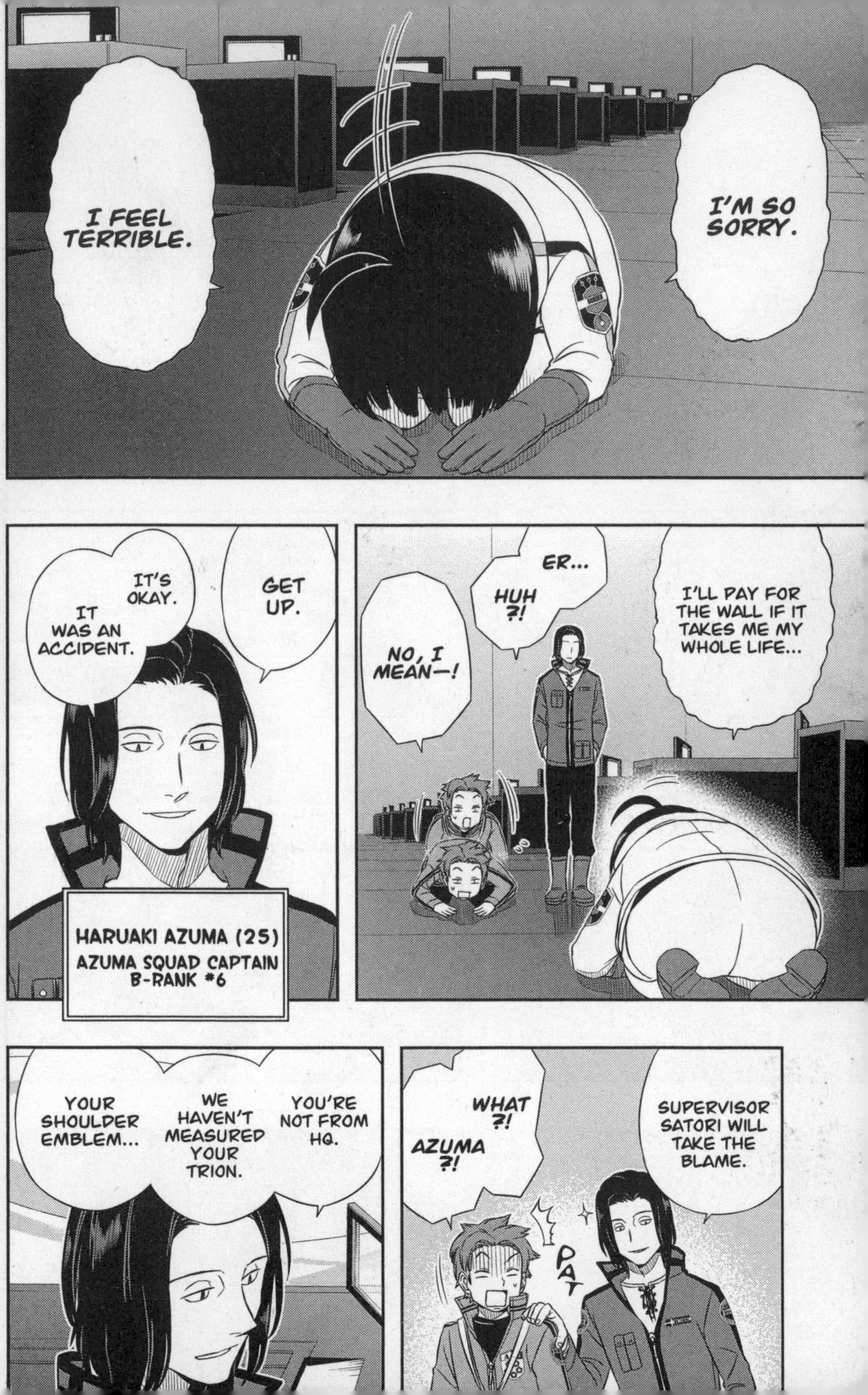
I'M SO SORRY.
I FEEL TERRIBLE.
I'LL PAY FOR THE WALL IF IT TAKES ME MY WHOLE LIFE...
ER...
HUH ?!
NO, I MEAN—!
GET UP.
IT'S OKAY.
IT WAS AN ACCIDENT.
HARUAKI AZUMA (25)
AZUMA SQUAD CAPTAIN
B-RANK #6
SUPERVISOR SATORI WILL TAKE THE BLAME.
WHAT ?!
AZUMA ?!
PAT
YOU'RE NOT FROM HQ.
WE HAVEN'T MEASURED YOUR TRION.
YOUR SHOULDER EMBLEM...

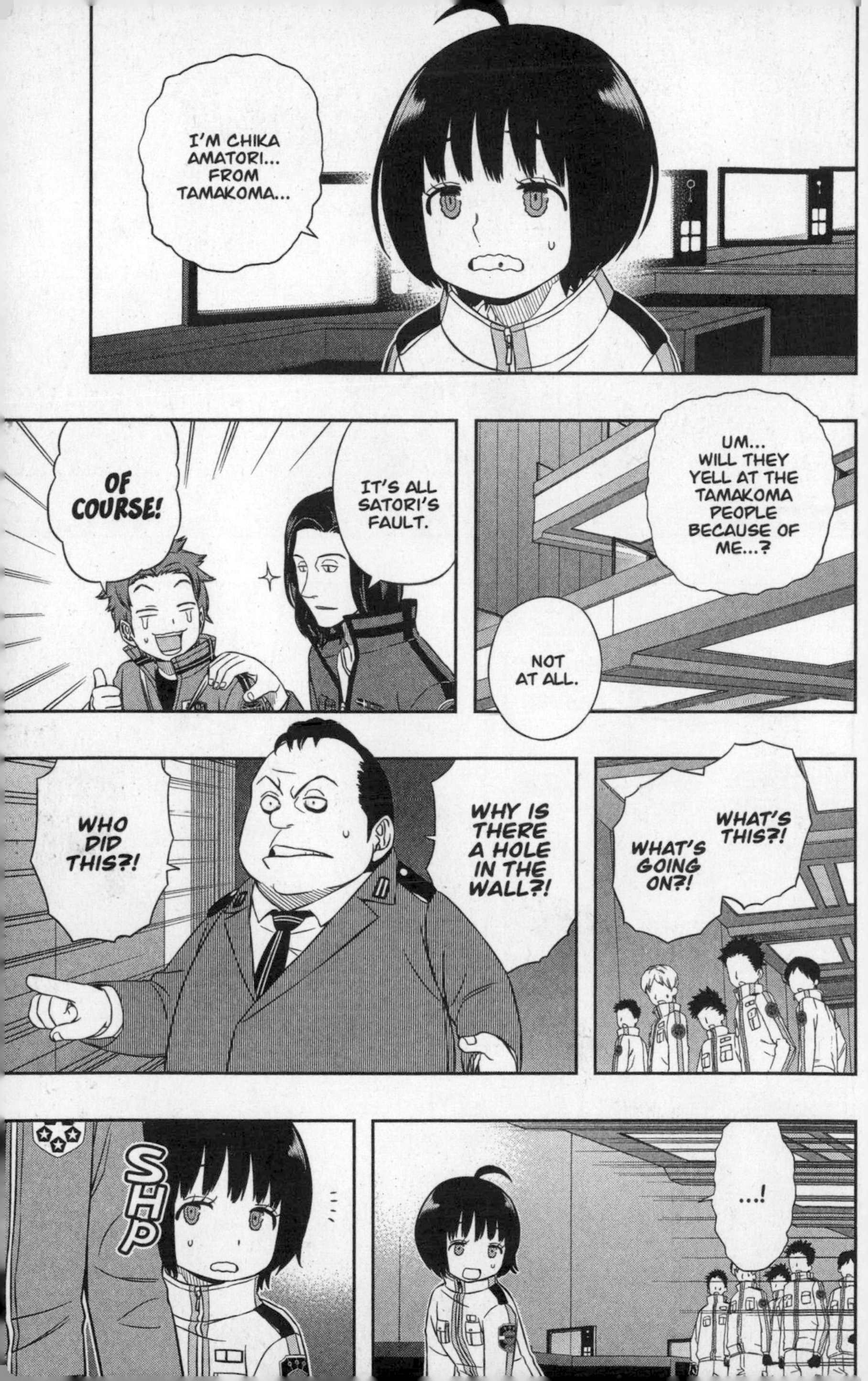
I'M CHIKA AMATORI... FROM TAMAKOMA...
UM... WILL THEY YELL AT THE TAMAKOMA PEOPLE BECAUSE OF ME...?
NOT AT ALL.
IT'S ALL SATORI'S FAULT.
OF COURSE!
WHAT'S THIS?!
WHAT'S GOING ON?!
WHY IS THERE A HOLE IN THE WALL?!
WHO DID THIS?!
...!
SHP

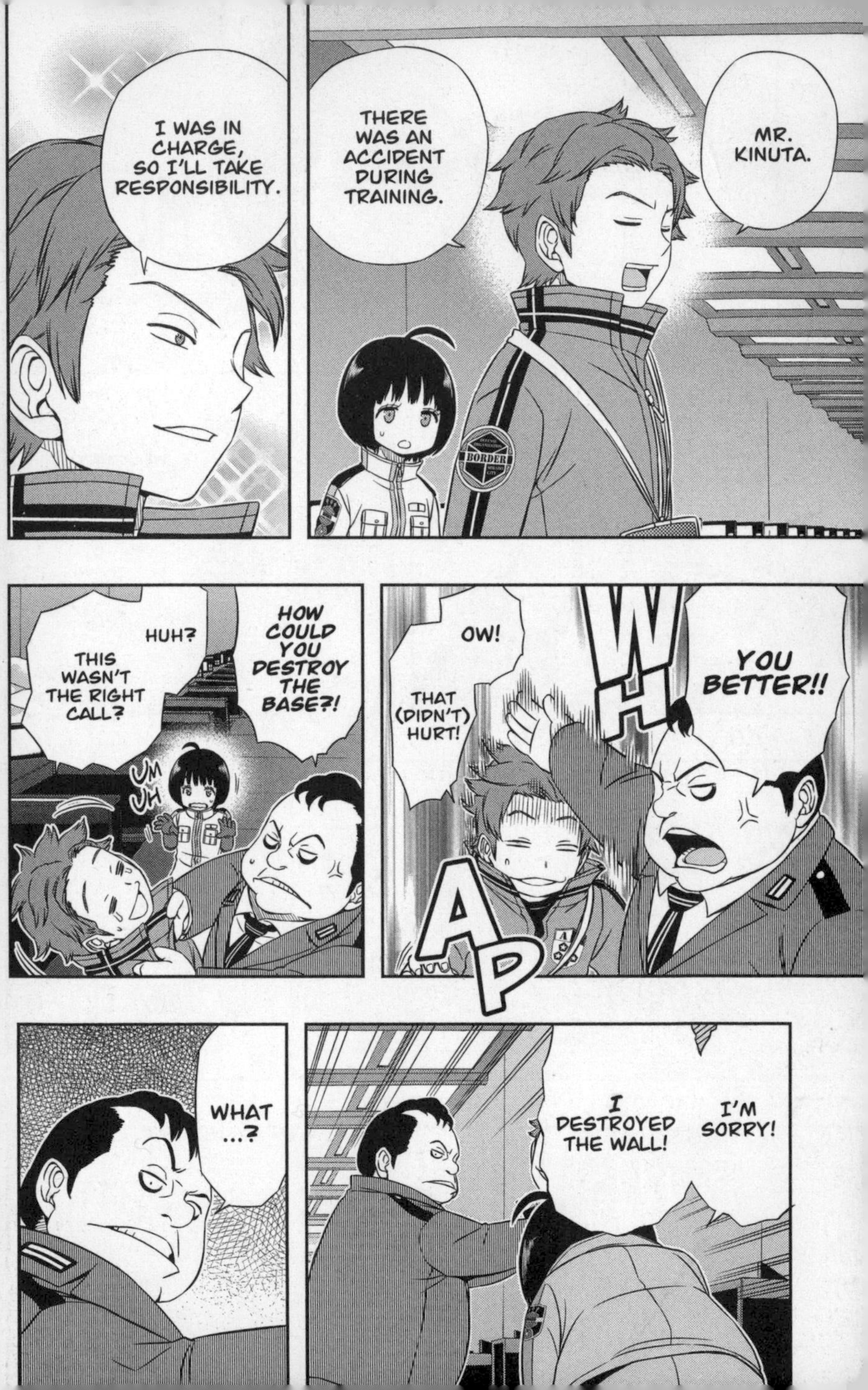
MR. KINUTA.
THERE WAS AN ACCIDENT DURING TRAINING.
I WAS IN CHARGE, SO I'LL TAKE RESPONSIBILITY.
YOU BETTER!!
WHAP
OW!
THAT (DIDN'T) HURT!
HOW COULD YOU DESTROY THE BASE?!
HUH?
THIS WASN'T THE RIGHT CALL?
UM UH
I'M SORRY!
I DESTROYED THE WALL!
WHAT ...?

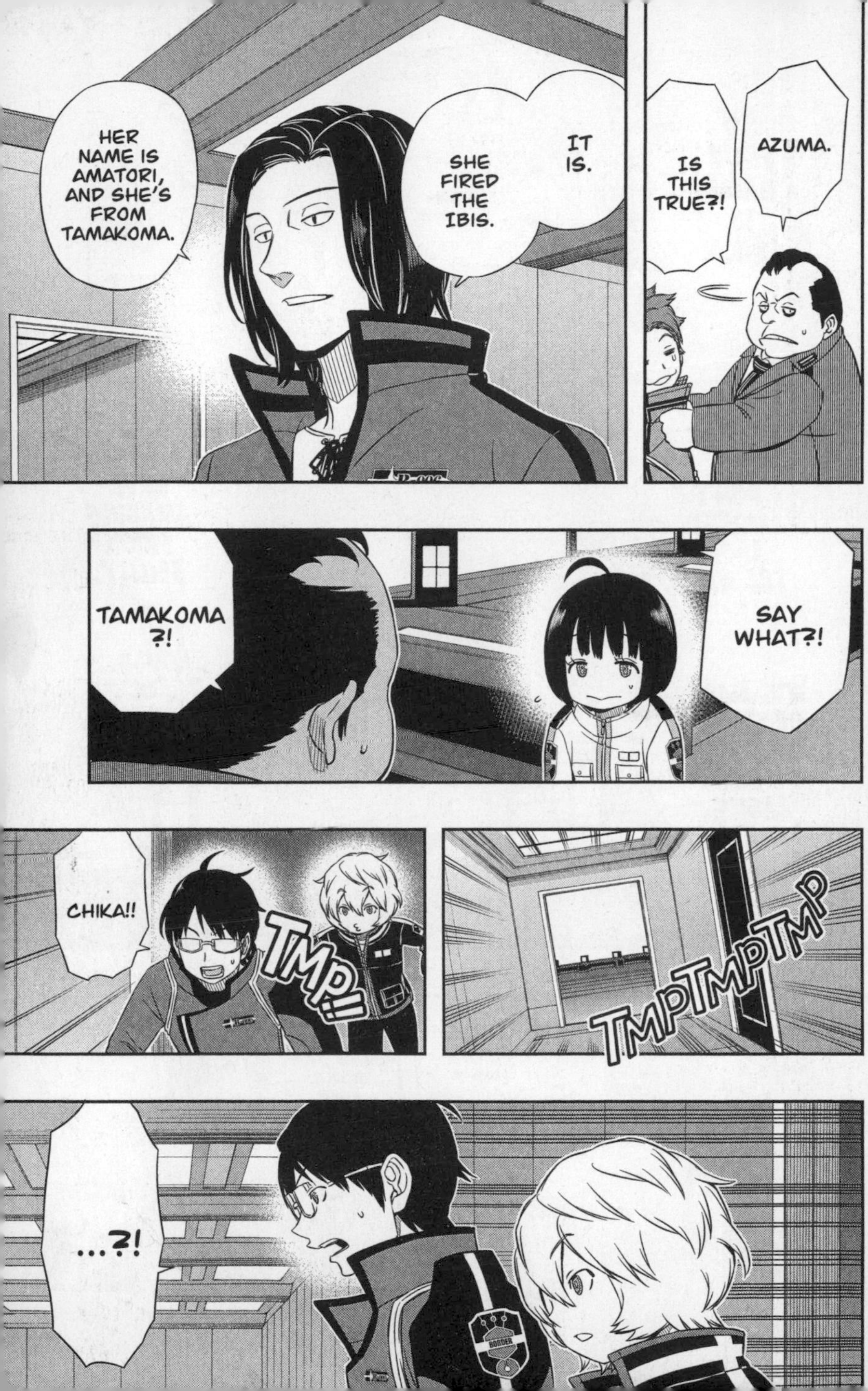
AZUMA.
IS THIS TRUE?!
IT IS.
SHE FIRED THE IBIS.
HER NAME IS AMATORI, AND SHE'S FROM TAMAKOMA.
SAY WHAT?!
TAMAKOMA?!
TMPTMPTMP
TMP
CHIKA!!
...?!

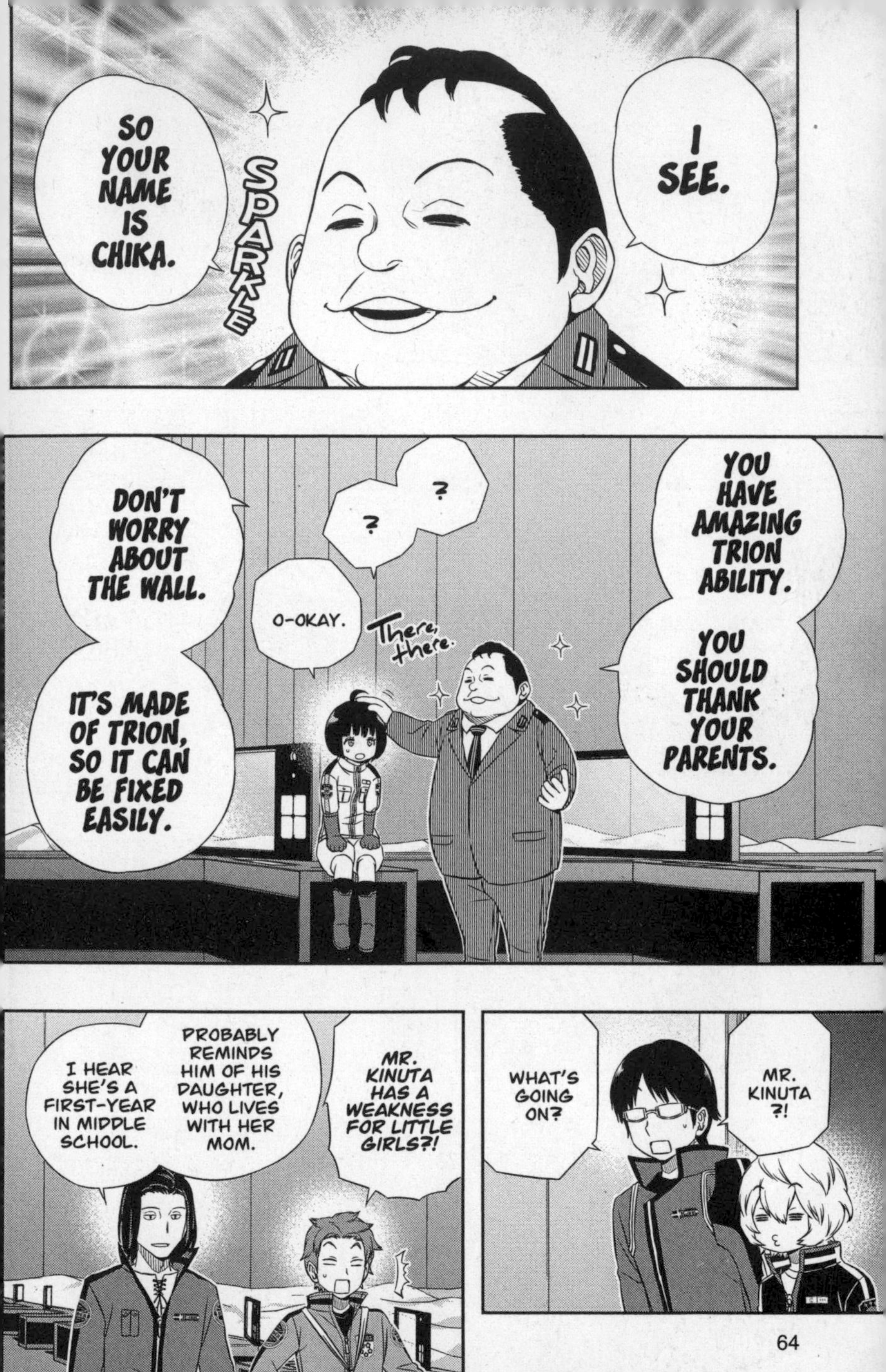
I SEE.
SPARKLE
SO YOUR NAME IS CHIKA.
YOU HAVE AMAZING TRION ABILITY.
YOU SHOULD THANK YOUR PARENTS.
There, there.
?
?
O-OKAY.
DON'T WORRY ABOUT THE WALL.
IT'S MADE OF TRION, SO IT CAN BE FIXED EASILY.
MR. KINUTA ?!
WHAT'S GOING ON?
MR. KINUTA HAS A WEAKNESS FOR LITTLE GIRLS?!
PROBABLY REMINDS HIM OF HIS DAUGHTER, WHO LIVES WITH HER MOM.
I HEAR SHE'S A FIRST-YEAR IN MIDDLE SCHOOL.

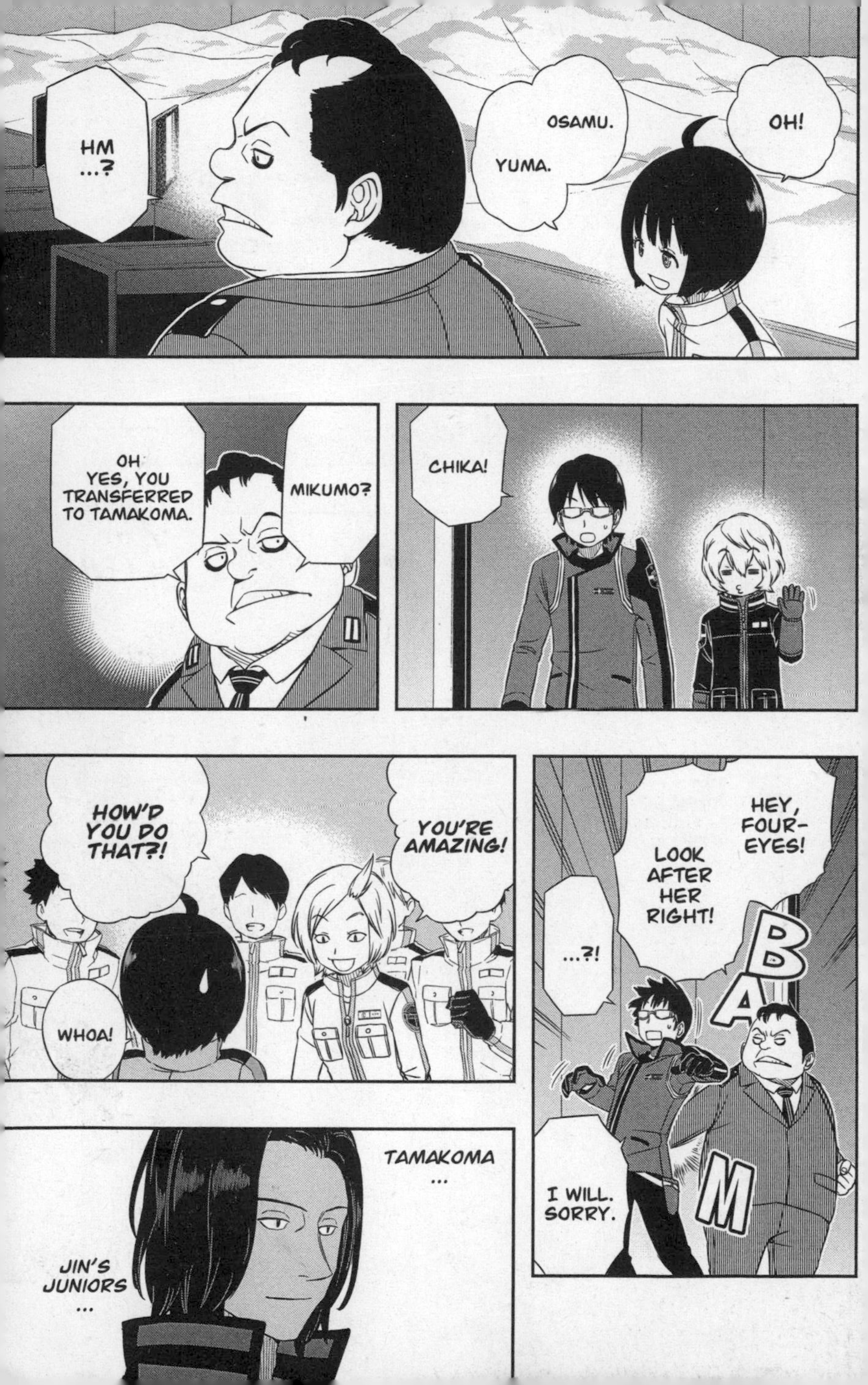
OH!
OSAMU. YUMA.
HM ...?
CHIKA!
MIKUMO?
OH YES, YOU TRANSFERRED TO TAMAKOMA.
HEY, FOUR-EYES!
LOOK AFTER HER RIGHT!
...?!
BAM
I WILL. SORRY.
YOU'RE AMAZING!
HOW'D YOU DO THAT?!
WHOA!
TAMAKOMA ...
JIN'S JUNIORS ...

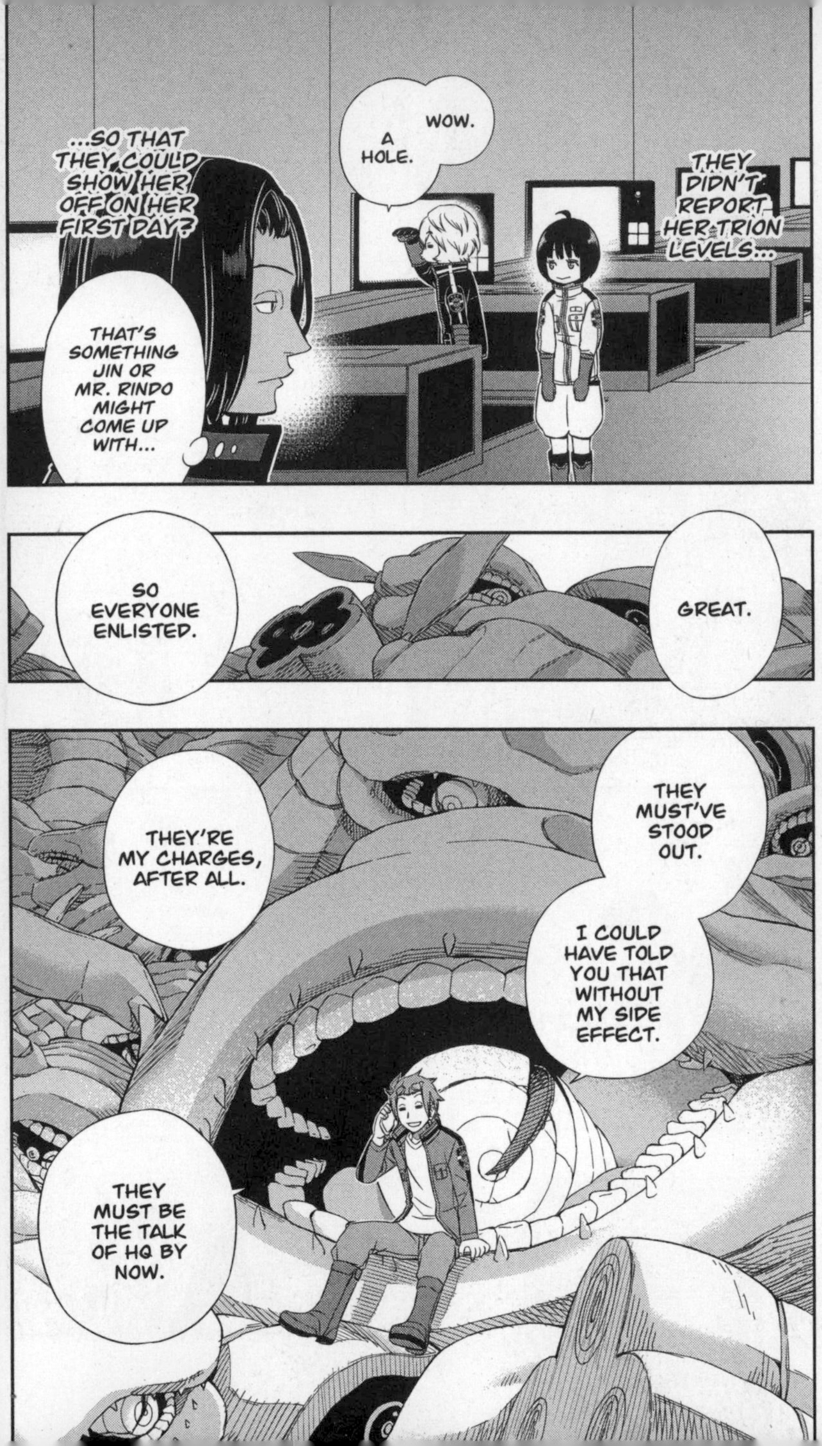
THEY DIDN'T REPORT HER TRION LEVELS...
WOW. A HOLE.
...SO THAT THEY COULD SHOW HER OFF ON HER FIRST DAY?
THAT'S SOMETHING JIN OR MR. RINDO MIGHT COME UP WITH...
GREAT.
SO EVERYONE ENLISTED.
THEY MUST'VE STOOD OUT.
I COULD HAVE TOLD YOU THAT WITHOUT MY SIDE EFFECT.
THEY'RE MY CHARGES, AFTER ALL.
THEY MUST BE THE TALK OF HQ BY NOW.

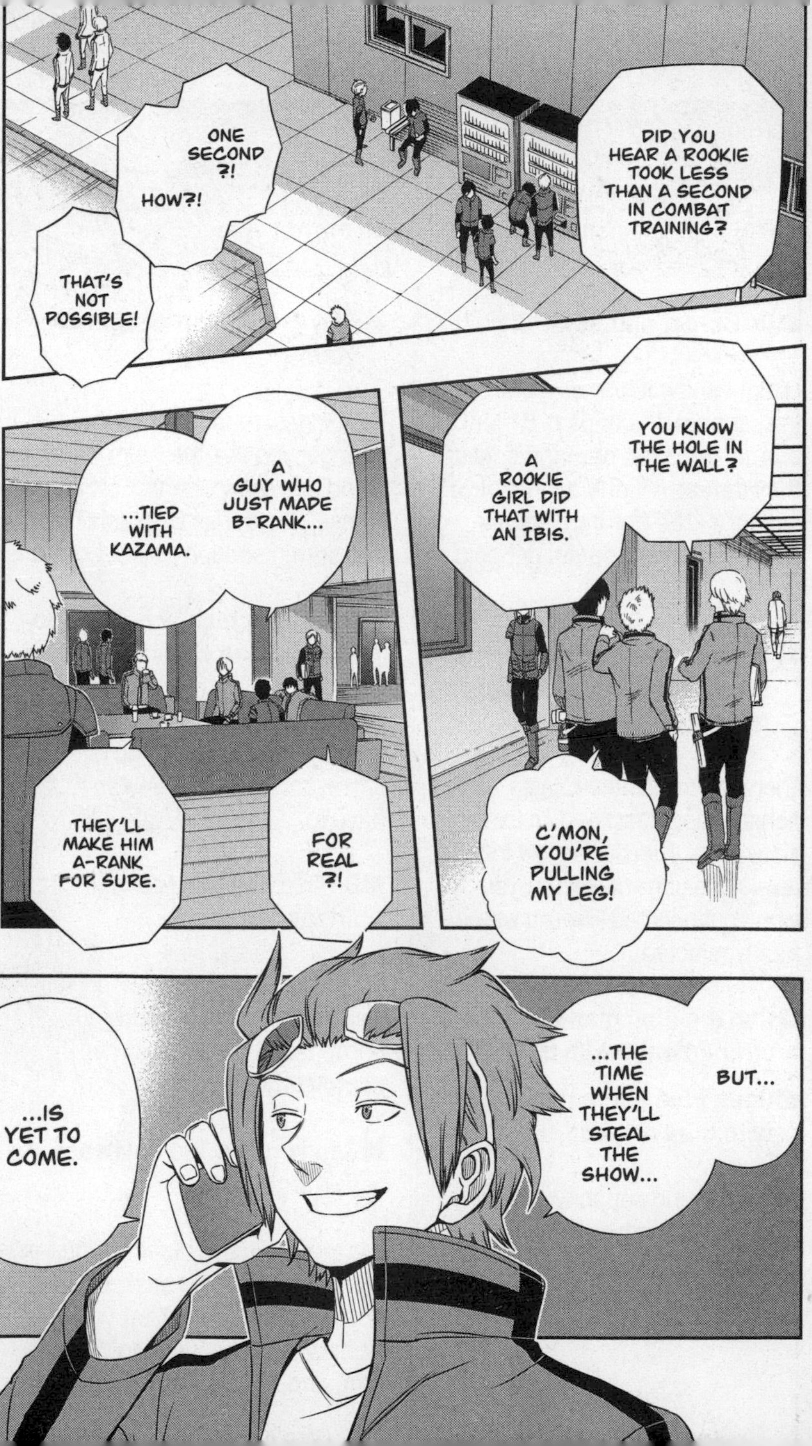
DID YOU HEAR A ROOKIE TOOK LESS THAN A SECOND IN COMBAT TRAINING?
ONE SECOND?!
HOW?!
THAT'S NOT POSSIBLE!
YOU KNOW THE HOLE IN THE WALL?
A ROOKIE GIRL DID THAT WITH AN IBIS.
C'MON, YOU'RE PULLING MY LEG!
A GUY WHO JUST MADE B-RANK...
...TIED WITH KAZAMA.
FOR REAL?!
THEY'LL MAKE HIM A-RANK FOR SURE.
BUT...
...THE TIME WHEN THEY'LL STEAL THE SHOW...
...IS YET TO COME.

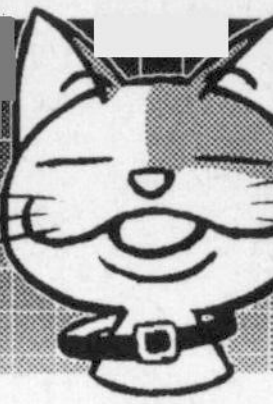

Q&A: Part 1

I sometimes answer these on my Twitter feed.

Do Border agents get paid?

I might show it one day, but yes, agents do get paid. B-Rank agents get a fee per Trion soldier they defeat. A-Rank agents have a salary + fee per Trion soldier. C-Rank trainees do not get paid.

Are there any requirements, like fitness tests, for applying to Border?

There are basic fitness tests, basic achievement tests and an interview. Other than having low Trion levels or a criminal record, you won't get rejected (Osamu was nearly rejected).

Can the Trion gland be strengthened with training?

Does Trion get replenished with time or sleep?

Just like lung capacity and muscle strength, it can be improved somewhat, and does recover with nutrition and rest.

■**Why are all Border agents young?**

The biggest reason is that the younger you are, the more your Trion gland can grow. Agents over age 20 whose growth has stopped often go into administration (like Sawamura).

■**Do Border high schoolers go to the same school?**

For better coordination of agent schedules, they often go to the same school, but they don't have to.

■**Do Trion bodies feel pain from Trigger attacks?**

There is a pain sensation that tells you what part of your body got damaged. This can be turned completely off.

■**Can you use Trion to heal damage?**

It is impossible to repair a Trion body. The combat body is basically disposable. Once destroyed, you need to create another one, which takes time and more Trion.

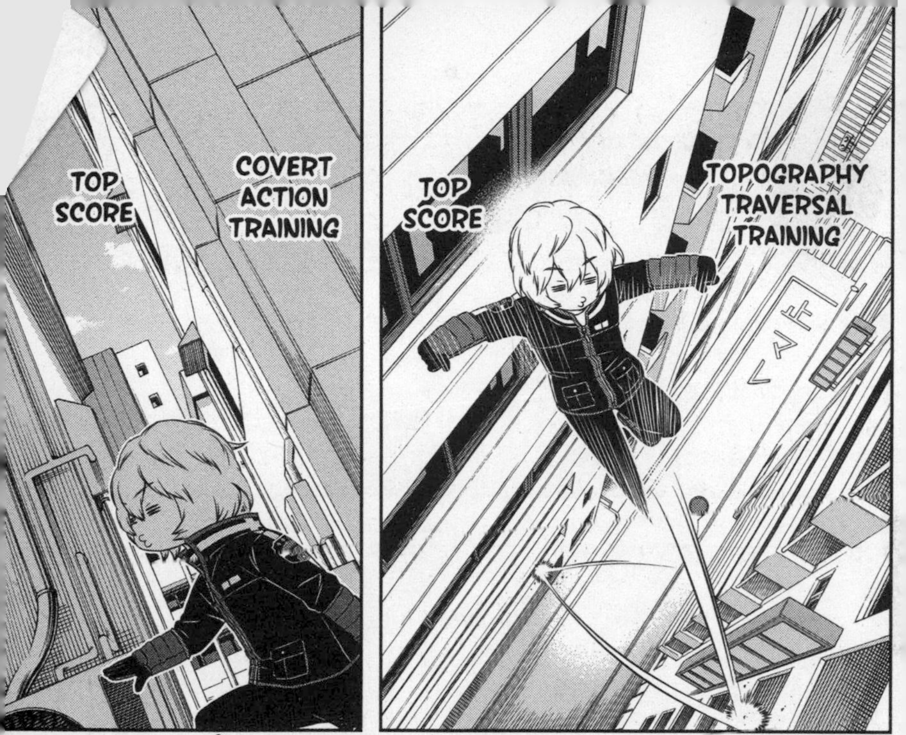
TOPOGRAPHY TRAVERSAL TRAINING
TOP SCORE
COVERT ACTION TRAINING
TOP SCORE

Chapter 38 Yuma Kuga: Part 6

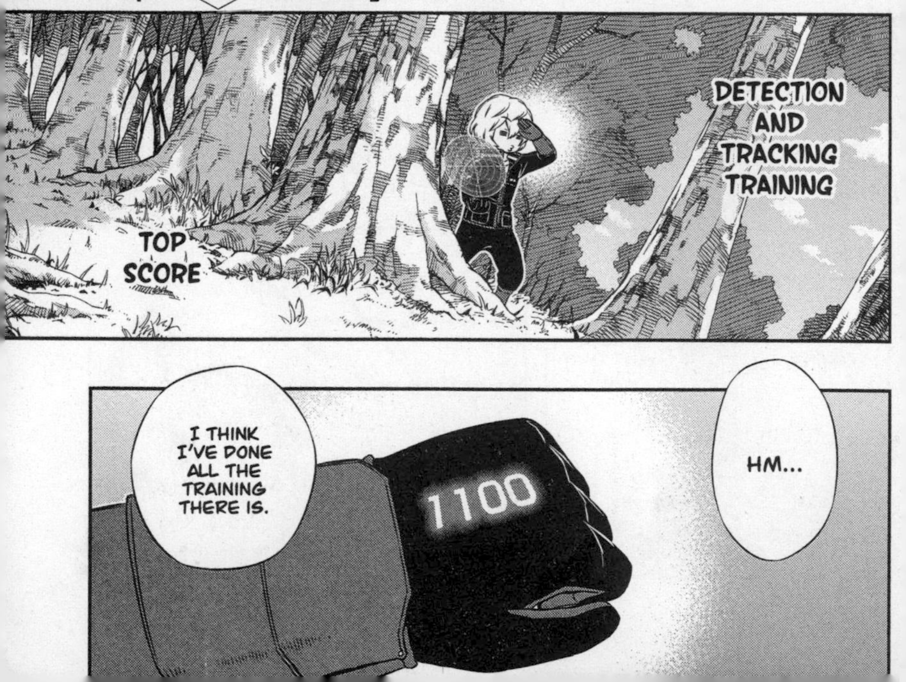
DETECTION AND TRACKING TRAINING
TOP SCORE
HM...
I THINK I'VE DONE ALL THE TRAINING THERE IS.
1100

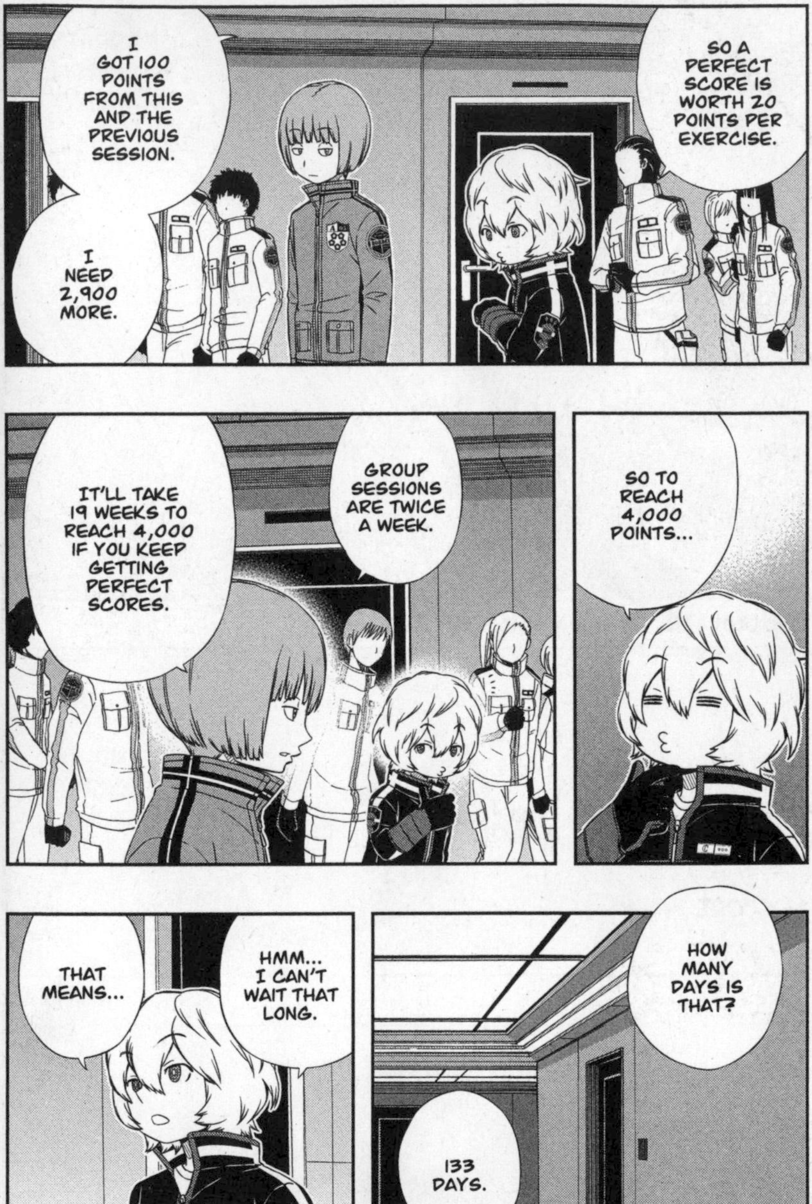
SO A PERFECT SCORE IS WORTH 20 POINTS PER EXERCISE.
I GOT 100 POINTS FROM THIS AND THE PREVIOUS SESSION.
I NEED 2,900 MORE.
SO TO REACH 4,000 POINTS...
GROUP SESSIONS ARE TWICE A WEEK.
IT'LL TAKE 19 WEEKS TO REACH 4,000 IF YOU KEEP GETTING PERFECT SCORES.
HOW MANY DAYS IS THAT?
133 DAYS.
HMM... I CAN'T WAIT THAT LONG.
THAT MEANS...

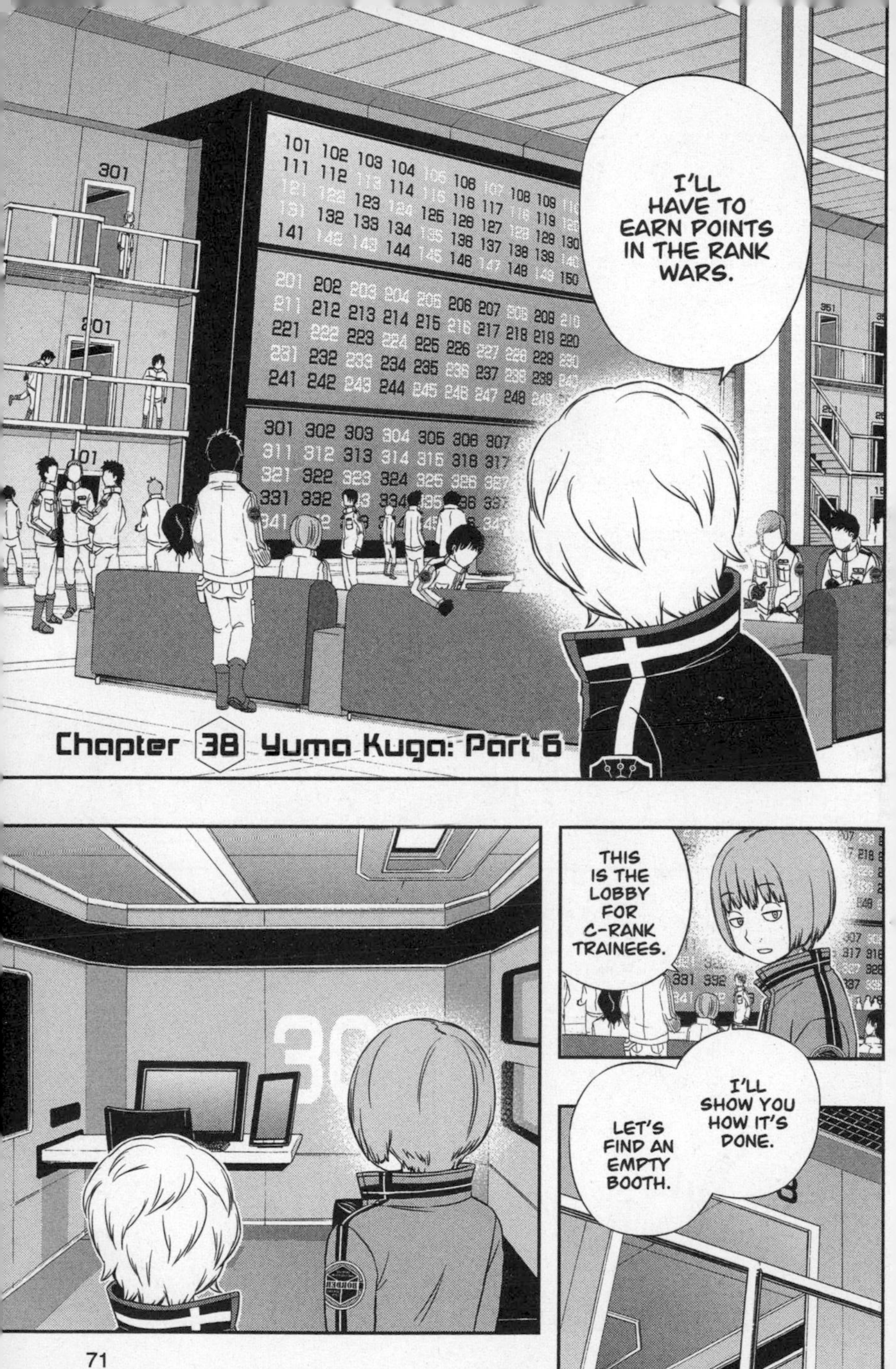
I'LL HAVE TO EARN POINTS IN THE RANK WARS.
Chapter 38 Yuma Kuga: Part 6
THIS IS THE LOBBY FOR C-RANK TRAINEES.
I'LL SHOW YOU HOW IT'S DONE.
LET'S FIND AN EMPTY BOOTH.

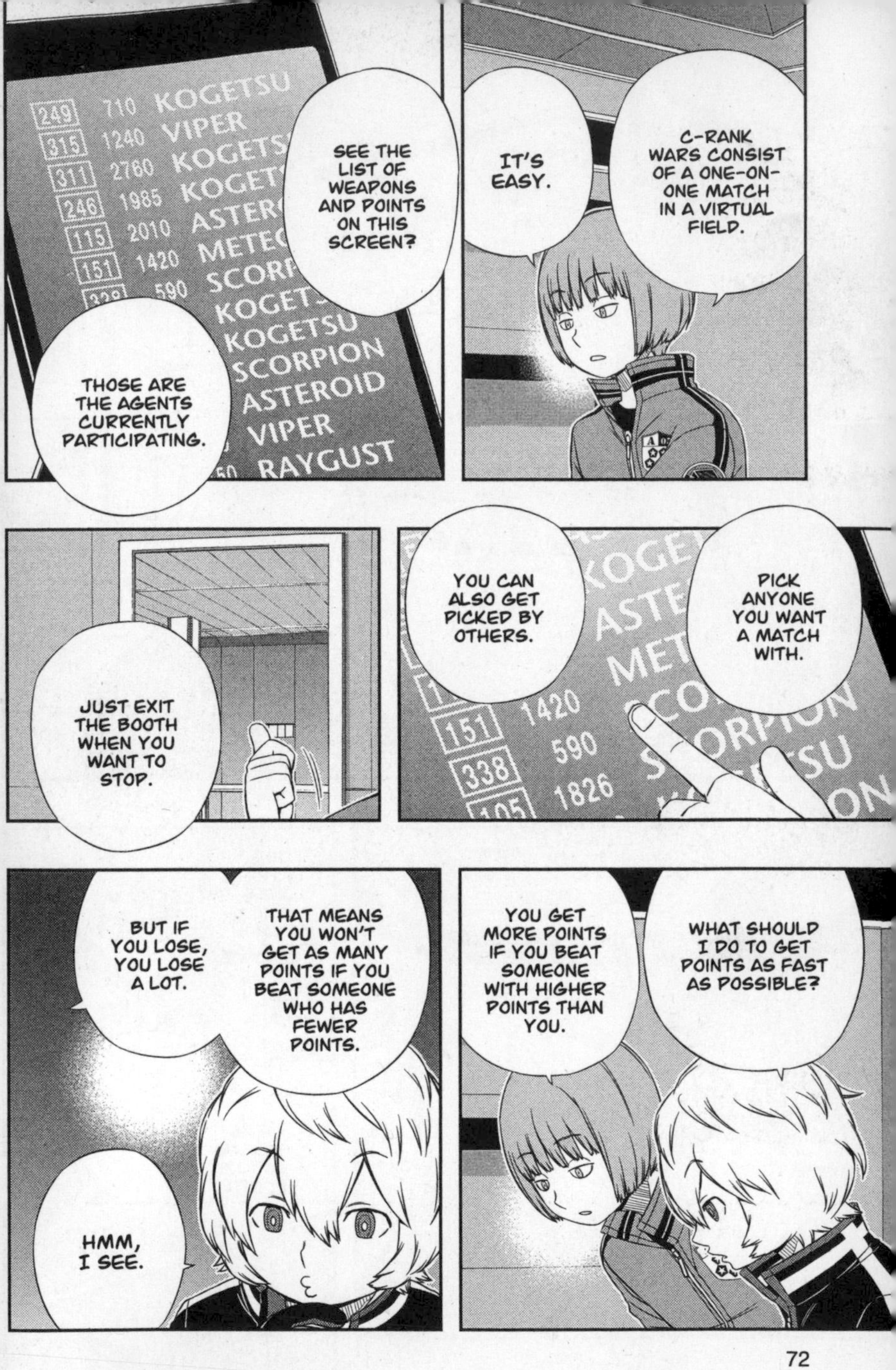
C-RANK WARS CONSIST OF A ONE-ON-ONE MATCH IN A VIRTUAL FIELD.
IT'S EASY.
SEE THE LIST OF WEAPONS AND POINTS ON THIS SCREEN?
249 710 KOGETSU
315 1240 VIPER
311 2760
246 1985
115 2010
151 1420
590
KOGETSU
SCORPION
ASTEROID
VIPER
RAYGUST
THOSE ARE THE AGENTS CURRENTLY PARTICIPATING.
PICK ANYONE YOU WANT A MATCH WITH.
YOU CAN ALSO GET PICKED BY OTHERS.
151 1420
338 590
1826
SCORPION
JUST EXIT THE BOOTH WHEN YOU WANT TO STOP.
WHAT SHOULD I DO TO GET POINTS AS FAST AS POSSIBLE?
YOU GET MORE POINTS IF YOU BEAT SOMEONE WITH HIGHER POINTS THAN YOU.
THAT MEANS YOU WON'T GET AS MANY POINTS IF YOU BEAT SOMEONE WHO HAS FEWER POINTS.
BUT IF YOU LOSE, YOU LOSE A LOT.
HMM, I SEE.

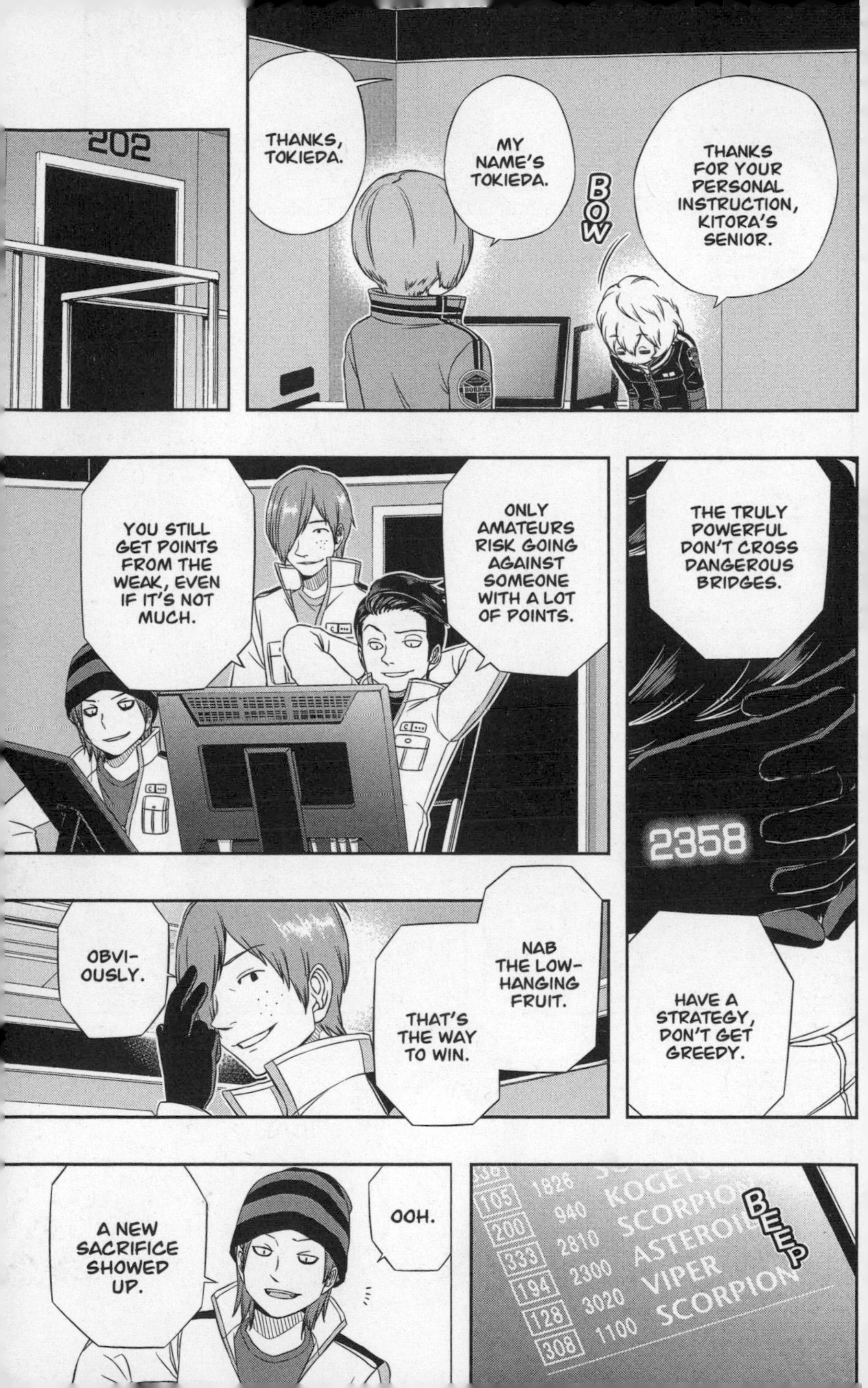
THANKS FOR YOUR PERSONAL INSTRUCTION, KITORA'S SENIOR.
BOW
MY NAME'S TOKIEDA.
THANKS, TOKIEDA.
202
THE TRULY POWERFUL DON'T CROSS DANGEROUS BRIDGES.
2358
HAVE A STRATEGY, DON'T GET GREEDY.
ONLY AMATEURS RISK GOING AGAINST SOMEONE WITH A LOT OF POINTS.
YOU STILL GET POINTS FROM THE WEAK, EVEN IF IT'S NOT MUCH.
NAB THE LOW-HANGING FRUIT.
THAT'S THE WAY TO WIN.
OBVI-OUSLY.
BEEP
105 940 KOGETS
200 2810 SCORPIO
333 2300 ASTEROI
194 3020 VIPER
128 1100 SCORPION
OOH.
A NEW SACRIFICE SHOWED UP.

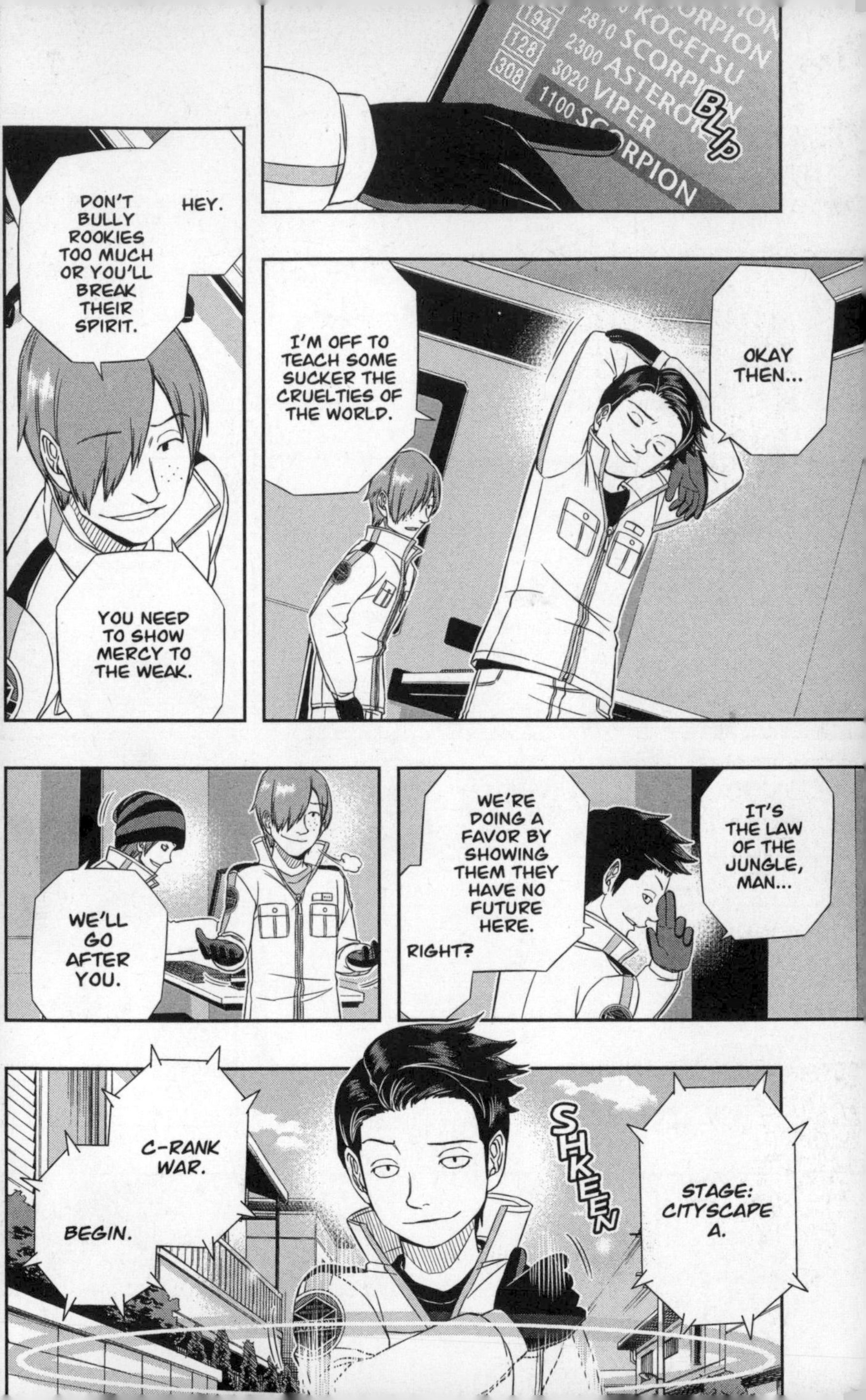
194
128
308
KOGETSU
2810 SCORPION
3020 VIPER
1100 SCORPION
BLIP
OKAY THEN...
I'M OFF TO TEACH SOME SUCKER THE CRUELTIES OF THE WORLD.
HEY.
DON'T BULLY ROOKIES TOO MUCH OR YOU'LL BREAK THEIR SPIRIT.
YOU NEED TO SHOW MERCY TO THE WEAK.
IT'S THE LAW OF THE JUNGLE, MAN...
WE'RE DOING A FAVOR BY SHOWING THEM THEY HAVE NO FUTURE HERE.
RIGHT?
WE'LL GO AFTER YOU.
STAGE: CITYSCAPE A.
SHKEEN
C-RANK WAR.
BEGIN.

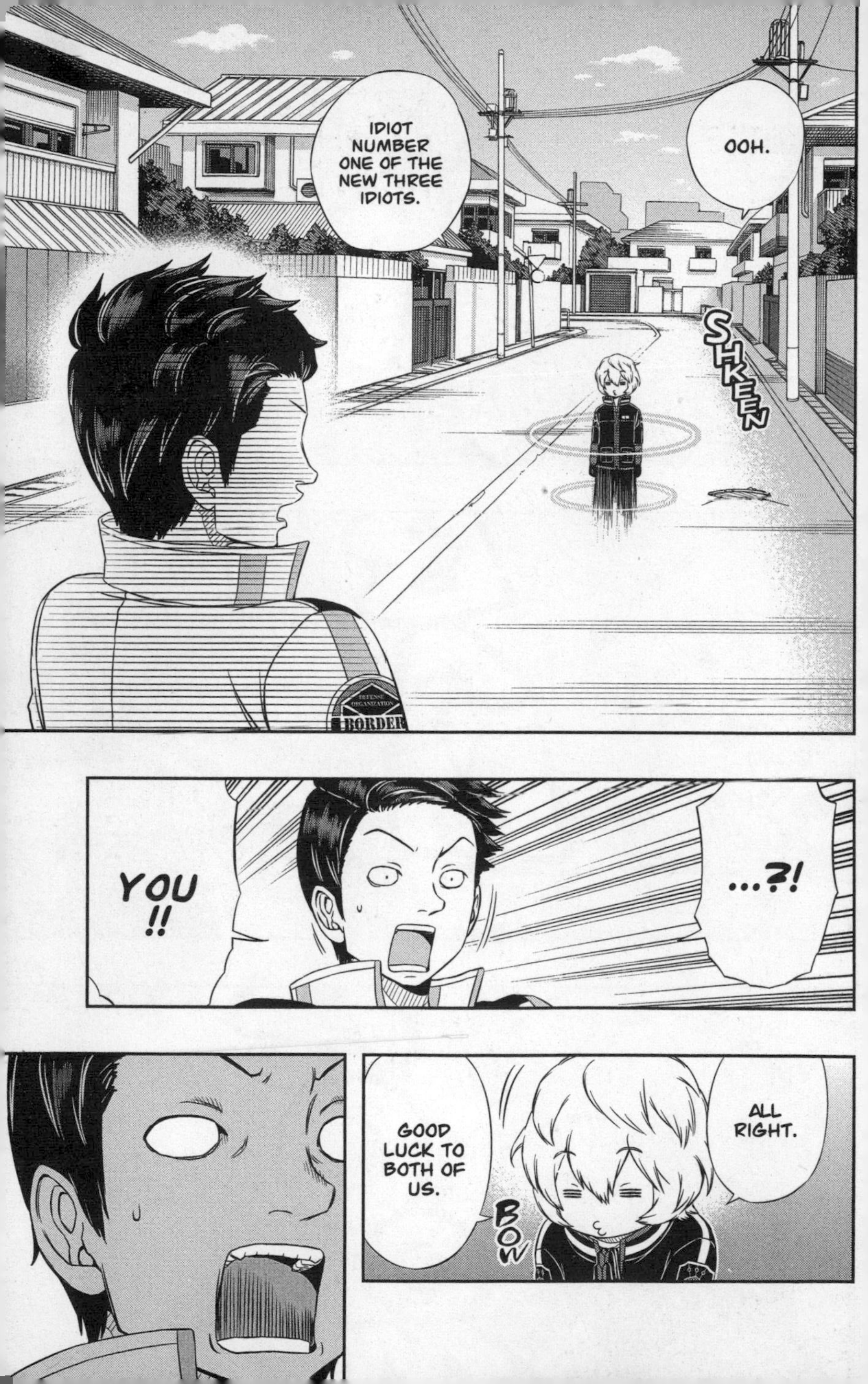
OOH.
IDIOT NUMBER ONE OF THE NEW THREE IDIOTS.
SHKEN
DEFENSE ORGANIZATION BORDER
...?!
YOU!!
ALL RIGHT.
BOW
GOOD LUCK TO BOTH OF US.

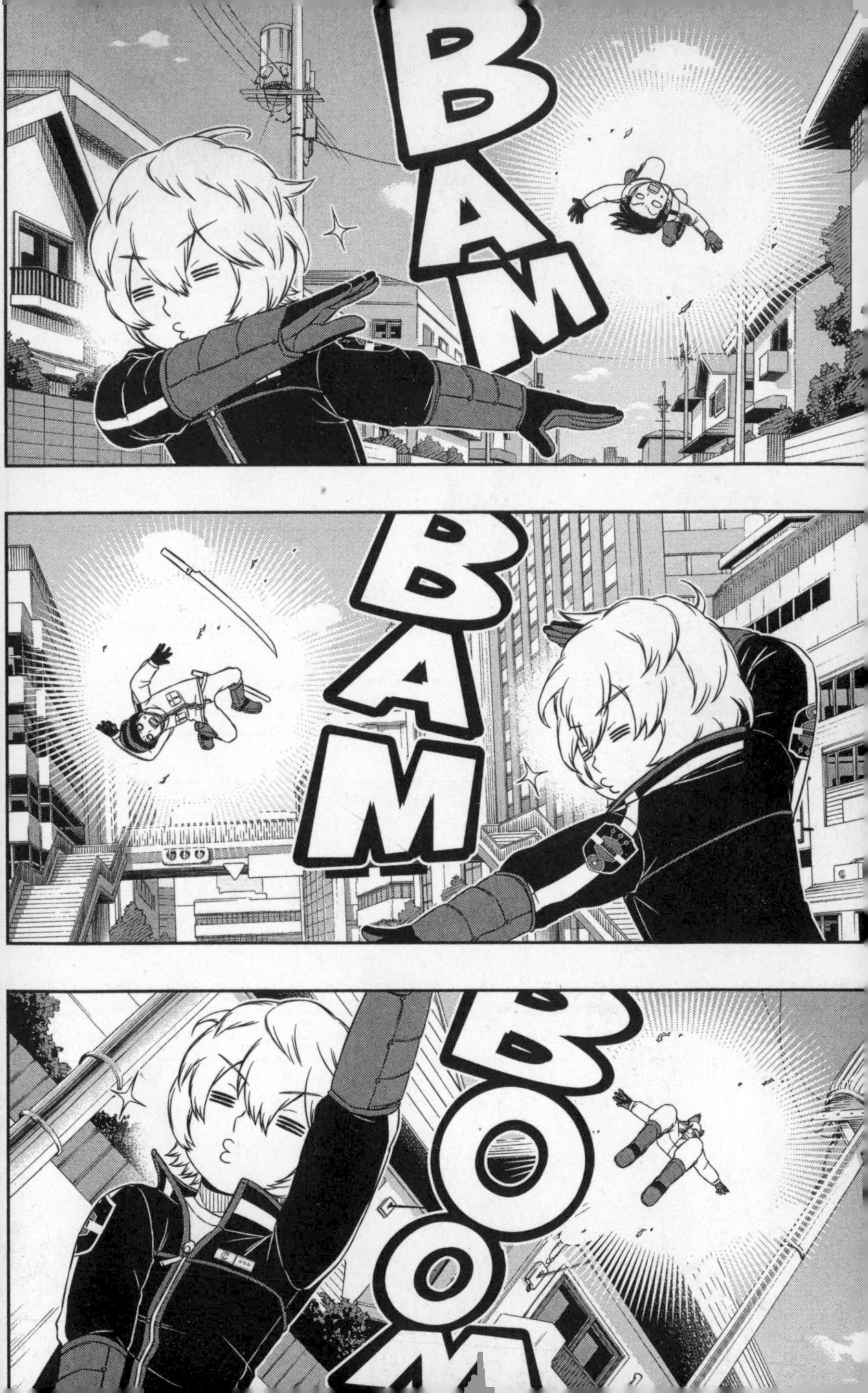
BAM
BAM
BOOM

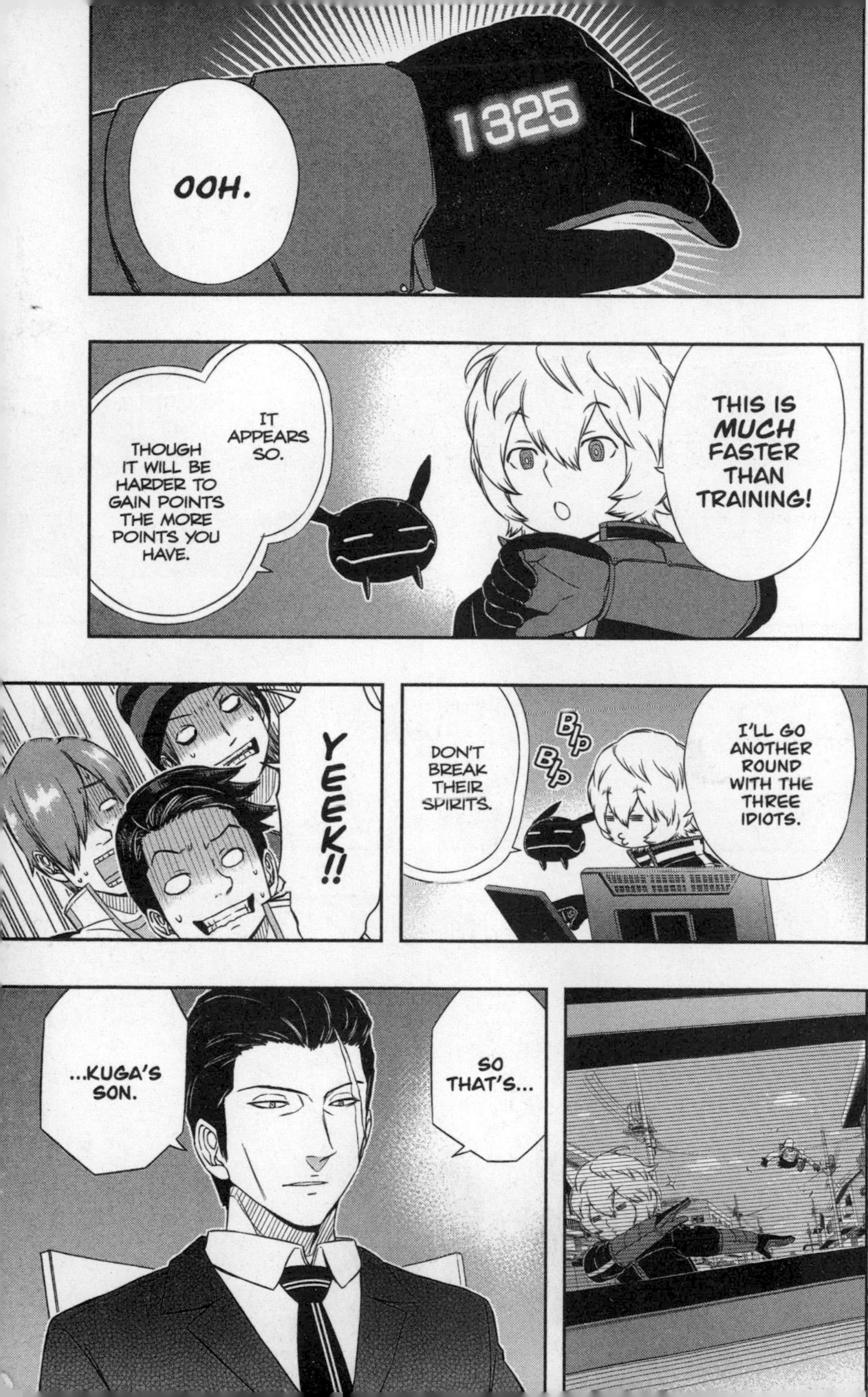
1325
OOH.
THIS IS MUCH FASTER THAN TRAINING!
IT APPEARS SO.
THOUGH IT WILL BE HARDER TO GAIN POINTS THE MORE POINTS YOU HAVE.
I'LL GO ANOTHER ROUND WITH THE THREE IDIOTS.
BIP BIP
DON'T BREAK THEIR SPIRITS.
YEEK!!
SO THAT'S...
...KUGA'S SON.

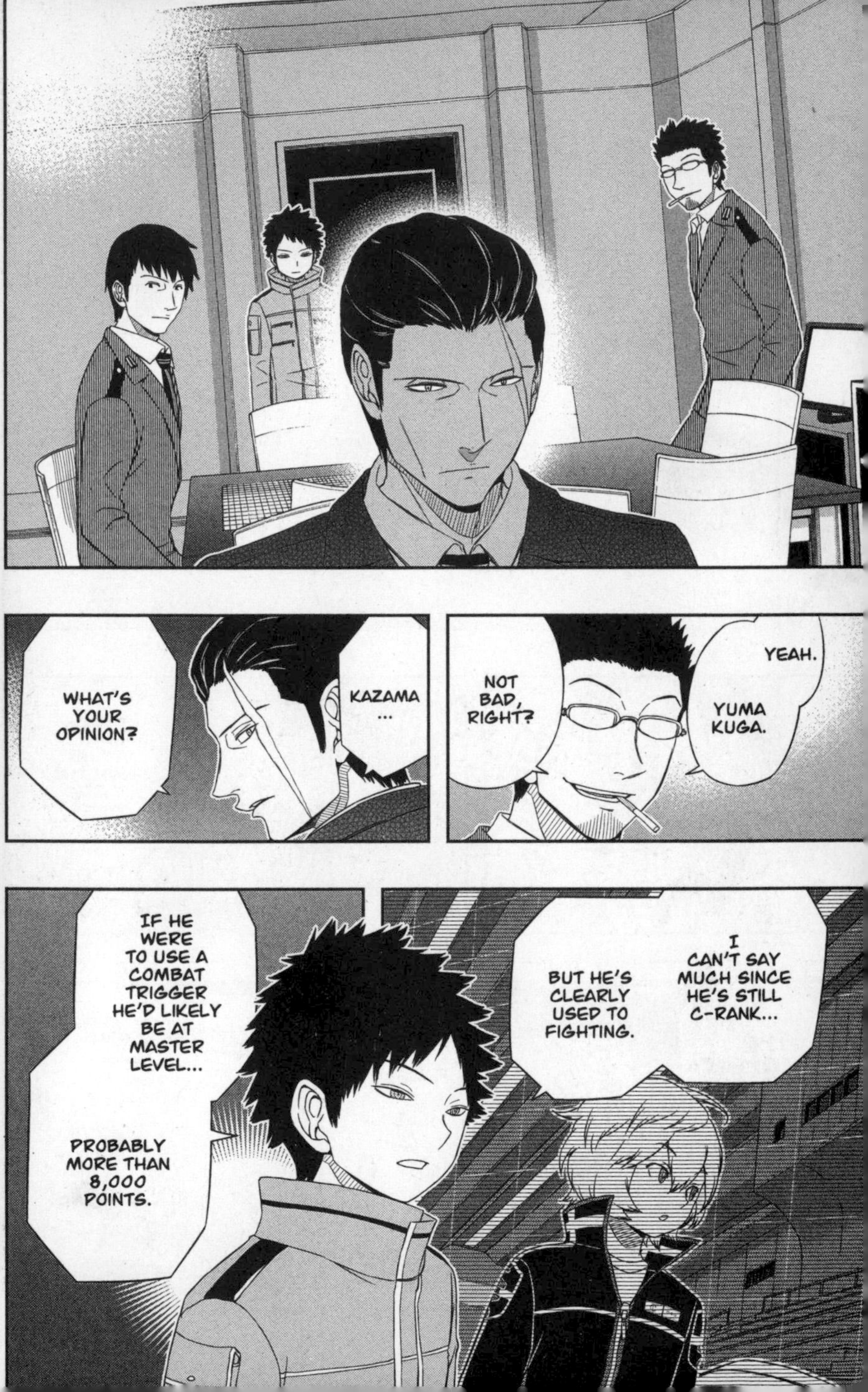

YEAH.
YUMA KUGA.
NOT BAD, RIGHT?
KAZAMA...
WHAT'S YOUR OPINION?
I CAN'T SAY MUCH SINCE HE'S STILL C-RANK...
BUT HE'S CLEARLY USED TO FIGHTING.
IF HE WERE TO USE A COMBAT TRIGGER HE'D LIKELY BE AT MASTER LEVEL...
PROBABLY MORE THAN 8,000 POINTS.

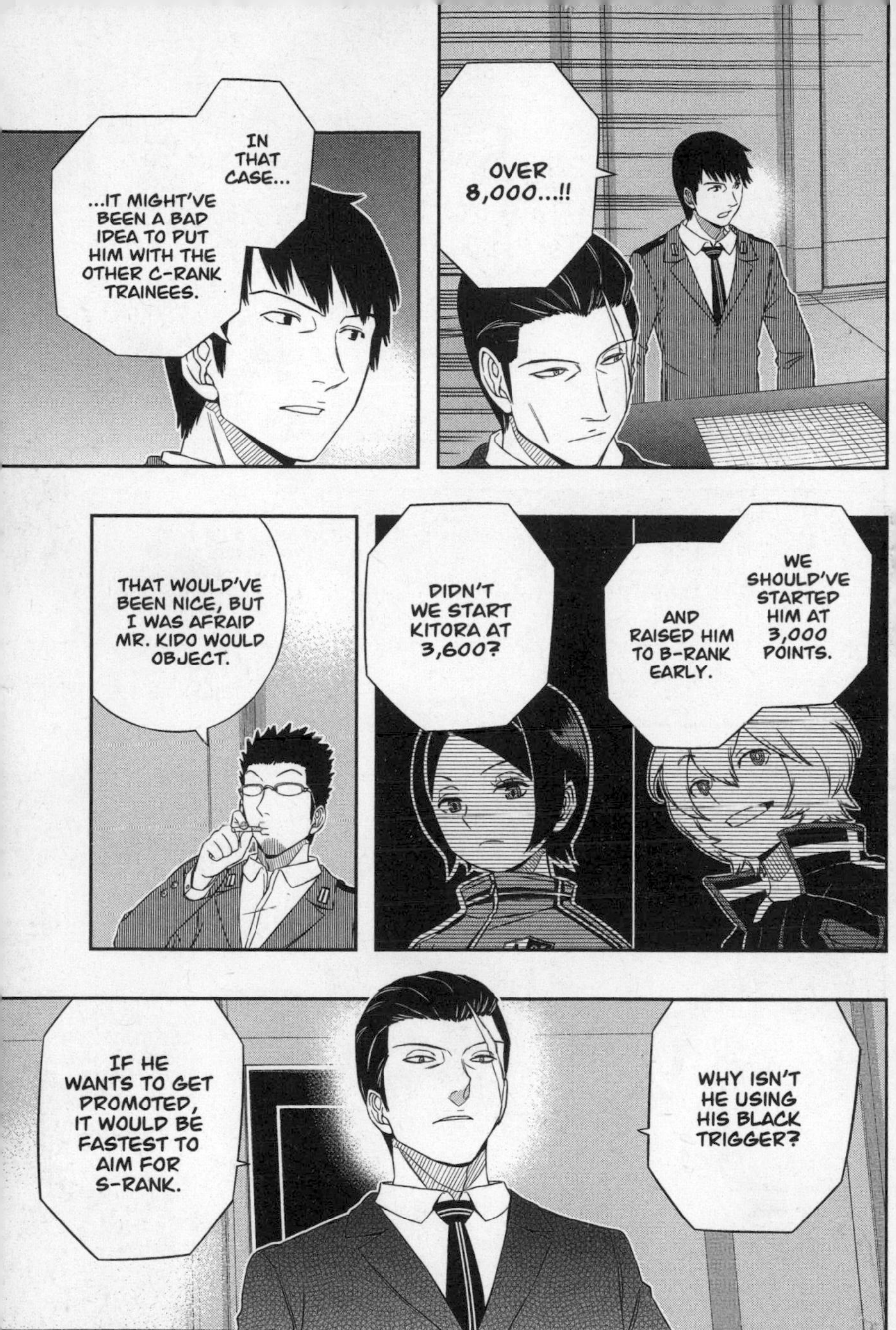

OVER 8,000...!!
IN THAT CASE...
...IT MIGHT'VE BEEN A BAD IDEA TO PUT HIM WITH THE OTHER C-RANK TRAINEES.
WE SHOULD'VE STARTED HIM AT 3,000 POINTS.
AND RAISED HIM TO B-RANK EARLY.
DIDN'T WE START KITORA AT 3,600?
THAT WOULD'VE BEEN NICE, BUT I WAS AFRAID MR. KIDO WOULD OBJECT.
WHY ISN'T HE USING HIS BLACK TRIGGER?
IF HE WANTS TO GET PROMOTED, IT WOULD BE FASTEST TO AIM FOR S-RANK.

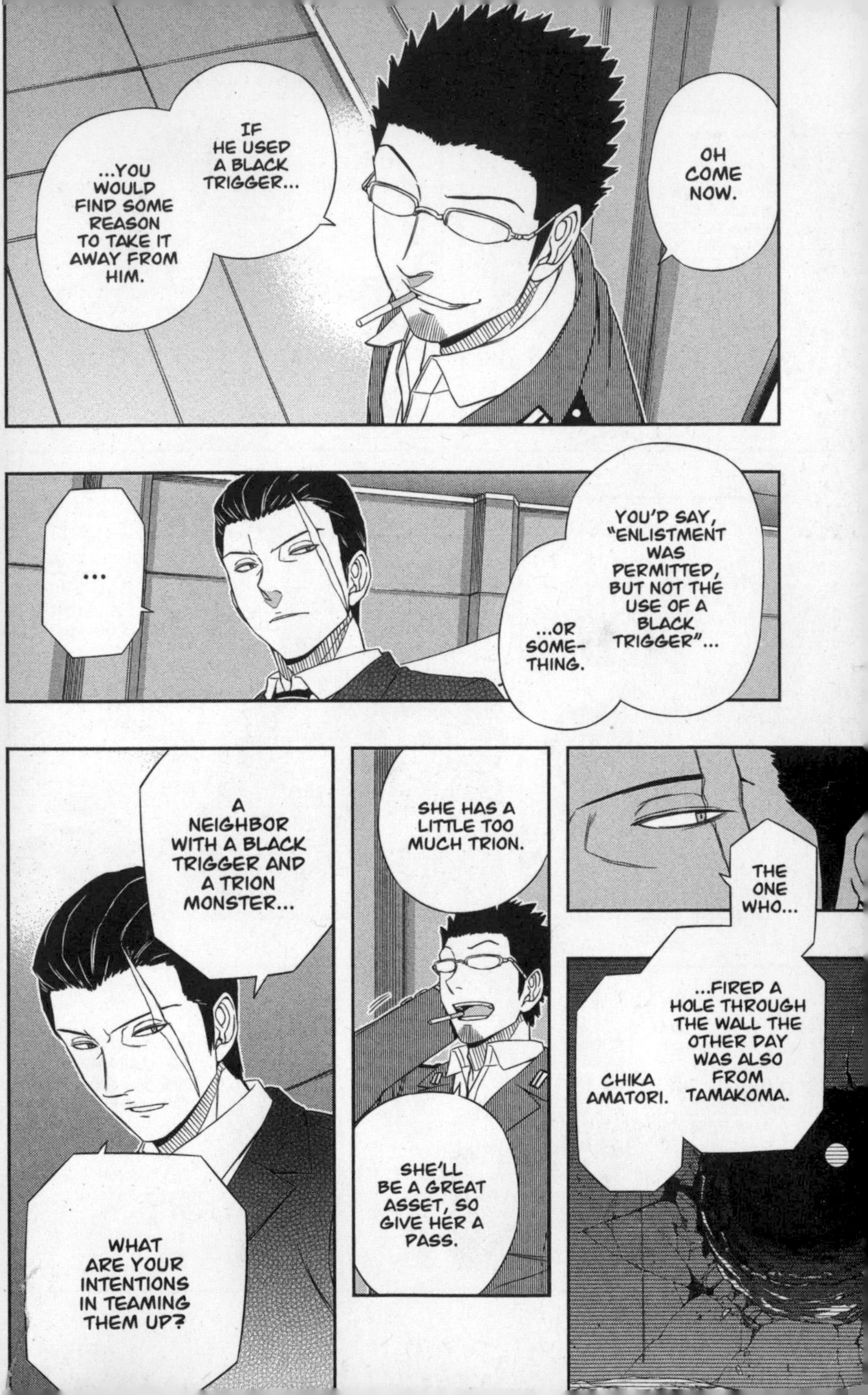
OH COME NOW.
IF HE USED A BLACK TRIGGER...
...YOU WOULD FIND SOME REASON TO TAKE IT AWAY FROM HIM.
YOU'D SAY, "ENLISTMENT WAS PERMITTED, BUT NOT THE USE OF A BLACK TRIGGER"...
...OR SOME-THING.
...
THE ONE WHO...
...FIRED A HOLE THROUGH THE WALL THE OTHER DAY WAS ALSO FROM TAMAKOMA.
CHIKA AMATORI.
SHE HAS A LITTLE TOO MUCH TRION.
SHE'LL BE A GREAT ASSET, SO GIVE HER A PASS.
A NEIGHBOR WITH A BLACK TRIGGER AND A TRION MONSTER...
WHAT ARE YOUR INTENTIONS IN TEAMING THEM UP?

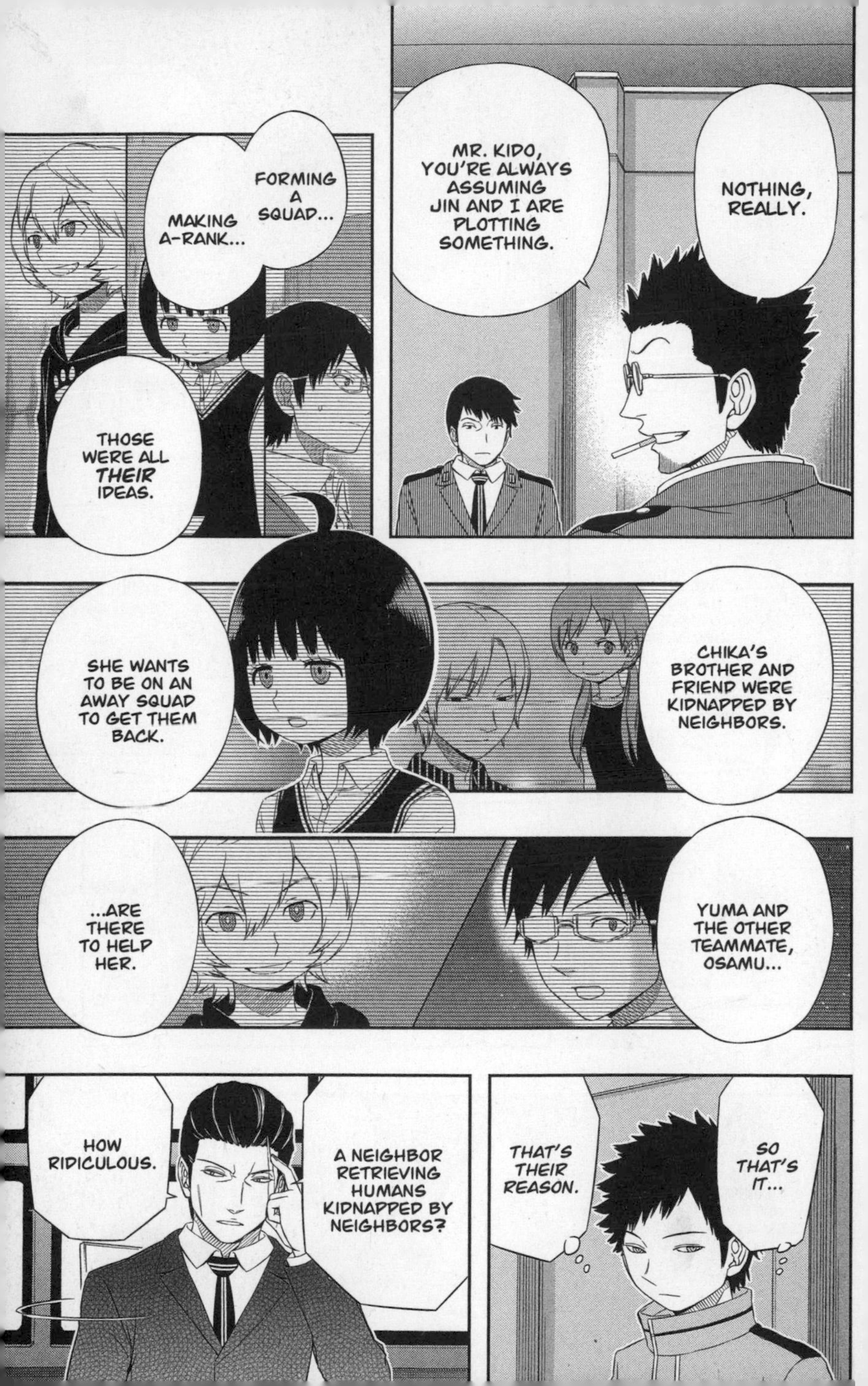
NOTHING, REALLY.
MR. KIDO, YOU'RE ALWAYS ASSUMING JIN AND I ARE PLOTTING SOMETHING.
FORMING A SQUAD...
MAKING A-RANK...
THOSE WERE ALL THEIR IDEAS.
CHIKA'S BROTHER AND FRIEND WERE KIDNAPPED BY NEIGHBORS.
SHE WANTS TO BE ON AN AWAY SQUAD TO GET THEM BACK.
YUMA AND THE OTHER TEAMMATE, OSAMU...
...ARE THERE TO HELP HER.
SO THAT'S IT...
THAT'S THEIR REASON.
A NEIGHBOR RETRIEVING HUMANS KIDNAPPED BY NEIGHBORS?
HOW RIDICULOUS.

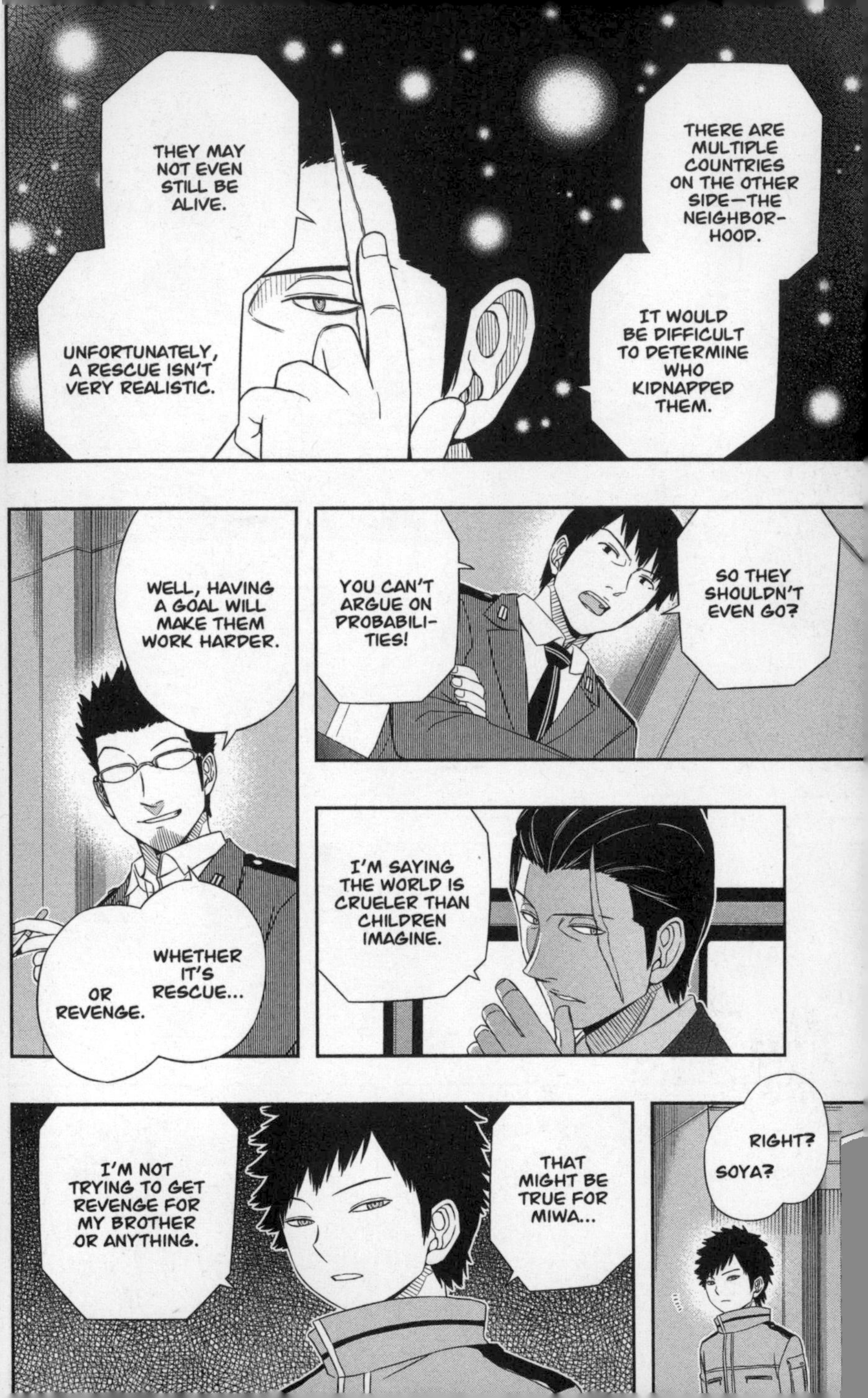
THERE ARE MULTIPLE COUNTRIES ON THE OTHER SIDE—THE NEIGHBOR-HOOD.
IT WOULD BE DIFFICULT TO DETERMINE WHO KIDNAPPED THEM.
THEY MAY NOT EVEN STILL BE ALIVE.
UNFORTUNATELY, A RESCUE ISN'T VERY REALISTIC.
SO THEY SHOULDN'T EVEN GO?
YOU CAN'T ARGUE ON PROBABILI-TIES!
I'M SAYING THE WORLD IS CRUELER THAN CHILDREN IMAGINE.
WELL, HAVING A GOAL WILL MAKE THEM WORK HARDER.
WHETHER IT'S RESCUE... OR REVENGE.
RIGHT? SOYA?
THAT MIGHT BE TRUE FOR MIWA...
I'M NOT TRYING TO GET REVENGE FOR MY BROTHER OR ANYTHING.

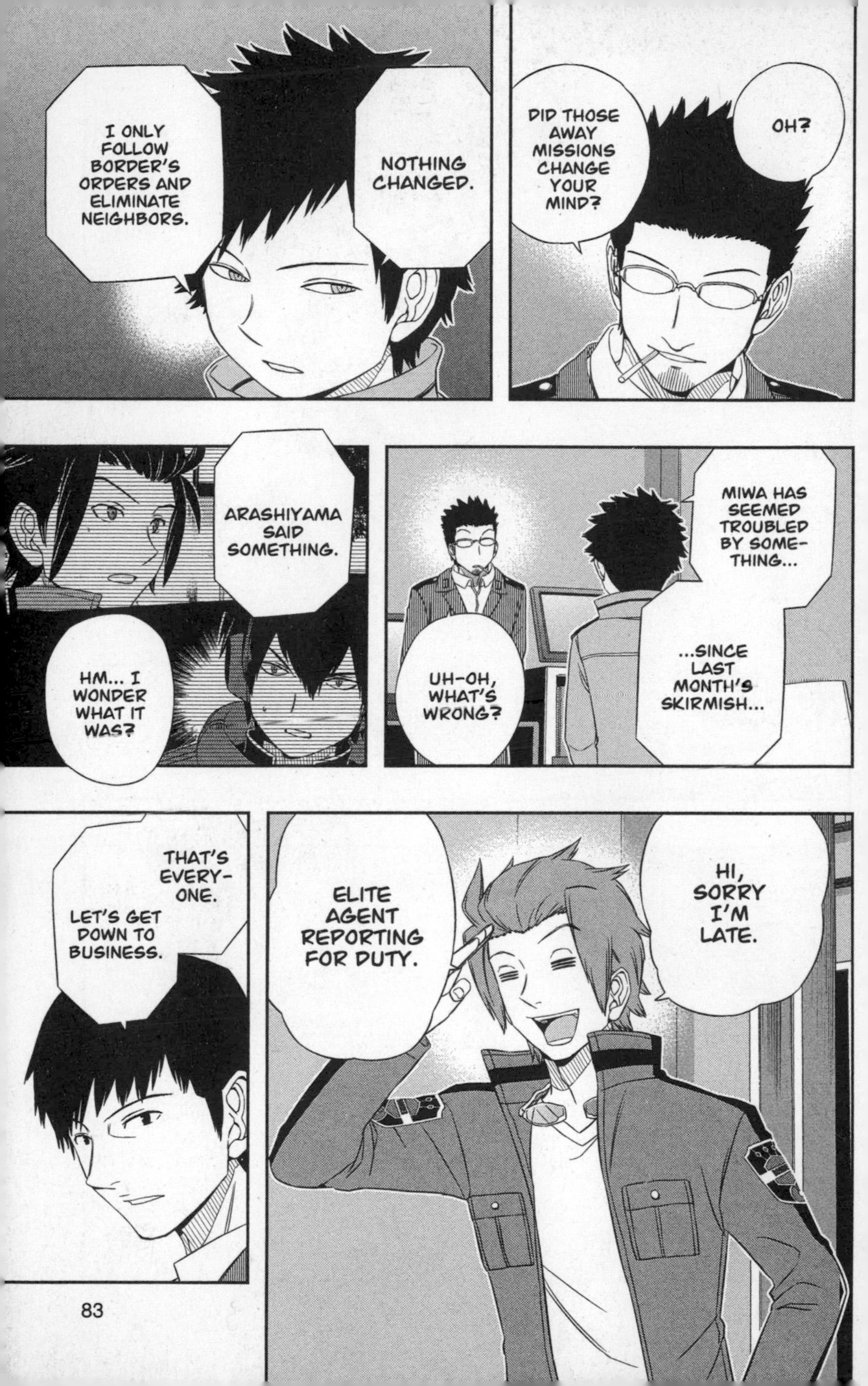
OH?
DID THOSE AWAY MISSIONS CHANGE YOUR MIND?
NOTHING CHANGED.
I ONLY FOLLOW BORDER'S ORDERS AND ELIMINATE NEIGHBORS.
MIWA HAS SEEMED TROUBLED BY SOME-THING...
...SINCE LAST MONTH'S SKIRMISH...
UH-OH, WHAT'S WRONG?
ARASHIYAMA SAID SOMETHING.
HM... I WONDER WHAT IT WAS?
HI, SORRY I'M LATE.
ELITE AGENT REPORTING FOR DUTY.
THAT'S EVERY-ONE.
LET'S GET DOWN TO BUSINESS.

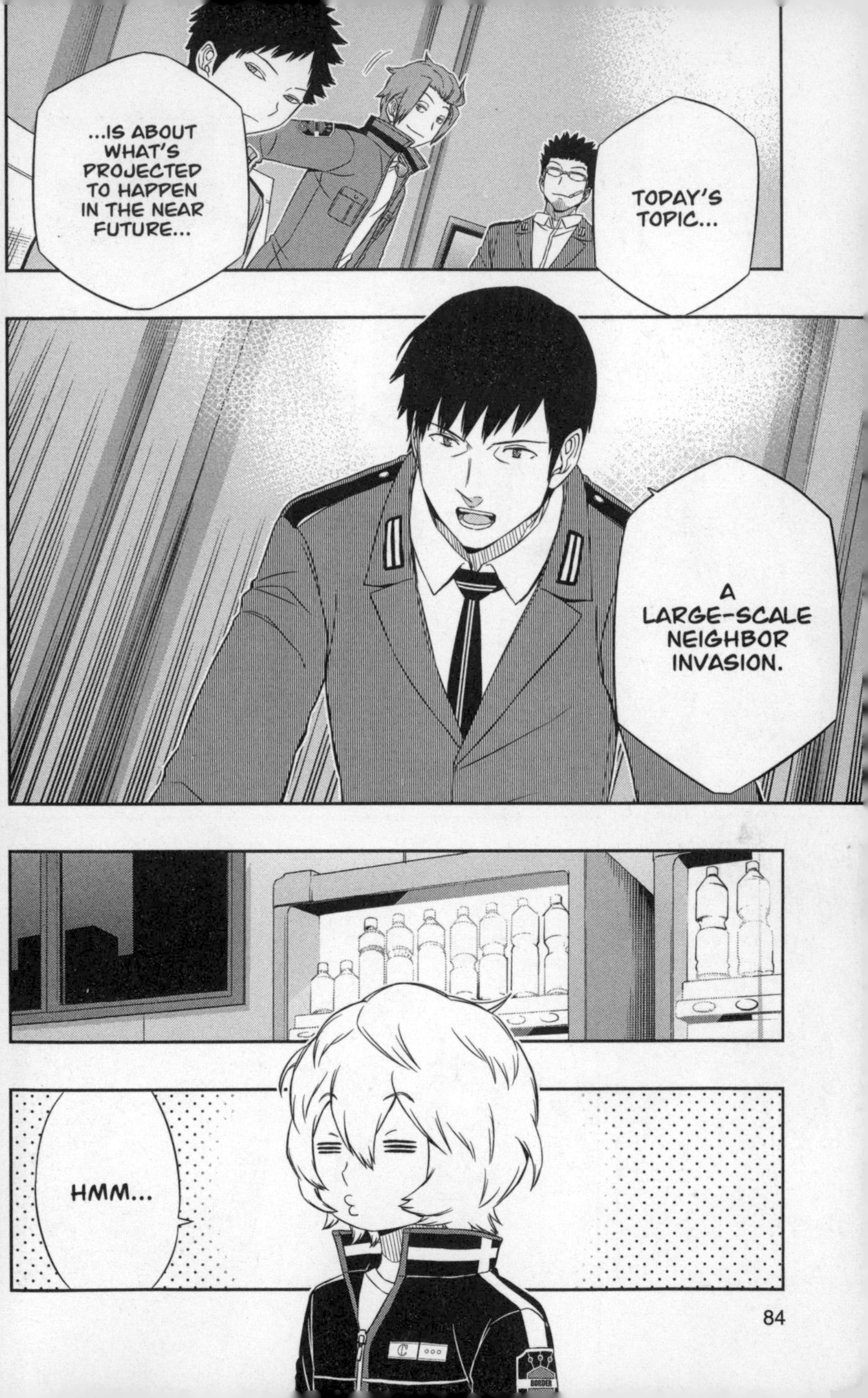
TODAY'S TOPIC...
...IS ABOUT WHAT'S PROJECTED TO HAPPEN IN THE NEAR FUTURE...
A LARGE-SCALE NEIGHBOR INVASION.
HMM...

READ THIS WAY

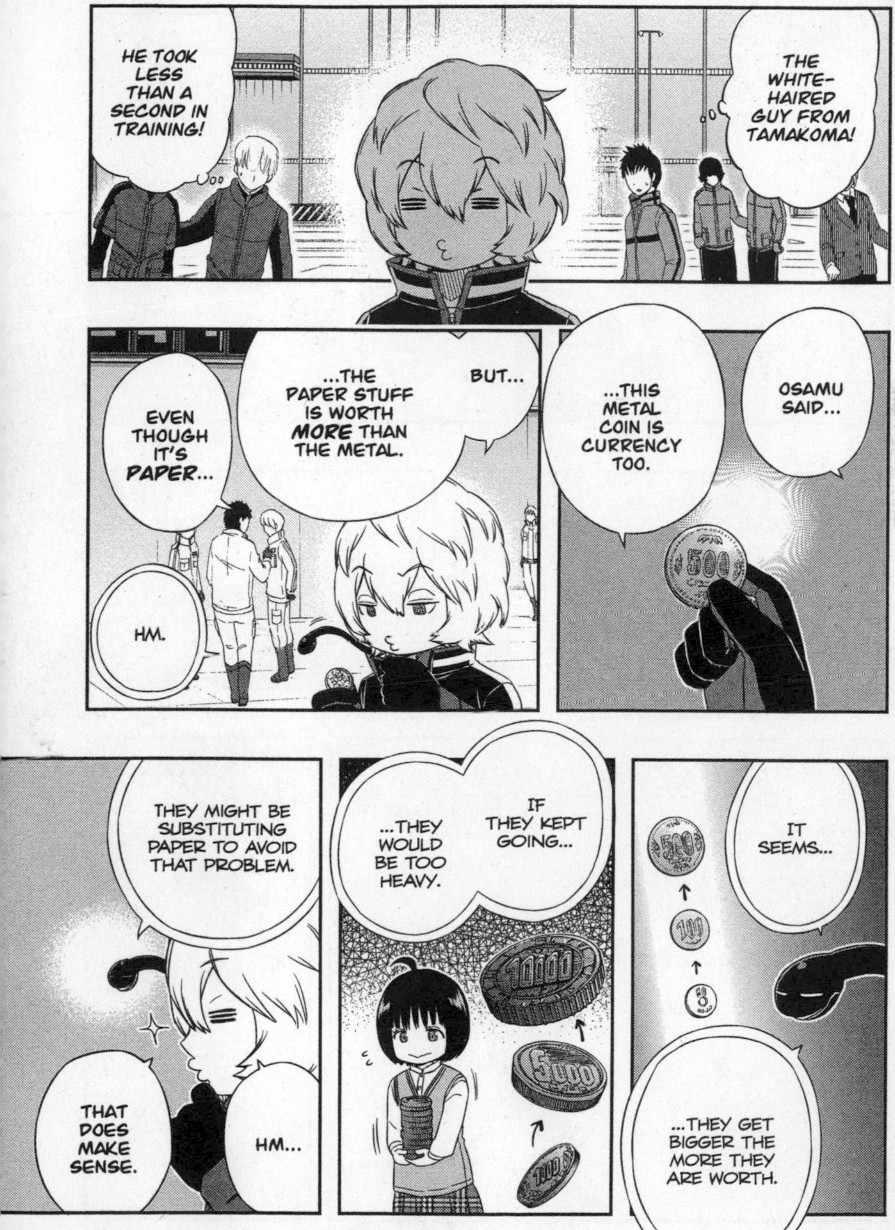
THE WHITE-HAIRED GUY FROM TAMAKOMA!
HE TOOK LESS THAN A SECOND IN TRAINING!
OSAMU SAID...
...THIS METAL COIN IS CURRENCY TOO.
BUT...
...THE PAPER STUFF IS WORTH MORE THAN THE METAL.
EVEN THOUGH IT'S PAPER...
HM.
IT SEEMS...
...THEY GET BIGGER THE MORE THEY ARE WORTH.
IF THEY KEPT GOING...
...THEY WOULD BE TOO HEAVY.
THEY MIGHT BE SUBSTITUTING PAPER TO AVOID THAT PROBLEM.
HM...
THAT DOES MAKE SENSE.

KATUNK
CLINK
CLINK
BUY SOMETHING AND YOU GET MORE MONEY.
ANOTHER MYSTERY.
IT WAS BROKEN DOWN...
...INTO "CHANGE."
CLINK
OOPS.
PLOP
TK
TOK
ROLL
TAP
HM...?

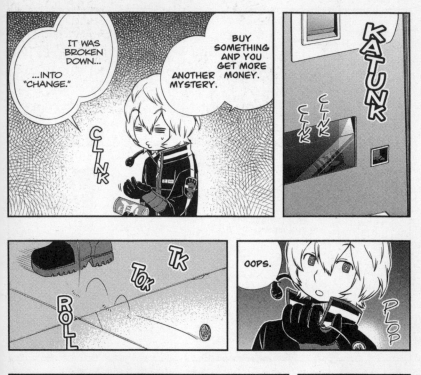

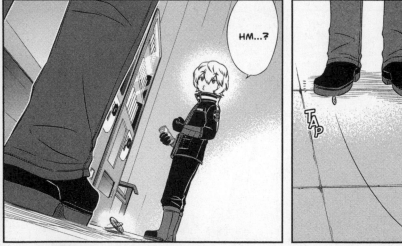

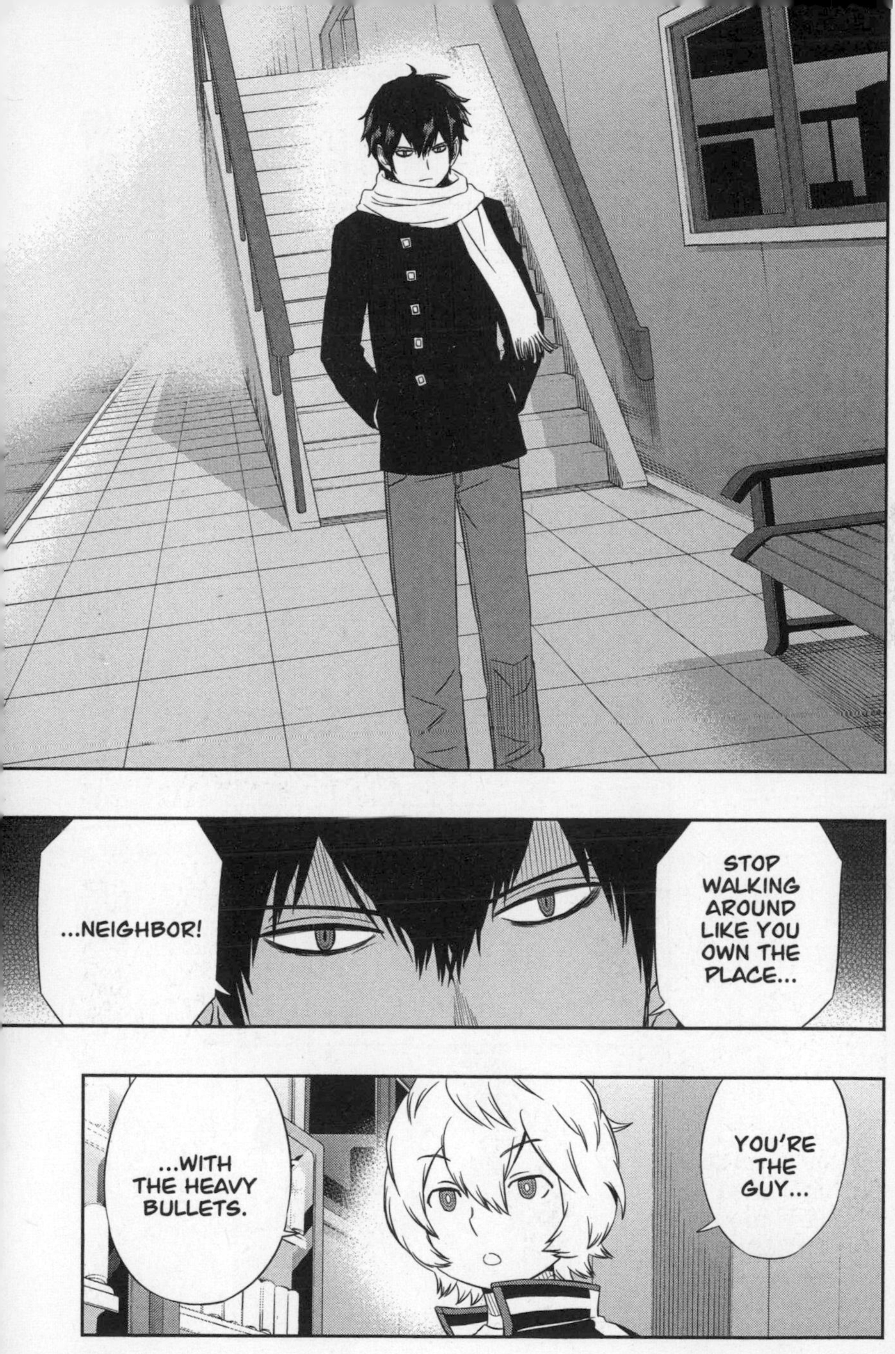
STOP WALKING AROUND LIKE YOU OWN THE PLACE...
...NEIGHBOR!
YOU'RE THE GUY...
...WITH THE HEAVY BULLETS.

■ 2014 *Weekly Shonen Jump* double issue 4-5
Christmas Strips

Cultural Exchange

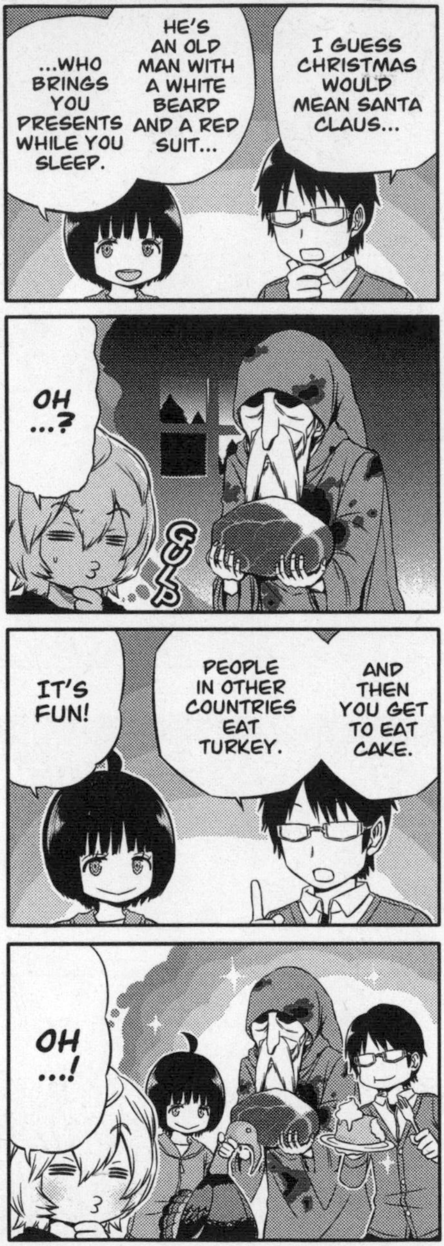
I GUESS CHRISTMAS WOULD MEAN SANTA CLAUS...
HE'S AN OLD MAN WITH A WHITE BEARD AND A RED SUIT...
...WHO BRINGS YOU PRESENTS WHILE YOU SLEEP.
OH ...?
GULP
AND THEN YOU GET TO EAT CAKE.
PEOPLE IN OTHER COUNTRIES EAT TURKEY.
IT'S FUN!
OH ...!

The strip was in color for *Jump*, so the meat looked meatier. To do this strip, I looked up what turkeys look like for the first time. They're gross.

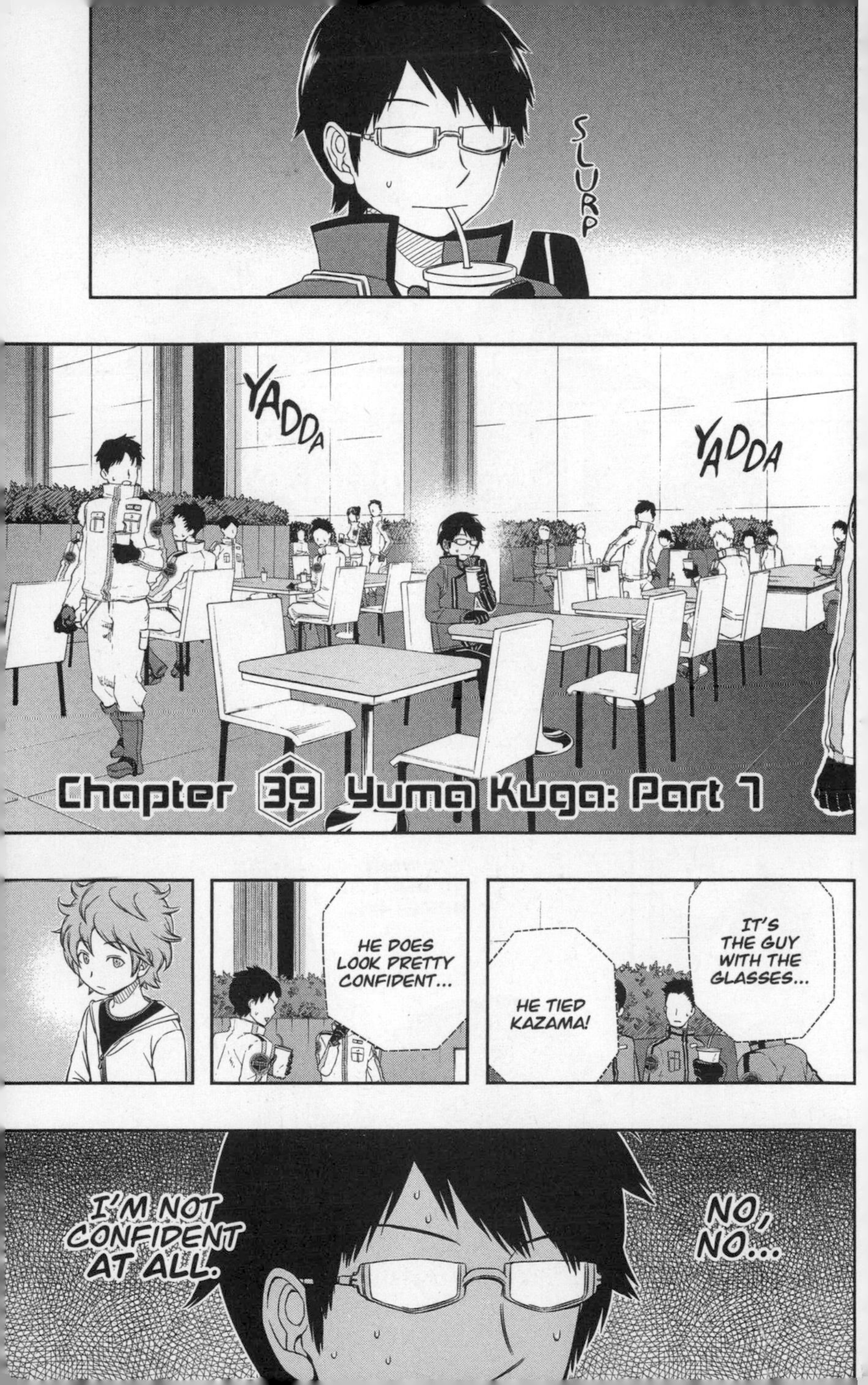
SLURP
YADDA
YADDA
Chapter 39 Yuma Kuga: Part 7
IT'S THE GUY WITH THE GLASSES...
HE TIED KAZAMA!
HE DOES LOOK PRETTY CONFIDENT...
NO, NO...
I'M NOT CONFIDENT AT ALL.

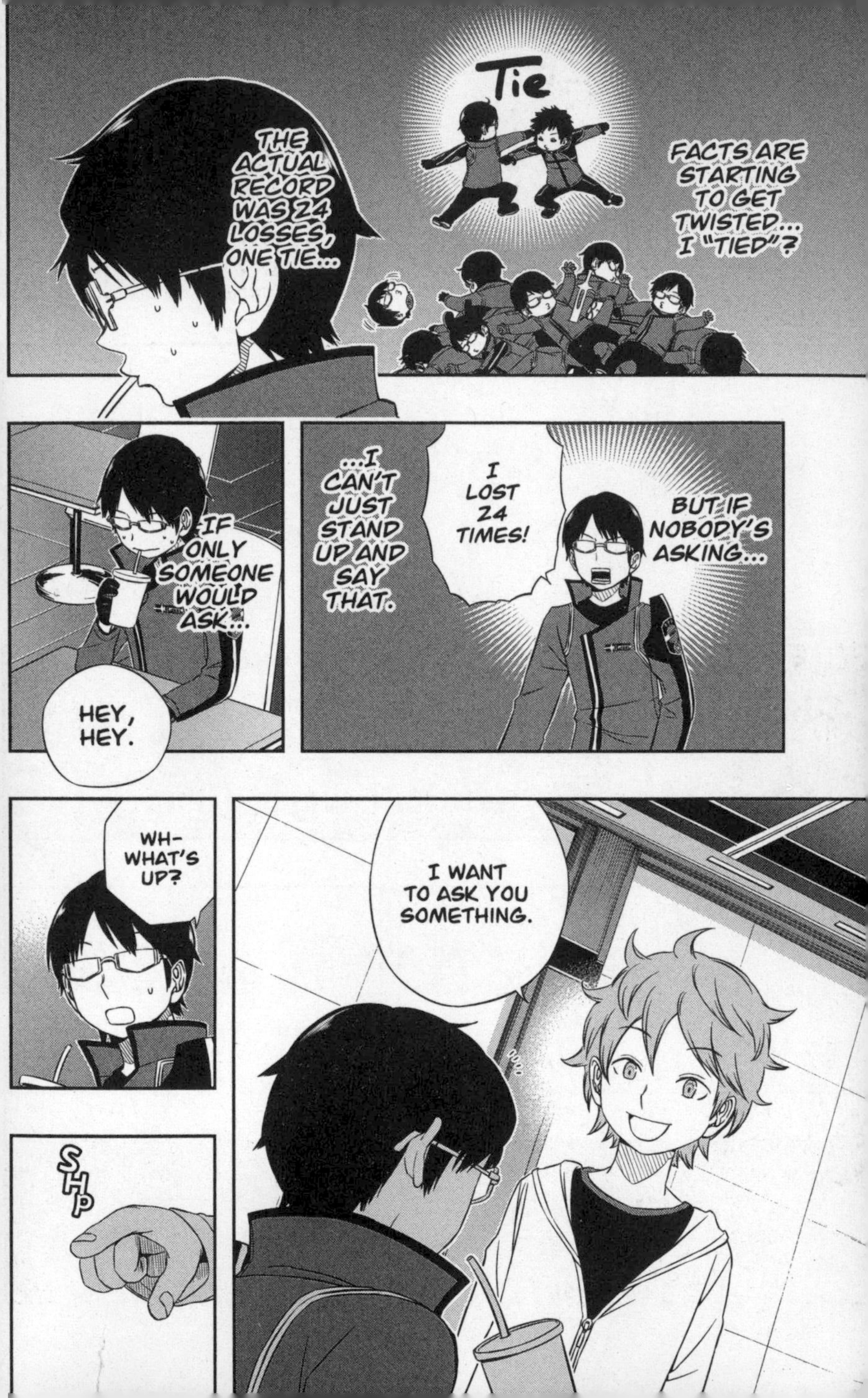
Tie
FACTS ARE STARTING TO GET TWISTED... I "TIED"?
THE ACTUAL RECORD WAS 24 LOSSES, ONE TIE...
BUT IF NOBODY'S ASKING...
I LOST 24 TIMES!
...I CAN'T JUST STAND UP AND SAY THAT.
IF ONLY SOMEONE WOULD ASK...
HEY, HEY.
I WANT TO ASK YOU SOMETHING.
WH- WHAT'S UP?
SHP

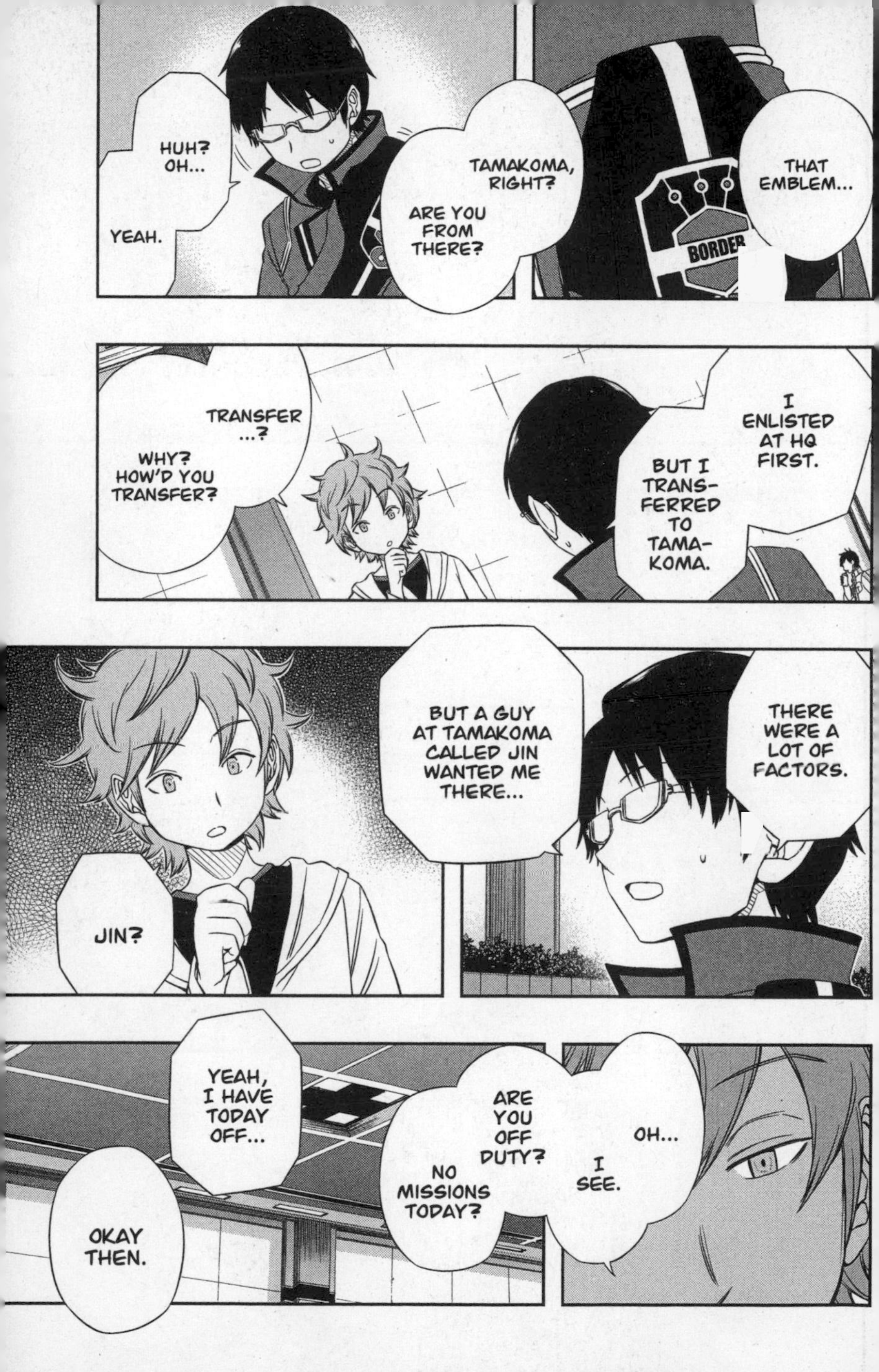
THAT EMBLEM...
TAMAKOMA, RIGHT?
ARE YOU FROM THERE?
HUH? OH...
YEAH.
I ENLISTED AT HQ FIRST.
BUT I TRANSFERRED TO TAMAKOMA.
TRANSFER ...?
WHY? HOW'D YOU TRANSFER?
THERE WERE A LOT OF FACTORS.
BUT A GUY AT TAMAKOMA CALLED JIN WANTED ME THERE...
JIN?
OH...
I SEE.
ARE YOU OFF DUTY?
NO MISSIONS TODAY?
YEAH, I HAVE TODAY OFF...
OKAY THEN.

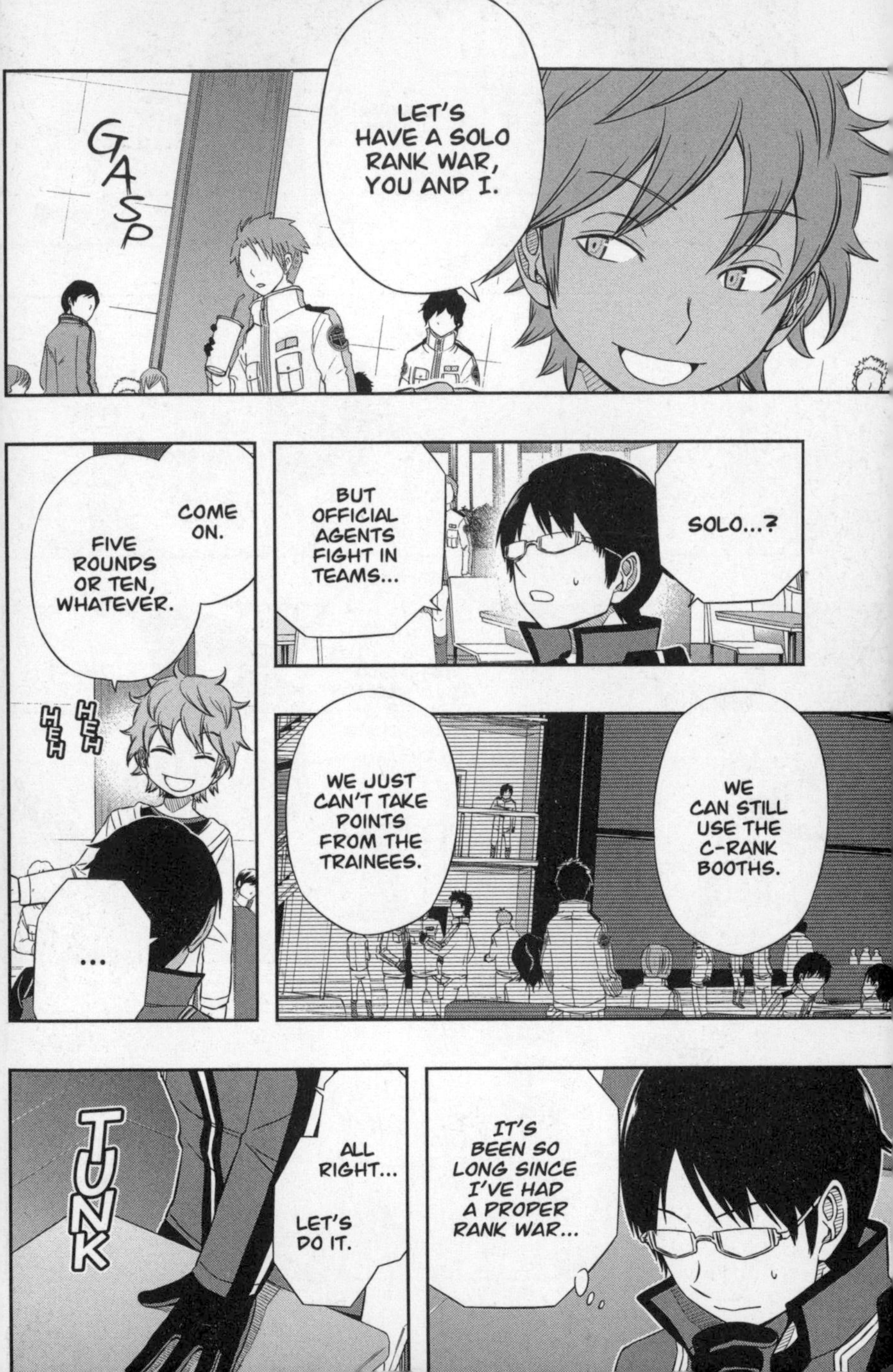
LET'S HAVE A SOLO RANK WAR, YOU AND I.
GASP
SOLO...?
BUT OFFICIAL AGENTS FIGHT IN TEAMS...
WE CAN STILL USE THE C-RANK BOOTHS.
WE JUST CAN'T TAKE POINTS FROM THE TRAINEES.
COME ON.
FIVE ROUNDS OR TEN, WHATEVER.
HEH HEH
...
IT'S BEEN SO LONG SINCE I'VE HAD A PROPER RANK WAR...
ALL RIGHT...
LET'S DO IT.
TUNK

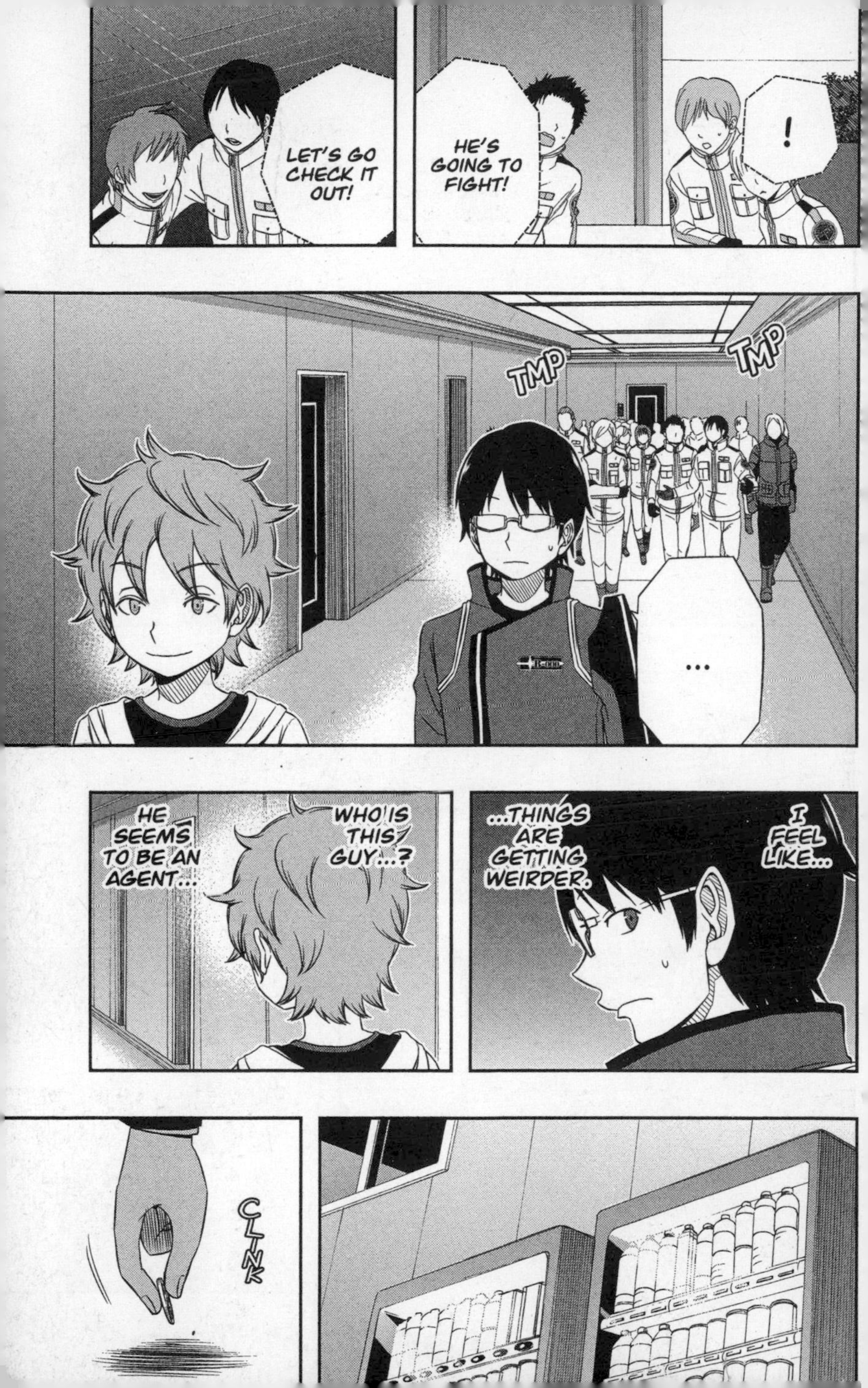
!
HE'S GOING TO FIGHT!
LET'S GO CHECK IT OUT!
TMP
TMP
...
I FEEL LIKE...
...THINGS ARE GETTING WEIRDER.
WHO IS THIS GUY...?
HE SEEMS TO BE AN AGENT...
CLINK

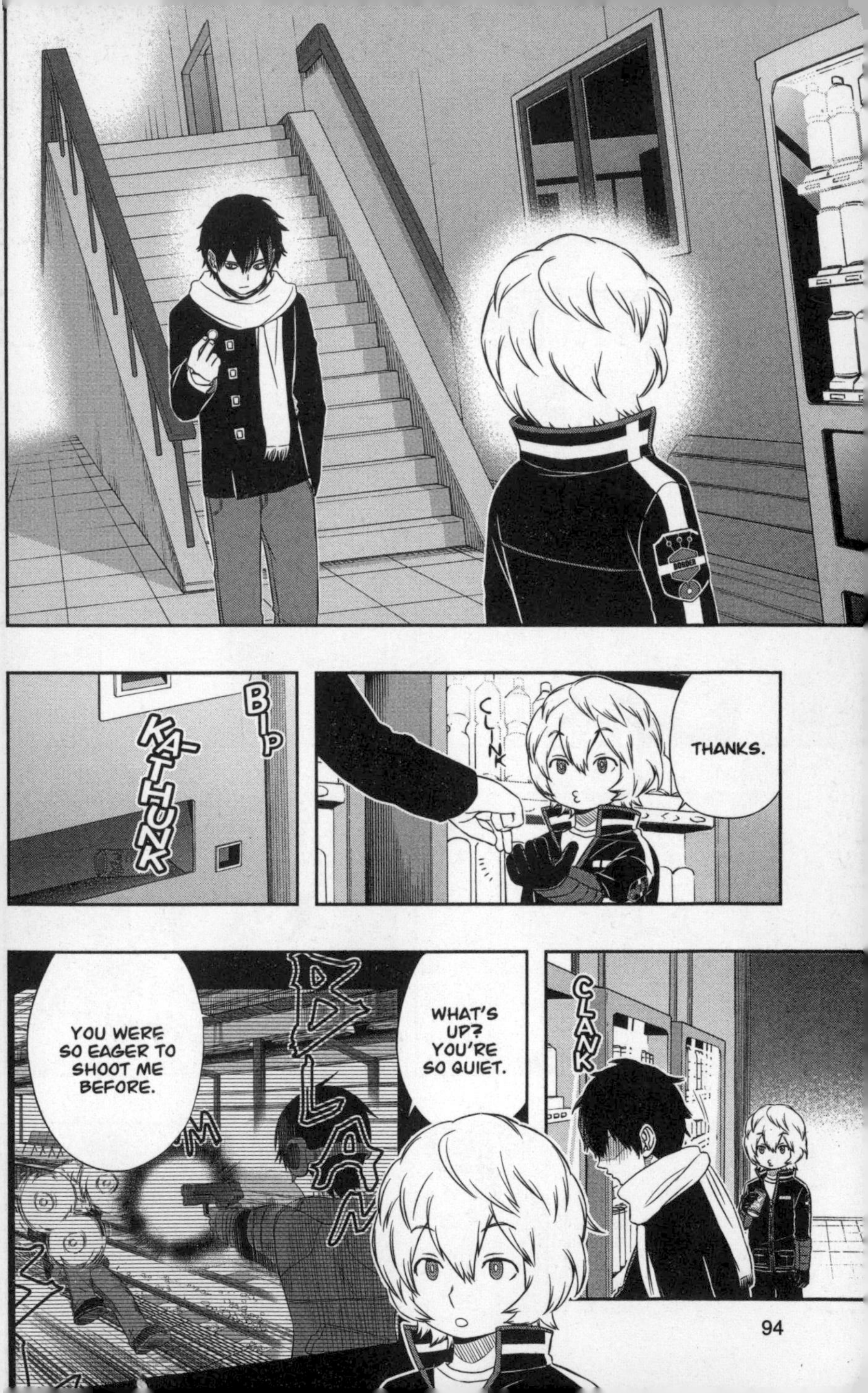
CLINK
THANKS.
BIP
KA-THUNK
CLANK
WHAT'S UP? YOU'RE SO QUIET.
YOU WERE SO EAGER TO SHOOT ME BEFORE.
BLAM

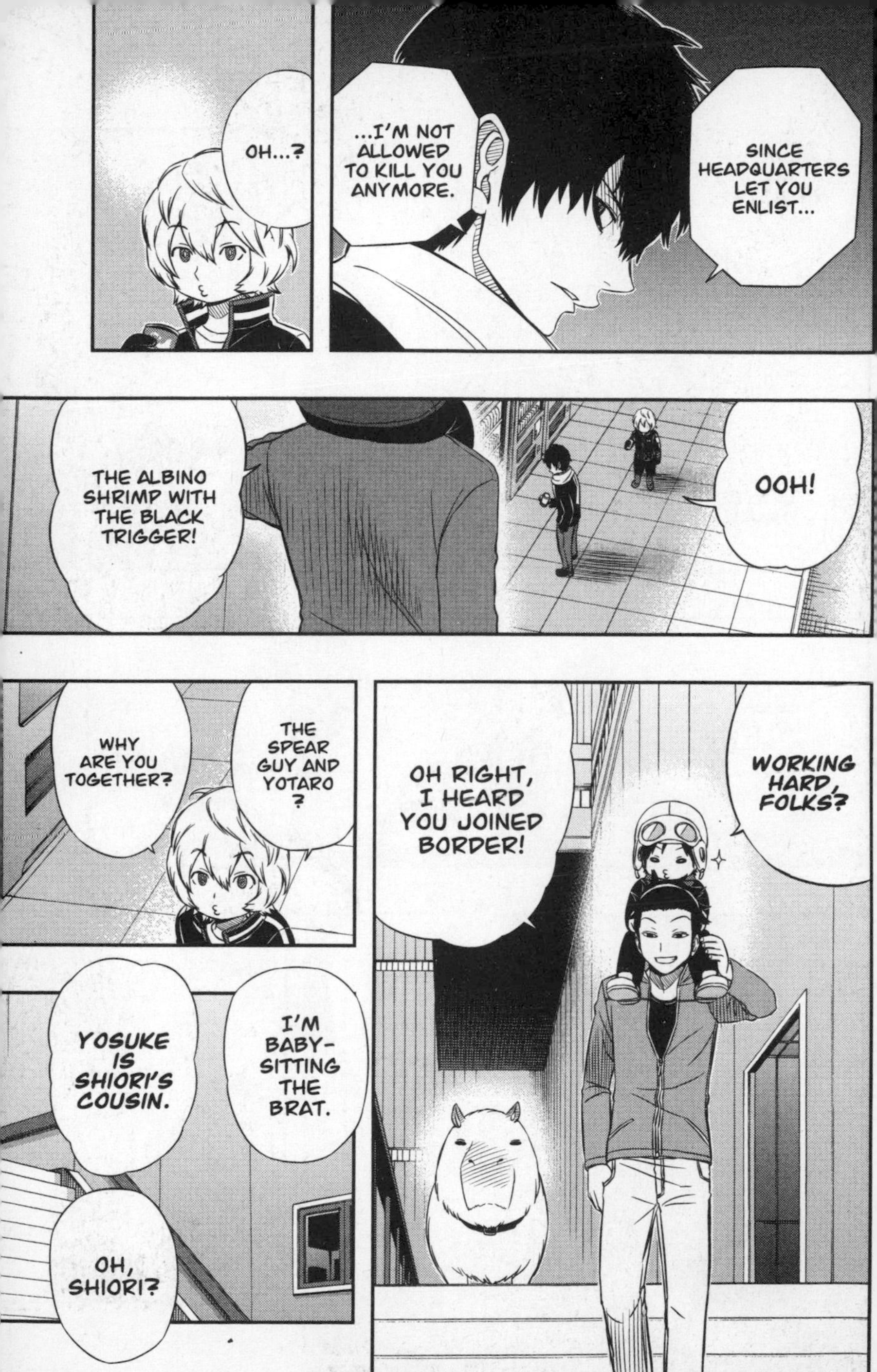
SINCE HEADQUARTERS LET YOU ENLIST...
...I'M NOT ALLOWED TO KILL YOU ANYMORE.
OH...?
OOH!
THE ALBINO SHRIMP WITH THE BLACK TRIGGER!
WORKING HARD, FOLKS?
OH RIGHT, I HEARD YOU JOINED BORDER!
THE SPEAR GUY AND YOTARO?
WHY ARE YOU TOGETHER?
I'M BABY-SITTING THE BRAT.
YOSUKE IS SHIORI'S COUSIN.
OH, SHIORI?

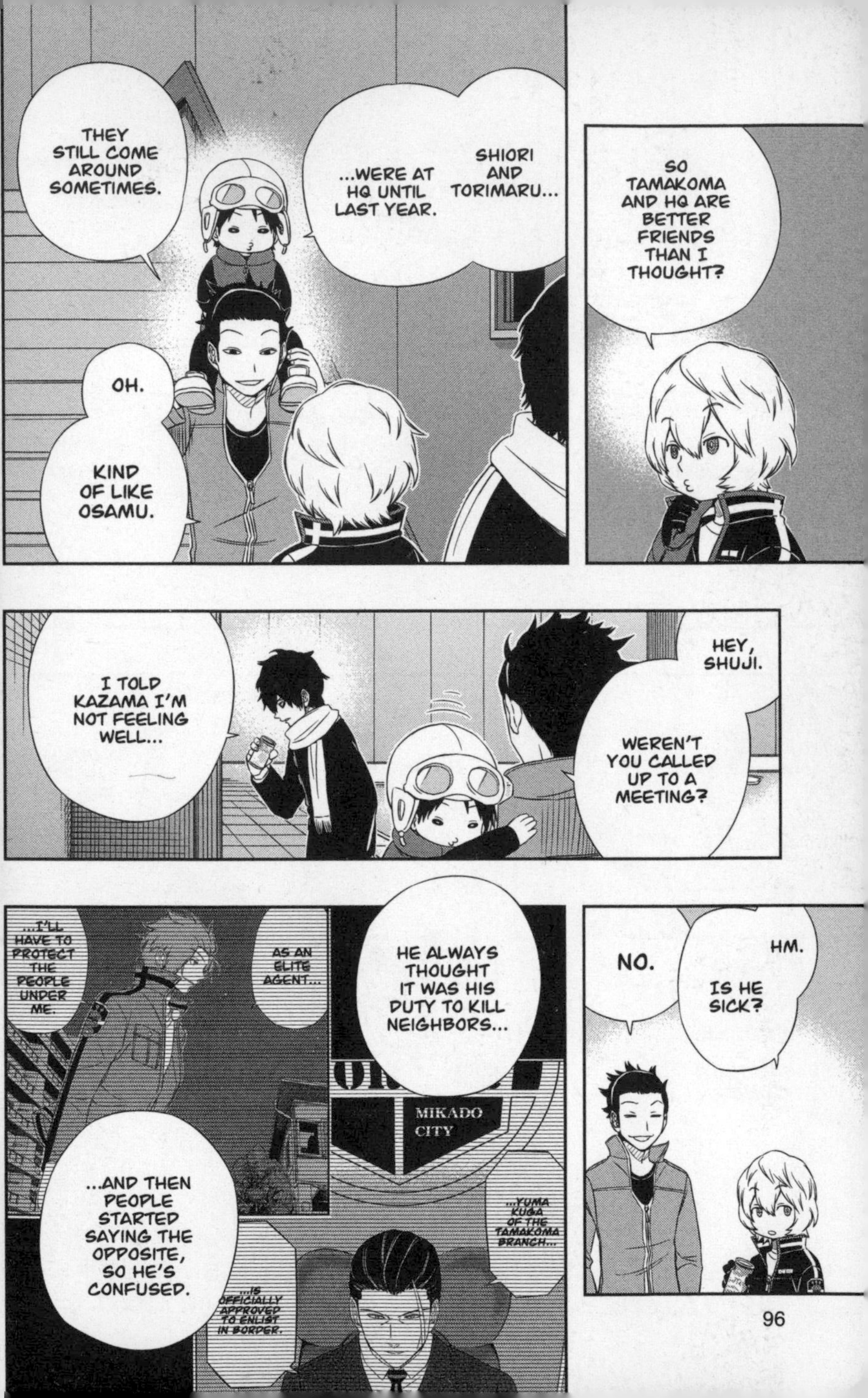
SO TAMAKOMA AND HQ ARE BETTER FRIENDS THAN I THOUGHT?
SHIORI AND TORIMARU...
...WERE AT HQ UNTIL LAST YEAR.
THEY STILL COME AROUND SOMETIMES.
OH.
KIND OF LIKE OSAMU.
HEY, SHUJI.
WEREN'T YOU CALLED UP TO A MEETING?
I TOLD KAZAMA I'M NOT FEELING WELL...
HM.
IS HE SICK?
NO.
HE ALWAYS THOUGHT IT WAS HIS DUTY TO KILL NEIGHBORS...
AS AN ELITE AGENT...
...I'LL HAVE TO PROTECT THE PEOPLE UNDER ME.
MIKADO CITY
...YUMA KUGA OF THE TAMAKOMA BRANCH...
...AND THEN PEOPLE STARTED SAYING THE OPPOSITE, SO HE'S CONFUSED.
...IS OFFICIALLY APPROVED TO ENLIST IN BORDER.

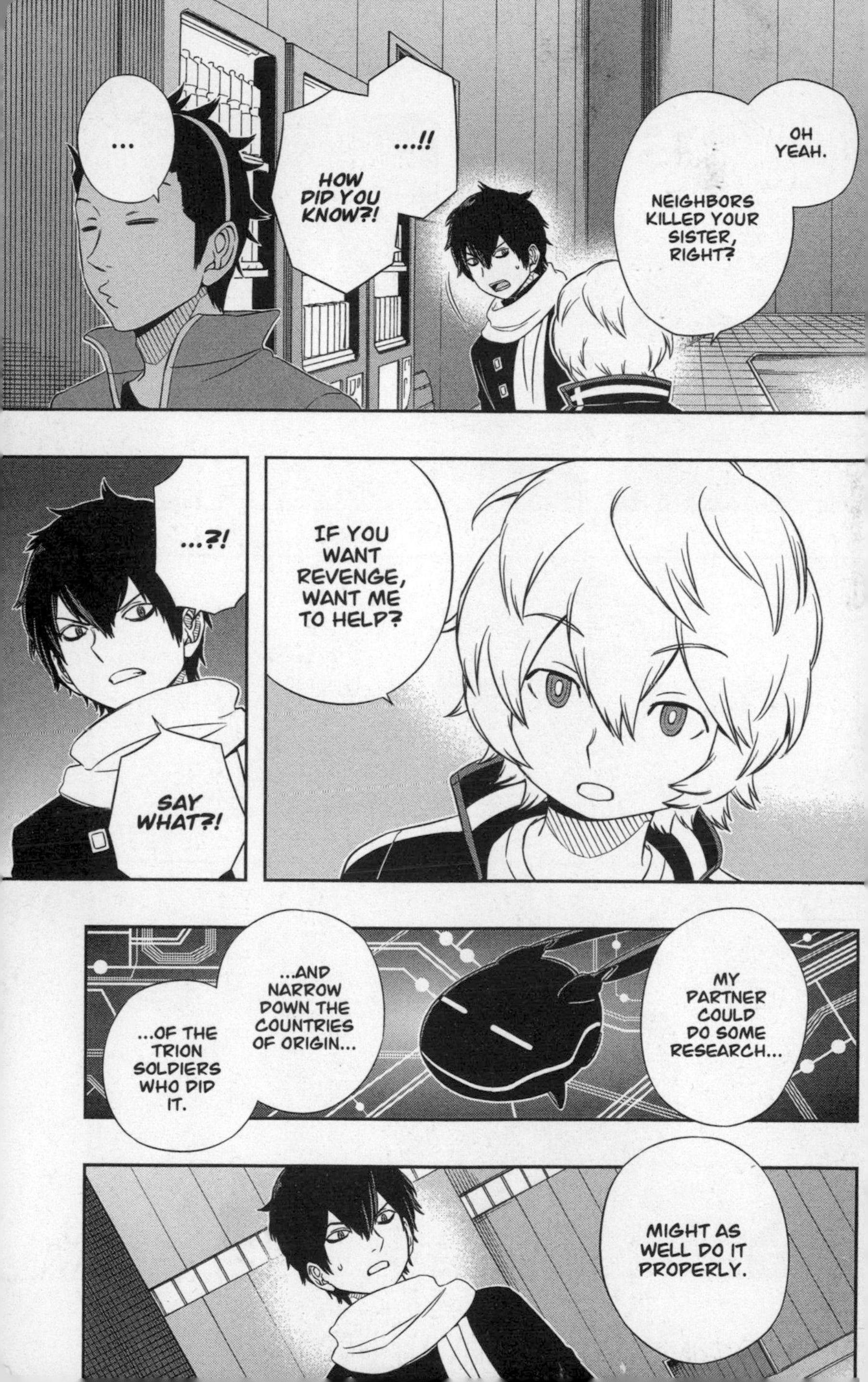
OH YEAH.
NEIGHBORS KILLED YOUR SISTER, RIGHT?
...!!
HOW DID YOU KNOW?!
...
IF YOU WANT REVENGE, WANT ME TO HELP?
...?!
SAY WHAT?!
MY PARTNER COULD DO SOME RESEARCH...
...AND NARROW DOWN THE COUNTRIES OF ORIGIN...
...OF THE TRION SOLDIERS WHO DID IT.
MIGHT AS WELL DO IT PROPERLY.

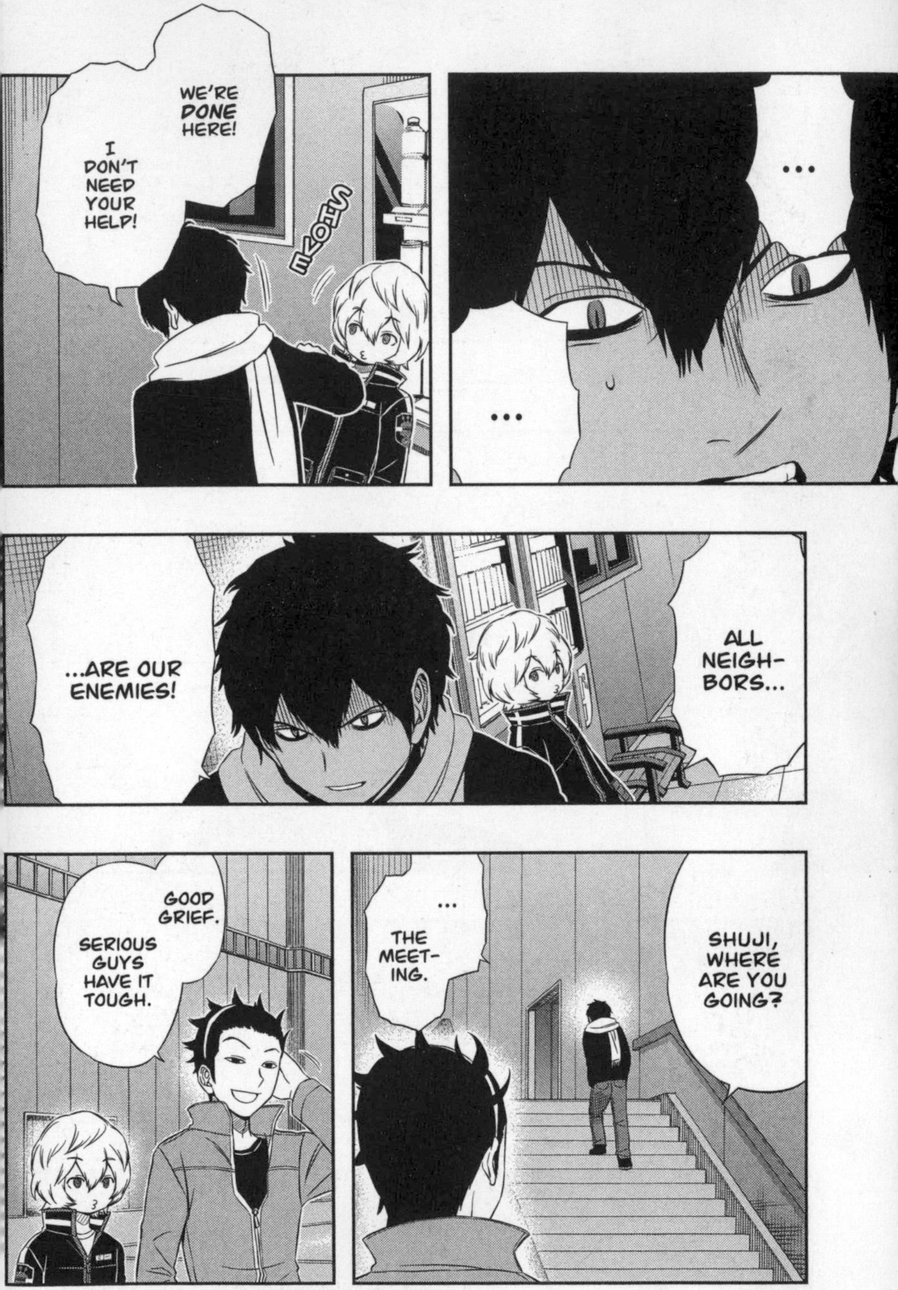
...
...
WE'RE DONE HERE!
I DON'T NEED YOUR HELP!
SHOVE
ALL NEIGH-BORS...
...ARE OUR ENEMIES!
SHUJI, WHERE ARE YOU GOING?
...
THE MEET-ING.
GOOD GRIEF.
SERIOUS GUYS HAVE IT TOUGH.

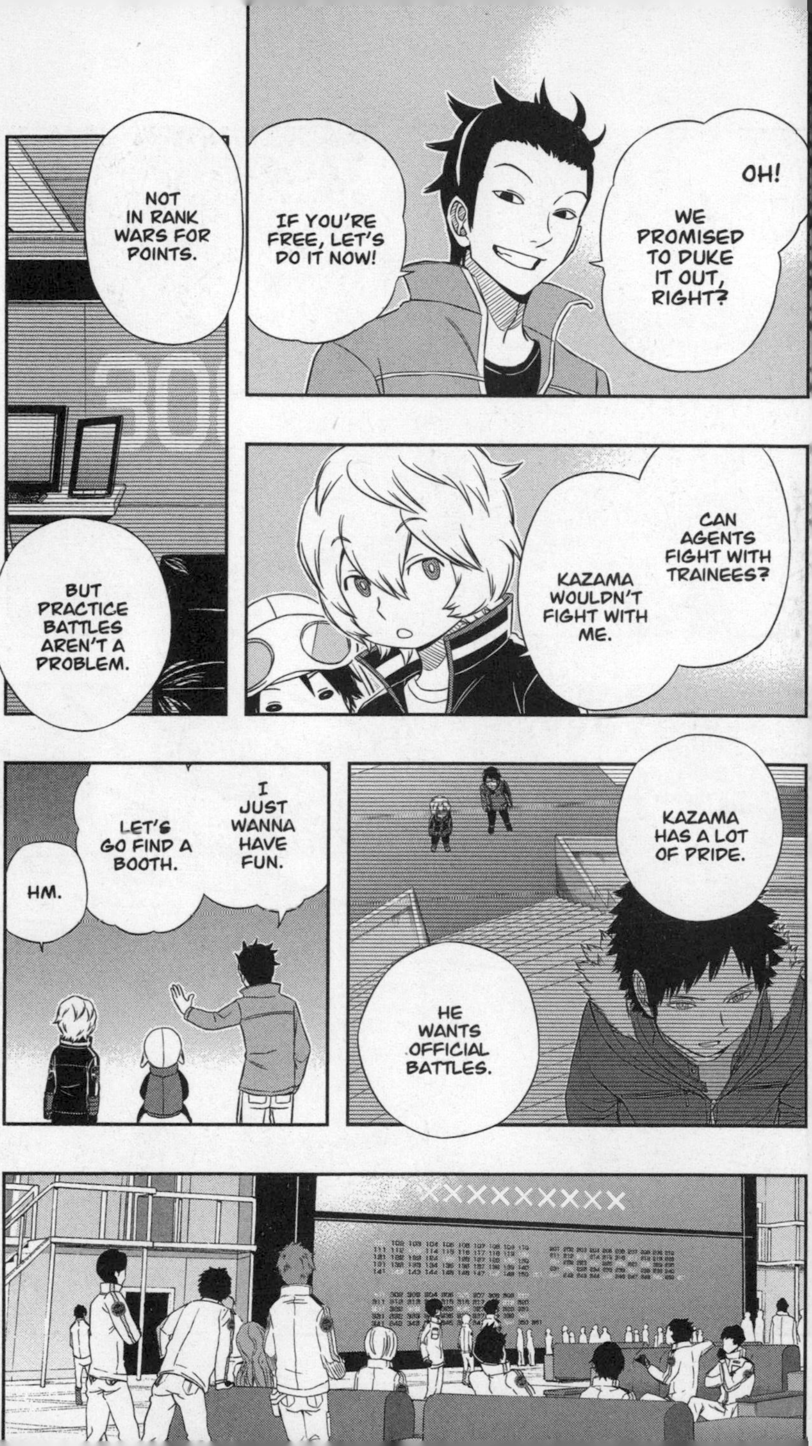
OH!
WE PROMISED TO DUKE IT OUT, RIGHT?
IF YOU'RE FREE, LET'S DO IT NOW!
CAN AGENTS FIGHT WITH TRAINEES?
KAZAMA WOULDN'T FIGHT WITH ME.
NOT IN RANK WARS FOR POINTS.
BUT PRACTICE BATTLES AREN'T A PROBLEM.
KAZAMA HAS A LOT OF PRIDE.
HE WANTS OFFICIAL BATTLES.
I JUST WANNA HAVE FUN.
LET'S GO FIND A BOOTH.
HM.

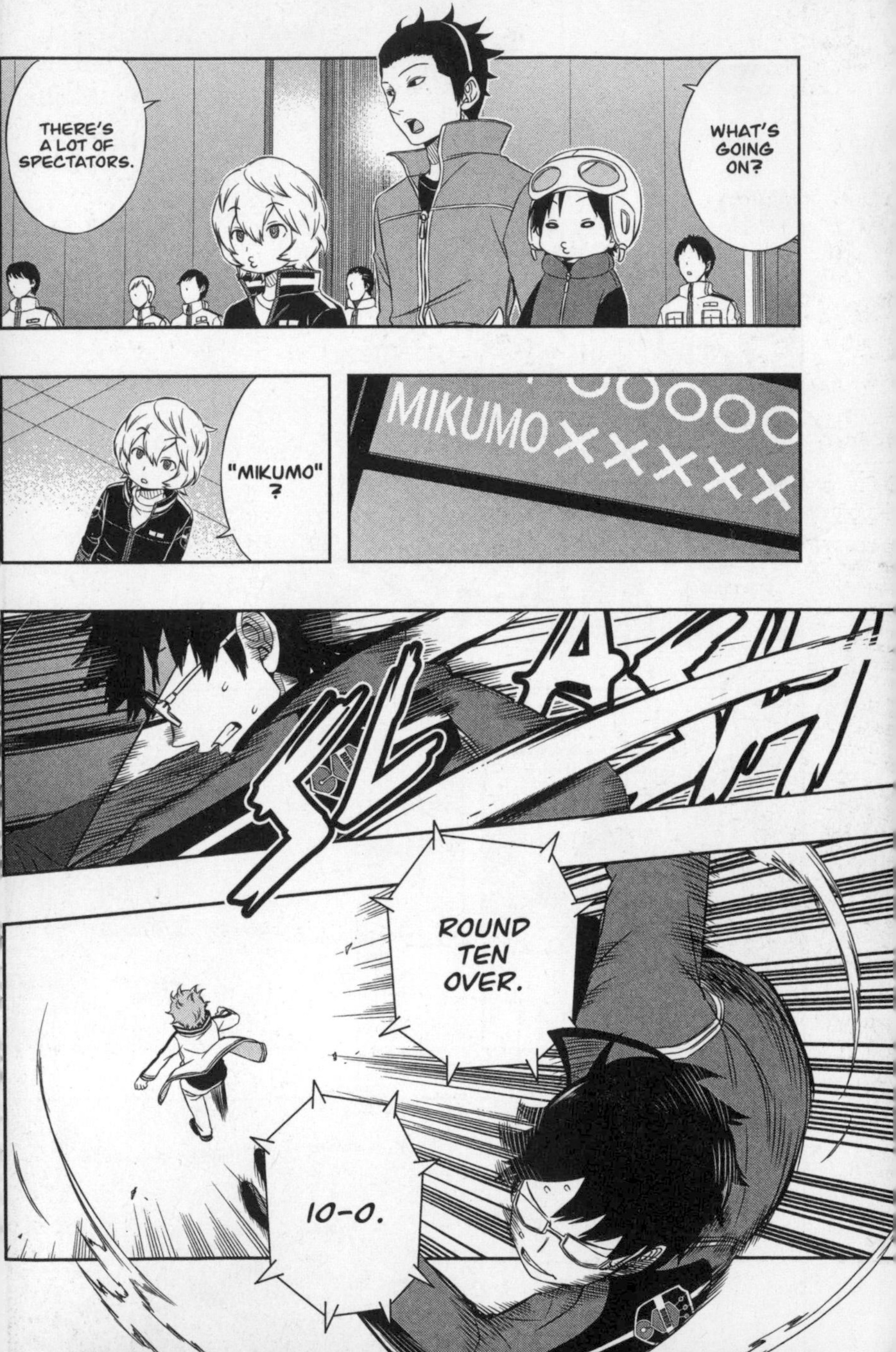
WHAT'S GOING ON?
THERE'S A LOT OF SPECTATORS.
MIKUMO
"MIKUMO"?
ROUND TEN OVER.
10-0.

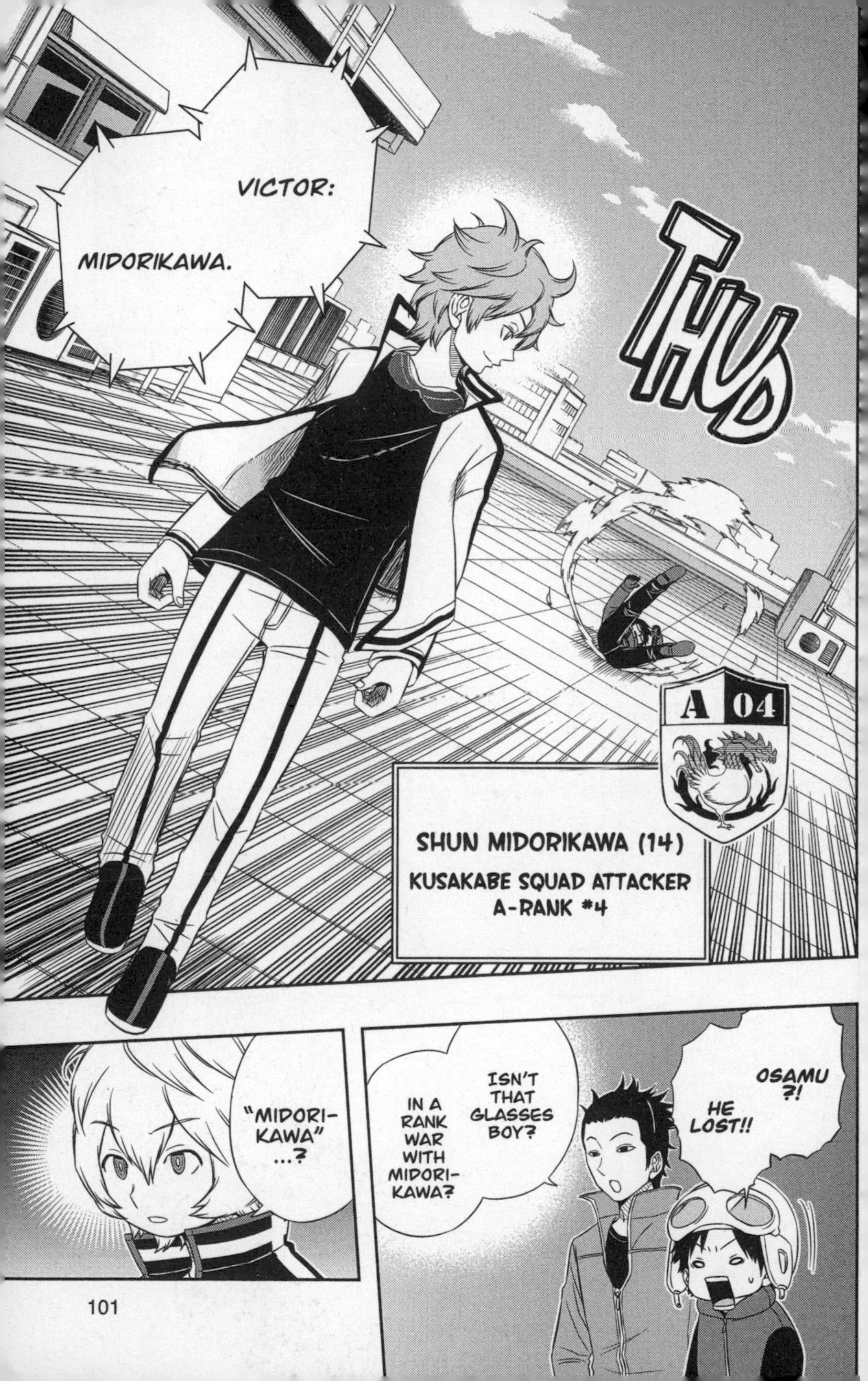
VICTOR: MIDORIKAWA.
THUD
A 04
SHUN MIDORIKAWA (14)
KUSAKABE SQUAD ATTACKER
A-RANK #4
OSAMU ?!
HE LOST!!
ISN'T THAT GLASSES BOY?
IN A RANK WAR WITH MIDORI-KAWA?
"MIDORI-KAWA" ...?

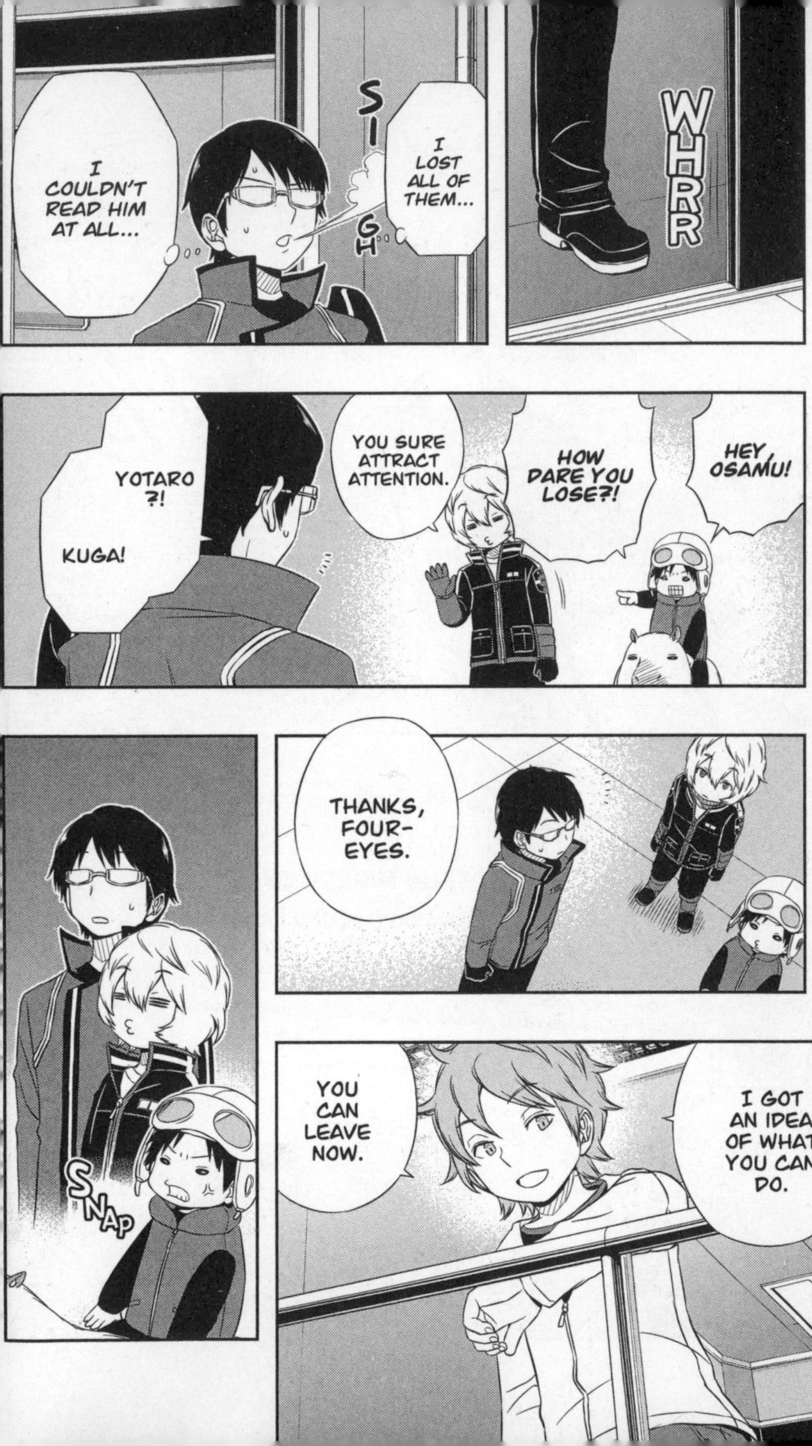
WHRRR
I LOST ALL OF THEM...
SIGH
I COULDN'T READ HIM AT ALL...
HEY, OSAMU!
HOW DARE YOU LOSE?!
YOU SURE ATTRACT ATTENTION.
YOTARO?! KUGA!
THANKS, FOUR-EYES.
I GOT AN IDEA OF WHAT YOU CAN DO.
YOU CAN LEAVE NOW.
SNAP

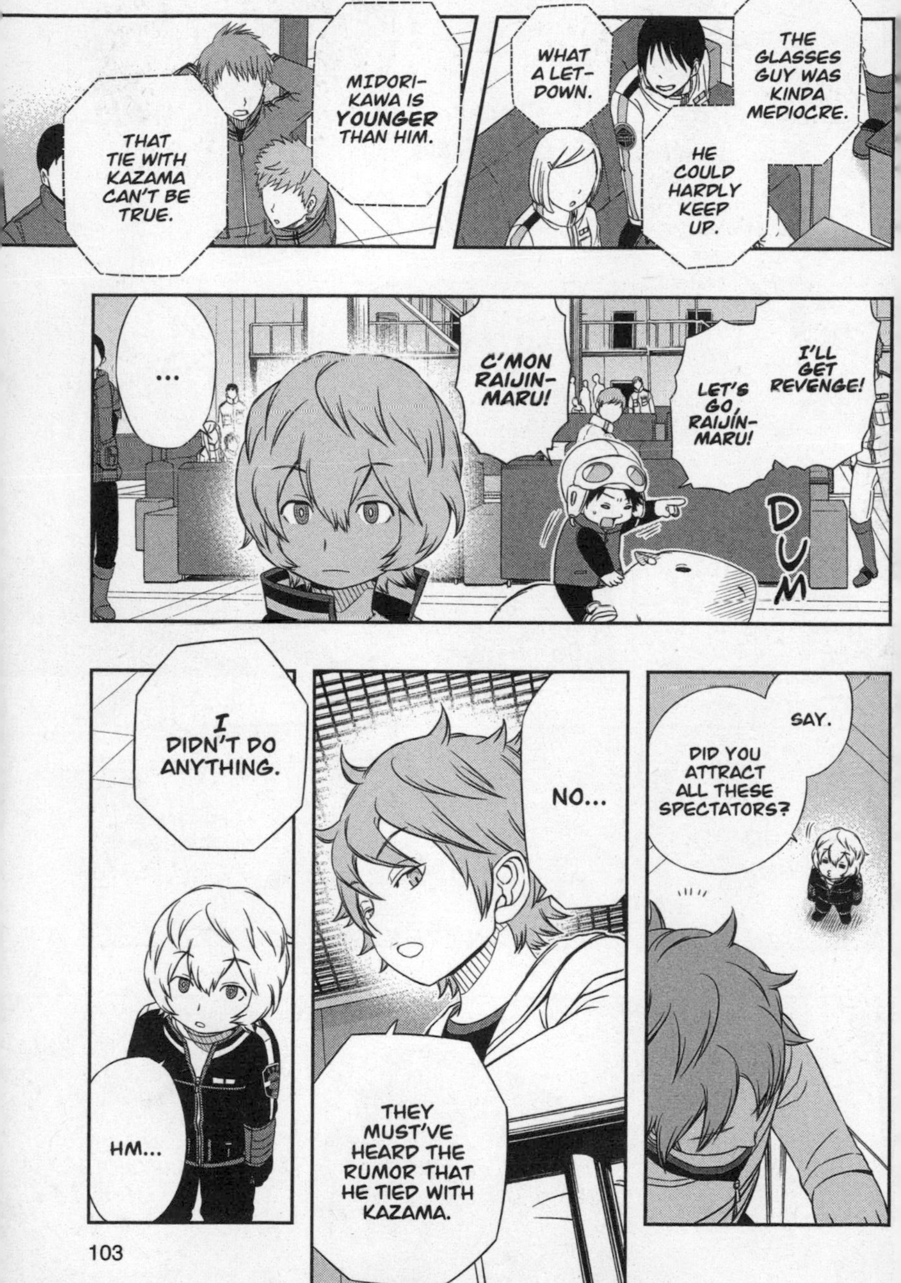
THE GLASSES GUY WAS KINDA MEDIOCRE.
WHAT A LET-DOWN.
HE COULD HARDLY KEEP UP.
MIDORI-KAWA IS YOUNGER THAN HIM.
THAT TIE WITH KAZAMA CAN'T BE TRUE.
I'LL GET REVENGE!
LET'S GO, RAIJIN-MARU!
C'MON RAIJIN-MARU!
...
DUM
SAY.
DID YOU ATTRACT ALL THESE SPECTATORS?
NO...
THEY MUST'VE HEARD THE RUMOR THAT HE TIED WITH KAZAMA.
I DIDN'T DO ANYTHING.
HM...

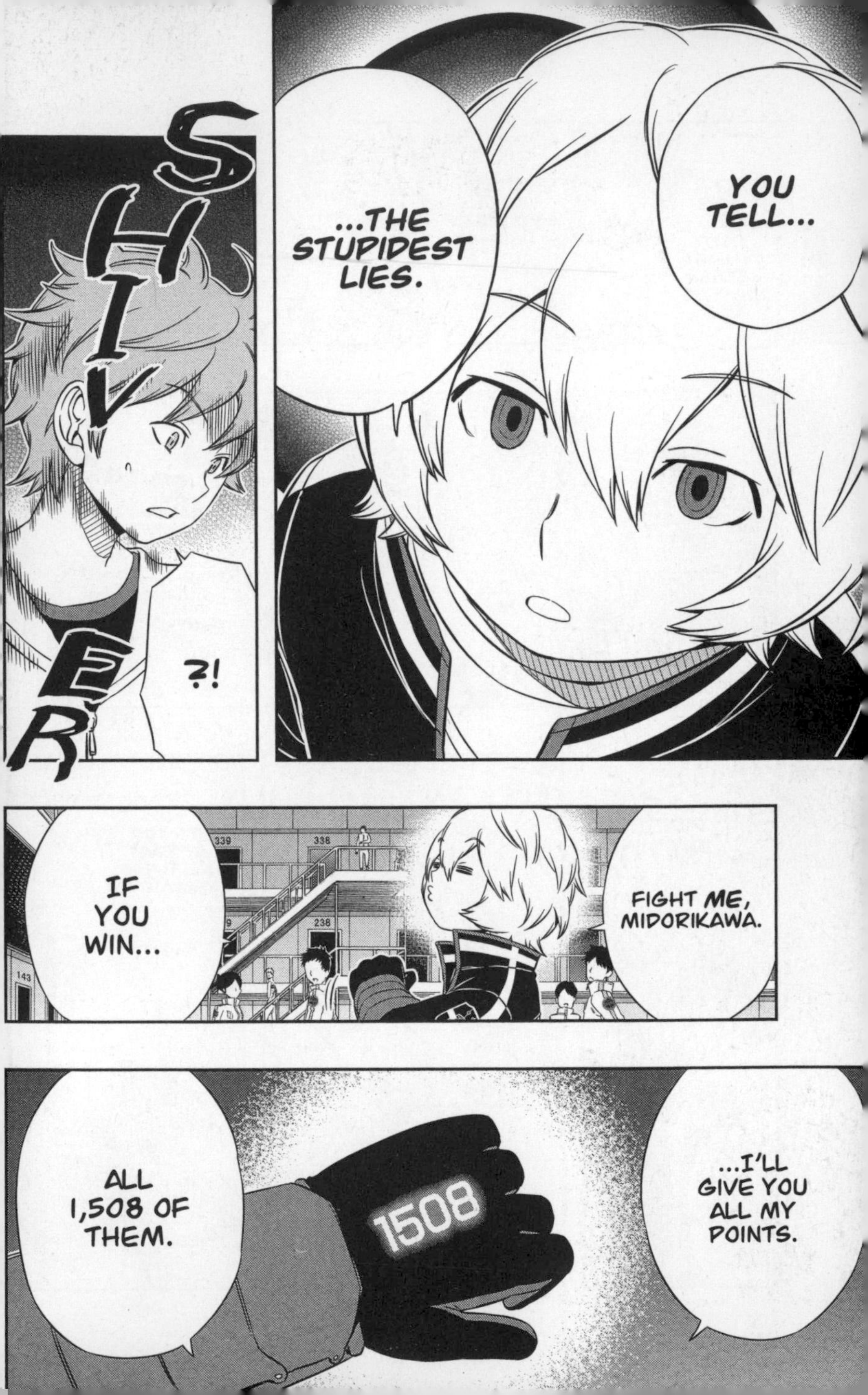
YOU TELL...
...THE STUPIDEST LIES.
SHIVER
?!
FIGHT ME, MIDORIKAWA.
IF YOU WIN...
...I'LL GIVE YOU ALL MY POINTS.
ALL 1,508 OF THEM.
1508

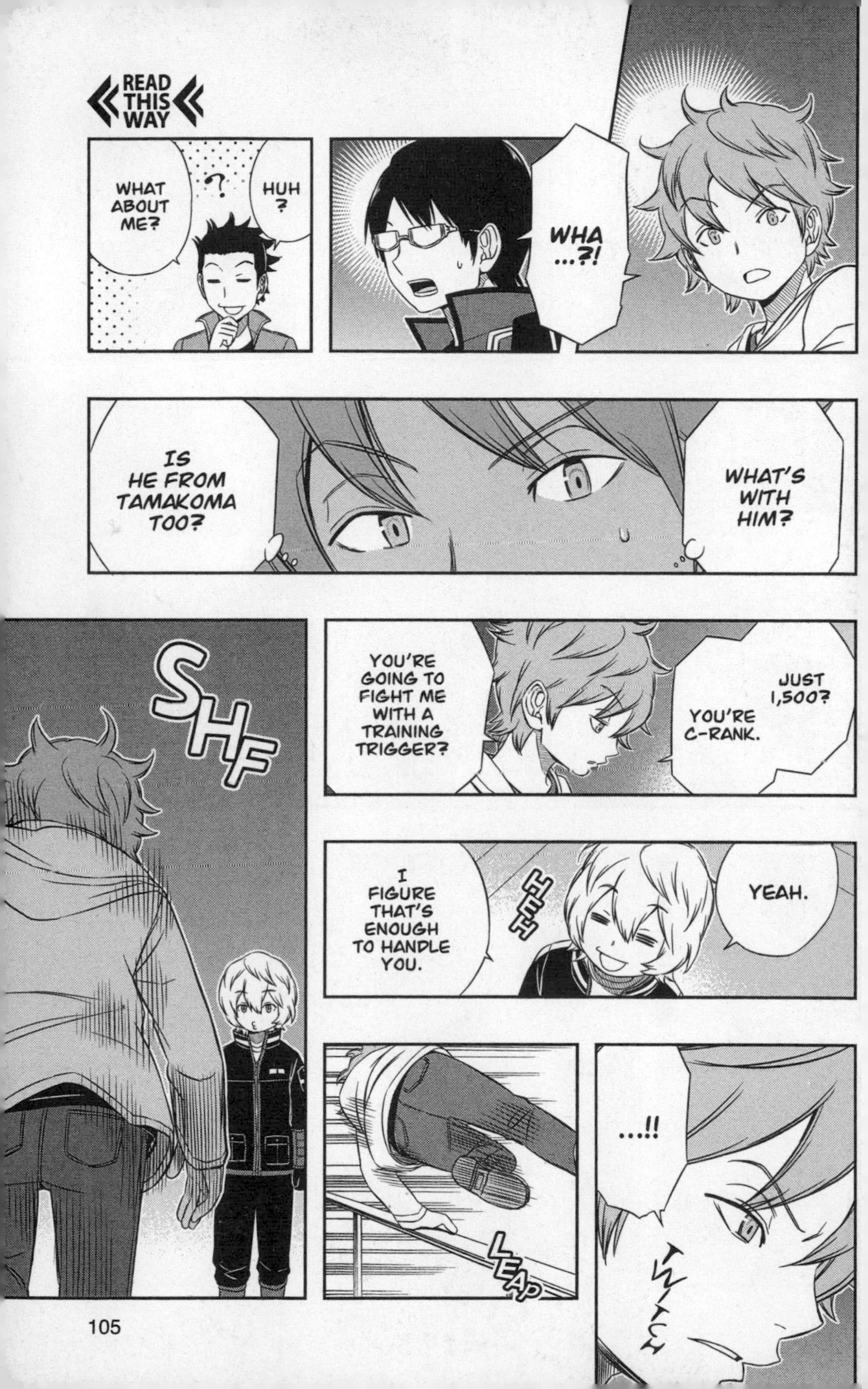
READ THIS WAY
WHA ...?!
HUH ?
?
WHAT ABOUT ME?
WHAT'S WITH HIM?
IS HE FROM TAMAKOMA TOO?
JUST 1,500?
YOU'RE C-RANK.
YOU'RE GOING TO FIGHT ME WITH A TRAINING TRIGGER?
YEAH.
HEH
I FIGURE THAT'S ENOUGH TO HANDLE YOU.
...!!
TWITCH
LEAP
SHF

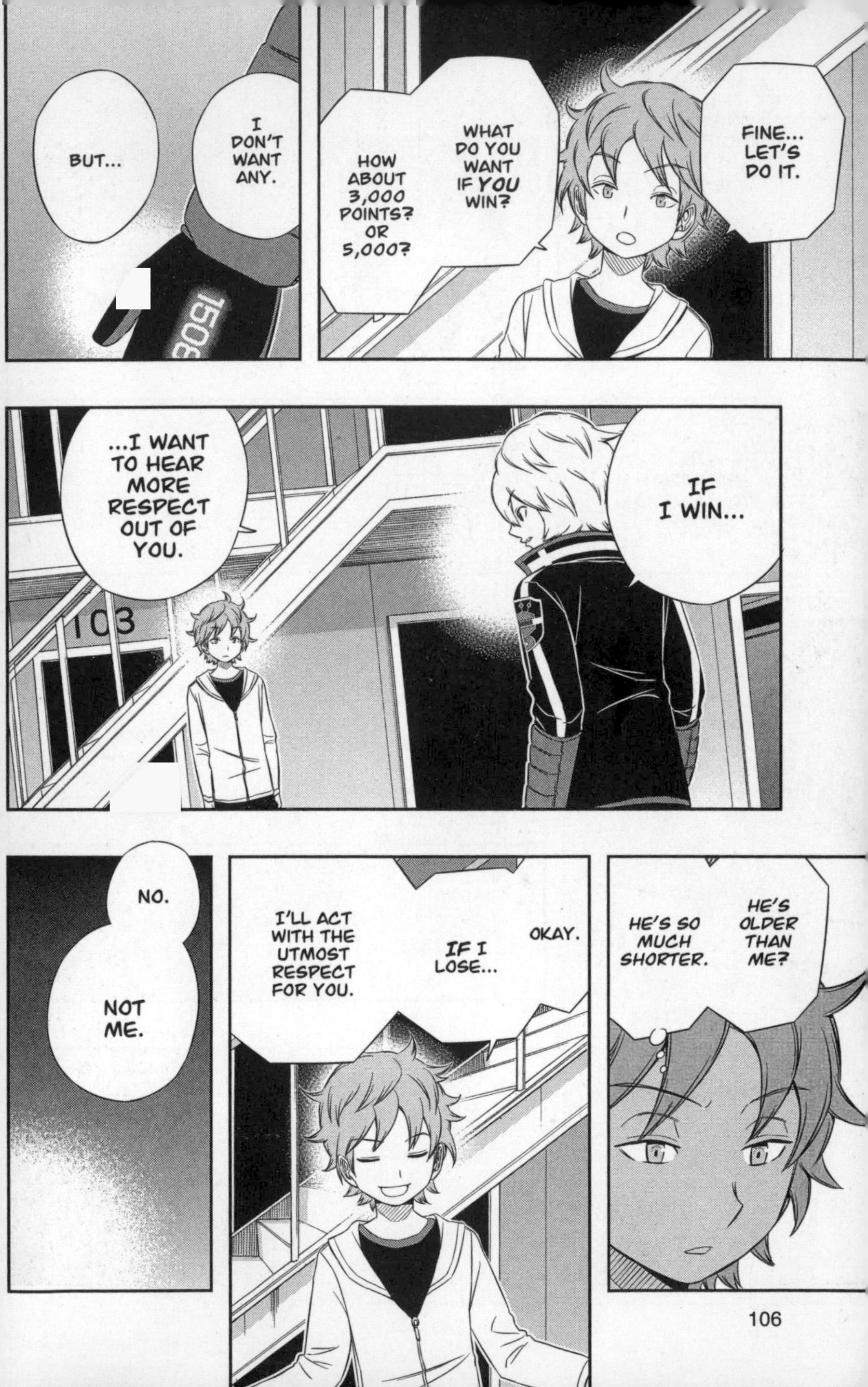
FINE... LET'S DO IT.
WHAT DO YOU WANT IF *YOU* WIN?
HOW ABOUT 3,000 POINTS? OR 5,000?
I DON'T WANT ANY.
BUT...
IF I WIN...
...I WANT TO HEAR MORE RESPECT OUT OF YOU.
103
HE'S OLDER THAN ME?
HE'S SO MUCH SHORTER.
OKAY.
IF I LOSE...
I'LL ACT WITH THE UTMOST RESPECT FOR YOU.
NO.
NOT ME.

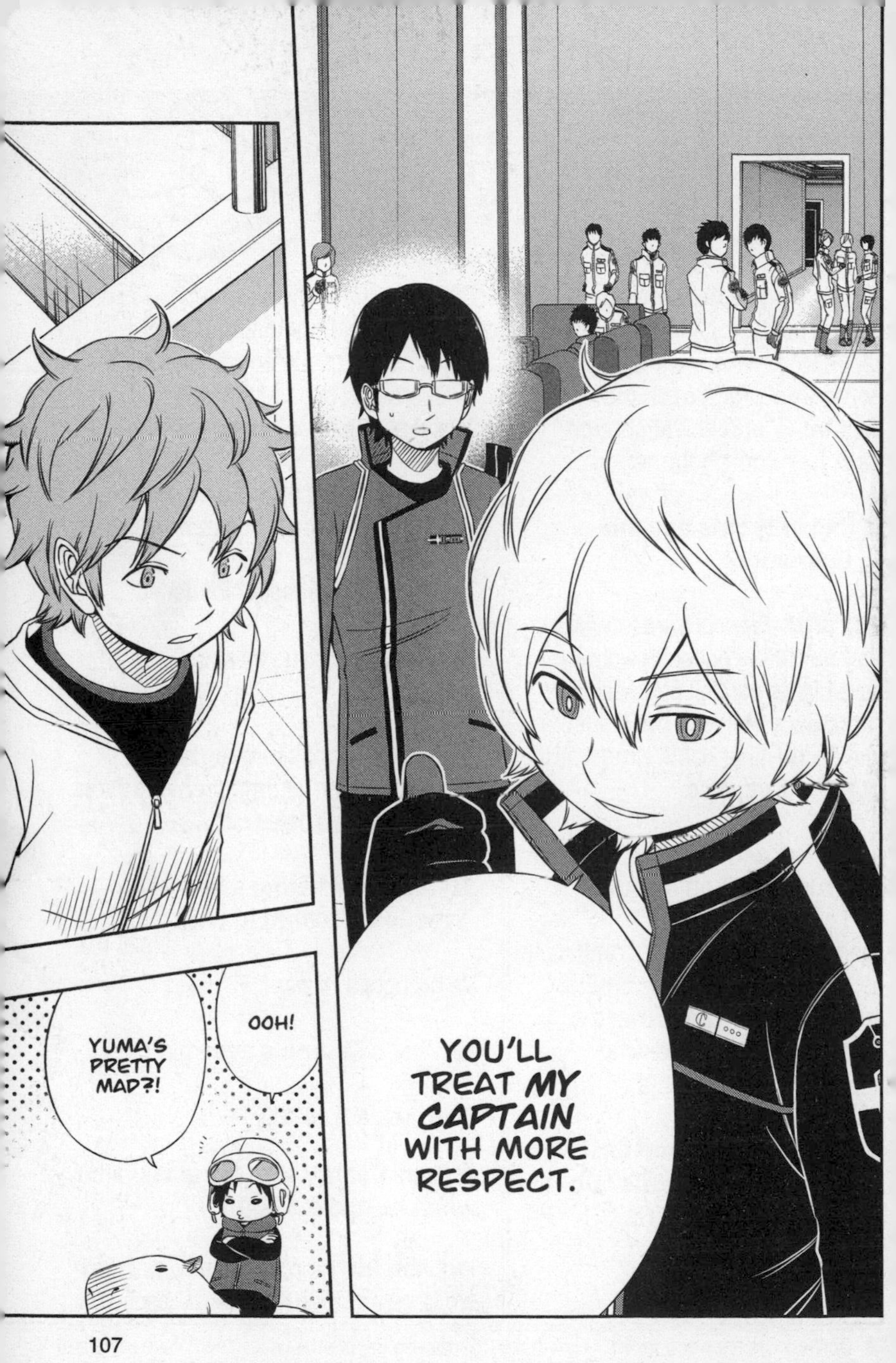
YOU'LL TREAT MY CAPTAIN WITH MORE RESPECT.
OOH!
YUMA'S PRETTY MAD?!

Q&A: Part 2

Since I'm sure not everyone reads Twitter.

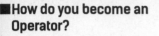

■ **How do you become an Operator?**

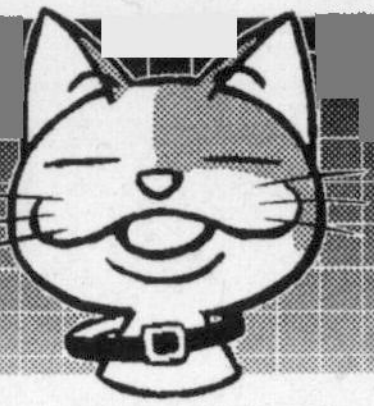

Some apply for it from the beginning, and some change track from combatants.

■ **Can only girls become Operators?**

Almost all Operators are female. They say this is because women have higher parallel processing capabilities. Men can be Operators too. On the other hand, almost all the engineers are male.

■ **Is there a limit to the number of members on a squad?**

A team of five, with four combatants and one Operator is the limit. Any more and it goes over the Operator's data processing capability.

■ **Why do Osamu and Chika have different outfits? Do they have free rein?**

Chika's outfit is the standard C-Rank female Sniper (up to junior high) uniform. Jin made adjustments to Osamu's. That's why it has Tamakoma's shoulder epaulette.

■ **Why is Narasaka the bamboo guy in the mushroom family?**

To avoid unnecessary bloodshed.

■ **Is Raijin-maru male or female?**

Raijin-maru looks female, but everyone at Tamakoma probably thinks Raijin-maru is male.

■ **Was Yuma eating a lunch made by Osamu in chapter 2?**

He brought it himself.

■ **What's Osamu's eyesight?**

Both eyes are 20/100.

■ **Does Osamu take his glasses off when he takes a bath?**

Probably not. He may even wear them while he's asleep. Perpetual Glasses.

■ I sometimes answer questions I get in my fan mail on my official Twitter feed. Make my editor happy by following me on Twitter. **World Trigger official Twitter account: @W_Trigger_off**

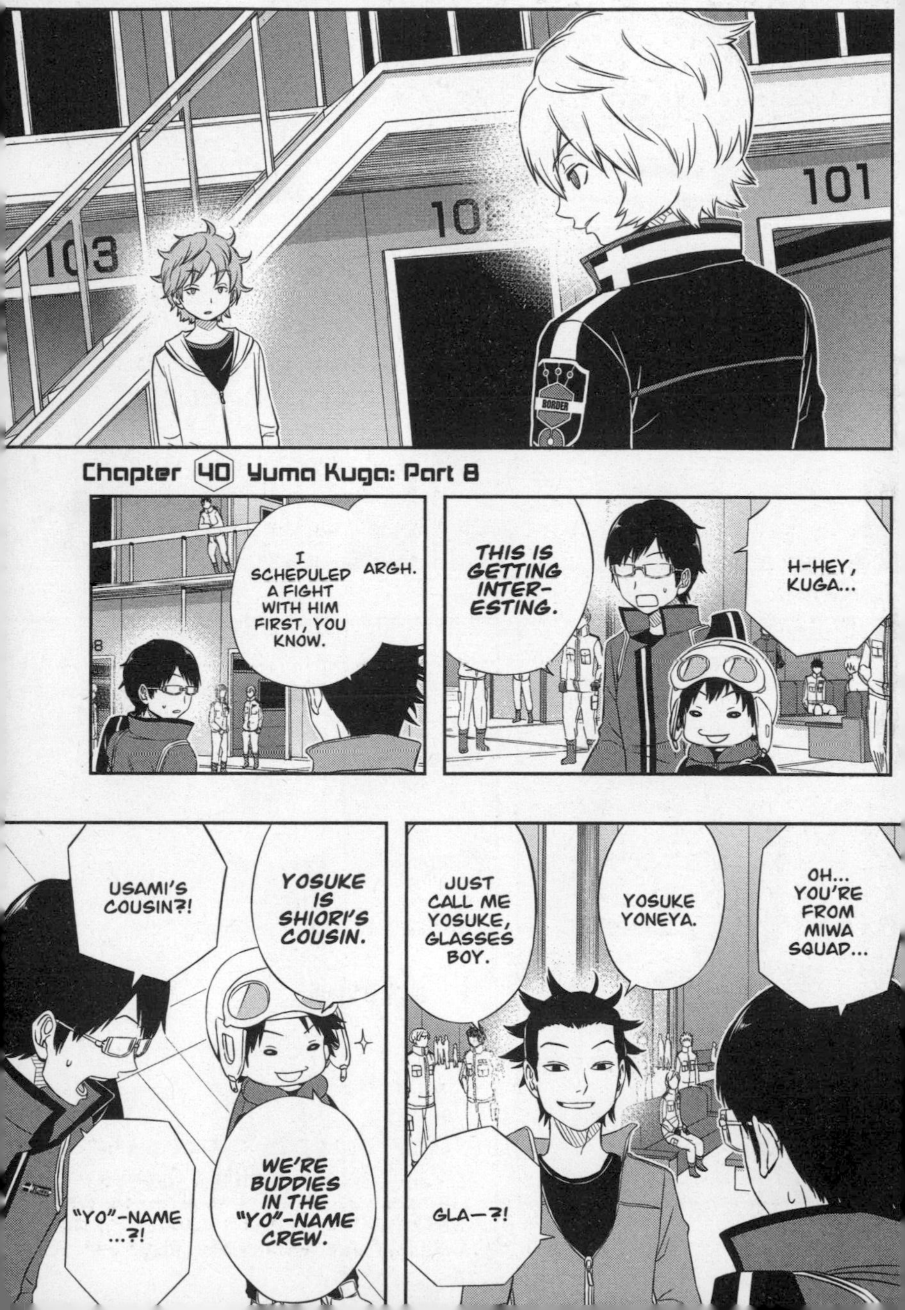

Chapter 40 Yuma Kuga: Part 8
H-HEY, KUGA...
THIS IS GETTING INTERESTING.
ARGH.
I SCHEDULED A FIGHT WITH HIM FIRST, YOU KNOW.
OH... YOU'RE FROM MIWA SQUAD...
YOSUKE YONEYA.
JUST CALL ME YOSUKE, GLASSES BOY.
GLA—?!
YOSUKE IS SHIORI'S COUSIN.
USAMI'S COUSIN?!
WE'RE BUDDIES IN THE "YO"-NAME CREW.
"YO"-NAME ...?!

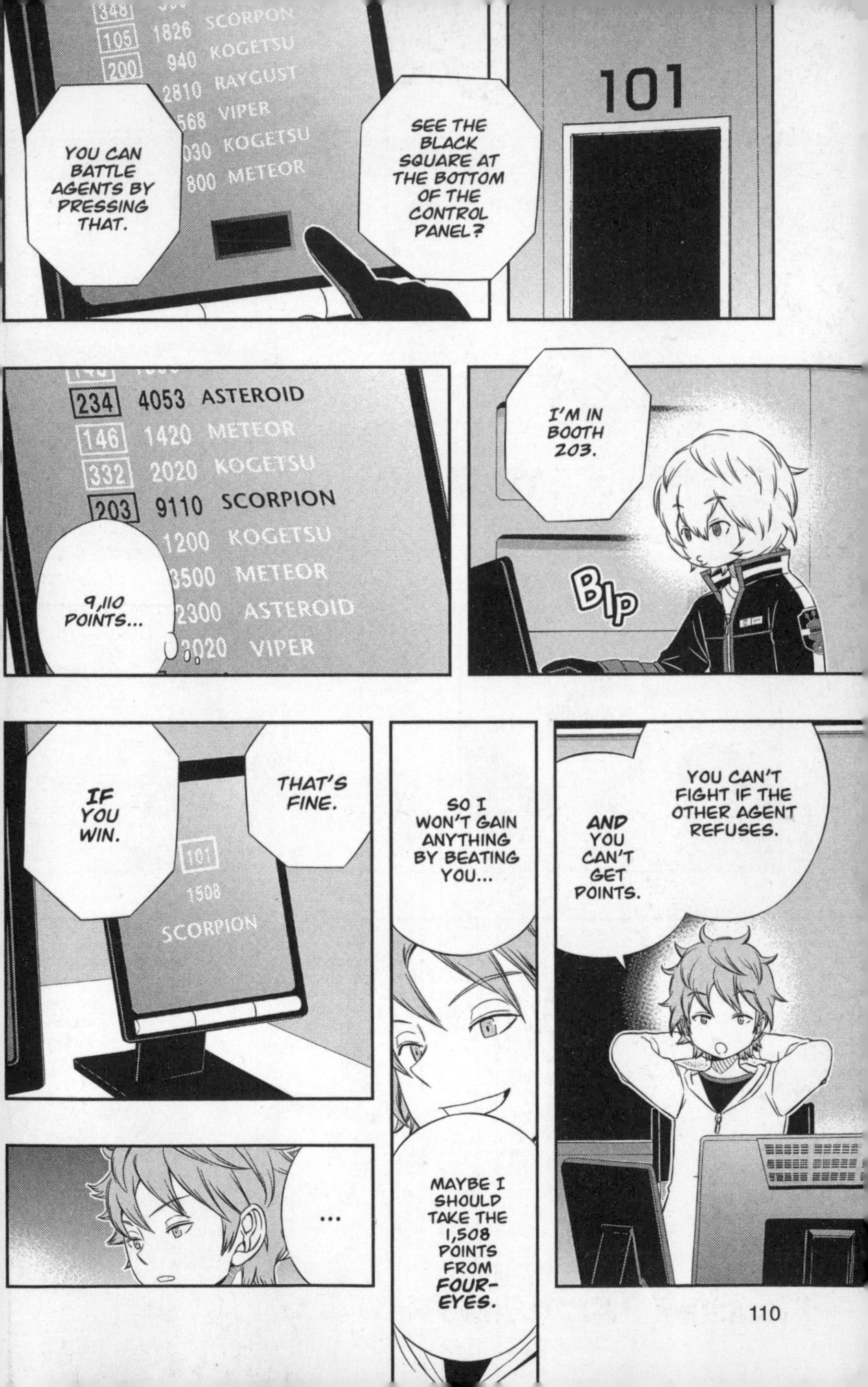
101
SEE THE BLACK SQUARE AT THE BOTTOM OF THE CONTROL PANEL?
YOU CAN BATTLE AGENTS BY PRESSING THAT.
105 1826 SCORPON
200 940 KOGETSU
2810 RAYGUST
568 VIPER
030 KOGETSU
800 METEOR
I'M IN BOOTH 203.
BLIP
234 4053 ASTEROID
146 1420 METEOR
332 2020 KOGETSU
203 9110 SCORPION
1200 KOGETSU
3500 METEOR
2300 ASTEROID
2020 VIPER
9,110 POINTS...
YOU CAN'T FIGHT IF THE OTHER AGENT REFUSES.
AND YOU CAN'T GET POINTS.
SO I WON'T GAIN ANYTHING BY BEATING YOU...
MAYBE I SHOULD TAKE THE 1,508 POINTS FROM FOUR-EYES.
THAT'S FINE.
IF YOU WIN.
101
1508
SCORPION
...

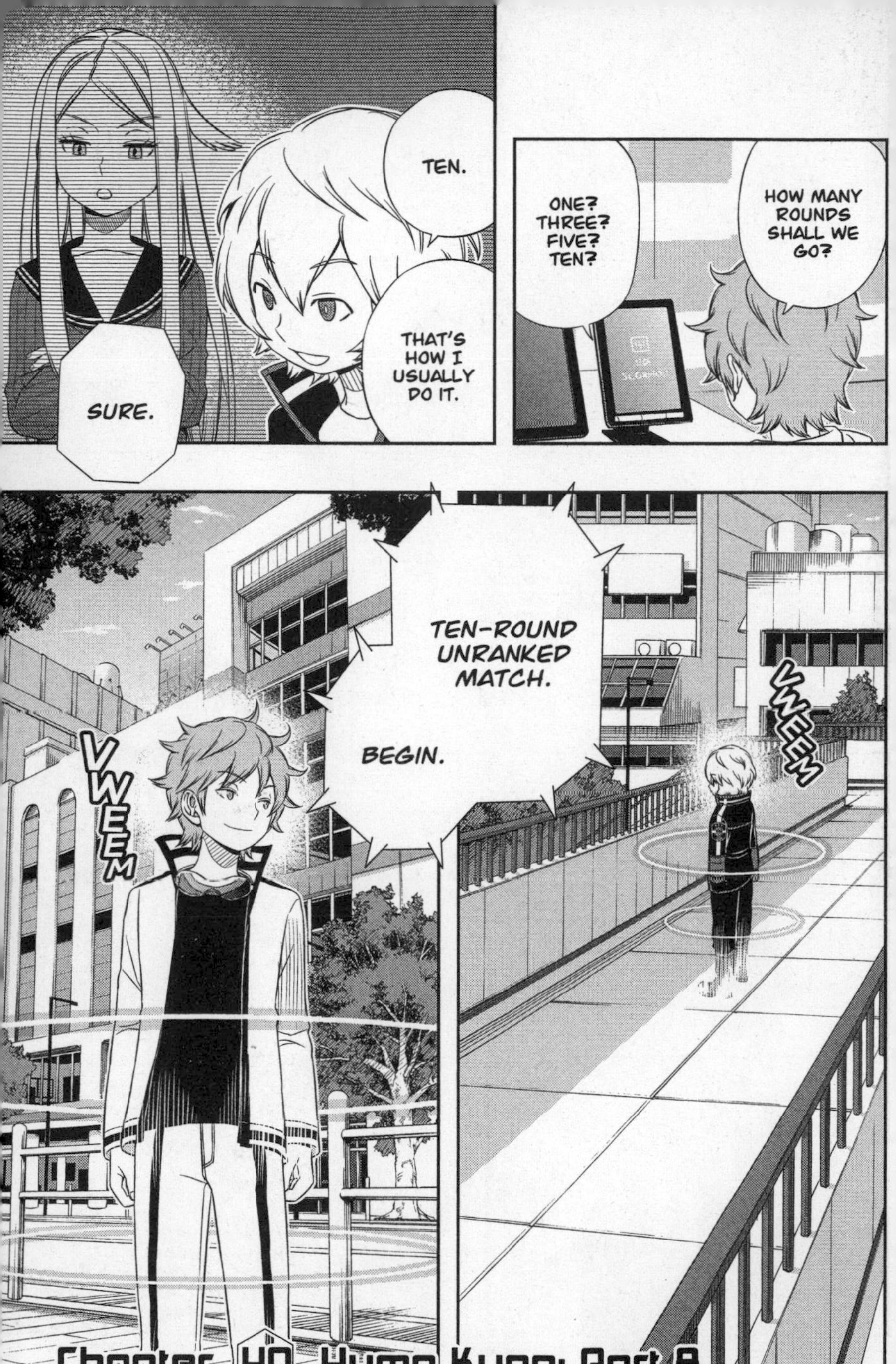
HOW MANY ROUNDS SHALL WE GO?
ONE? THREE? FIVE? TEN?
TEN.
THAT'S HOW I USUALLY DO IT.
SURE.
VWEEM
TEN-ROUND UNRANKED MATCH.
BEGIN.
VWEEM

Chapter 40 Yuma Kuga: Part 8

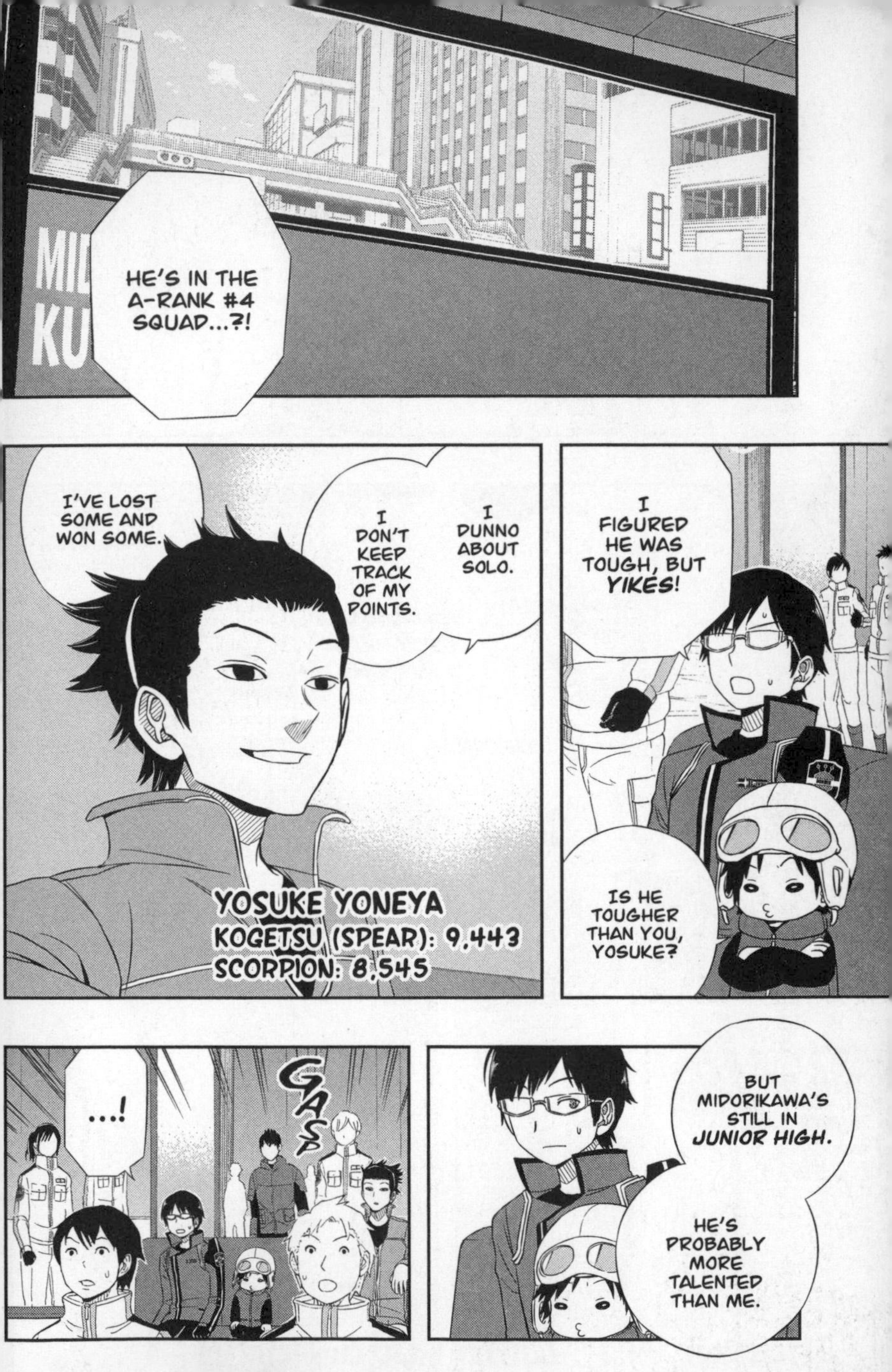
HE'S IN THE A-RANK #4 SQUAD...?!
I FIGURED HE WAS TOUGH, BUT YIKES!
IS HE TOUGHER THAN YOU, YOSUKE?
I DUNNO ABOUT SOLO.
I DON'T KEEP TRACK OF MY POINTS.
I'VE LOST SOME AND WON SOME.
YOSUKE YONEYA
KOGETSU (SPEAR): 9,443
SCORPION: 8,545
BUT MIDORIKAWA'S STILL IN JUNIOR HIGH.
HE'S PROBABLY MORE TALENTED THAN ME.
GASP
...!

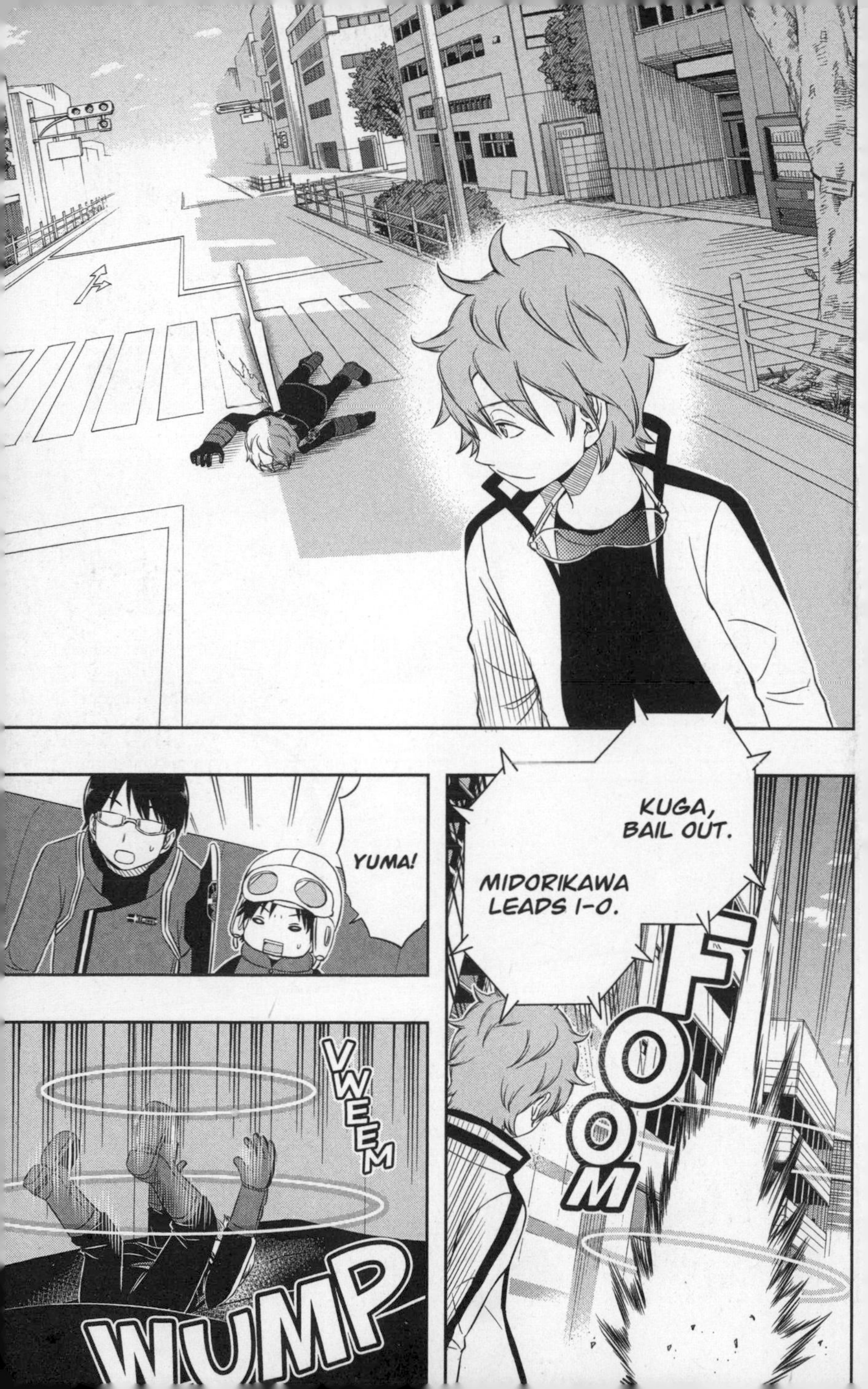
KUGA, BAIL OUT.
MIDORIKAWA LEADS 1-0.
FOOOM
YUMA!
VWEEM
WUMP

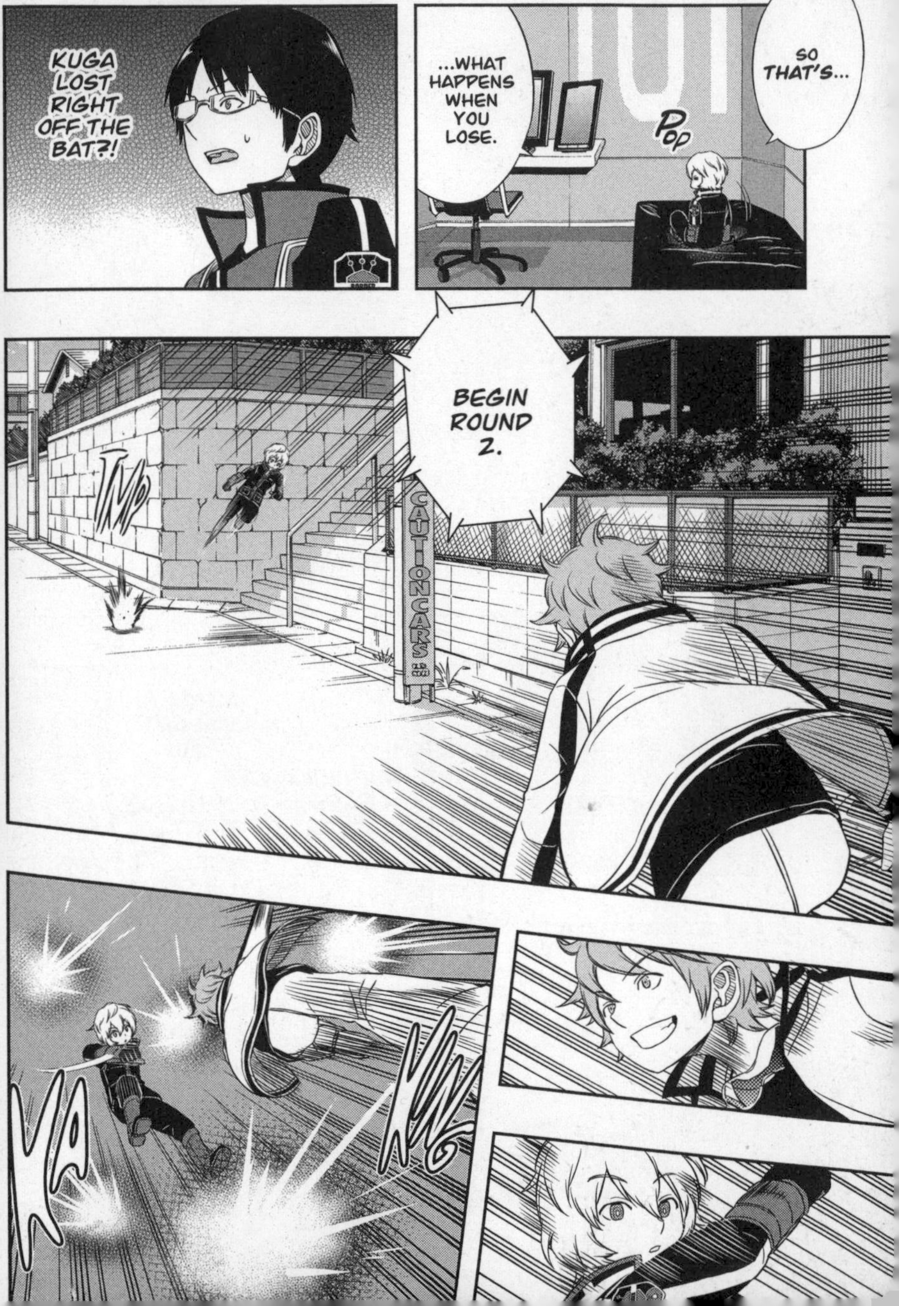
SO THAT'S...
...WHAT HAPPENS WHEN YOU LOSE.
POP
KUGA LOST RIGHT OFF THE BAT?!
BEGIN ROUND 2.
CAUTION CARS
TMP
KA

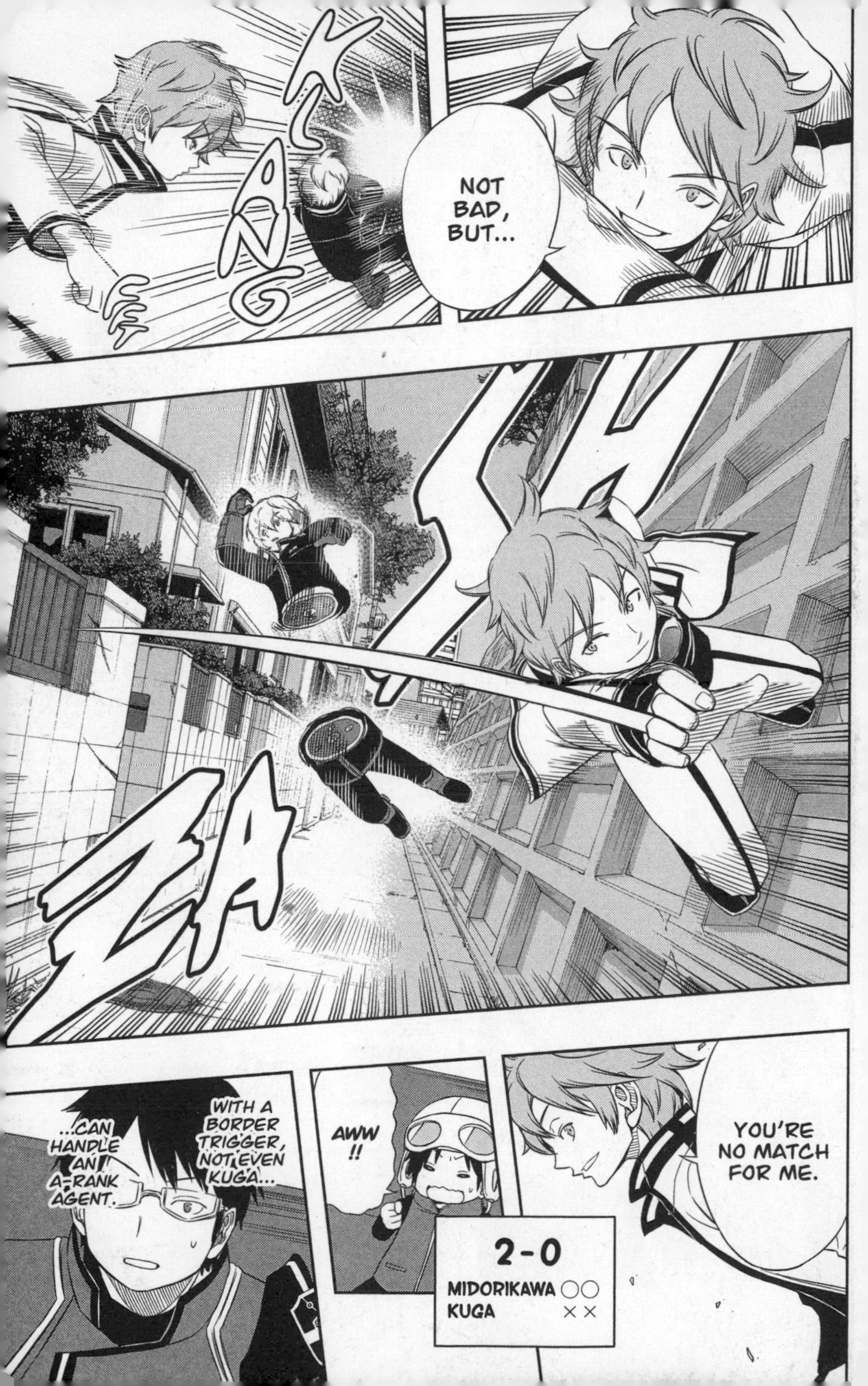
NOT BAD, BUT...
KLANG
YOU'RE NO MATCH FOR ME.
2-0
MIDORIKAWA ○○
KUGA ××
AWW !!
WITH A BORDER TRIGGER, NOT EVEN KUGA...
...CAN HANDLE AN A-RANK AGENT.

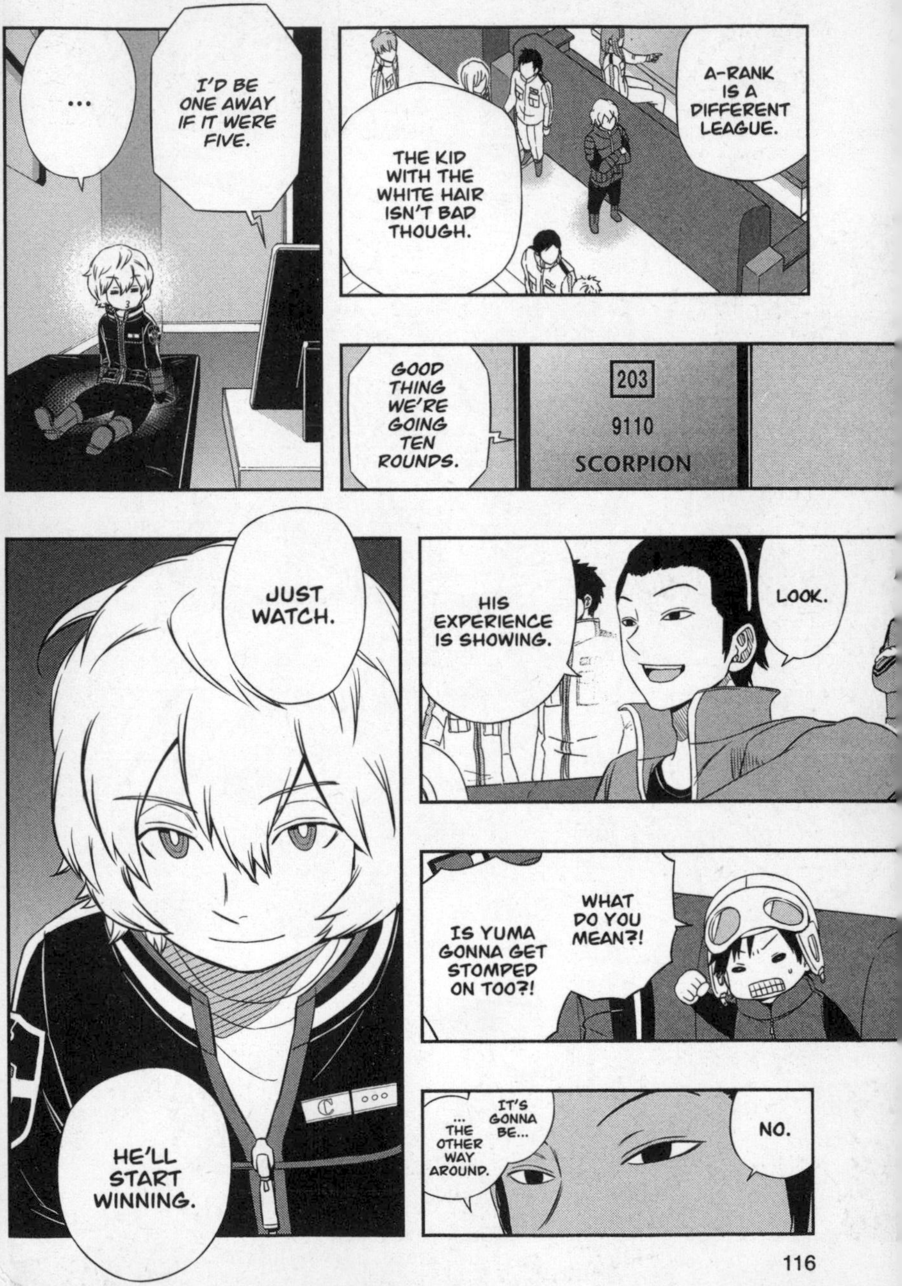
A-RANK IS A DIFFERENT LEAGUE.
THE KID WITH THE WHITE HAIR ISN'T BAD THOUGH.
203
9110
SCORPION
GOOD THING WE'RE GOING TEN ROUNDS.
I'D BE ONE AWAY IF IT WERE FIVE.
...
LOOK.
HIS EXPERIENCE IS SHOWING.
WHAT DO YOU MEAN?!
IS YUMA GONNA GET STOMPED ON TOO?!
NO.
IT'S GONNA BE...
...THE OTHER WAY AROUND.
JUST WATCH.
HE'LL START WINNING.

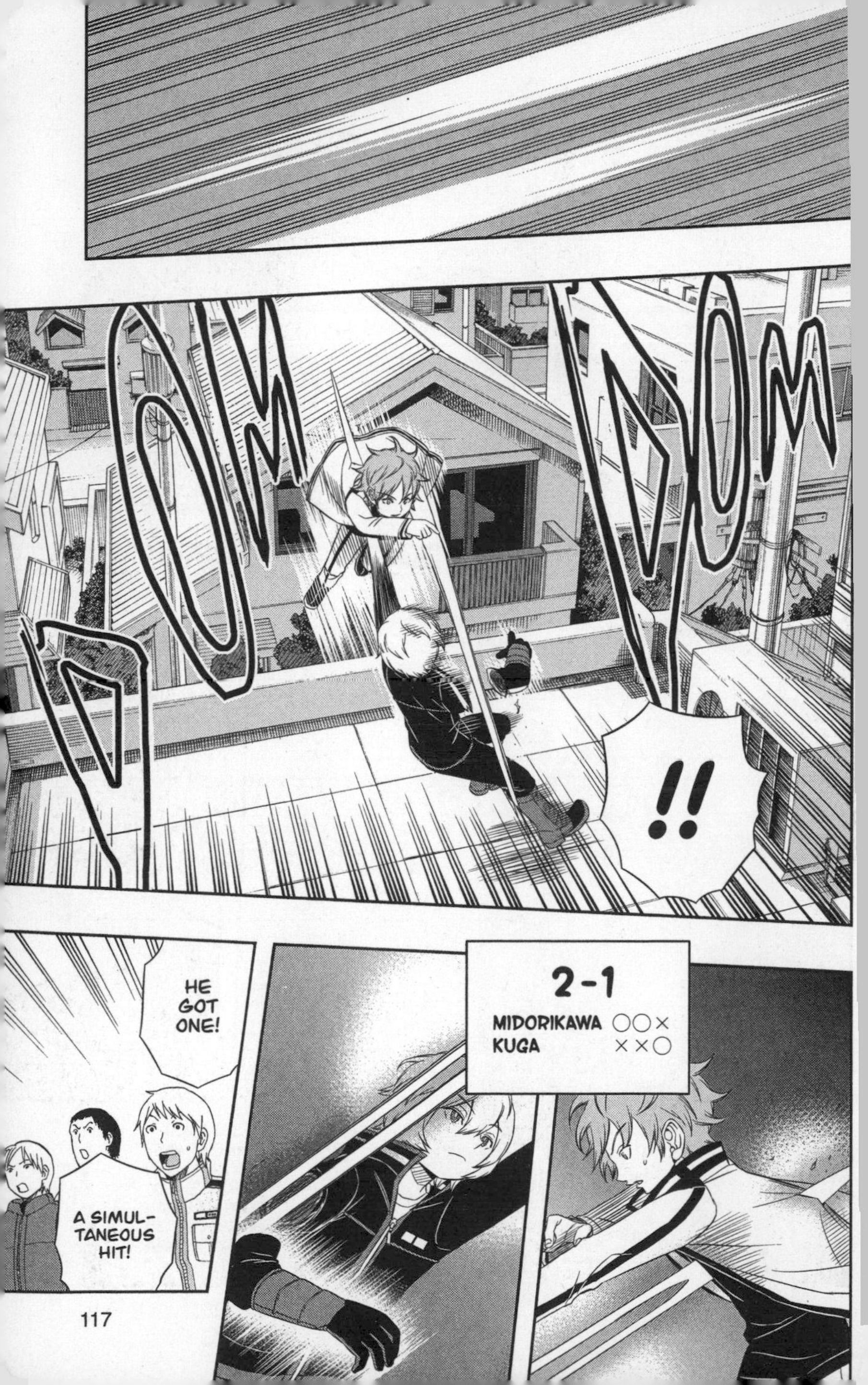
DOM
!!
DOM
2-1
MIDORIKAWA ○○×
KUGA ××○
HE GOT ONE!
A SIMUL-TANEOUS HIT!

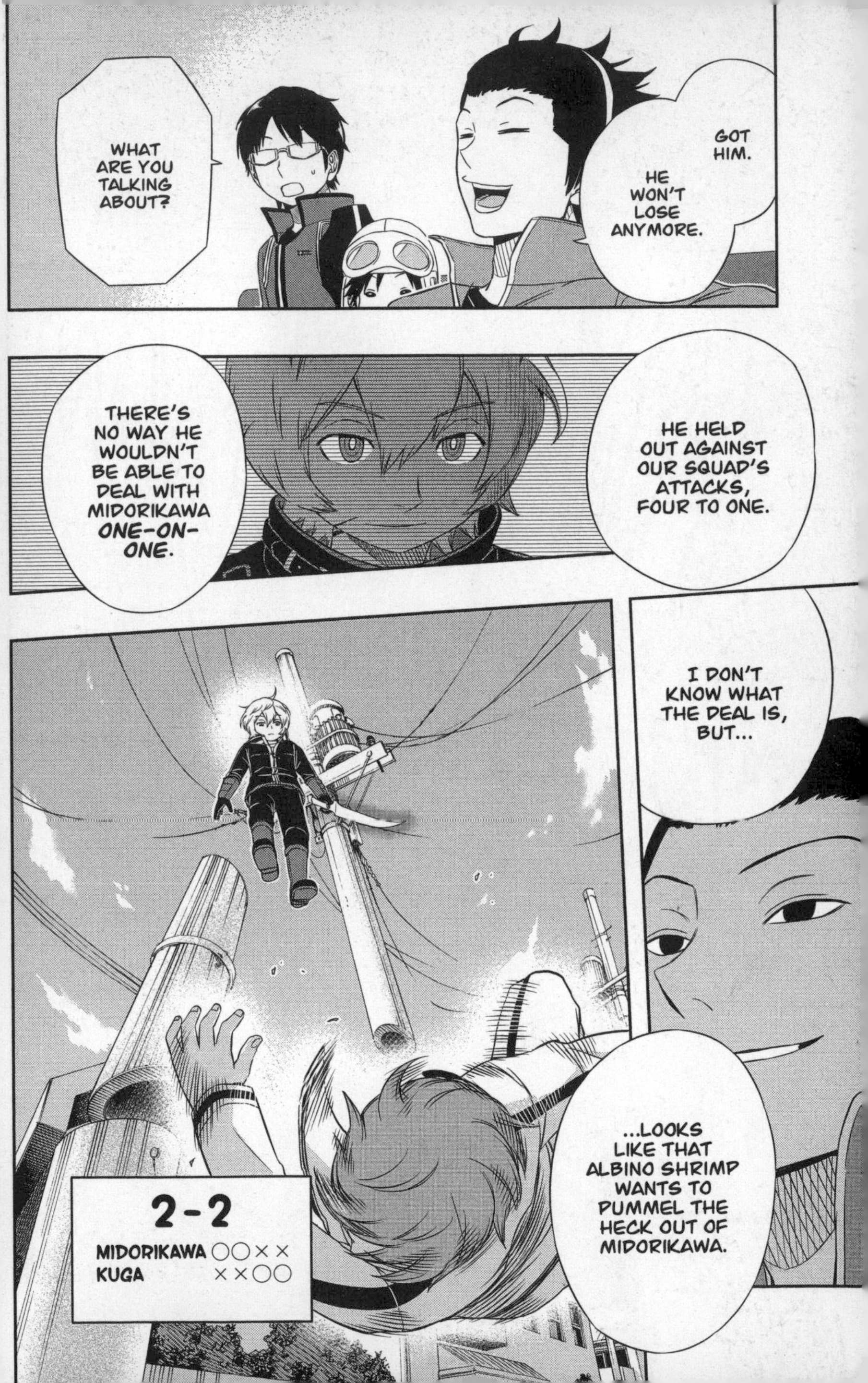
GOT HIM.
HE WON'T LOSE ANYMORE.
WHAT ARE YOU TALKING ABOUT?
HE HELD OUT AGAINST OUR SQUAD'S ATTACKS, FOUR TO ONE.
THERE'S NO WAY HE WOULDN'T BE ABLE TO DEAL WITH MIDORIKAWA ONE-ON-ONE.
I DON'T KNOW WHAT THE DEAL IS, BUT...
...LOOKS LIKE THAT ALBINO SHRIMP WANTS TO PUMMEL THE HECK OUT OF MIDORIKAWA.
2-2
MIDORIKAWA ○○××
KUGA ××○○

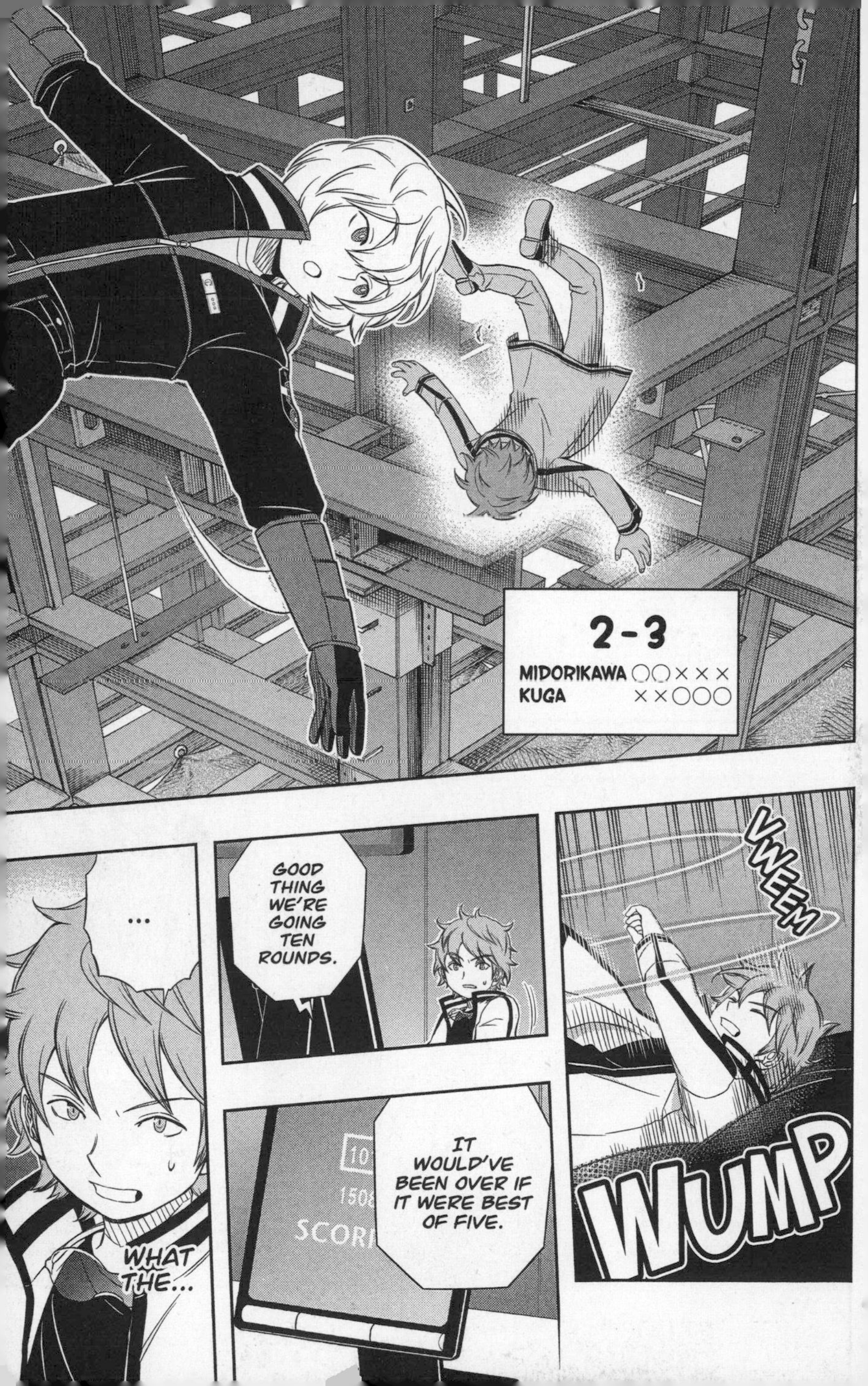
2-3
MIDORIKAWA ○○×××
KUGA ××○○○
VWEEM
WUMP
GOOD THING WE'RE GOING TEN ROUNDS.
IT WOULD'VE BEEN OVER IF IT WERE BEST OF FIVE.
...
WHAT THE...

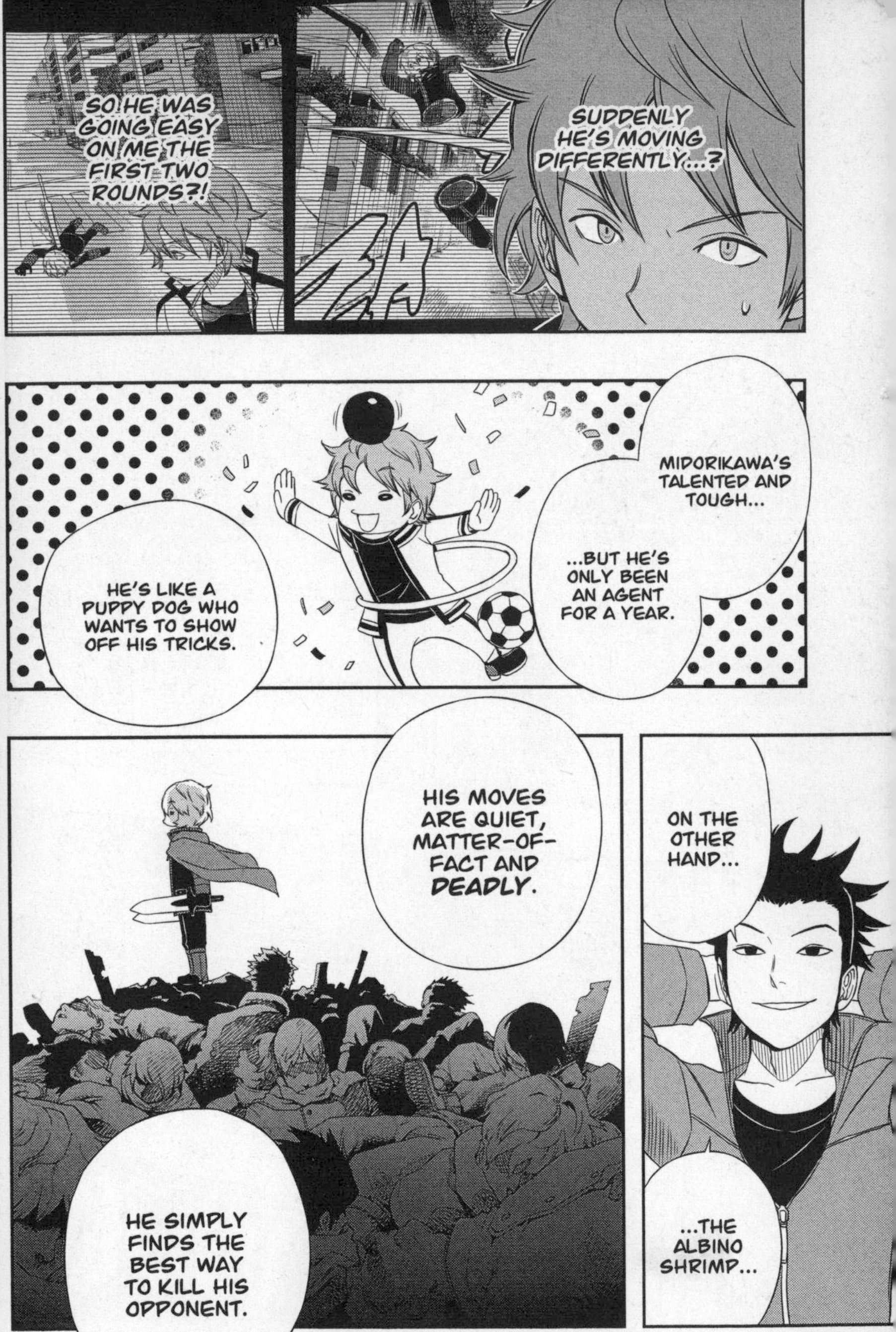
SUDDENLY HE'S MOVING DIFFERENTLY...?
SO HE WAS GOING EASY ON ME THE FIRST TWO ROUNDS?!
MIDORIKAWA'S TALENTED AND TOUGH...
...BUT HE'S ONLY BEEN AN AGENT FOR A YEAR.
HE'S LIKE A PUPPY DOG WHO WANTS TO SHOW OFF HIS TRICKS.
ON THE OTHER HAND...
...THE ALBINO SHRIMP...
HIS MOVES ARE QUIET, MATTER-OF-FACT AND DEADLY.
HE SIMPLY FINDS THE BEST WAY TO KILL HIS OPPONENT.

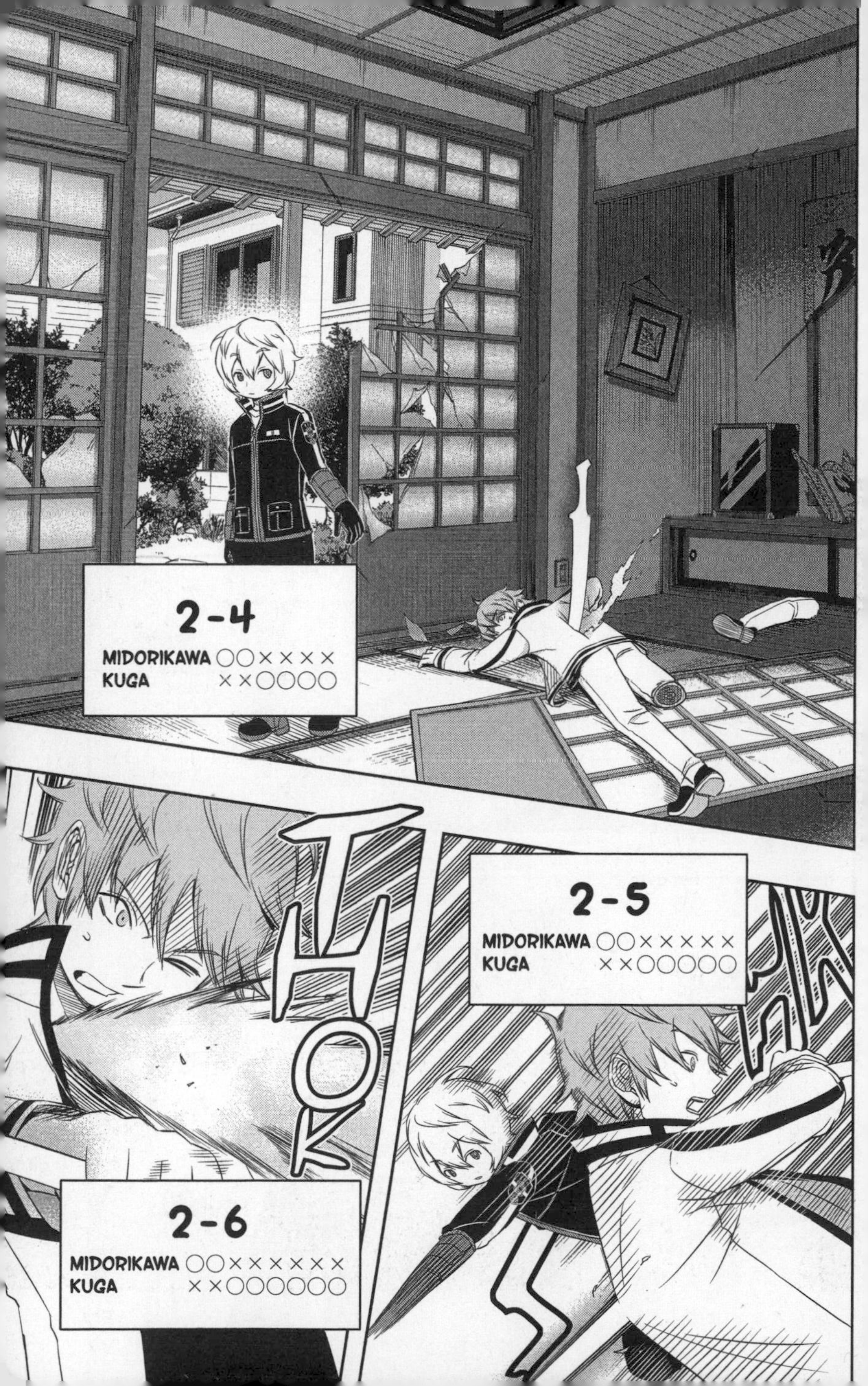
2-4
MIDORIKAWA ○○××××
KUGA ××○○○○
2-5
MIDORIKAWA ○○×××××
KUGA ××○○○○○
THOK
2-6
MIDORIKAWA ○○××××××
KUGA ××○○○○○○

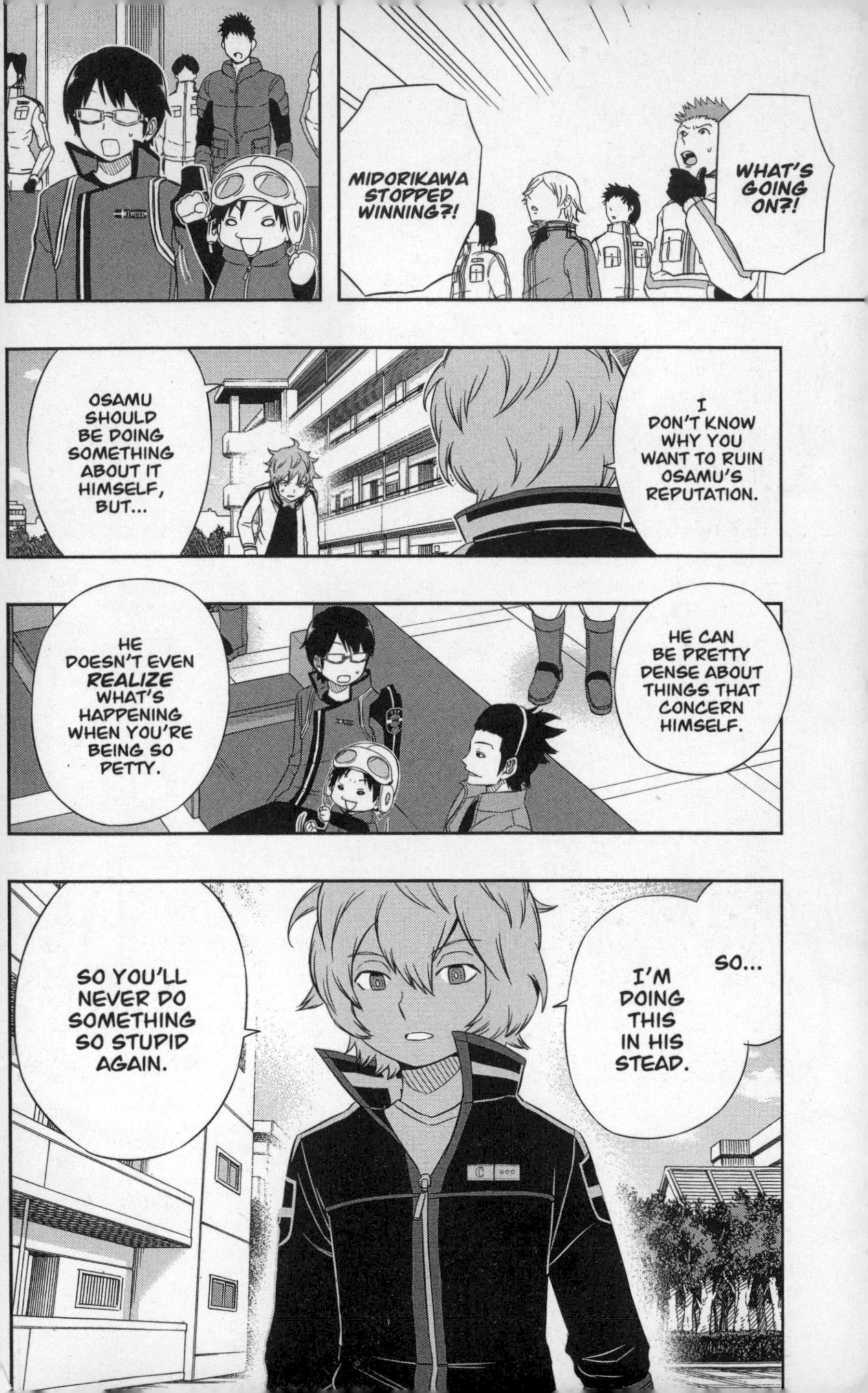
WHAT'S GOING ON?!
MIDORIKAWA STOPPED WINNING?!
I DON'T KNOW WHY YOU WANT TO RUIN OSAMU'S REPUTATION.
OSAMU SHOULD BE DOING SOMETHING ABOUT IT HIMSELF, BUT...
HE CAN BE PRETTY DENSE ABOUT THINGS THAT CONCERN HIMSELF.
HE DOESN'T EVEN REALIZE WHAT'S HAPPENING WHEN YOU'RE BEING SO PETTY.
SO...
I'M DOING THIS IN HIS STEAD.
SO YOU'LL NEVER DO SOMETHING SO STUPID AGAIN.

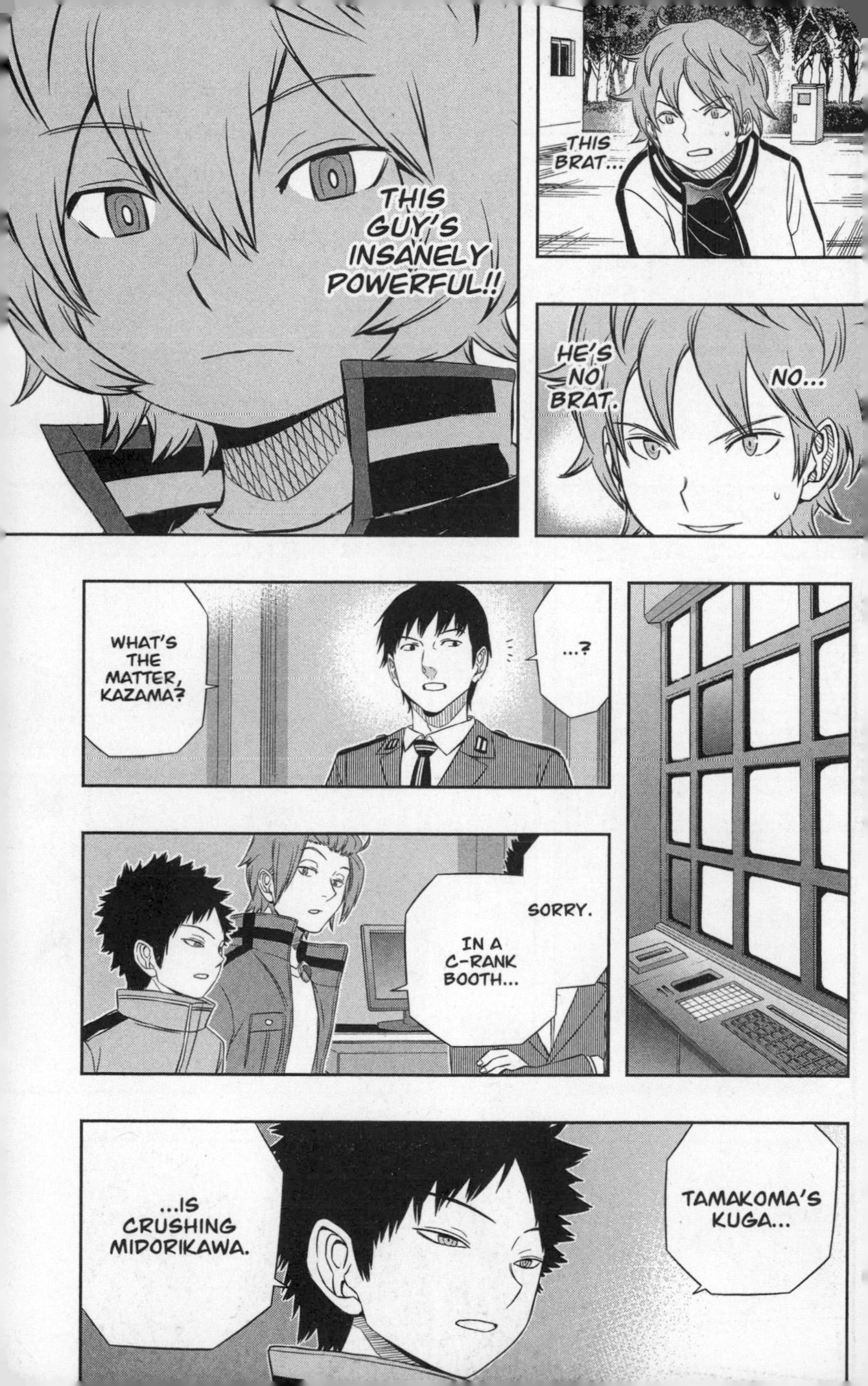
THIS BRAT...
NO...
HE'S NO BRAT.
THIS GUY'S INSANELY POWERFUL!!
...?
WHAT'S THE MATTER, KAZAMA?
SORRY.
IN A C-RANK BOOTH...
TAMAKOMA'S KUGA...
...IS CRUSHING MIDORIKAWA.

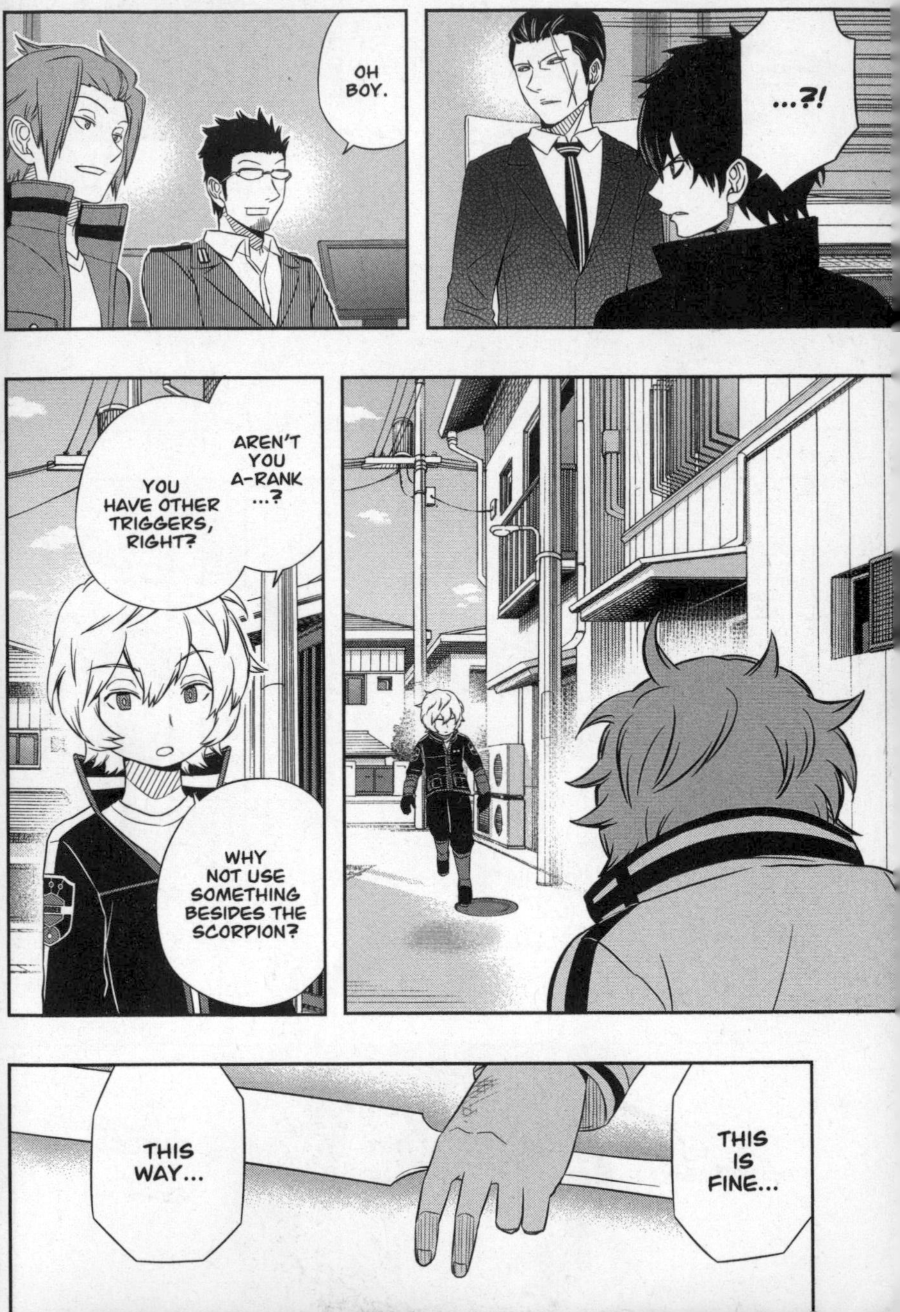
...?!
OH BOY.
AREN'T YOU A-RANK ...?
YOU HAVE OTHER TRIGGERS, RIGHT?
WHY NOT USE SOMETHING BESIDES THE SCORPION?
THIS IS FINE...
THIS WAY...

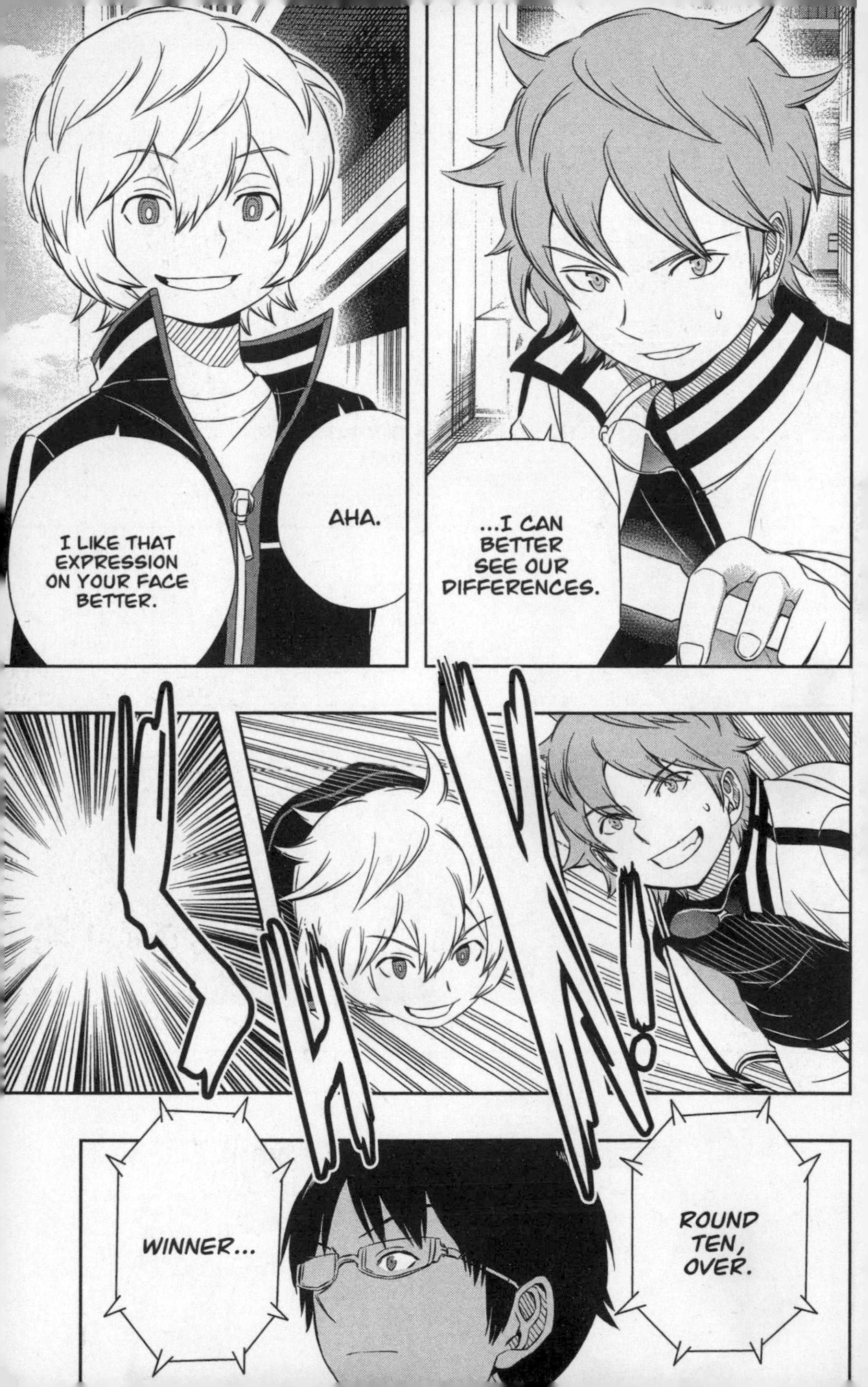
...I CAN BETTER SEE OUR DIFFERENCES.
AHA.
I LIKE THAT EXPRESSION ON YOUR FACE BETTER.
ROUND TEN, OVER.
WINNER...

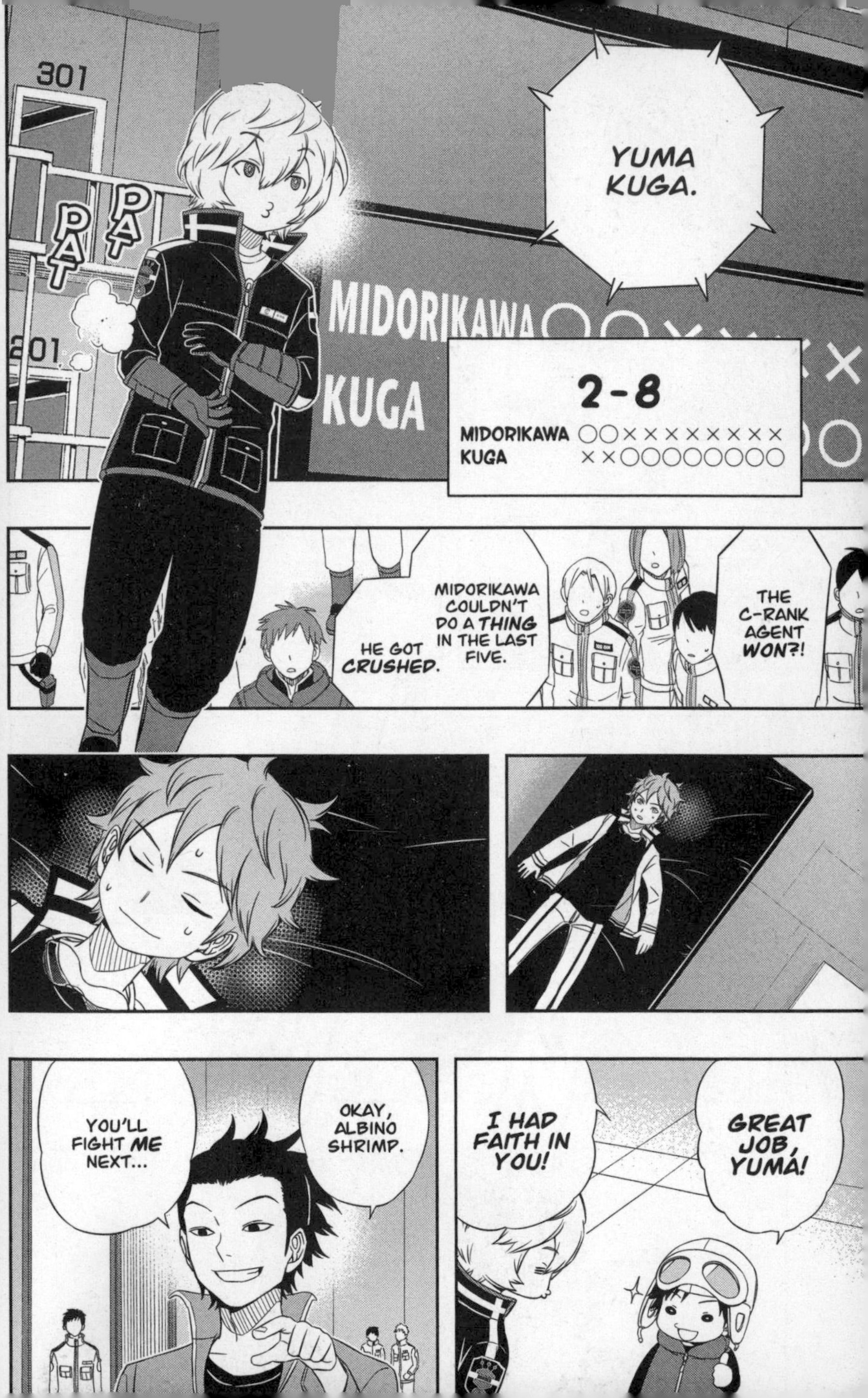
YUMA KUGA.
2-8
MIDORIKAWA ○○××××××××
KUGA ××○○○○○○○○
MIDORIKAWA
KUGA
PAT PAT
301
201
THE C-RANK AGENT WON?!
MIDORIKAWA COULDN'T DO A THING IN THE LAST FIVE.
HE GOT CRUSHED.
GREAT JOB, YUMA!
I HAD FAITH IN YOU!
OKAY, ALBINO SHRIMP.
YOU'LL FIGHT ME NEXT...

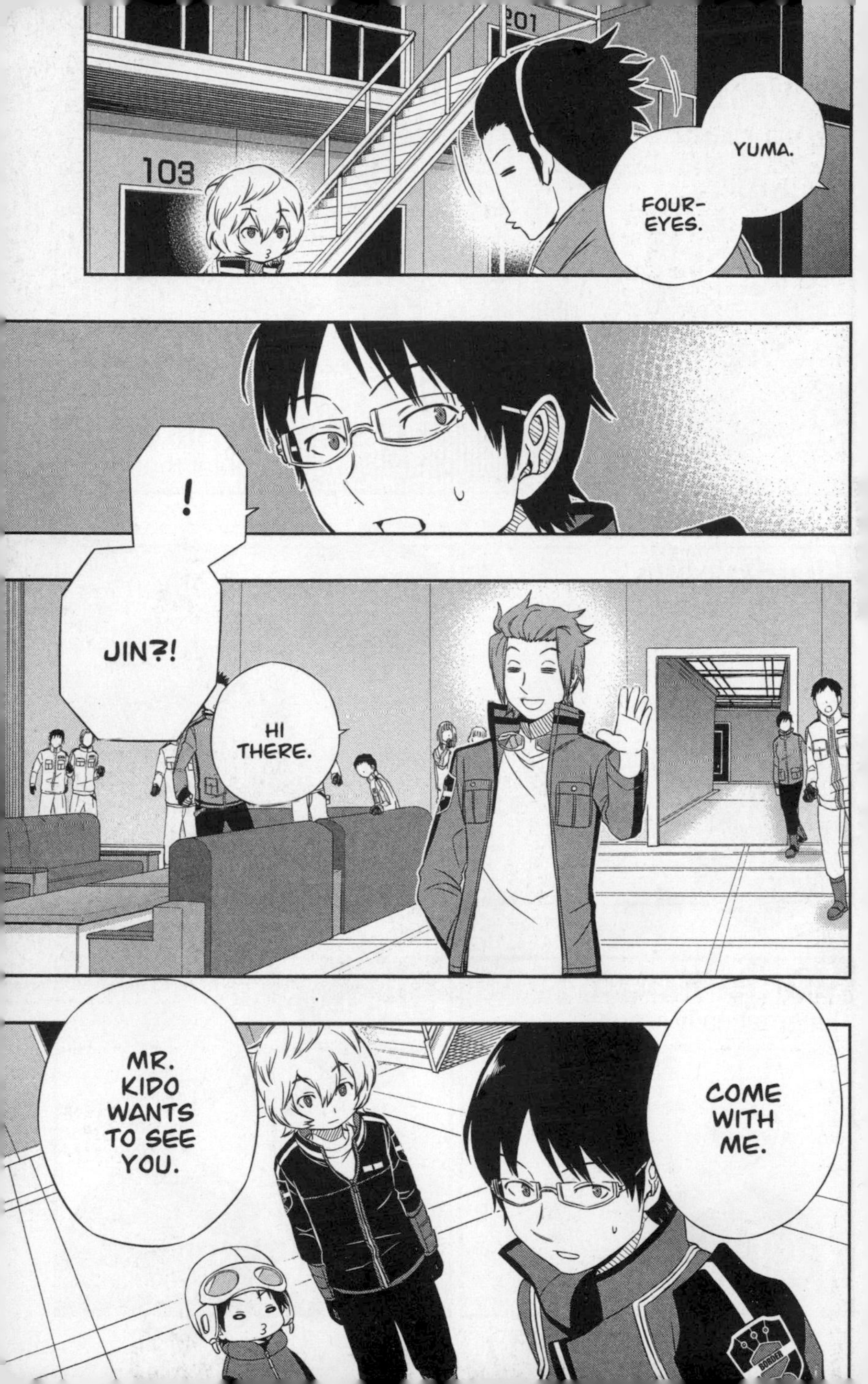
201
103
YUMA.
FOUR-EYES.
!
JIN?!
HI THERE.
COME WITH ME.
MR. KIDO WANTS TO SEE YOU.

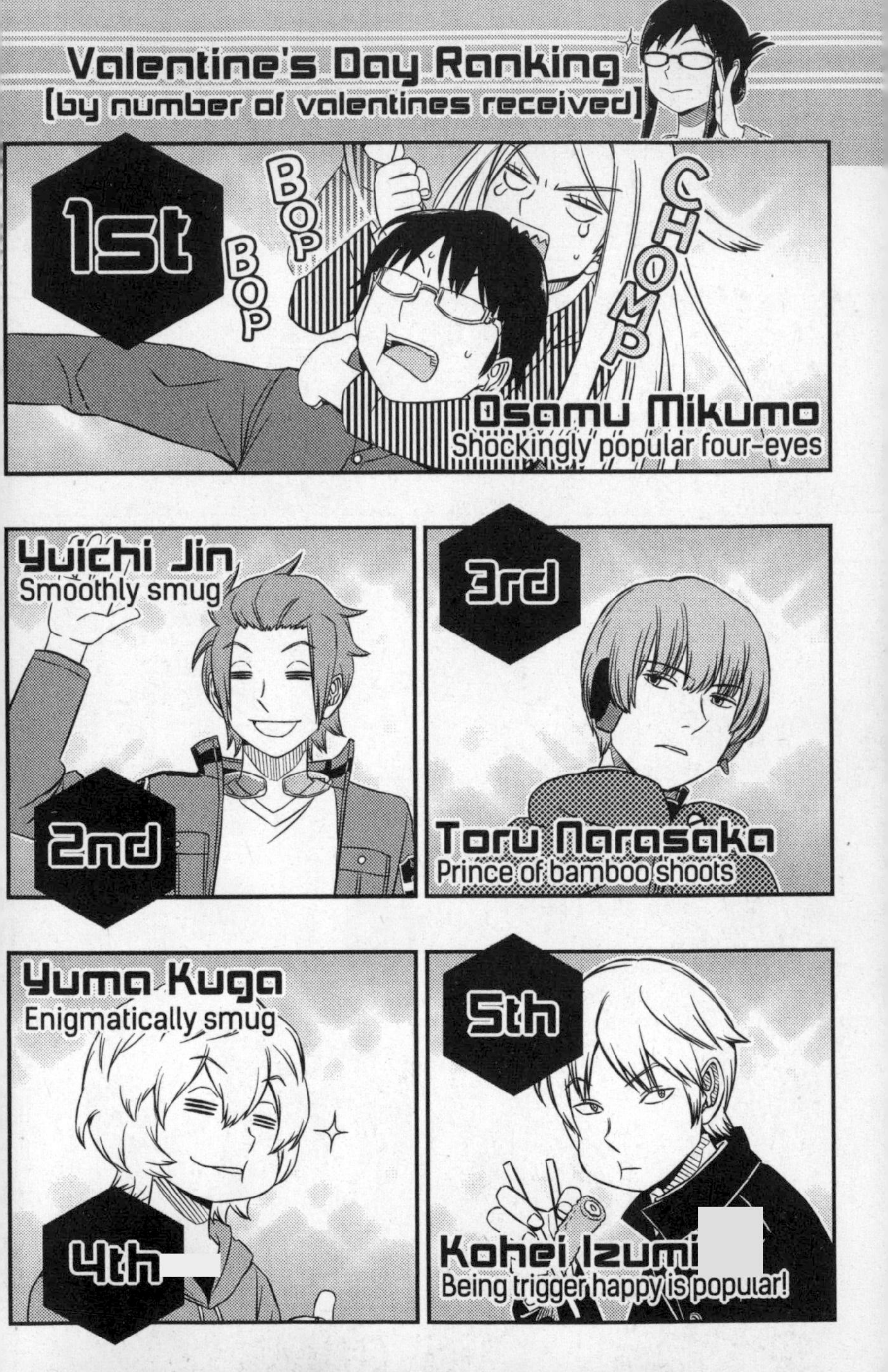
Valentine's Day Ranking
[by number of valentines received]
CHOMP
BOP
BOP
1st
Osamu Mikumo
Shockingly popular four-eyes
3rd
Toru Narasaka
Prince of bamboo shoots
Yuichi Jin
Smoothly smug
2nd
5th
Kohei Izumi
Being trigger happy is popular!
Yuma Kuga
Enigmatically smug
4th

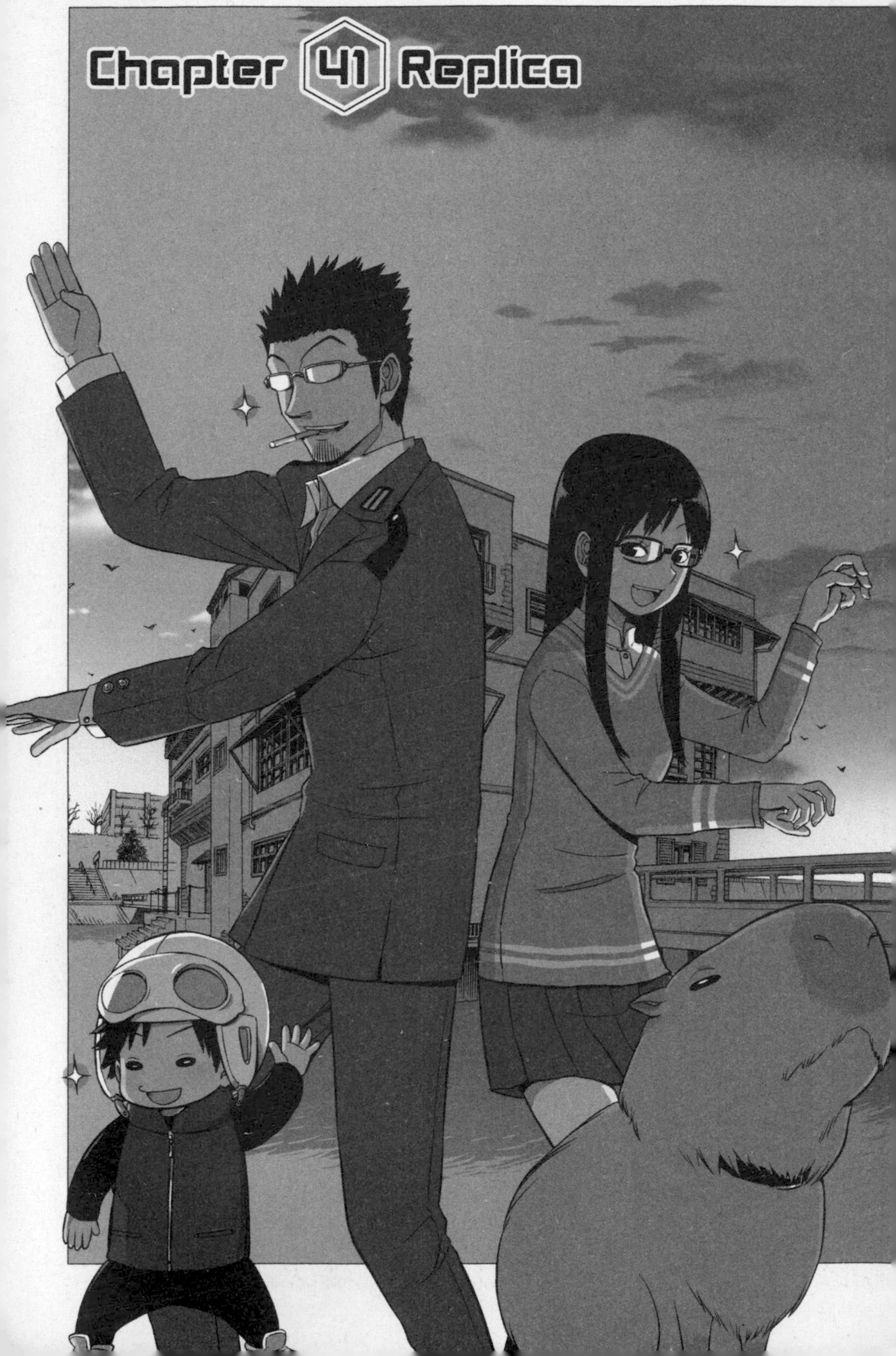
Chapter 41 Replica

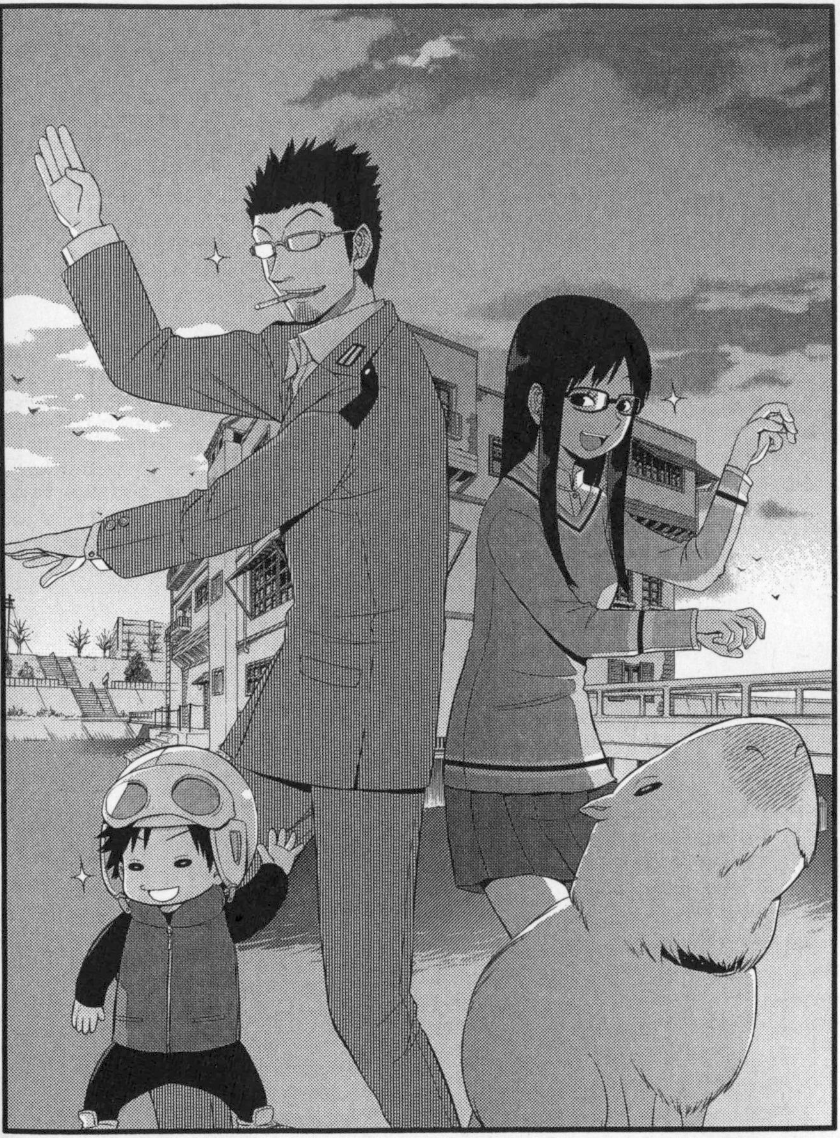

■ 2014 *Weekly Shonen Jump* issue 1, center color page (seventh one)
This is a self-parody of the two-page spread poster in the same issue. I was working on it at the same time as the poster, so my schedule was hell, but I had fun. I put the morning glow on the left and the sunset on the right, but it doesn't show at all in black and white. So sad.

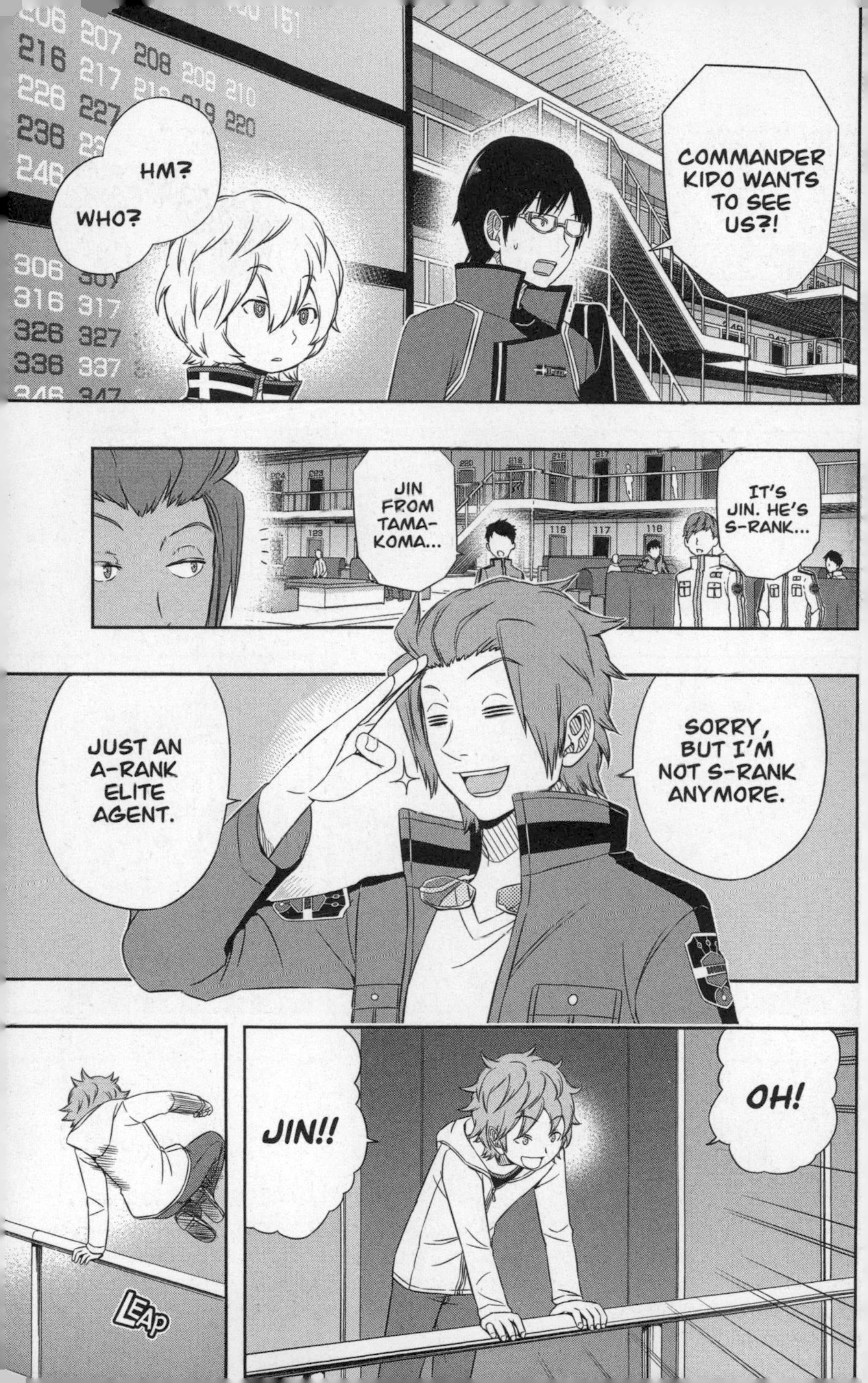
COMMANDER KIDO WANTS TO SEE US?!
HM?
WHO?
IT'S JIN. HE'S S-RANK...
JIN FROM TAMA-KOMA...
SORRY, BUT I'M NOT S-RANK ANYMORE.
JUST AN A-RANK ELITE AGENT.
OH!
JIN!!
LEAP

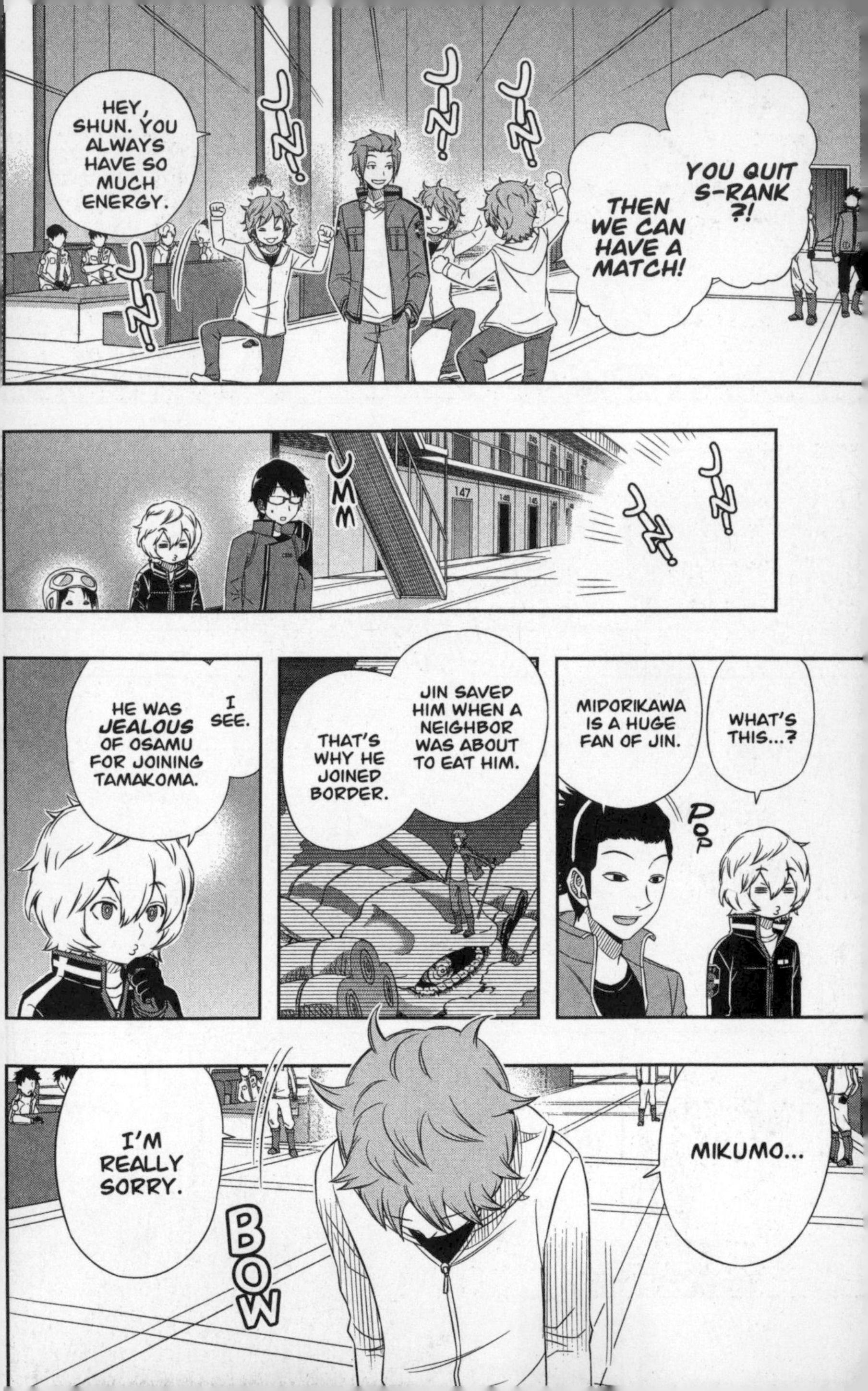
YOU QUIT S-RANK ?!
THEN WE CAN HAVE A MATCH!
JIN!
JIN!
JIN!
HEY, SHUN. YOU ALWAYS HAVE SO MUCH ENERGY.
JIN!
JIN!
JIN!
UMM
WHAT'S THIS...?
MIDORIKAWA IS A HUGE FAN OF JIN.
POP
JIN SAVED HIM WHEN A NEIGHBOR WAS ABOUT TO EAT HIM.
THAT'S WHY HE JOINED BORDER.
I SEE.
HE WAS *JEALOUS* OF OSAMU FOR JOINING TAMAKOMA.
MIKUMO...
BOW
I'M REALLY SORRY.

READ THIS WAY

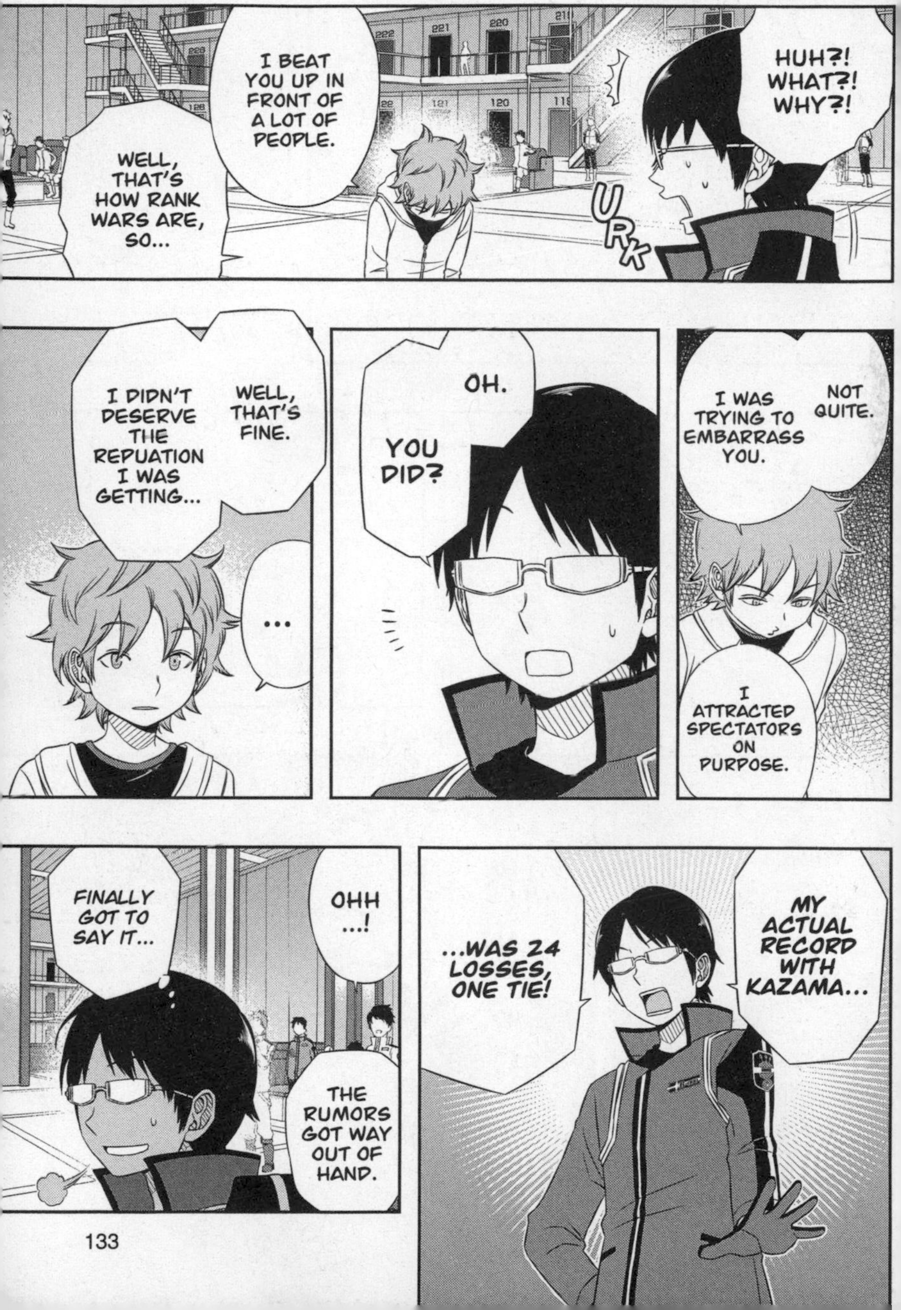
HUH?! WHAT?! WHY?!
URK
I BEAT YOU UP IN FRONT OF A LOT OF PEOPLE.
WELL, THAT'S HOW RANK WARS ARE, SO...
NOT QUITE.
I WAS TRYING TO EMBARRASS YOU.
I ATTRACTED SPECTATORS ON PURPOSE.
OH.
YOU DID?
WELL, THAT'S FINE.
I DIDN'T DESERVE THE REPUATION I WAS GETTING...
...
MY ACTUAL RECORD WITH KAZAMA...
...WAS 24 LOSSES, ONE TIE!
OHH ...!
FINALLY GOT TO SAY IT...
THE RUMORS GOT WAY OUT OF HAND.

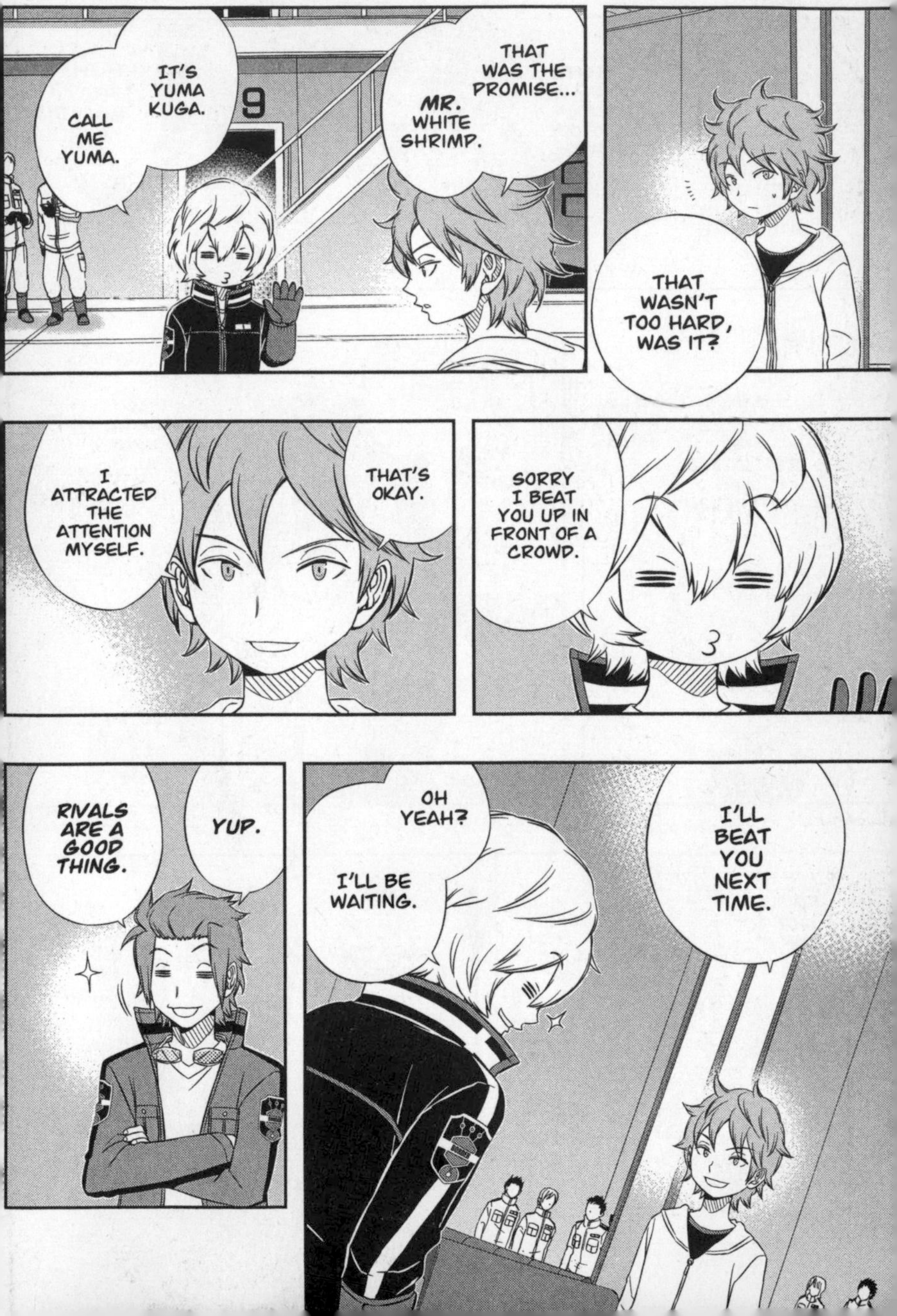
THAT WASN'T TOO HARD, WAS IT?
THAT WAS THE PROMISE...
MR. WHITE SHRIMP.
IT'S YUMA KUGA.
CALL ME YUMA.
SORRY I BEAT YOU UP IN FRONT OF A CROWD.
THAT'S OKAY.
I ATTRACTED THE ATTENTION MYSELF.
I'LL BEAT YOU NEXT TIME.
OH YEAH?
I'LL BE WAITING.
YUP.
RIVALS ARE A GOOD THING.

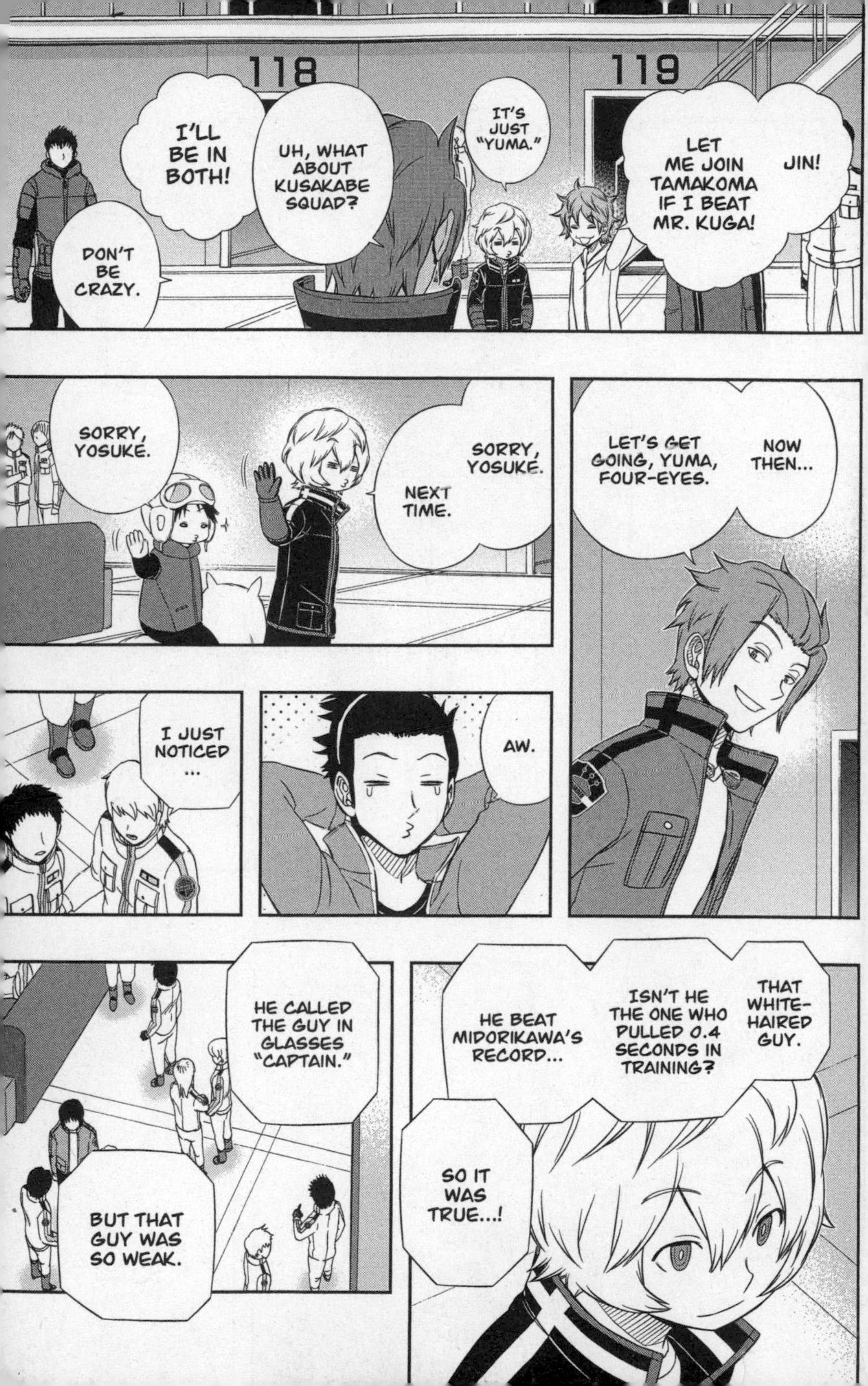
JIN!
LET ME JOIN TAMAKOMA IF I BEAT MR. KUGA!
IT'S JUST "YUMA."
UH, WHAT ABOUT KUSAKABE SQUAD?
I'LL BE IN BOTH!
DON'T BE CRAZY.
NOW THEN...
LET'S GET GOING, YUMA, FOUR-EYES.
SORRY, YOSUKE.
NEXT TIME.
SORRY, YOSUKE.
AW.
I JUST NOTICED ...
THAT WHITE-HAIRED GUY.
ISN'T HE THE ONE WHO PULLED 0.4 SECONDS IN TRAINING?
HE BEAT MIDORIKAWA'S RECORD...
SO IT WAS TRUE...!
HE CALLED THE GUY IN GLASSES "CAPTAIN."
BUT THAT GUY WAS SO WEAK.

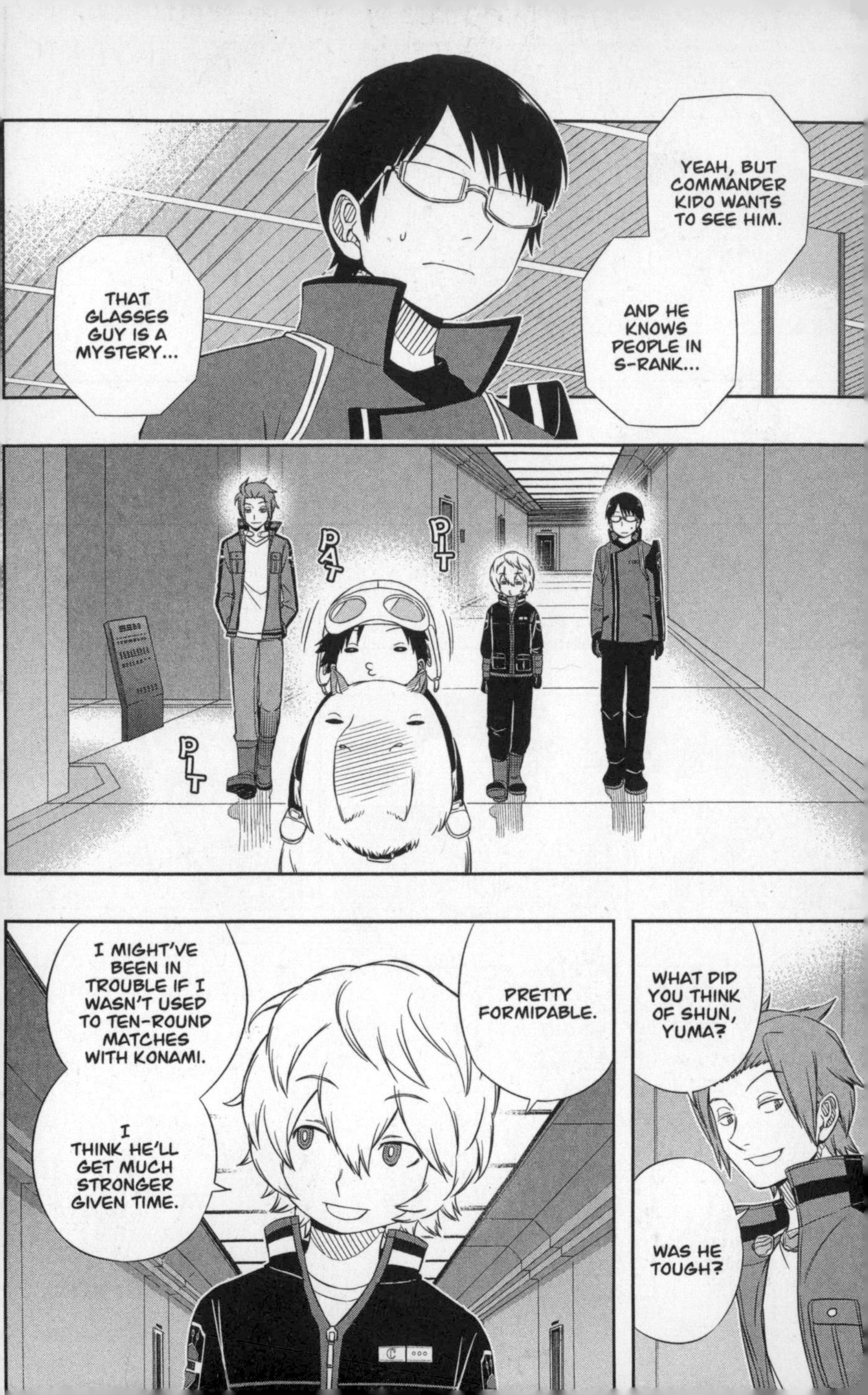
YEAH, BUT COMMANDER KIDO WANTS TO SEE HIM.
AND HE KNOWS PEOPLE IN S-RANK...
THAT GLASSES GUY IS A MYSTERY...
PIT
PAT
PIT
WHAT DID YOU THINK OF SHUN, YUMA?
WAS HE TOUGH?
PRETTY FORMIDABLE.
I MIGHT'VE BEEN IN TROUBLE IF I WASN'T USED TO TEN-ROUND MATCHES WITH KONAMI.
I THINK HE'LL GET MUCH STRONGER GIVEN TIME.

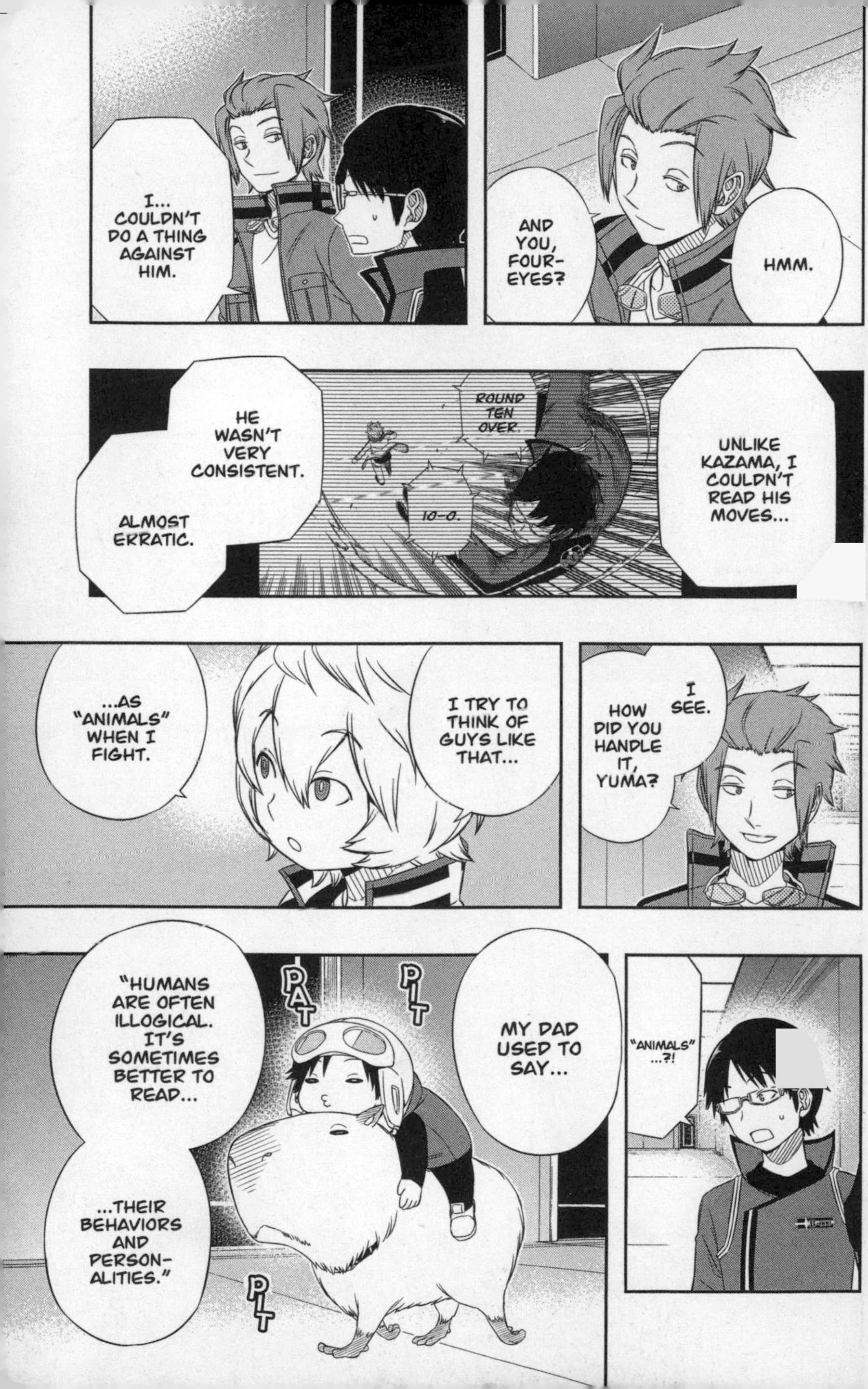
HMM.
AND YOU, FOUR-EYES?
I... COULDN'T DO A THING AGAINST HIM.
UNLIKE KAZAMA, I COULDN'T READ HIS MOVES...
ROUND TEN OVER.
10-0.
HE WASN'T VERY CONSISTENT.
ALMOST ERRATIC.
I SEE.
HOW DID YOU HANDLE IT, YUMA?
I TRY TO THINK OF GUYS LIKE THAT...
...AS "ANIMALS" WHEN I FIGHT.
"ANIMALS" ...?!
MY DAD USED TO SAY...
PIT
PAT
"HUMANS ARE OFTEN ILLOGICAL. IT'S SOMETIMES BETTER TO READ...
...THEIR BEHAVIORS AND PERSON-ALITIES."
PIT

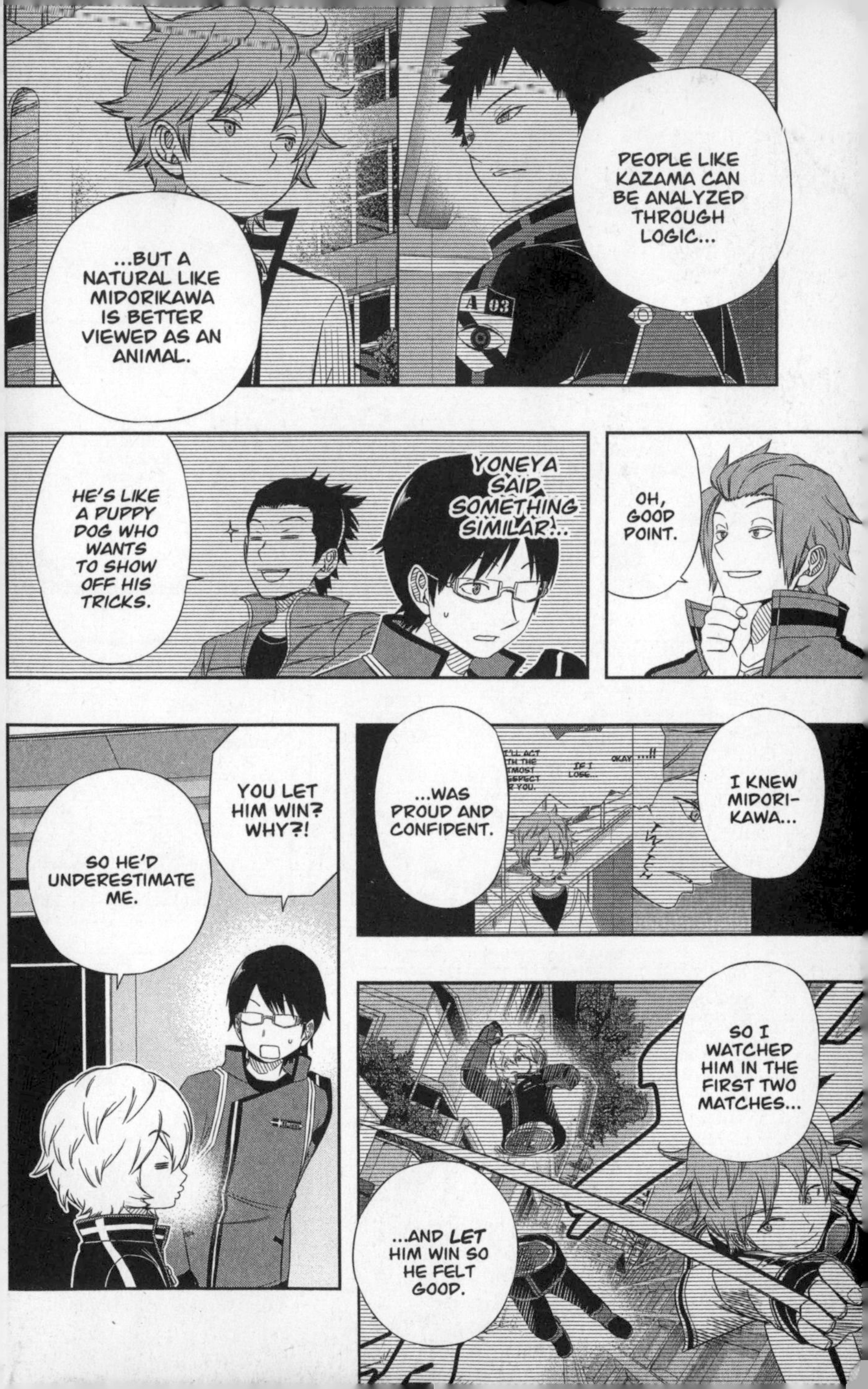
PEOPLE LIKE KAZAMA CAN BE ANALYZED THROUGH LOGIC...
...BUT A NATURAL LIKE MIDORIKAWA IS BETTER VIEWED AS AN ANIMAL.
OH, GOOD POINT.
YONEYA SAID SOMETHING SIMILAR...
HE'S LIKE A PUPPY DOG WHO WANTS TO SHOW OFF HIS TRICKS.
I KNEW MIDORI-KAWA...
OKAY...!!
IF I LOSE...
...WAS PROUD AND CONFIDENT.
SO I WATCHED HIM IN THE FIRST TWO MATCHES...
...AND LET HIM WIN SO HE FELT GOOD.
YOU LET HIM WIN? WHY?!
SO HE'D UNDERESTIMATE ME.

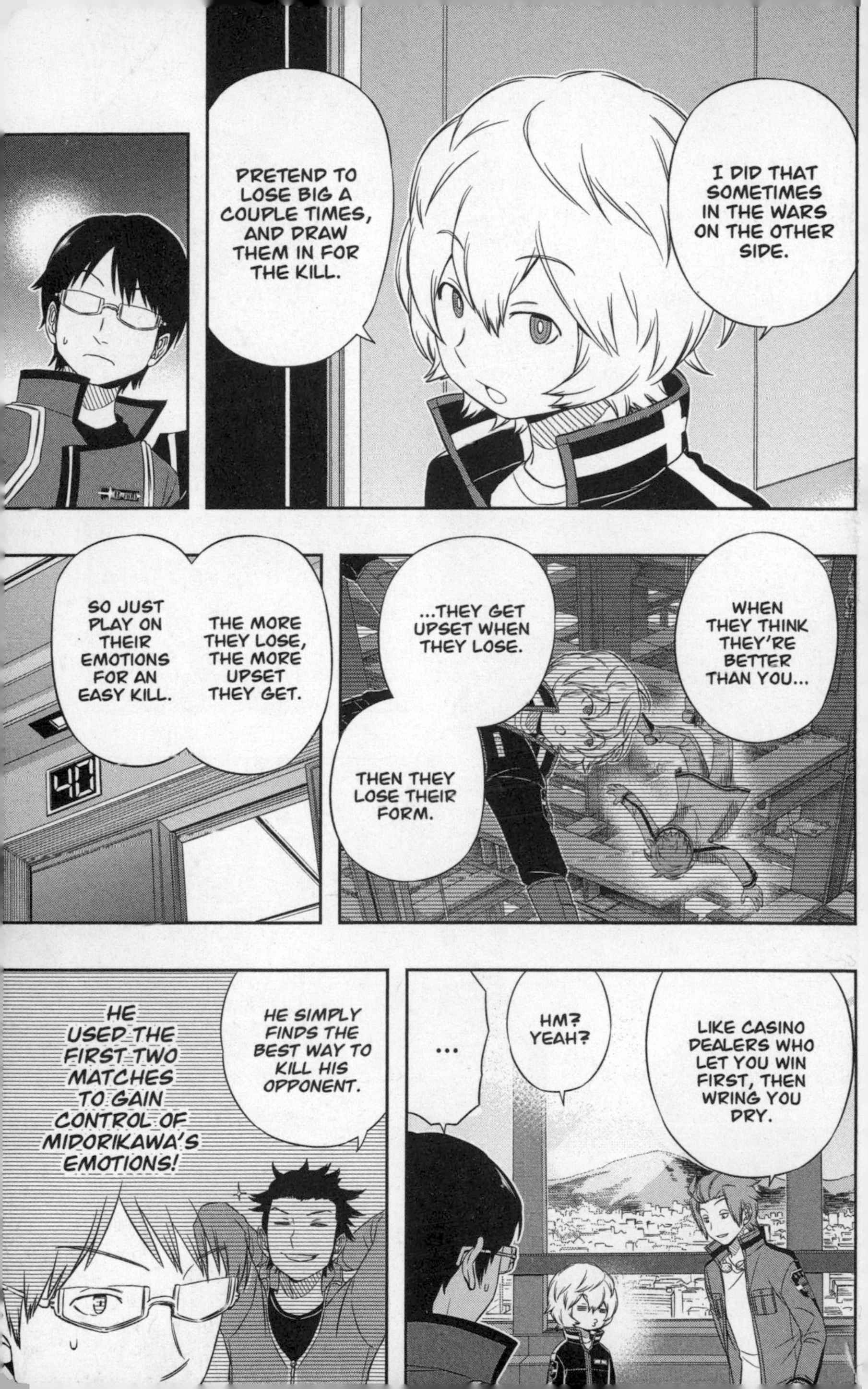

I DID THAT SOMETIMES IN THE WARS ON THE OTHER SIDE.
PRETEND TO LOSE BIG A COUPLE TIMES, AND DRAW THEM IN FOR THE KILL.
WHEN THEY THINK THEY'RE BETTER THAN YOU...
...THEY GET UPSET WHEN THEY LOSE.
THEN THEY LOSE THEIR FORM.
THE MORE THEY LOSE, THE MORE UPSET THEY GET.
SO JUST PLAY ON THEIR EMOTIONS FOR AN EASY KILL.
LIKE CASINO DEALERS WHO LET YOU WIN FIRST, THEN WRING YOU DRY.
HM? YEAH?
...
HE SIMPLY FINDS THE BEST WAY TO KILL HIS OPPONENT.
HE USED THE FIRST TWO MATCHES TO GAIN CONTROL OF MIDORIKAWA'S EMOTIONS!

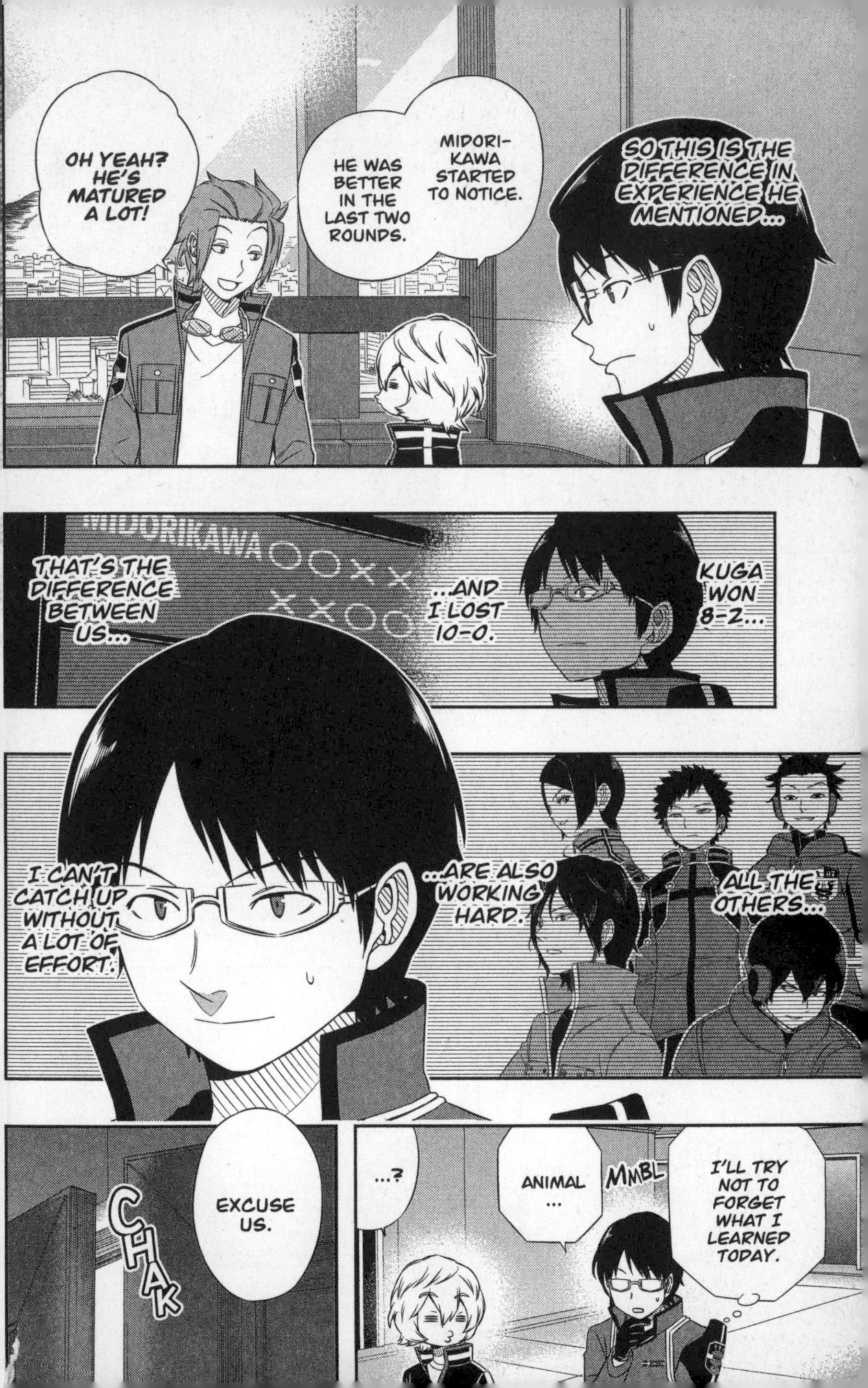
SO THIS IS THE DIFFERENCE IN EXPERIENCE HE MENTIONED...
MIDORI-KAWA STARTED TO NOTICE.
HE WAS BETTER IN THE LAST TWO ROUNDS.
OH YEAH? HE'S MATURED A LOT!
KUGA WON 8-2...
...AND I LOST 10-0.
MIDORIKAWA
THAT'S THE DIFFERENCE BETWEEN US...
ALL THE OTHERS...
...ARE ALSO WORKING HARD.
I CAN'T CATCH UP WITHOUT A LOT OF EFFORT.
I'LL TRY NOT TO FORGET WHAT I LEARNED TODAY.
MMBL
ANIMAL...
...?
EXCUSE US.
CHAK

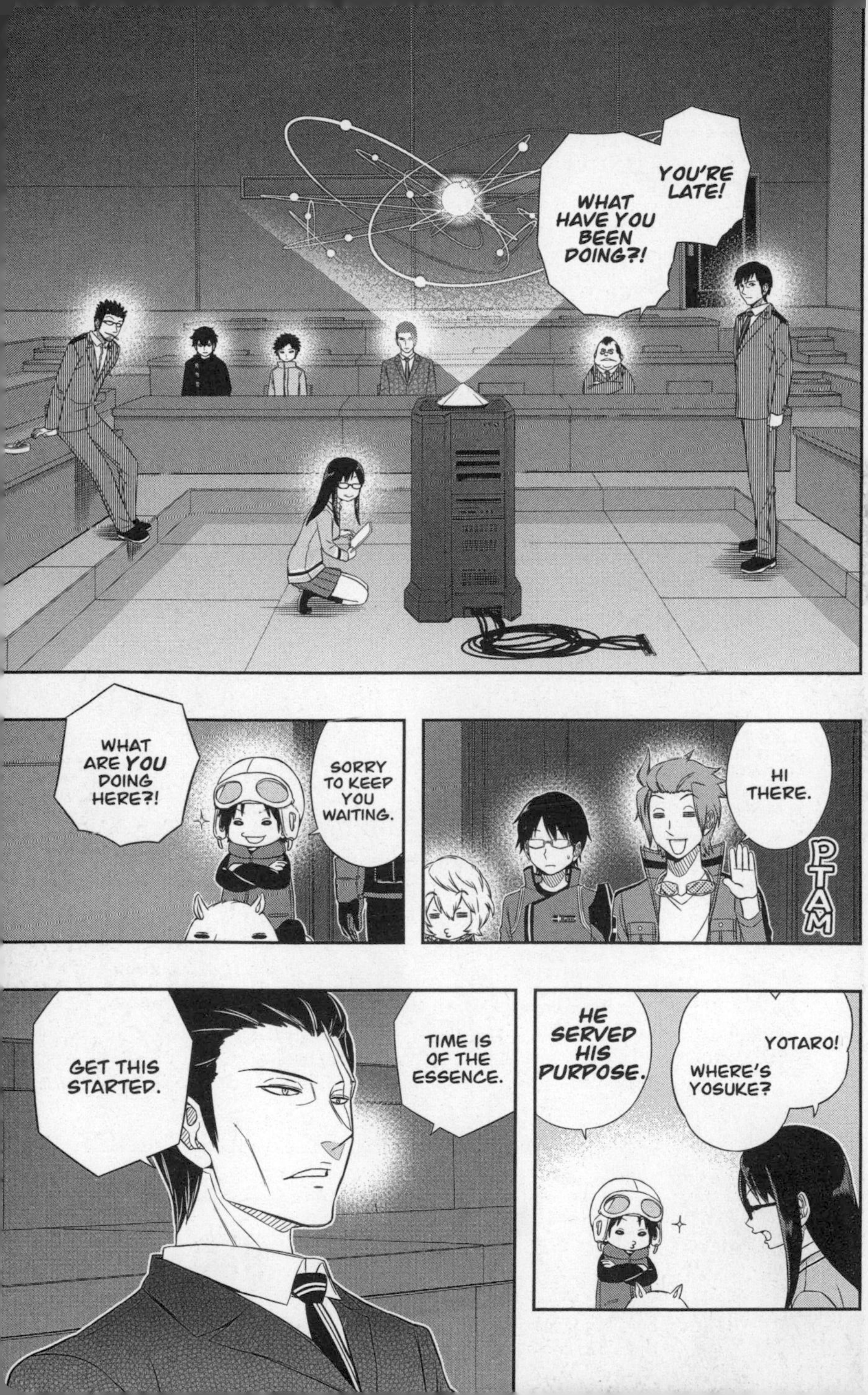
YOU'RE LATE!
WHAT HAVE YOU BEEN DOING?!
HI THERE.
PTAM
SORRY TO KEEP YOU WAITING.
WHAT ARE YOU DOING HERE?!
YOTARO!
WHERE'S YOSUKE?
HE SERVED HIS PURPOSE.
TIME IS OF THE ESSENCE.
GET THIS STARTED.

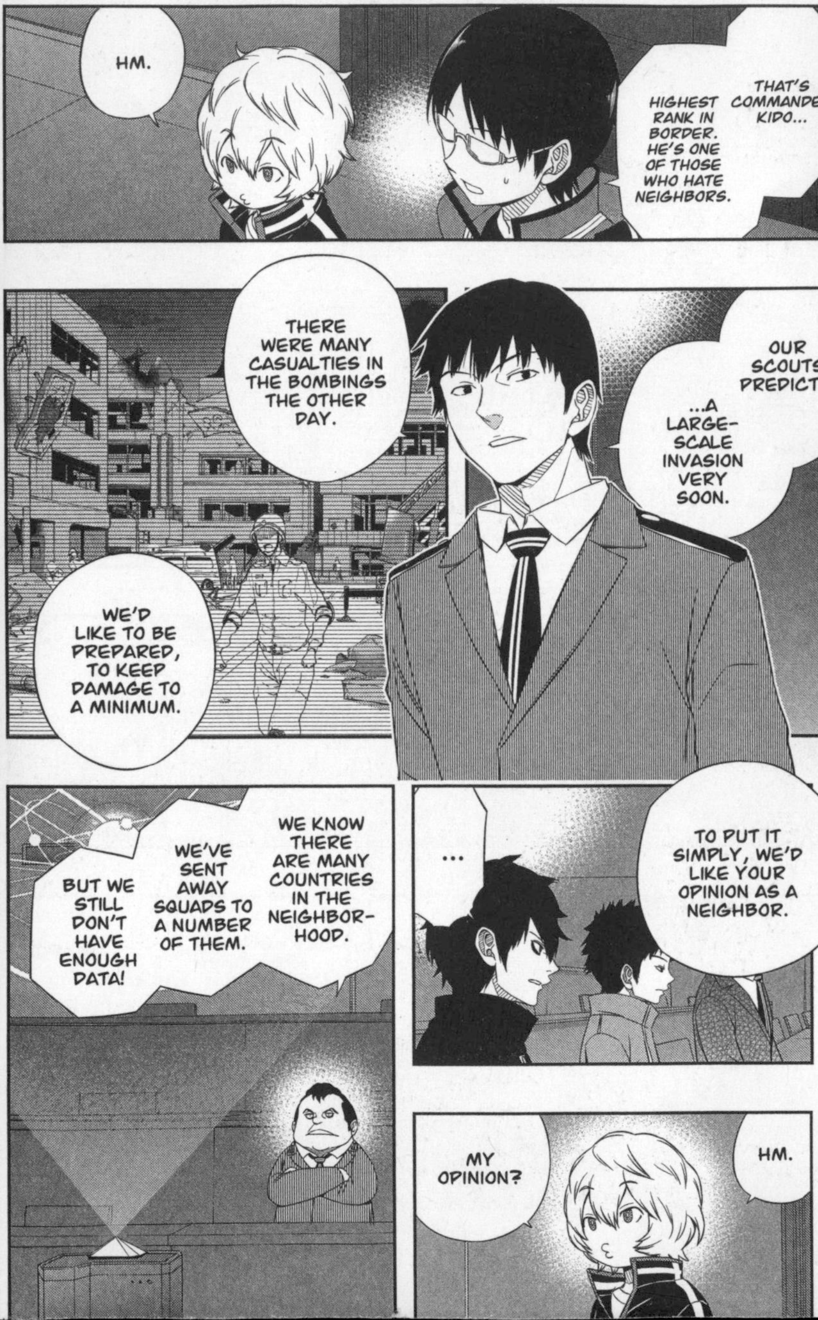
THAT'S COMMANDER KIDO...
HIGHEST RANK IN BORDER. HE'S ONE OF THOSE WHO HATE NEIGHBORS.
HM.
OUR SCOUTS PREDICT...
...A LARGE-SCALE INVASION VERY SOON.
THERE WERE MANY CASUALTIES IN THE BOMBINGS THE OTHER DAY.
WE'D LIKE TO BE PREPARED, TO KEEP DAMAGE TO A MINIMUM.
TO PUT IT SIMPLY, WE'D LIKE YOUR OPINION AS A NEIGHBOR.
...
HM.
MY OPINION?
WE KNOW THERE ARE MANY COUNTRIES IN THE NEIGHBORHOOD.
WE'VE SENT AWAY SQUADS TO A NUMBER OF THEM.
BUT WE STILL DON'T HAVE ENOUGH DATA!

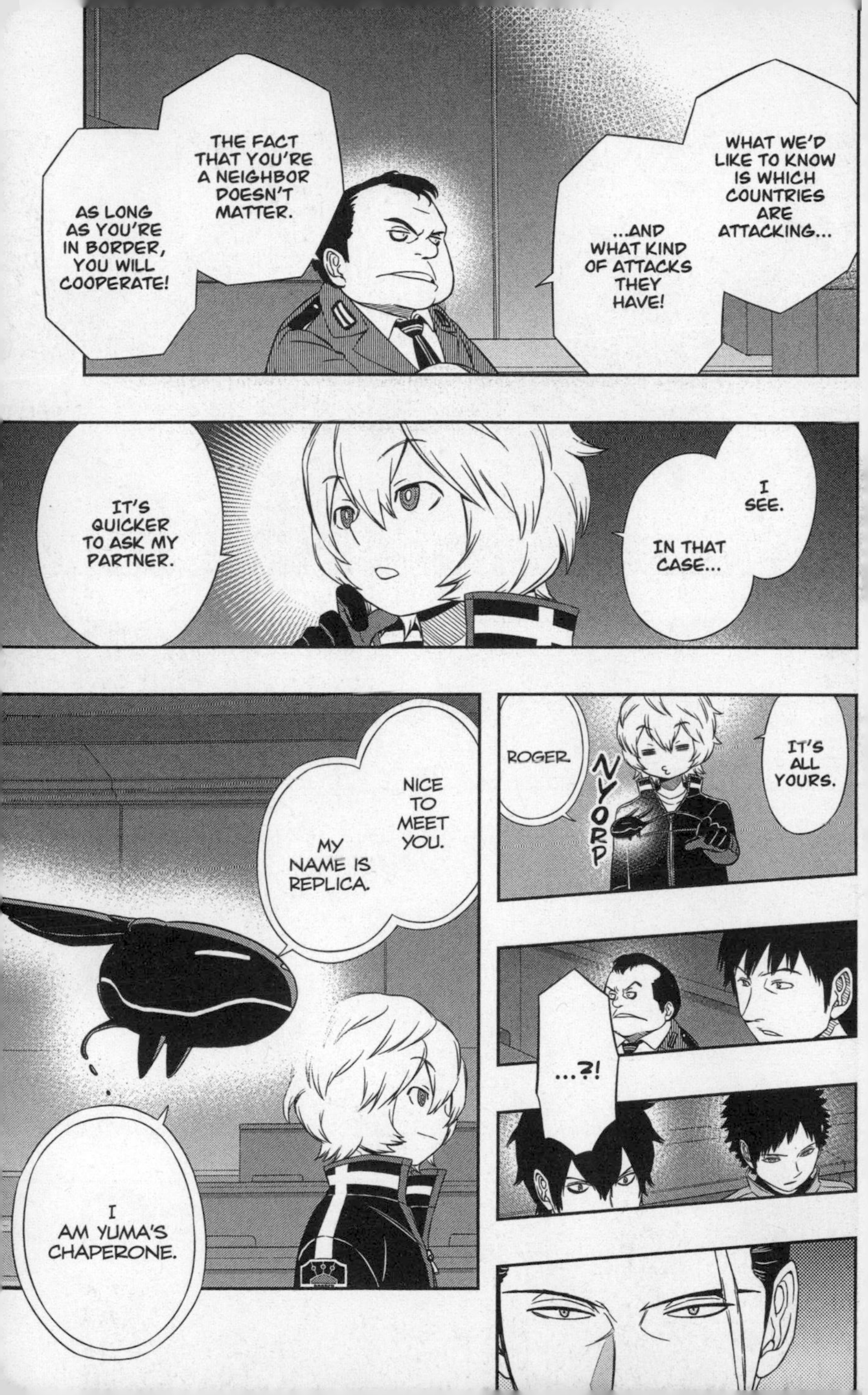
WHAT WE'D LIKE TO KNOW IS WHICH COUNTRIES ARE ATTACKING...
...AND WHAT KIND OF ATTACKS THEY HAVE!
THE FACT THAT YOU'RE A NEIGHBOR DOESN'T MATTER.
AS LONG AS YOU'RE IN BORDER, YOU WILL COOPERATE!
I SEE.
IN THAT CASE...
IT'S QUICKER TO ASK MY PARTNER.
IT'S ALL YOURS.
NYORP
ROGER.
...?!
NICE TO MEET YOU.
MY NAME IS REPLICA.
I AM YUMA'S CHAPERONE.

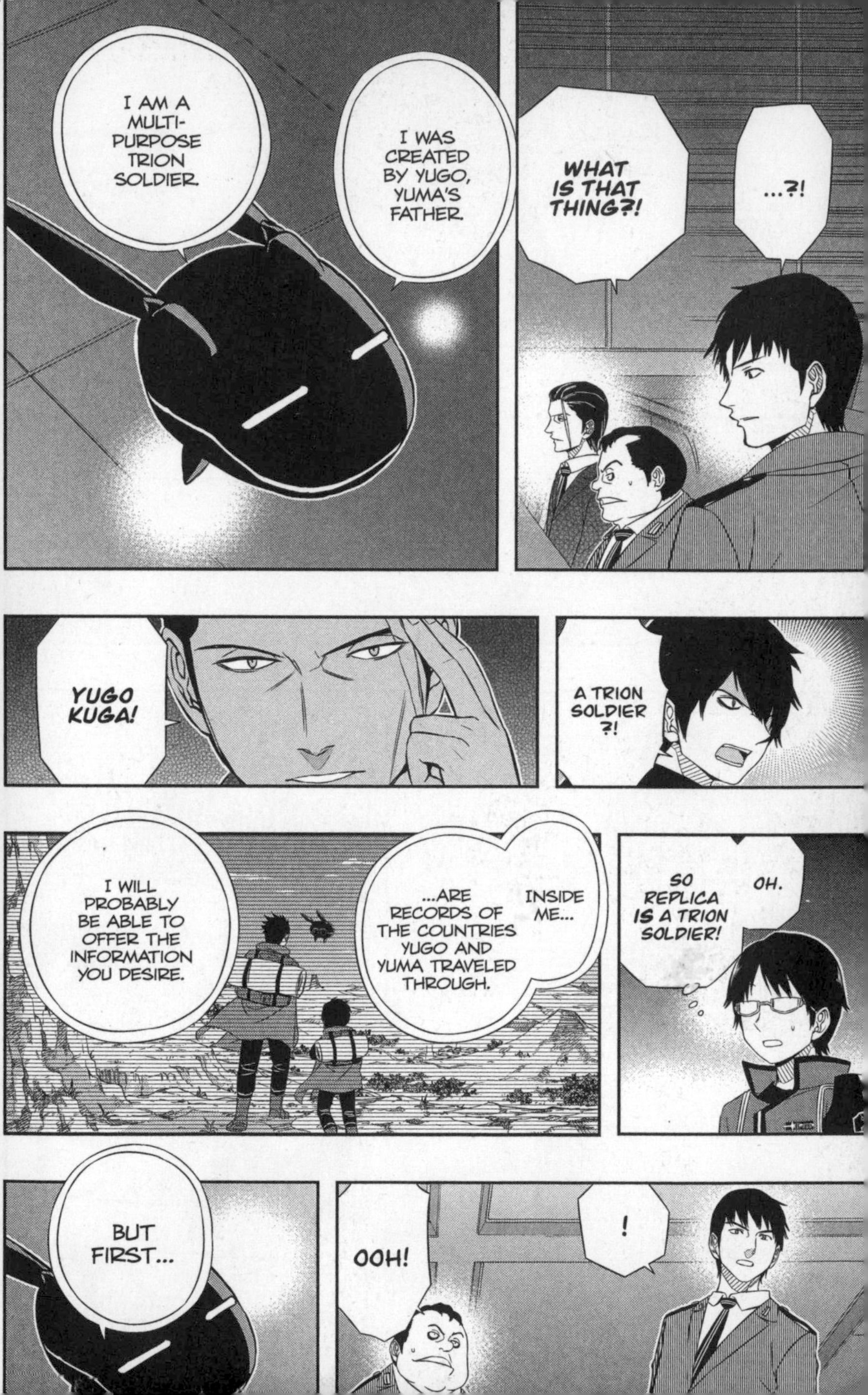
...?!
WHAT IS THAT THING?!
I AM A MULTI-PURPOSE TRION SOLDIER.
I WAS CREATED BY YUGO, YUMA'S FATHER.
A TRION SOLDIER ?!
YUGO KUGA!
OH.
SO REPLICA IS A TRION SOLDIER!
INSIDE ME...
...ARE RECORDS OF THE COUNTRIES YUGO AND YUMA TRAVELED THROUGH.
I WILL PROBABLY BE ABLE TO OFFER THE INFORMATION YOU DESIRE.
!
OOH!
BUT FIRST...

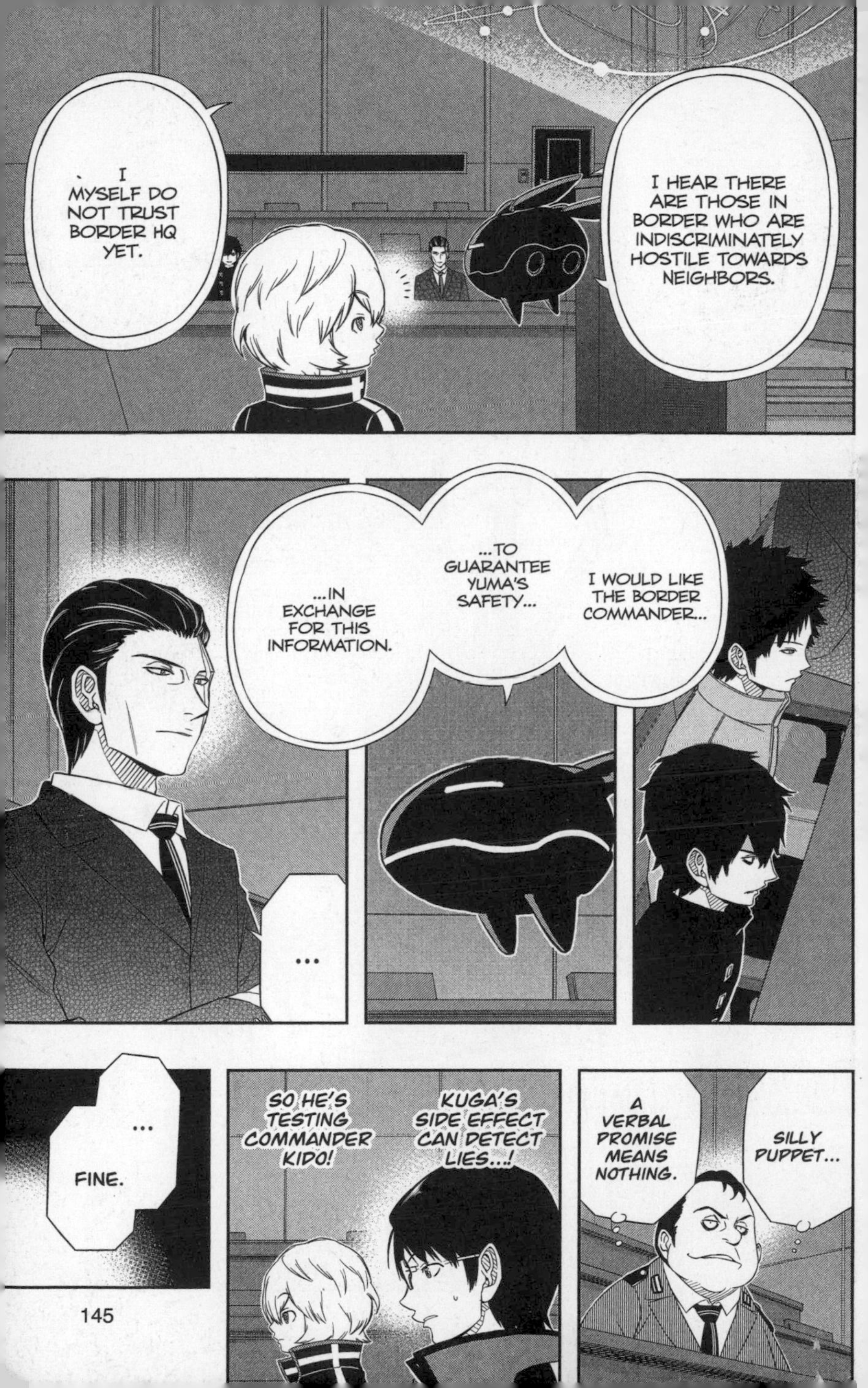
I HEAR THERE ARE THOSE IN BORDER WHO ARE INDISCRIMINATELY HOSTILE TOWARDS NEIGHBORS.
I MYSELF DO NOT TRUST BORDER HQ YET.
I WOULD LIKE THE BORDER COMMANDER...
...TO GUARANTEE YUMA'S SAFETY...
...IN EXCHANGE FOR THIS INFORMATION.
...
SILLY PUPPET...
A VERBAL PROMISE MEANS NOTHING.
KUGA'S SIDE EFFECT CAN DETECT LIES...!
SO HE'S TESTING COMMANDER KIDO!
...
FINE.

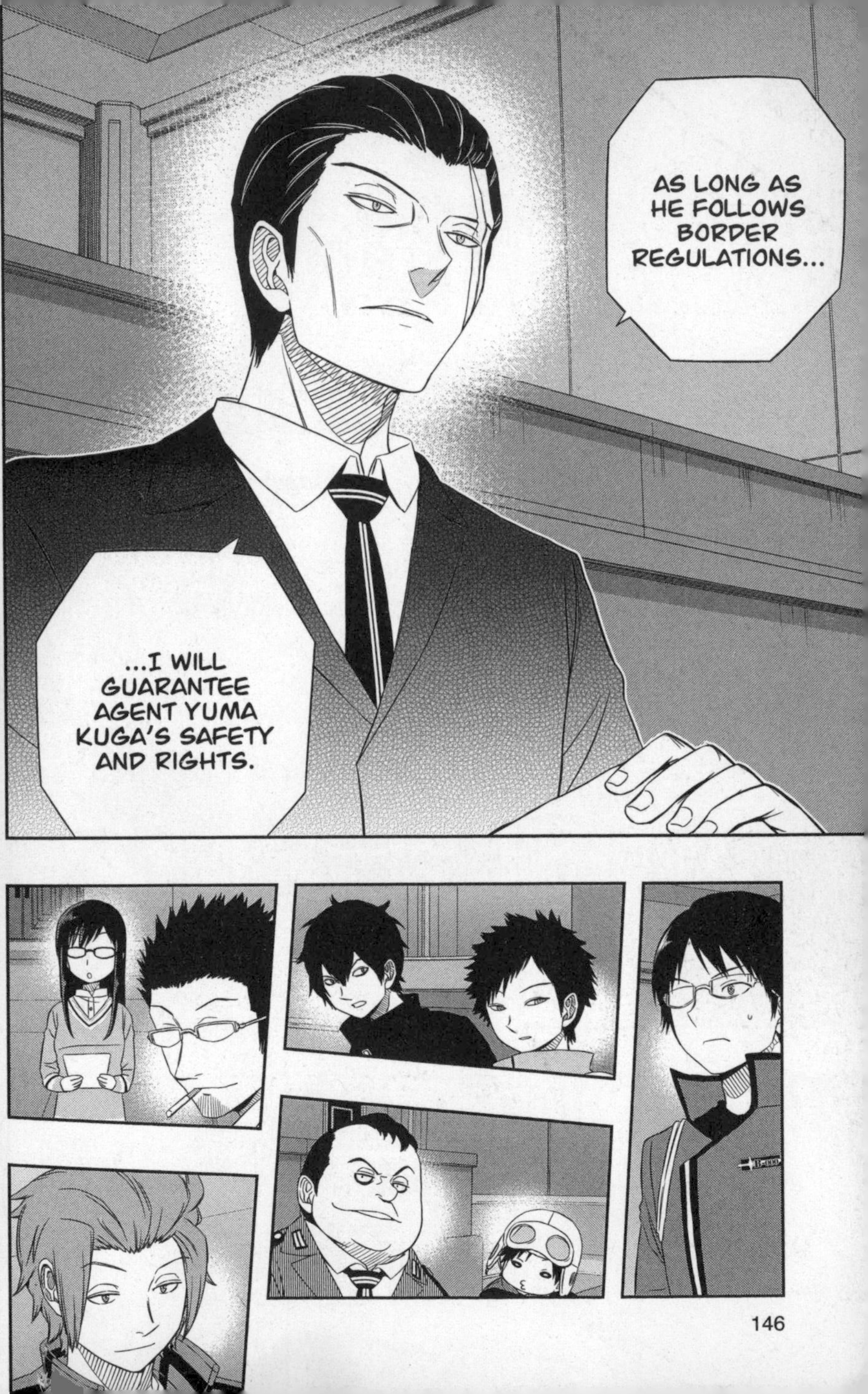
AS LONG AS HE FOLLOWS BORDER REGULATIONS...
...I WILL GUARANTEE AGENT YUMA KUGA'S SAFETY AND RIGHTS.

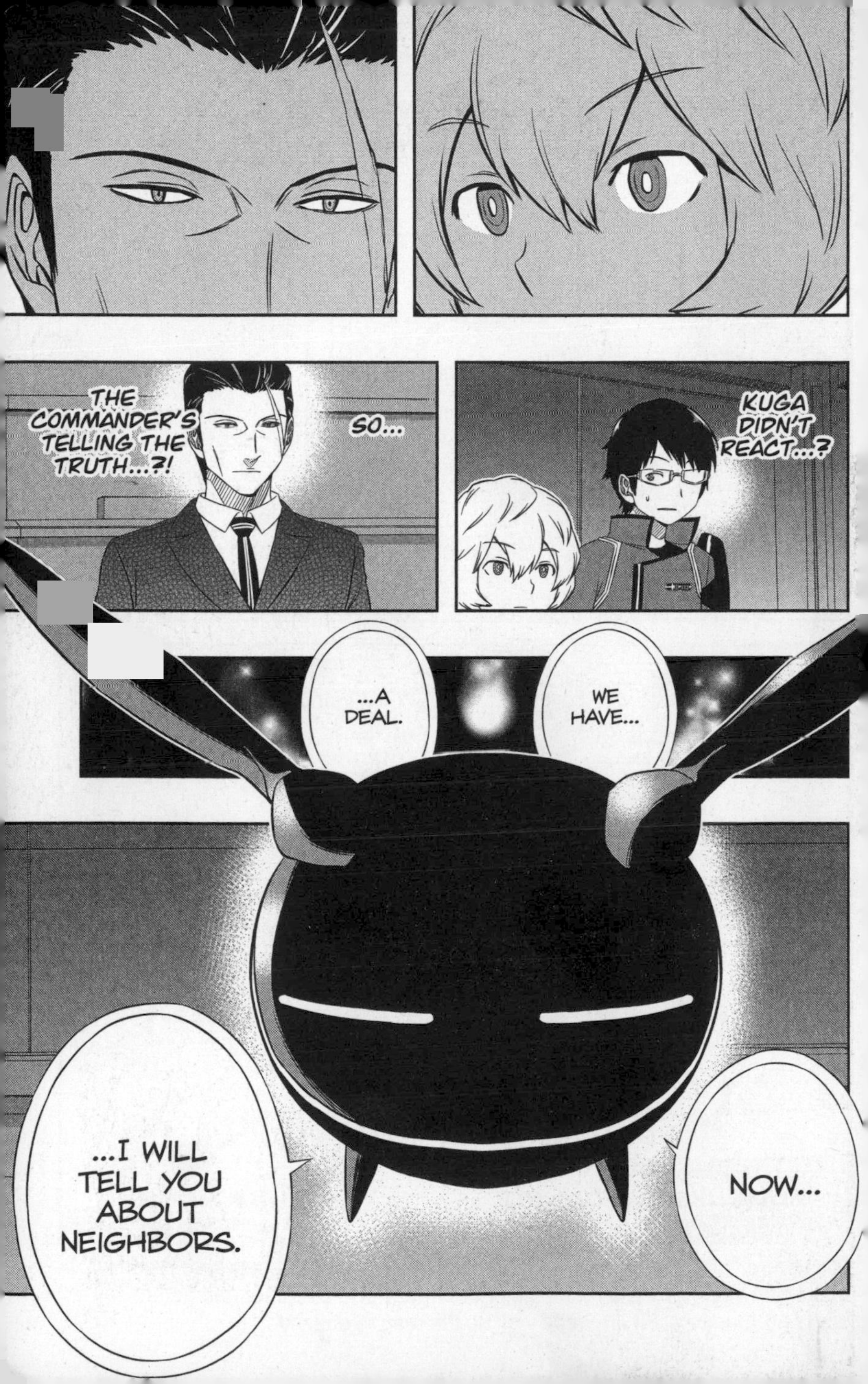
KUGA DIDN'T REACT...?
SO...
THE COMMANDER'S TELLING THE TRUTH...?!
WE HAVE...
...A DEAL.
NOW...
...I WILL TELL YOU ABOUT NEIGHBORS.

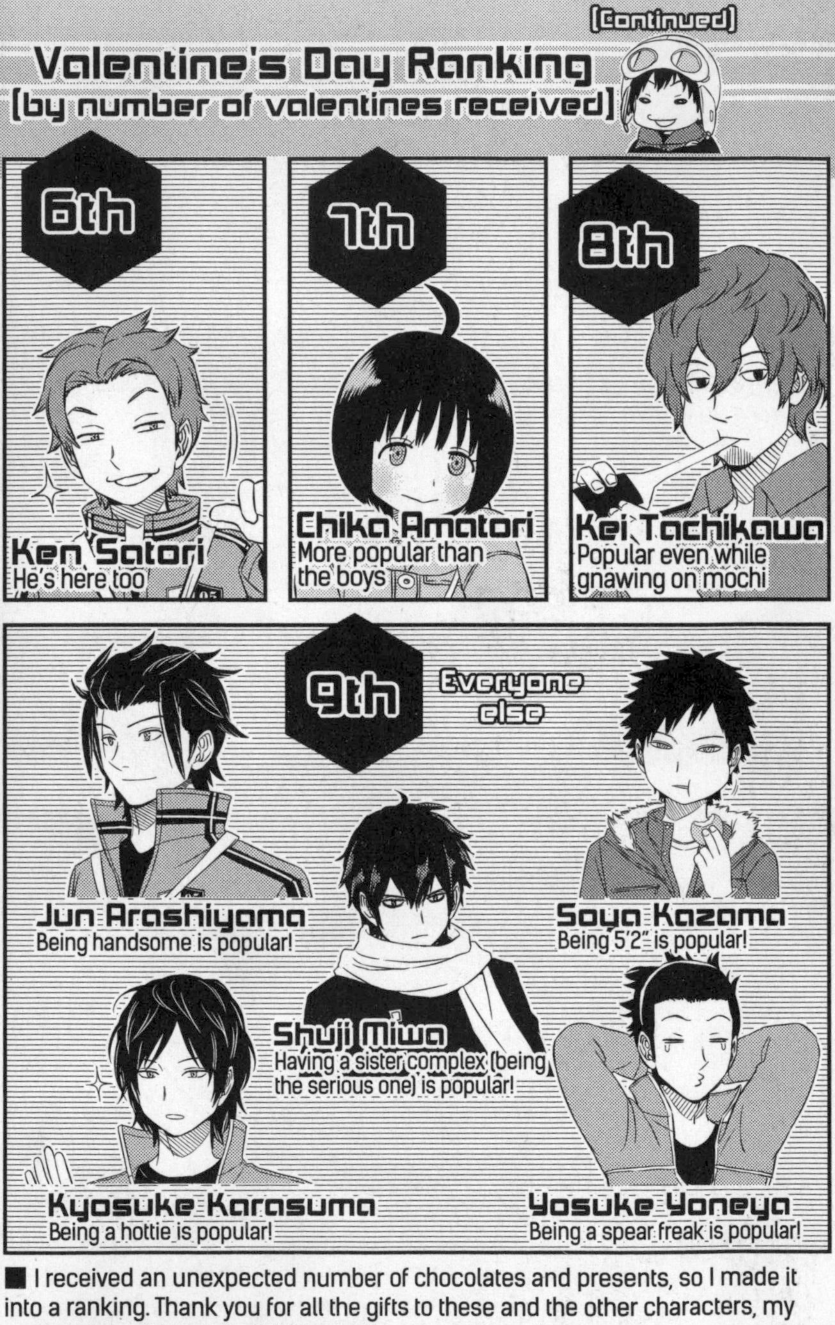
(Continued)
Valentine's Day Ranking
(by number of valentines received)
6th
Ken Satori
He's here too
7th
Chika Amatori
More popular than the boys
8th
Kei Tachikawa
Popular even while gnawing on mochi
9th
Everyone else
Jun Arashiyama
Being handsome is popular!
Soya Kazama
Being 5'2" is popular!
Shuji Miwa
Having a sister complex (being the serious one) is popular!
Kyosuke Karasuma
Being a hottie is popular!
Yosuke Yoneya
Being a spear freak is popular!

■ I received an unexpected number of chocolates and presents, so I made it into a ranking. Thank you for all the gifts to these and the other characters, my staff and me. We ate it all. We're well on the road to obesity.

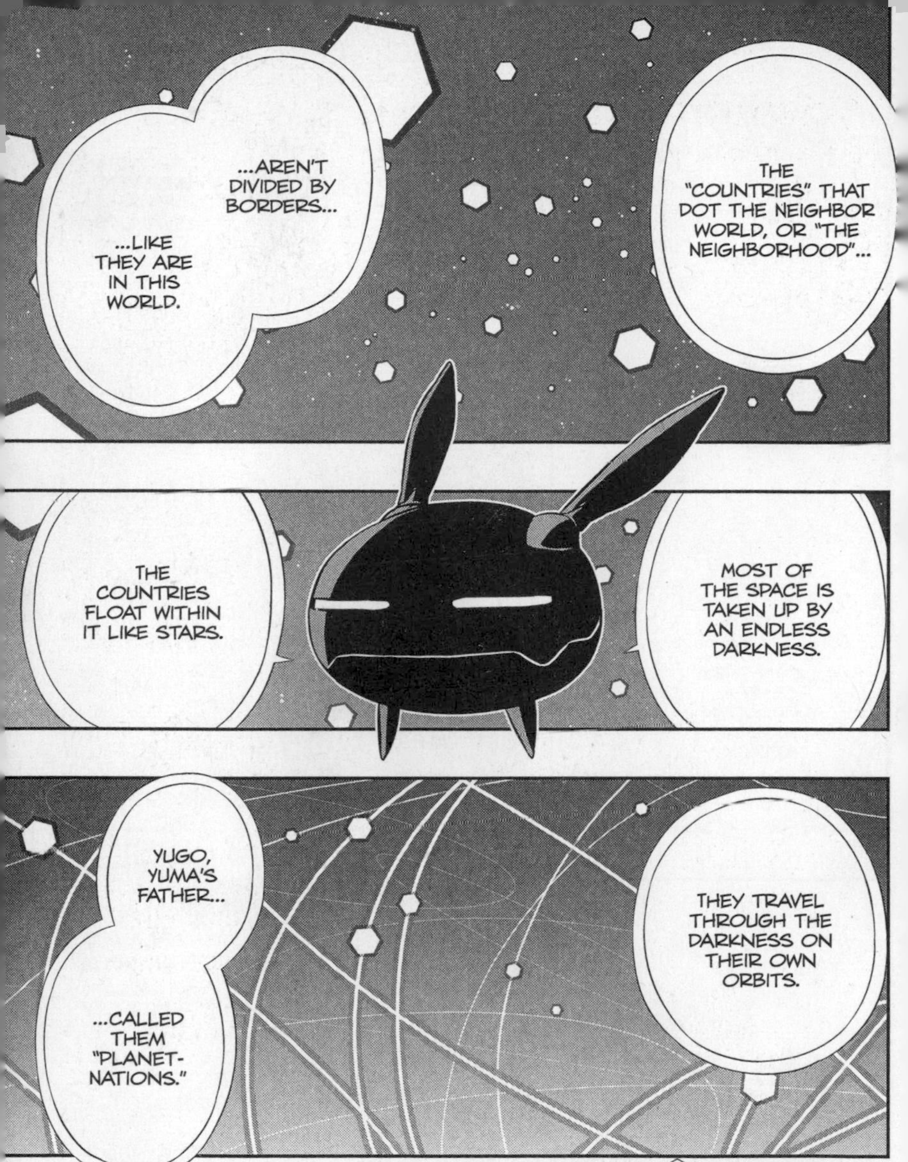
THE "COUNTRIES" THAT DOT THE NEIGHBOR WORLD, OR "THE NEIGHBORHOOD"...
...AREN'T DIVIDED BY BORDERS...
...LIKE THEY ARE IN THIS WORLD.
MOST OF THE SPACE IS TAKEN UP BY AN ENDLESS DARKNESS.
THE COUNTRIES FLOAT WITHIN IT LIKE STARS.
THEY TRAVEL THROUGH THE DARKNESS ON THEIR OWN ORBITS.
YUGO, YUMA'S FATHER...
...CALLED THEM "PLANET-NATIONS."

Chapter 42 Replica: Part 2

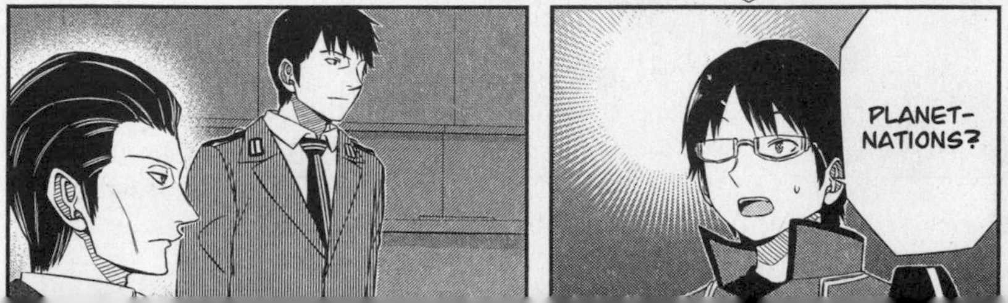
PLANET-NATIONS?

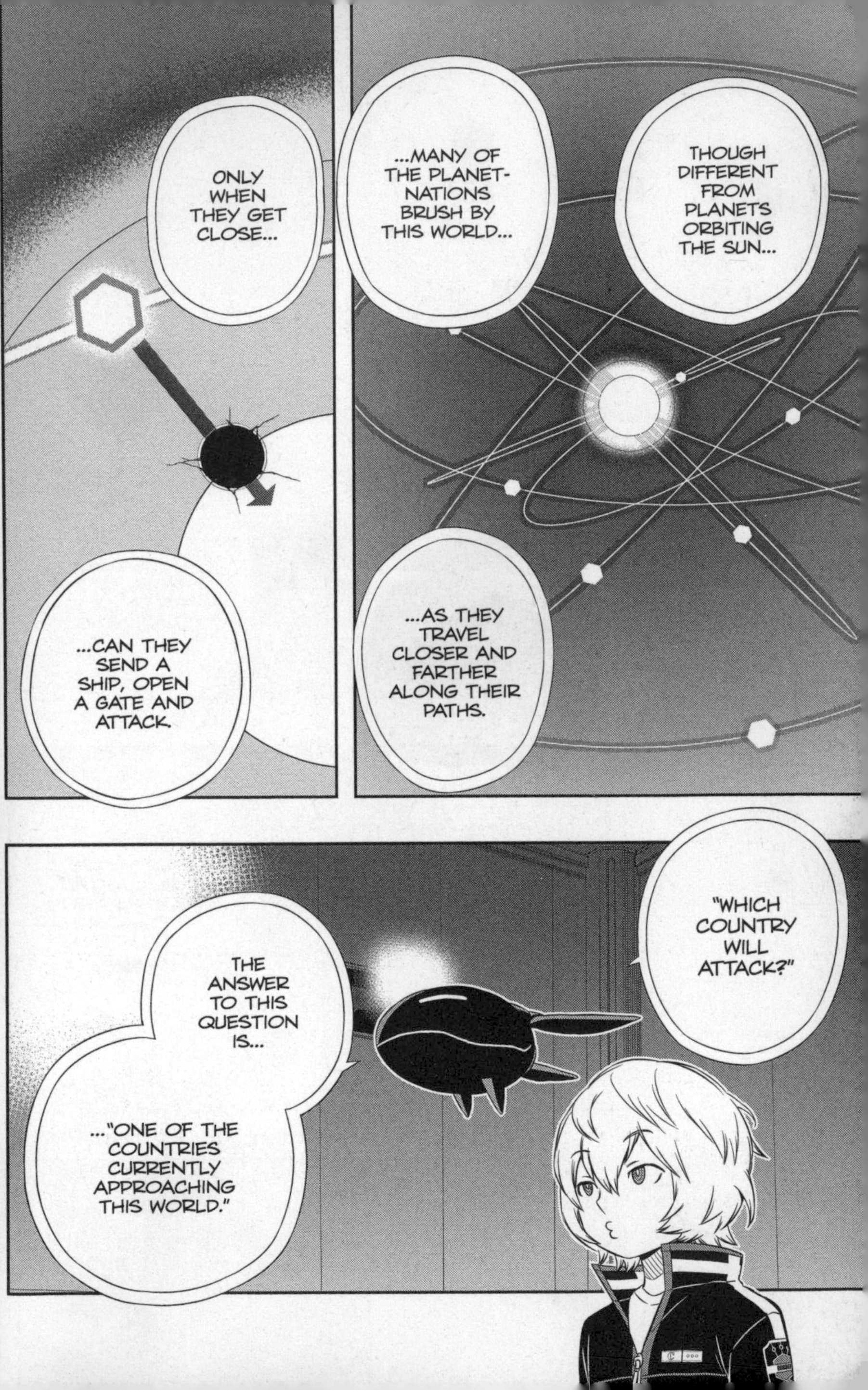
THOUGH DIFFERENT FROM PLANETS ORBITING THE SUN...
...MANY OF THE PLANET-NATIONS BRUSH BY THIS WORLD...
...AS THEY TRAVEL CLOSER AND FARTHER ALONG THEIR PATHS.
ONLY WHEN THEY GET CLOSE...
...CAN THEY SEND A SHIP, OPEN A GATE AND ATTACK.
"WHICH COUNTRY WILL ATTACK?"
THE ANSWER TO THIS QUESTION IS...
..."ONE OF THE COUNTRIES CURRENTLY APPROACHING THIS WORLD."

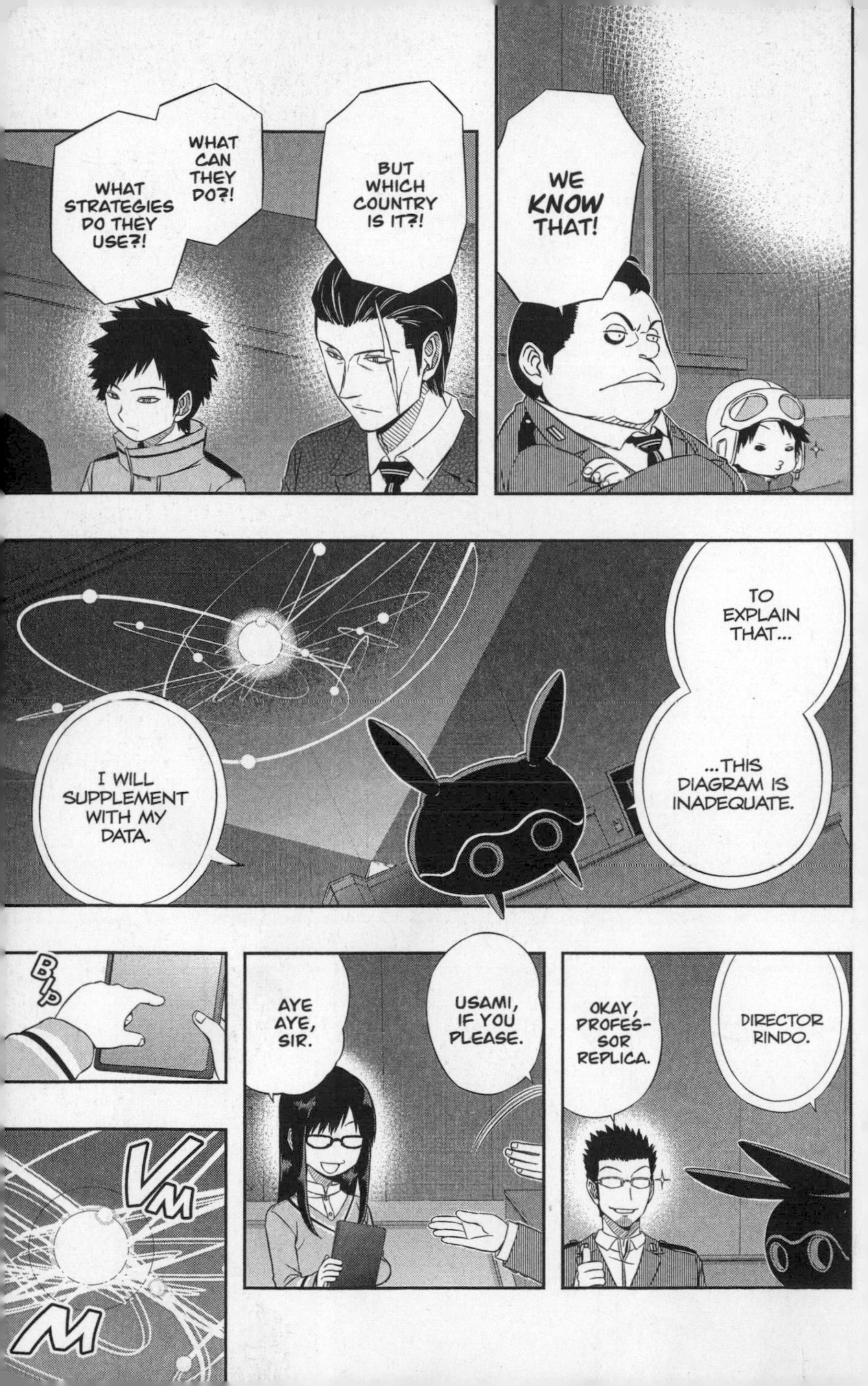
WE KNOW THAT!
BUT WHICH COUNTRY IS IT?!
WHAT CAN THEY DO?!
WHAT STRATEGIES DO THEY USE?!
TO EXPLAIN THAT...
...THIS DIAGRAM IS INADEQUATE.
I WILL SUPPLEMENT WITH MY DATA.
DIRECTOR RINDO.
OKAY, PROFES-SOR REPLICA.
USAMI, IF YOU PLEASE.
AYE AYE, SIR.
BIP
VMM

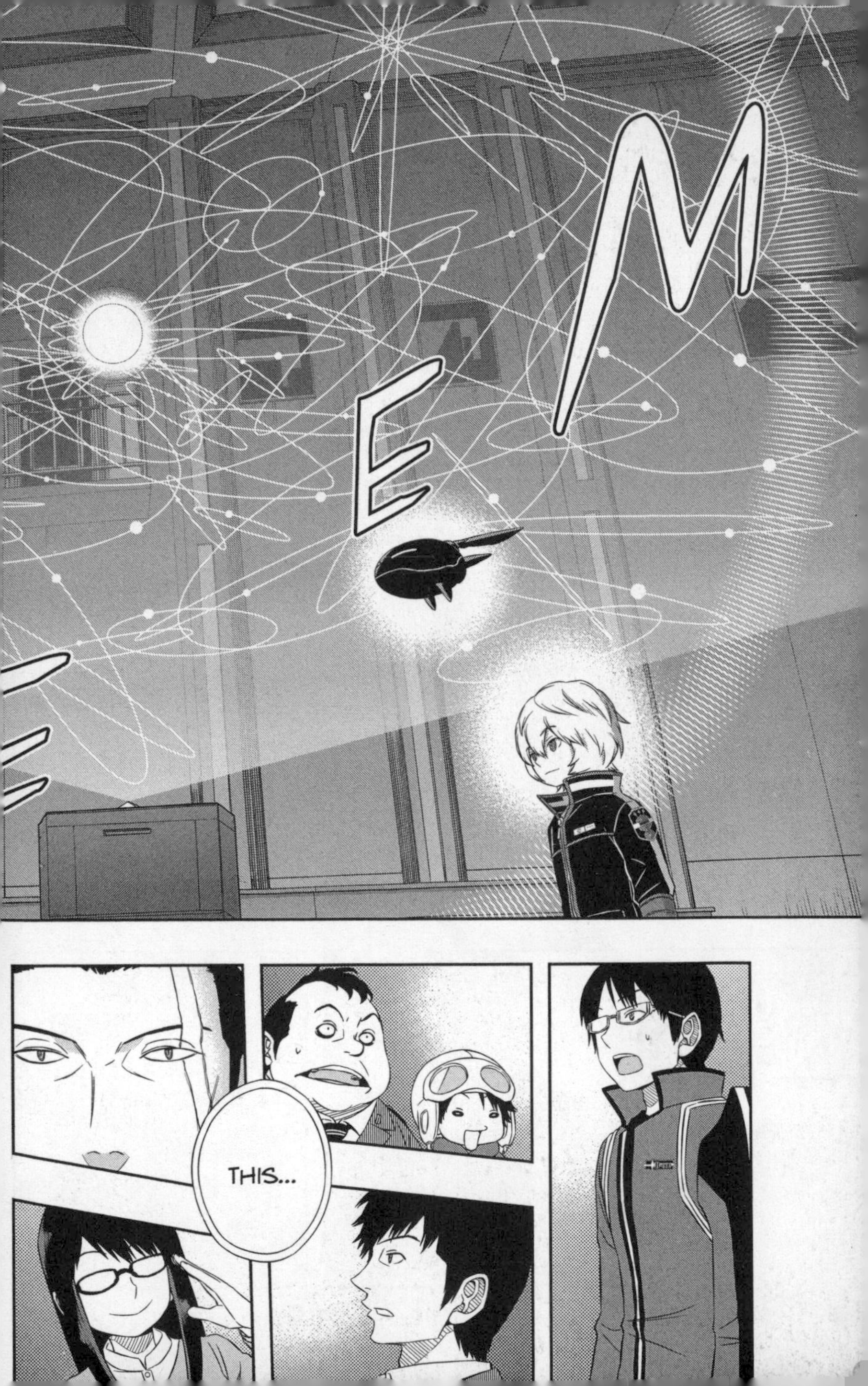
THIS...

Chapter 42 Replica: Part 2

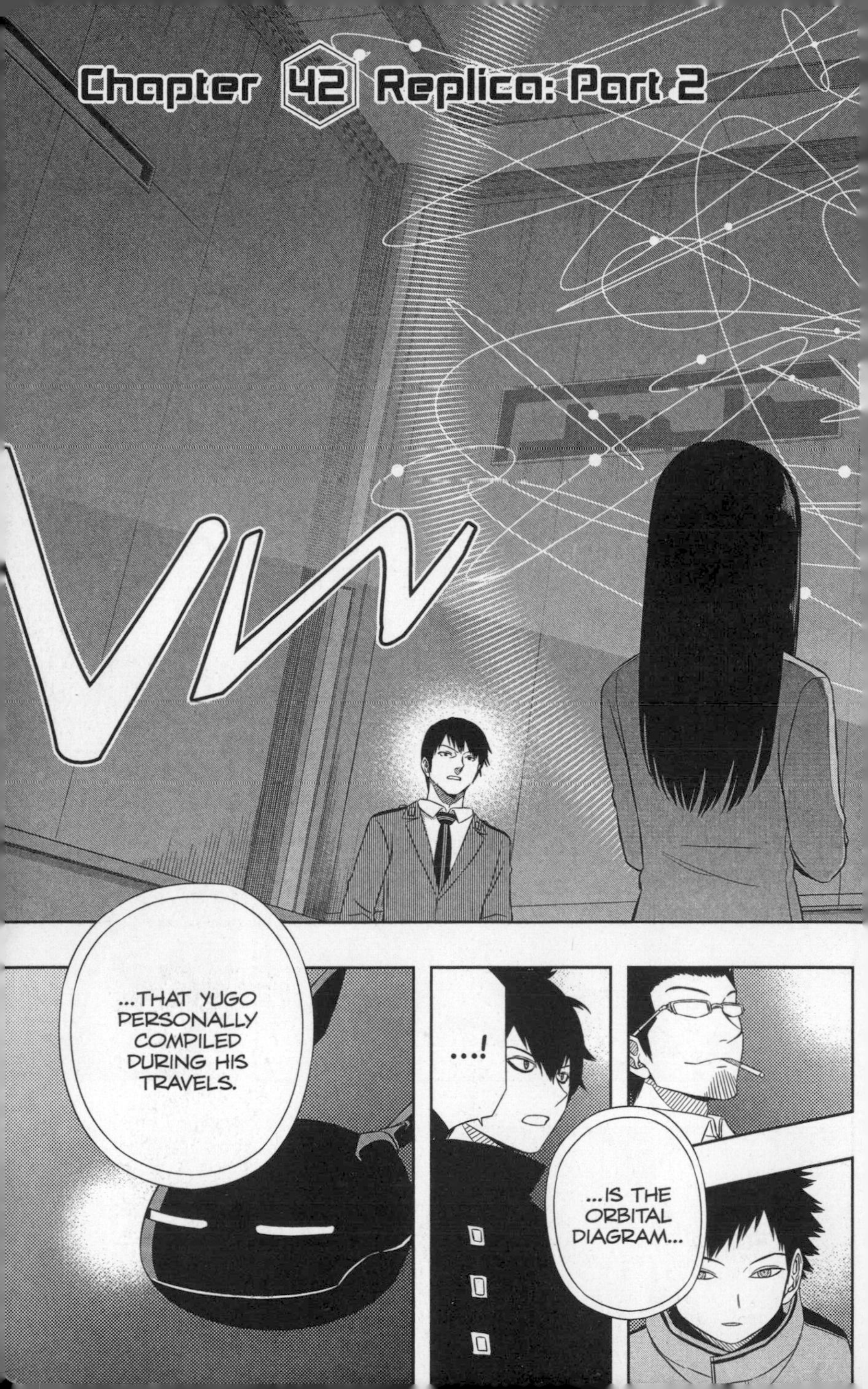
VVN
...IS THE ORBITAL DIAGRAM...
...!
...THAT YUGO PERSONALLY COMPILED DURING HIS TRAVELS.

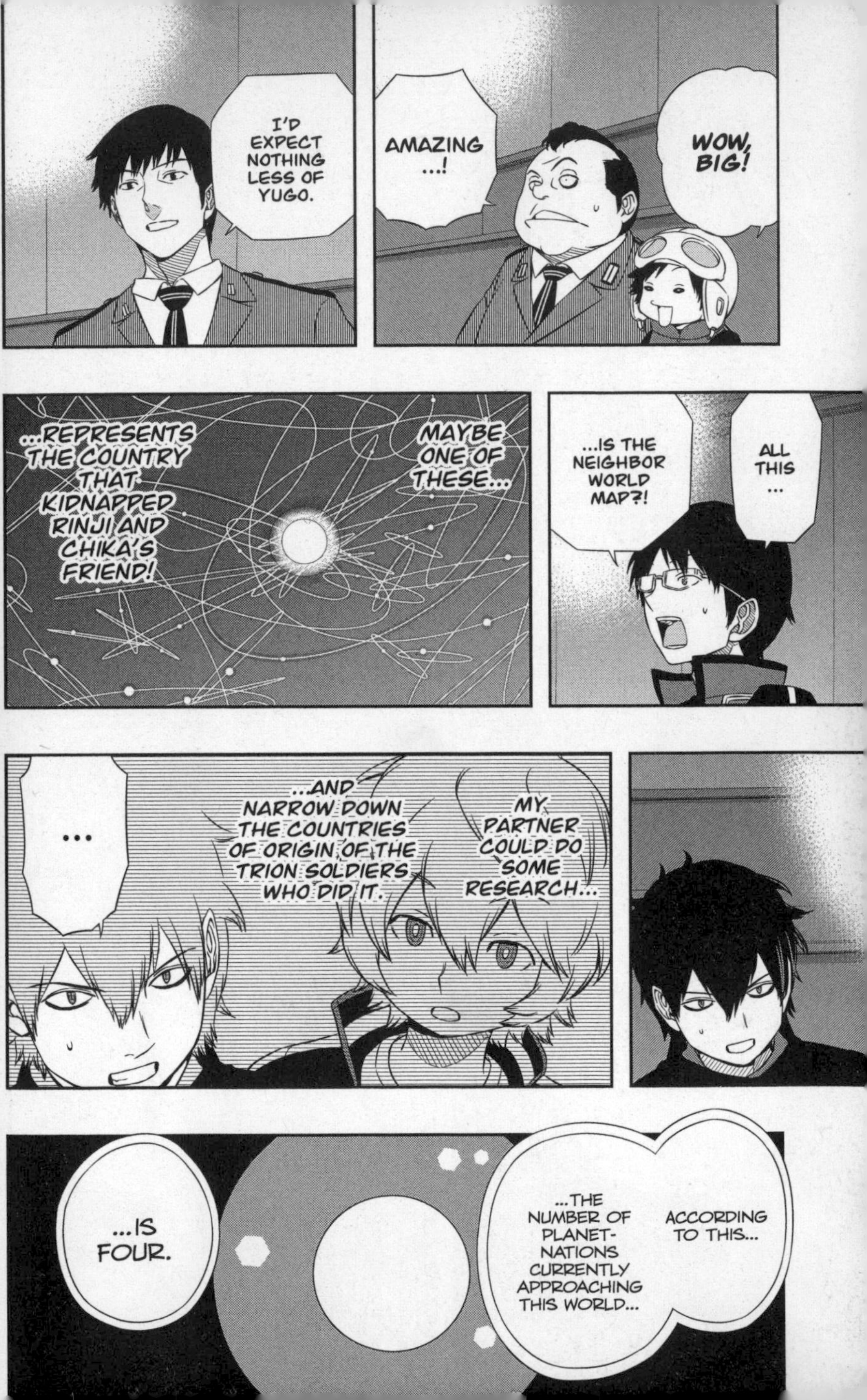
WOW, BIG!
AMAZING ...!
I'D EXPECT NOTHING LESS OF YUGO.
ALL THIS ...
...IS THE NEIGHBOR WORLD MAP?!
MAYBE ONE OF THESE...
...REPRESENTS THE COUNTRY THAT KIDNAPPED RINJI AND CHIKA'S FRIEND!
MY PARTNER COULD DO SOME RESEARCH...
...AND NARROW DOWN THE COUNTRIES OF ORIGIN OF THE TRION SOLDIERS WHO DID IT.
...
ACCORDING TO THIS...
...THE NUMBER OF PLANET-NATIONS CURRENTLY APPROACHING THIS WORLD...
...IS FOUR.

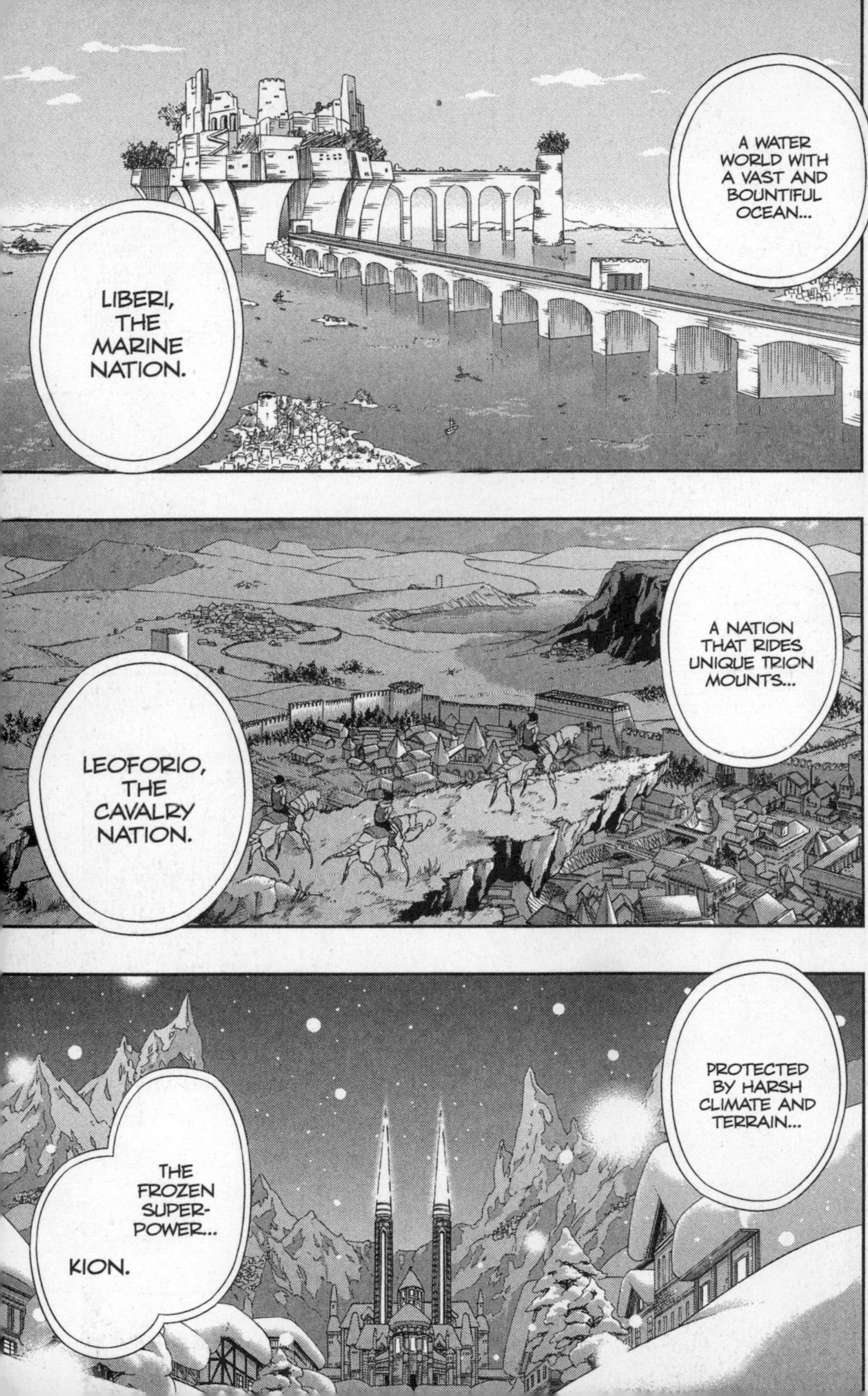
A WATER WORLD WITH A VAST AND BOUNTIFUL OCEAN...
LIBERI, THE MARINE NATION.
A NATION THAT RIDES UNIQUE TRION MOUNTS...
LEOFORIO, THE CAVALRY NATION.
PROTECTED BY HARSH CLIMATE AND TERRAIN...
THE FROZEN SUPER-POWER...
KION.

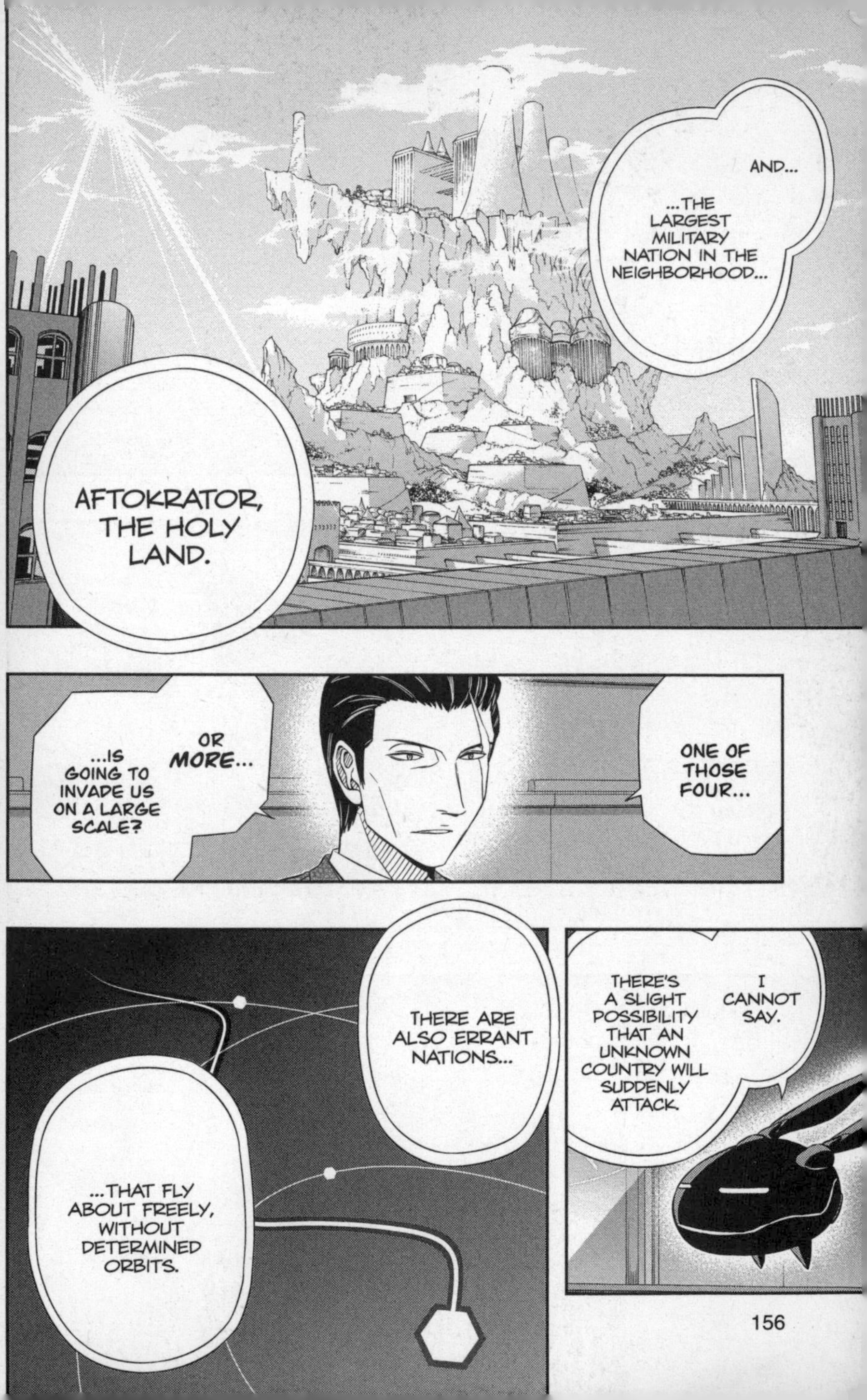
AND...
...THE LARGEST MILITARY NATION IN THE NEIGHBORHOOD...
AFTOKRATOR, THE HOLY LAND.
ONE OF THOSE FOUR...
OR MORE...
...IS GOING TO INVADE US ON A LARGE SCALE?
I CANNOT SAY.
THERE'S A SLIGHT POSSIBILITY THAT AN UNKNOWN COUNTRY WILL SUDDENLY ATTACK.
THERE ARE ALSO ERRANT NATIONS...
...THAT FLY ABOUT FREELY, WITHOUT DETERMINED ORBITS.

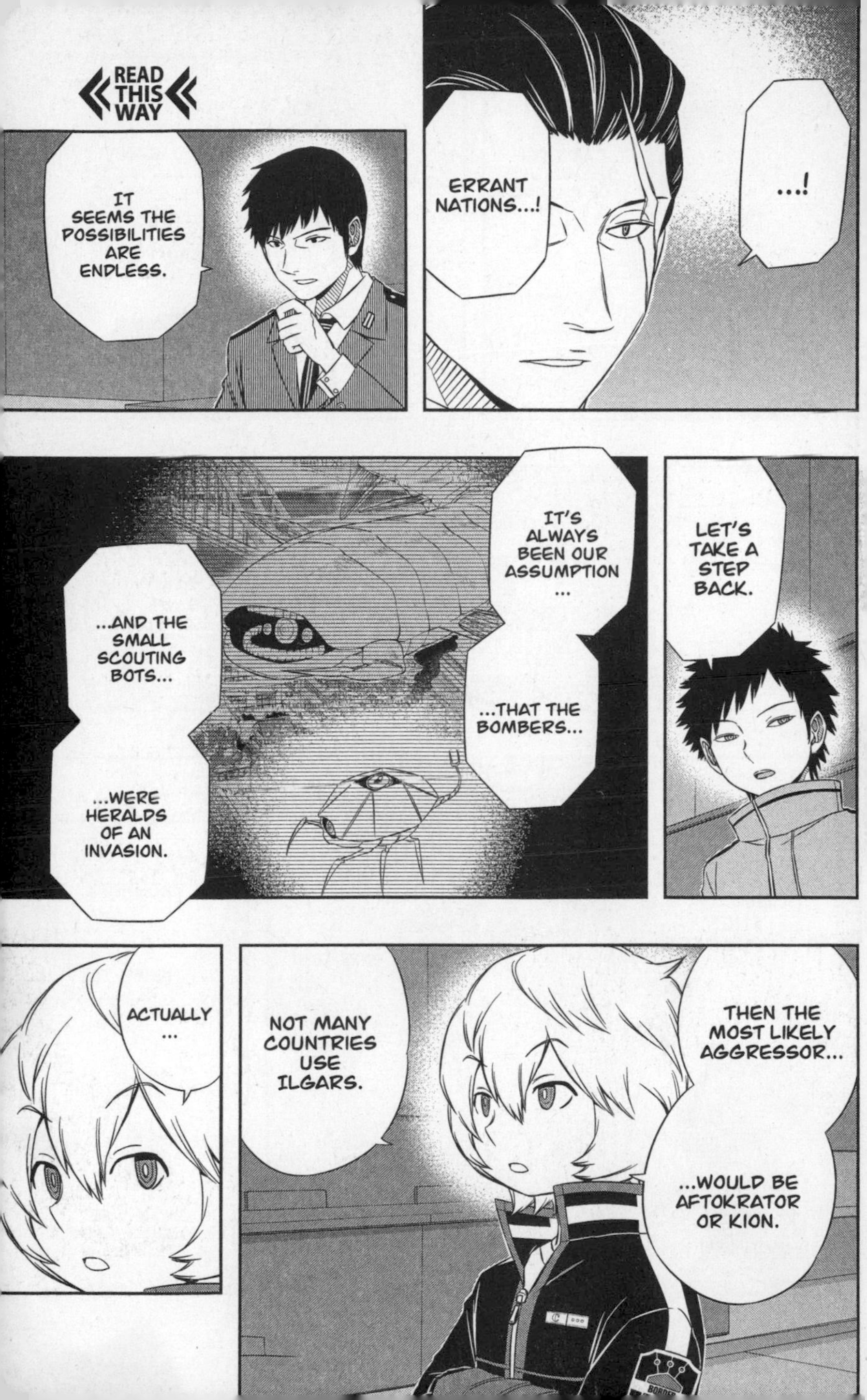
READ THIS WAY
...!
ERRANT NATIONS...!
IT SEEMS THE POSSIBILITIES ARE ENDLESS.
LET'S TAKE A STEP BACK.
IT'S ALWAYS BEEN OUR ASSUMPTION ...
...THAT THE BOMBERS...
...AND THE SMALL SCOUTING BOTS...
...WERE HERALDS OF AN INVASION.
THEN THE MOST LIKELY AGGRESSOR...
...WOULD BE AFTOKRATOR OR KION.
NOT MANY COUNTRIES USE ILGARS.
ACTUALLY ...

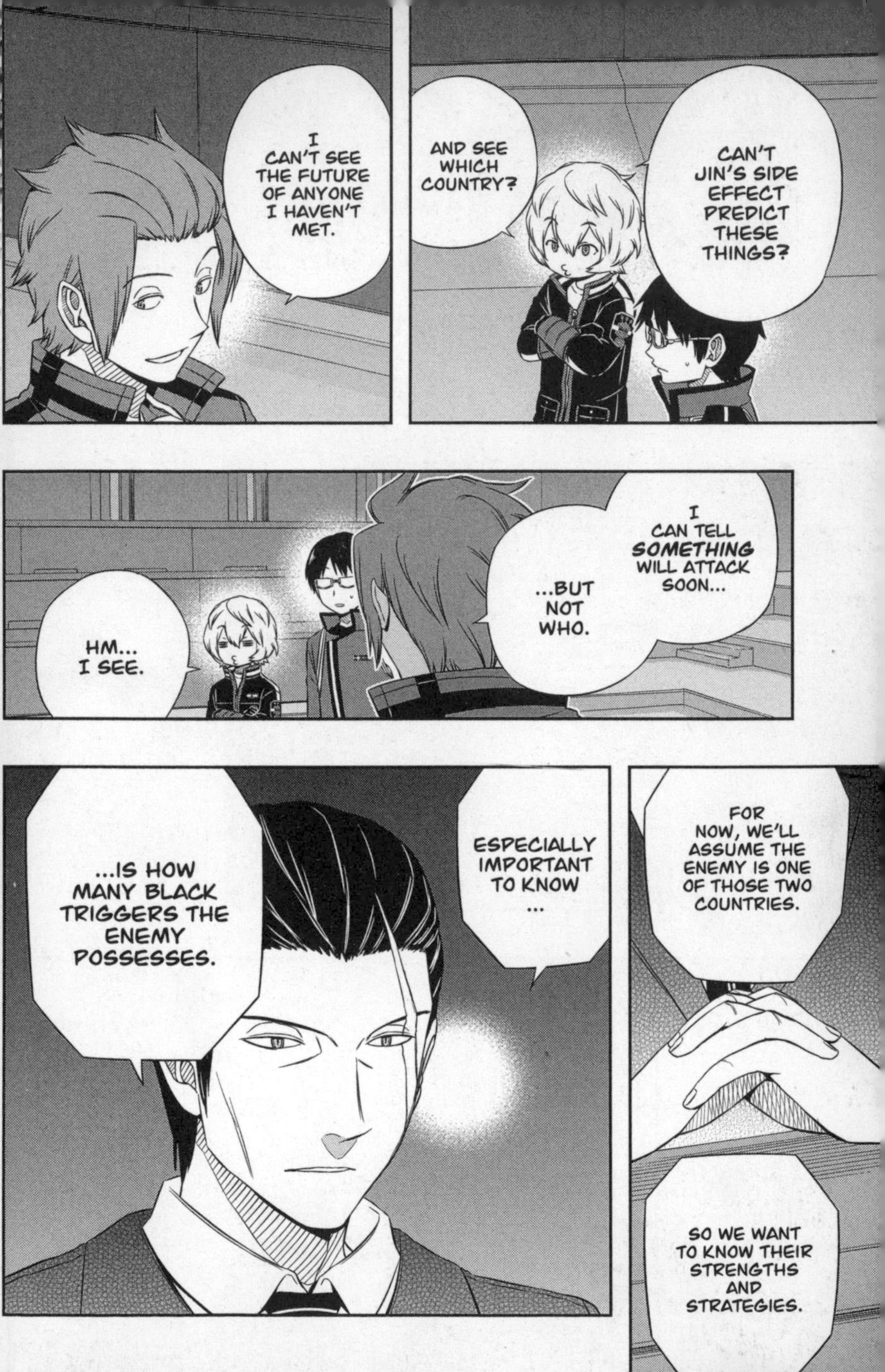
CAN'T JIN'S SIDE EFFECT PREDICT THESE THINGS?
AND SEE WHICH COUNTRY?
I CAN'T SEE THE FUTURE OF ANYONE I HAVEN'T MET.
I CAN TELL **SOMETHING** WILL ATTACK SOON...
...BUT NOT WHO.
HM... I SEE.
FOR NOW, WE'LL ASSUME THE ENEMY IS ONE OF THOSE TWO COUNTRIES.
SO WE WANT TO KNOW THEIR STRENGTHS AND STRATEGIES.
ESPECIALLY IMPORTANT TO KNOW ...
...IS HOW MANY BLACK TRIGGERS THE ENEMY POSSESSES.

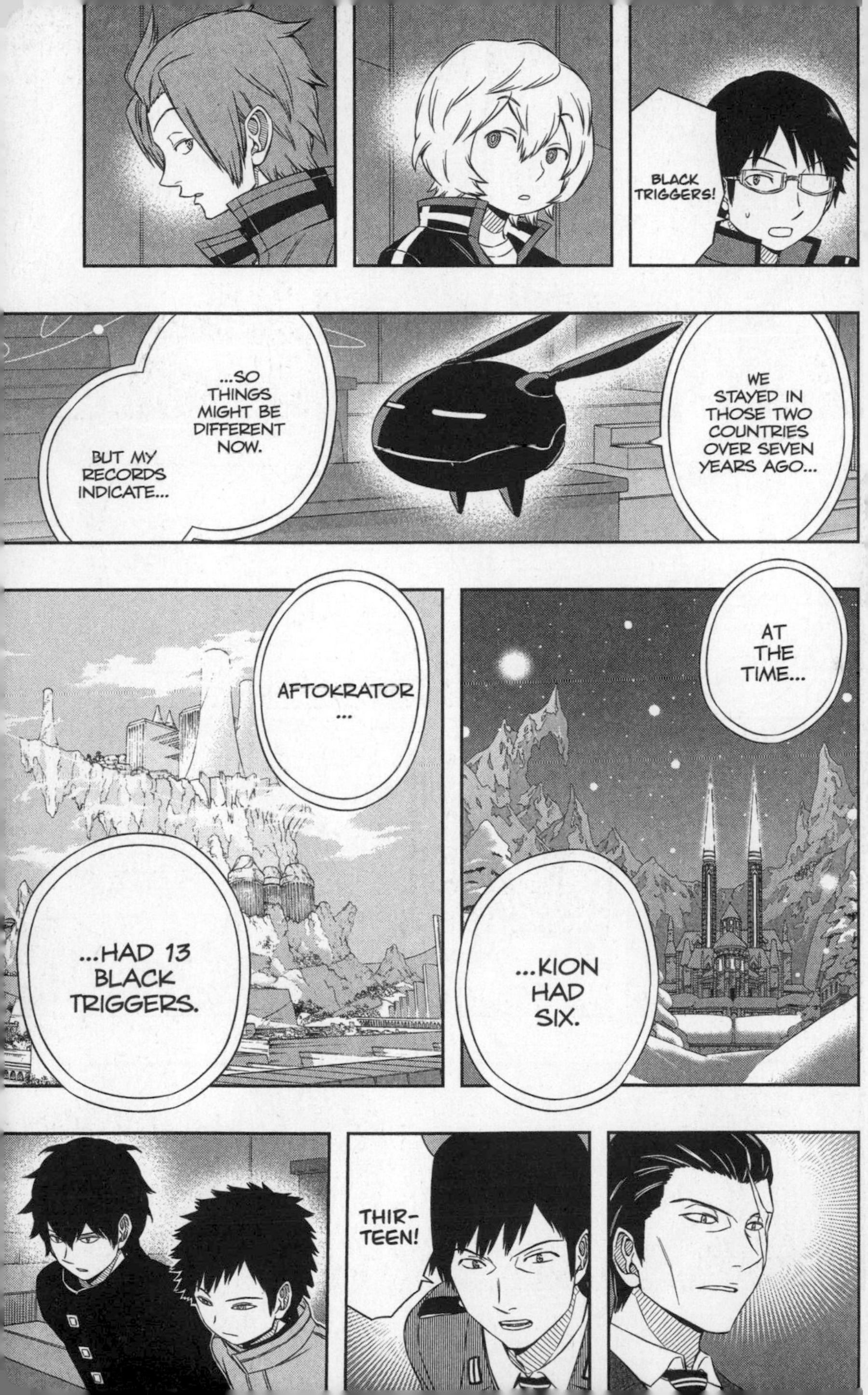
BLACK TRIGGERS!
WE STAYED IN THOSE TWO COUNTRIES OVER SEVEN YEARS AGO...
...SO THINGS MIGHT BE DIFFERENT NOW.
BUT MY RECORDS INDICATE...
AT THE TIME...
...KION HAD SIX.
AFTOKRATOR ...
...HAD 13 BLACK TRIGGERS.
THIR-TEEN!

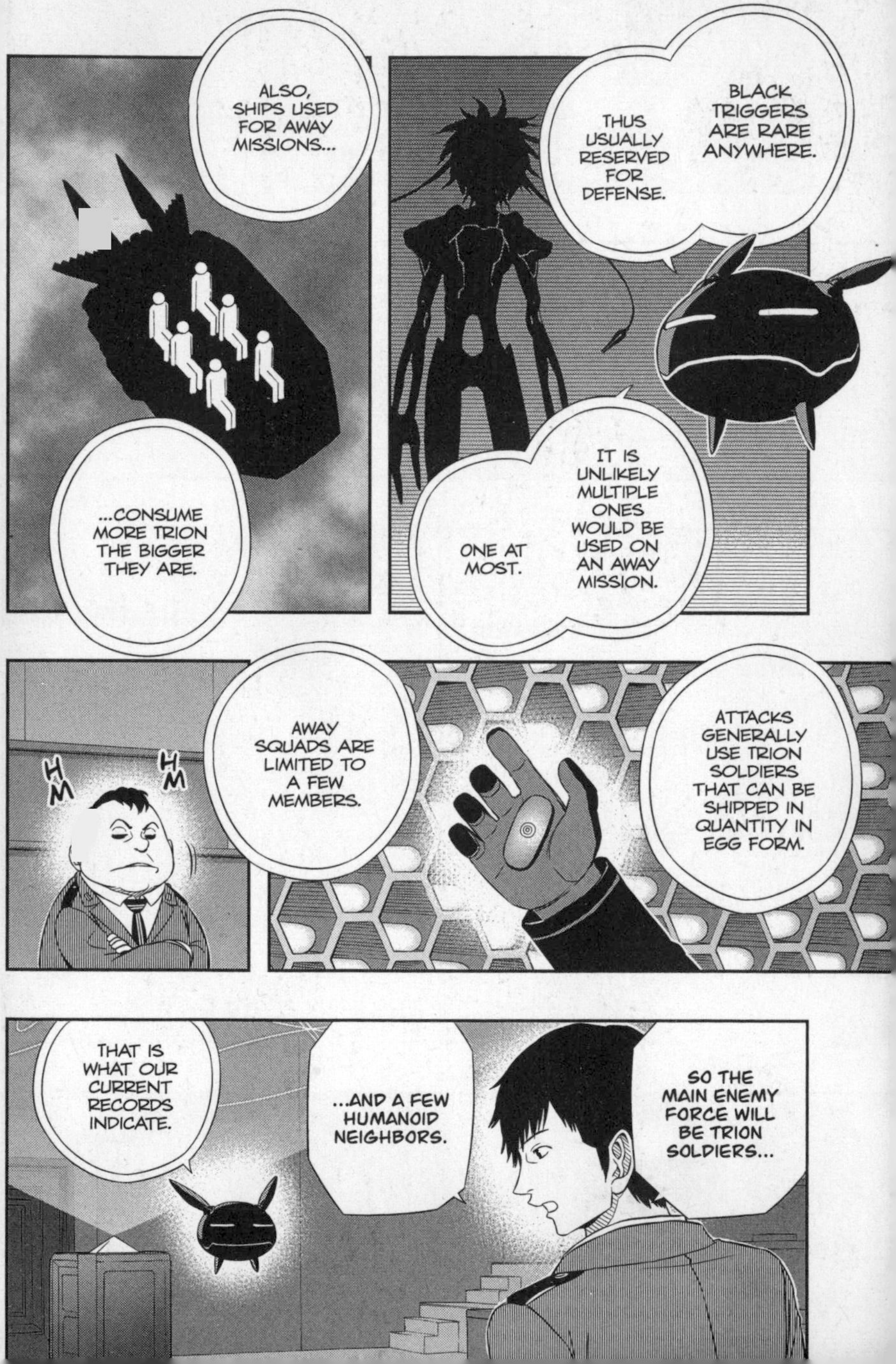
BLACK TRIGGERS ARE RARE ANYWHERE.
THUS USUALLY RESERVED FOR DEFENSE.
IT IS UNLIKELY MULTIPLE ONES WOULD BE USED ON AN AWAY MISSION.
ONE AT MOST.
ALSO, SHIPS USED FOR AWAY MISSIONS...
...CONSUME MORE TRION THE BIGGER THEY ARE.
ATTACKS GENERALLY USE TRION SOLDIERS THAT CAN BE SHIPPED IN QUANTITY IN EGG FORM.
AWAY SQUADS ARE LIMITED TO A FEW MEMBERS.
HM
HM
SO THE MAIN ENEMY FORCE WILL BE TRION SOLDIERS...
...AND A FEW HUMANOID NEIGHBORS.
THAT IS WHAT OUR CURRENT RECORDS INDICATE.

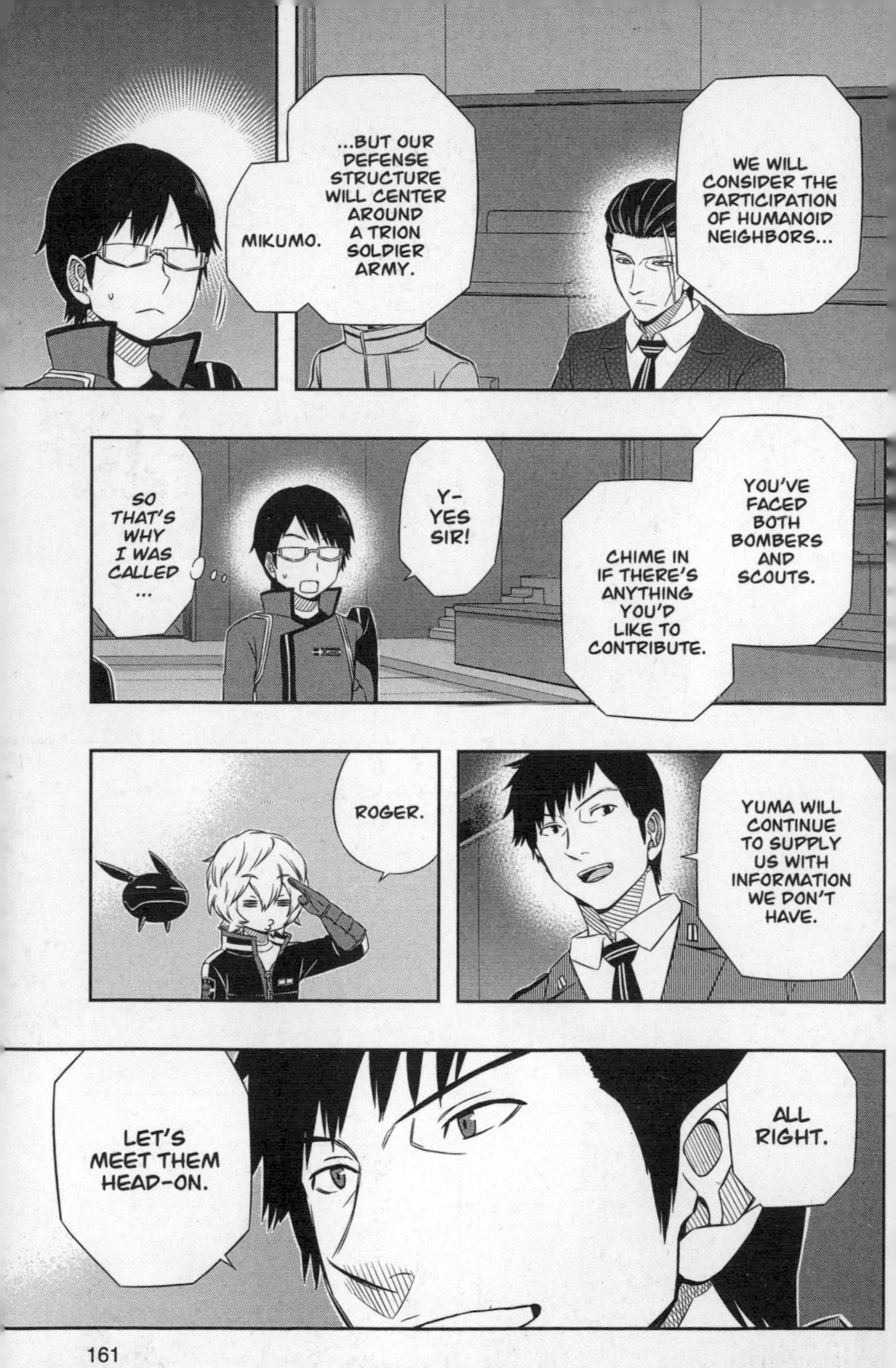
WE WILL CONSIDER THE PARTICIPATION OF HUMANOID NEIGHBORS...
...BUT OUR DEFENSE STRUCTURE WILL CENTER AROUND A TRION SOLDIER ARMY.
MIKUMO.
YOU'VE FACED BOTH BOMBERS AND SCOUTS.
CHIME IN IF THERE'S ANYTHING YOU'D LIKE TO CONTRIBUTE.
Y-YES SIR!
SO THAT'S WHY I WAS CALLED...
YUMA WILL CONTINUE TO SUPPLY US WITH INFORMATION WE DON'T HAVE.
ROGER.
ALL RIGHT.
LET'S MEET THEM HEAD-ON.

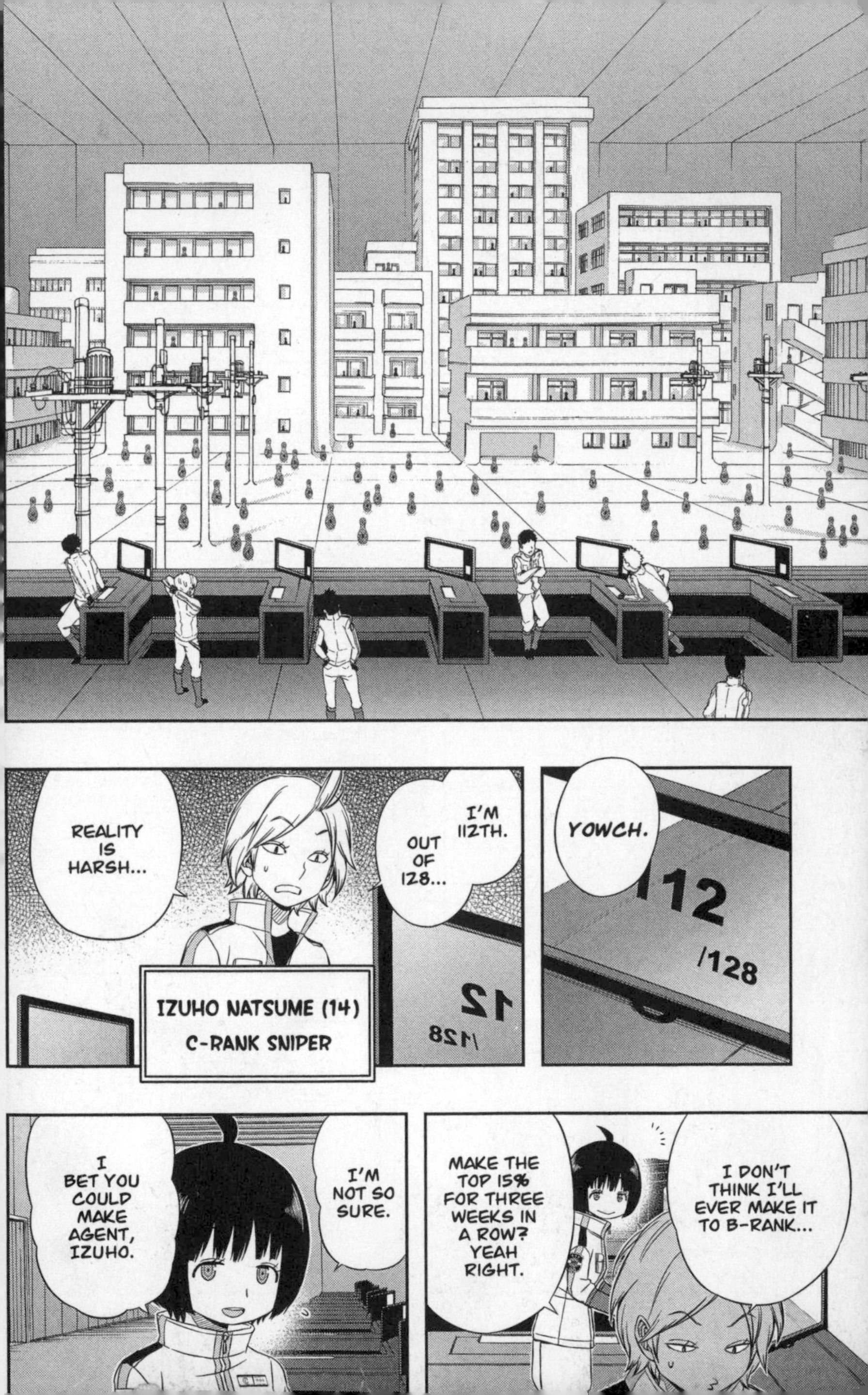
YOWCH.
112
/128
I'M 112TH.
OUT OF 128...
REALITY IS HARSH...
IZUHO NATSUME (14)
C-RANK SNIPER
I DON'T THINK I'LL EVER MAKE IT TO B-RANK...
MAKE THE TOP 15% FOR THREE WEEKS IN A ROW? YEAH RIGHT.
I'M NOT SO SURE.
I BET YOU COULD MAKE AGENT, IZUHO.

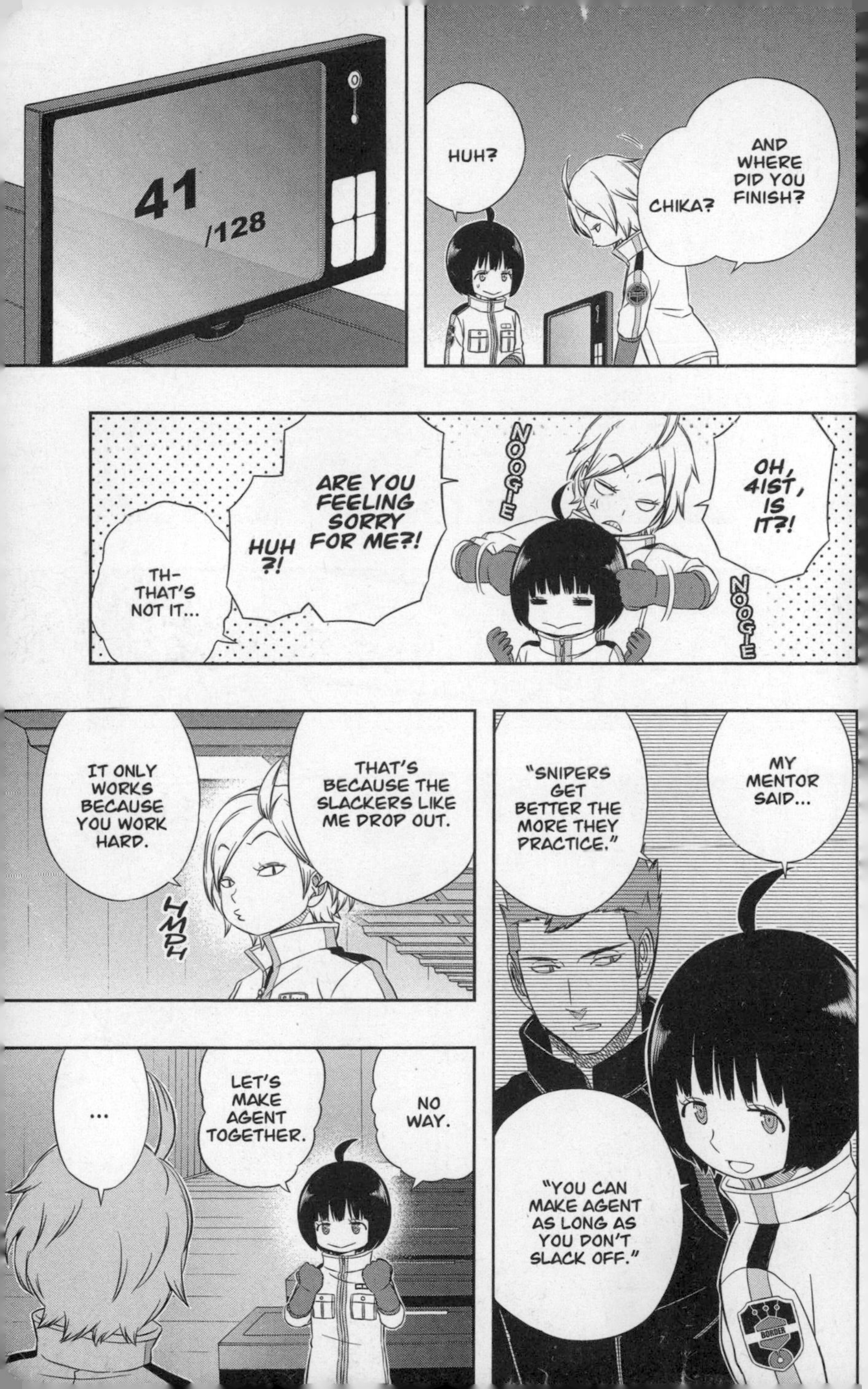
CHIKA? AND WHERE DID YOU FINISH?
HUH?
41
/128
OH, 41ST, IS IT?!
NOOGIE
NOOGIE
ARE YOU FEELING SORRY FOR ME?!
HUH?!
TH-THAT'S NOT IT...
MY MENTOR SAID...
"SNIPERS GET BETTER THE MORE THEY PRACTICE."
"YOU CAN MAKE AGENT AS LONG AS YOU DON'T SLACK OFF."
BORDER
THAT'S BECAUSE THE SLACKERS LIKE ME DROP OUT.
IT ONLY WORKS BECAUSE YOU WORK HARD.
HMPH
NO WAY.
LET'S MAKE AGENT TOGETHER.
...

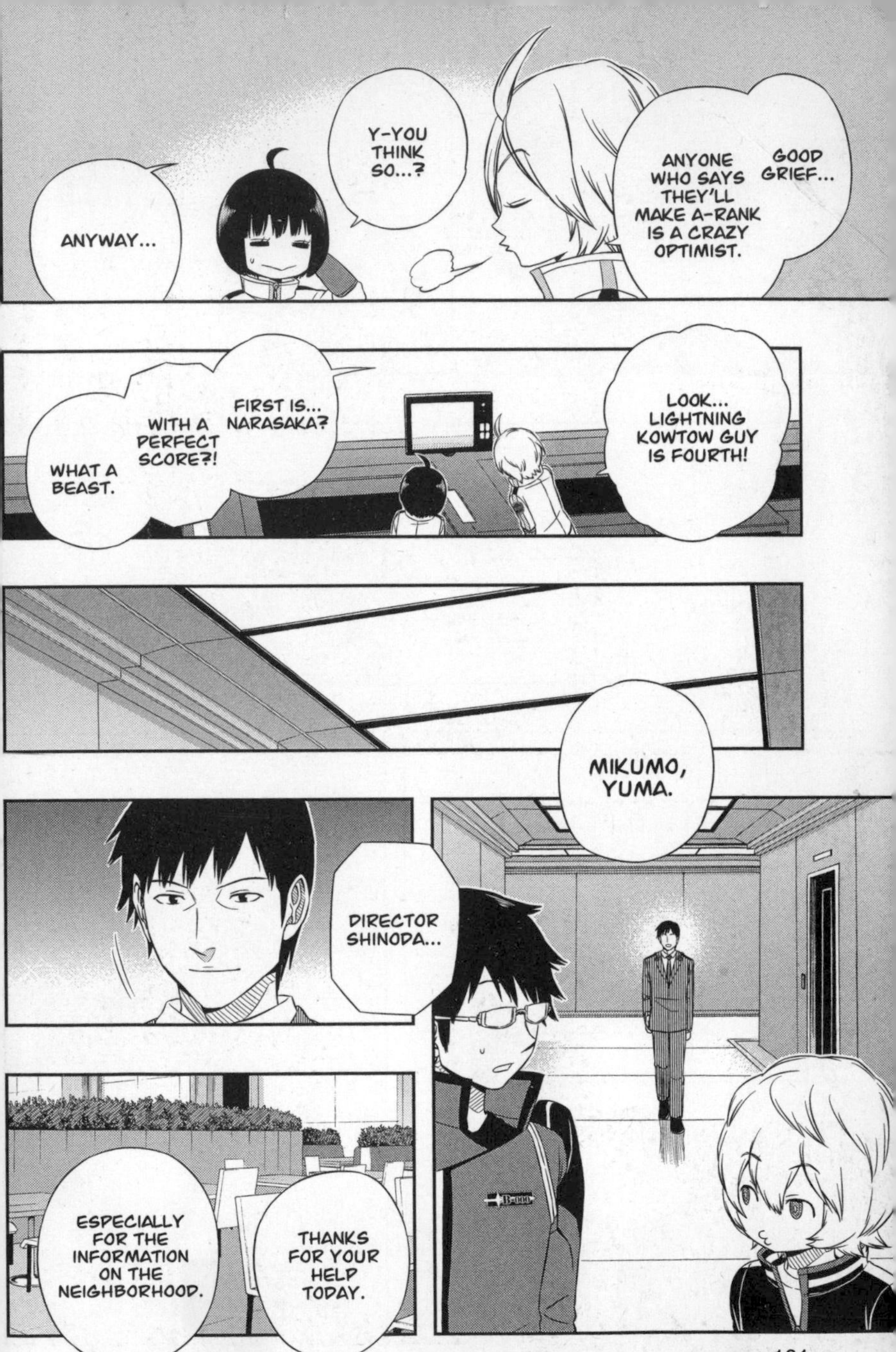
GOOD GRIEF...
ANYONE WHO SAYS THEY'LL MAKE A-RANK IS A CRAZY OPTIMIST.
Y-YOU THINK SO...?
ANYWAY...
LOOK... LIGHTNING KOWTOW GUY IS FOURTH!
FIRST IS... NARASAKA?
WITH A PERFECT SCORE?!
WHAT A BEAST.
MIKUMO, YUMA.
DIRECTOR SHINODA...
THANKS FOR YOUR HELP TODAY.
ESPECIALLY FOR THE INFORMATION ON THE NEIGHBORHOOD.

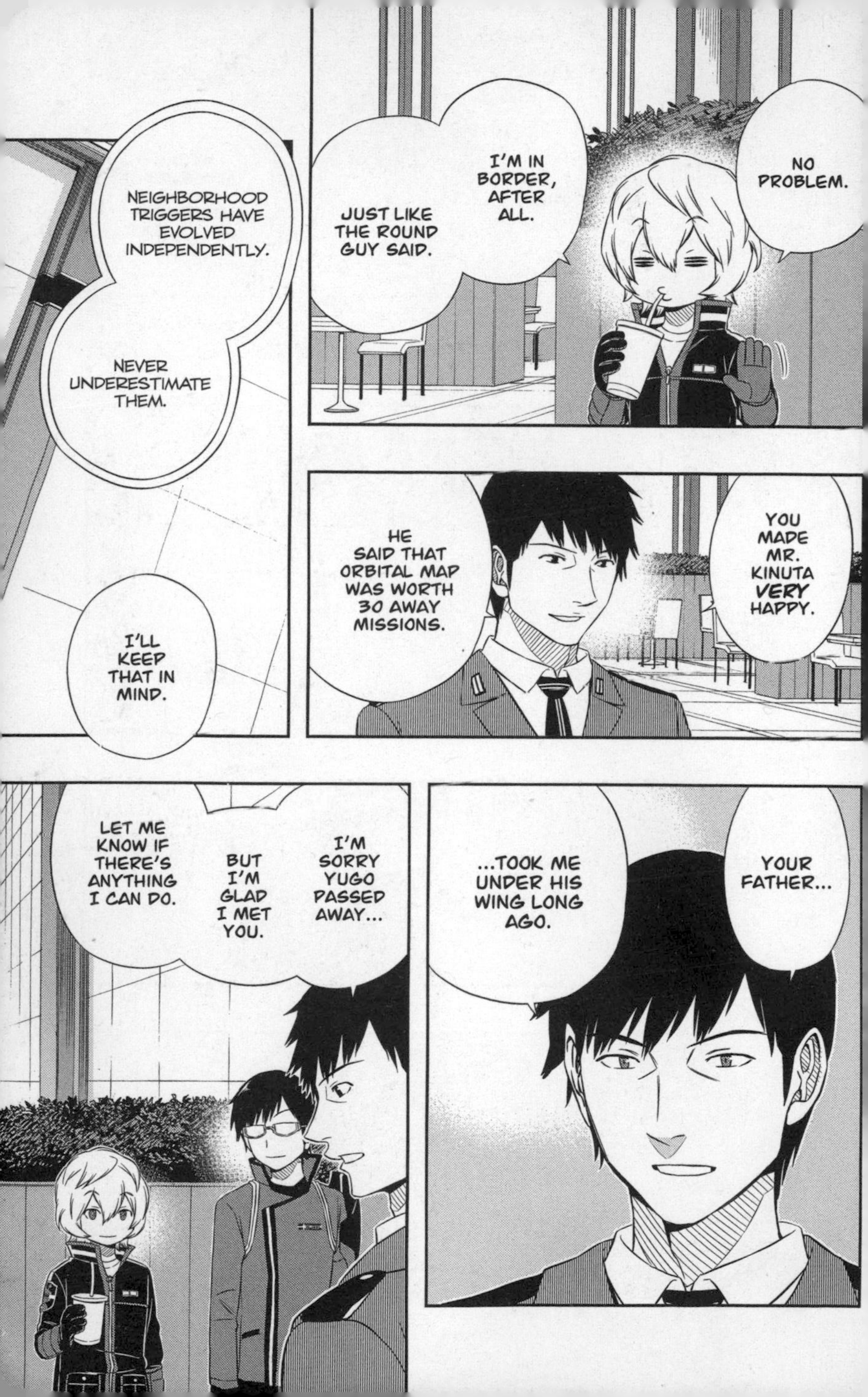
NO PROBLEM.
I'M IN BORDER, AFTER ALL.
JUST LIKE THE ROUND GUY SAID.
YOU MADE MR. KINUTA **VERY** HAPPY.
HE SAID THAT ORBITAL MAP WAS WORTH 30 AWAY MISSIONS.
NEIGHBORHOOD TRIGGERS HAVE EVOLVED INDEPENDENTLY.
NEVER UNDERESTIMATE THEM.
I'LL KEEP THAT IN MIND.
YOUR FATHER...
...TOOK ME UNDER HIS WING LONG AGO.
I'M SORRY YUGO PASSED AWAY...
BUT I'M GLAD I MET YOU.
LET ME KNOW IF THERE'S ANYTHING I CAN DO.

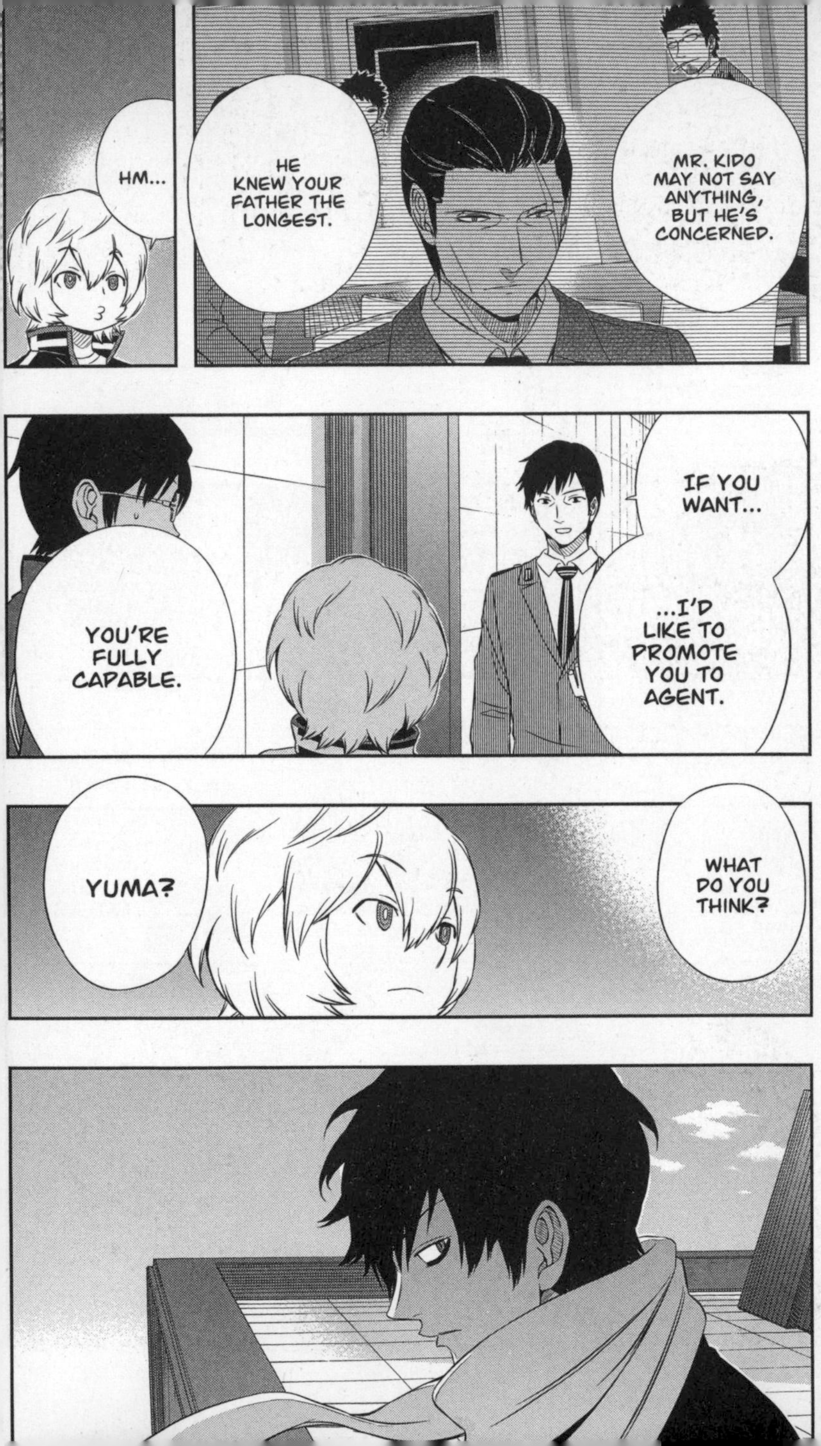
MR. KIDO MAY NOT SAY ANYTHING, BUT HE'S CONCERNED.
HE KNEW YOUR FATHER THE LONGEST.
HM...
IF YOU WANT...
...I'D LIKE TO PROMOTE YOU TO AGENT.
YOU'RE FULLY CAPABLE.
WHAT DO YOU THINK?
YUMA?

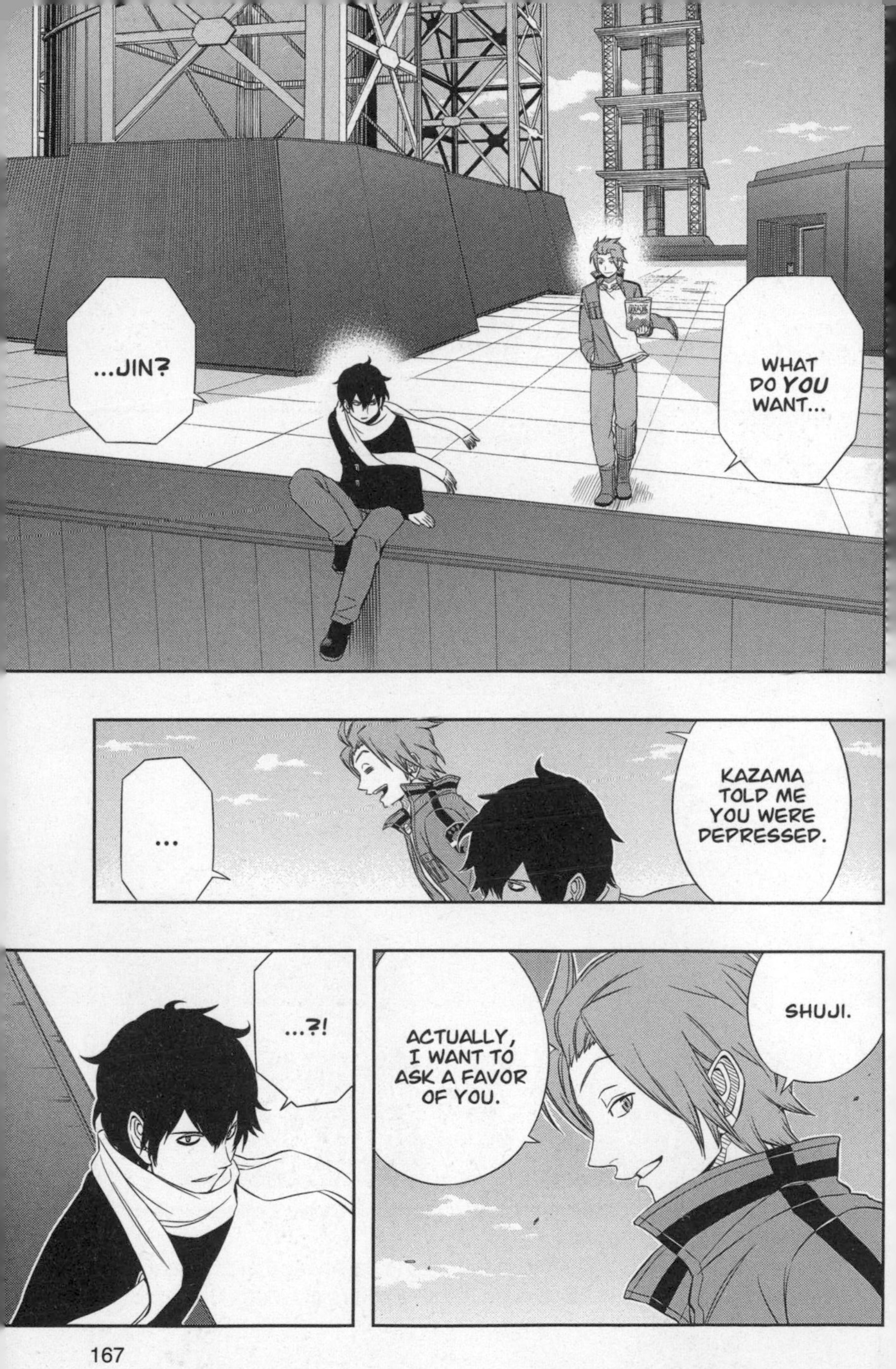
...JIN?
WHAT DO YOU WANT...
KAZAMA TOLD ME YOU WERE DEPRESSED.
...
SHUJI.
ACTUALLY, I WANT TO ASK A FAVOR OF YOU.
...?!

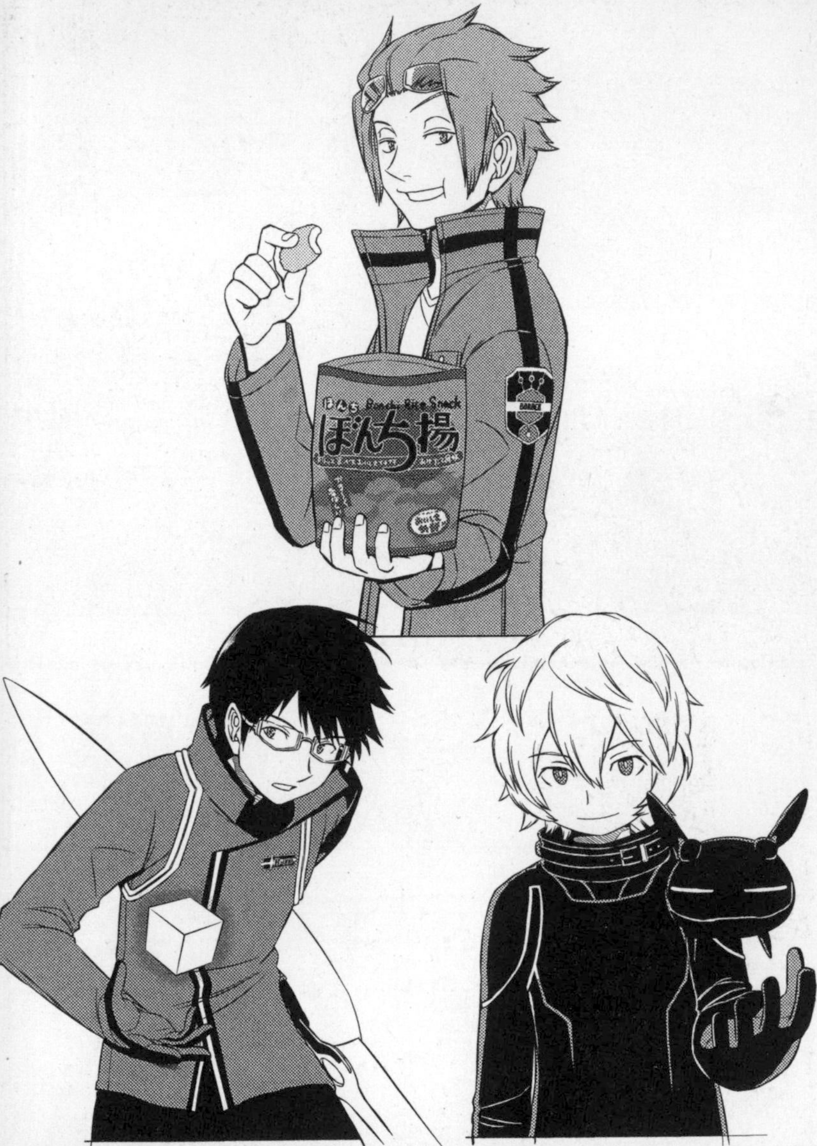
Bonchi Rice Snack
ぼんち揚

■ 2014 Bonchi fried rice crackers / *World Trigger* collaboration packages (three types)

I had a surprising collaboration with Bonchi, the company that makes the fried rice crackers. I intend to keep making the characters eat them. Osamu looks so cool here.

Chapter 43 Yuichi Jin: Part 7

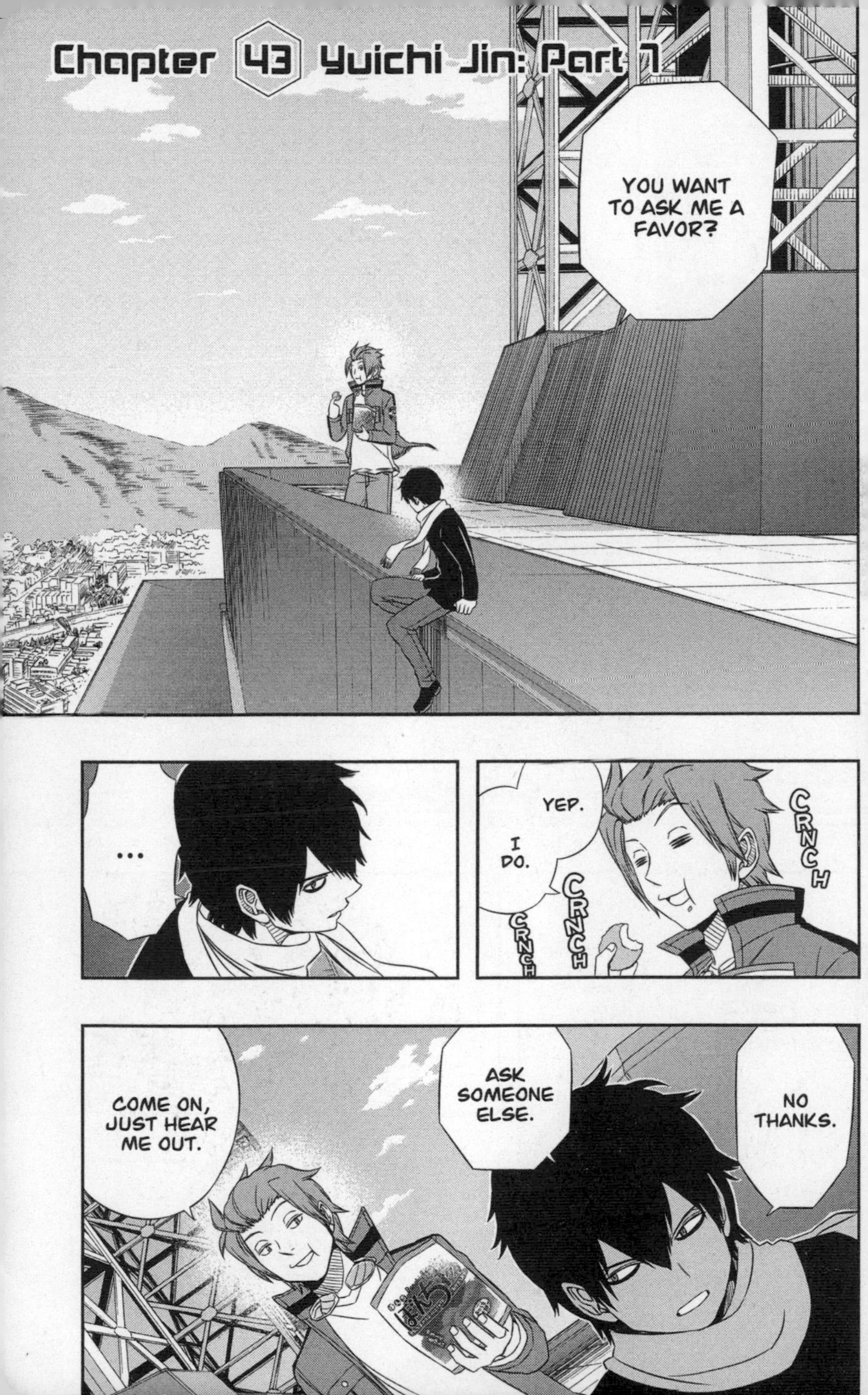
YOU WANT TO ASK ME A FAVOR?
YEP.
I DO.
CRNCH
CRNCH
CRNCH
...
NO THANKS.
ASK SOMEONE ELSE.
COME ON, JUST HEAR ME OUT.

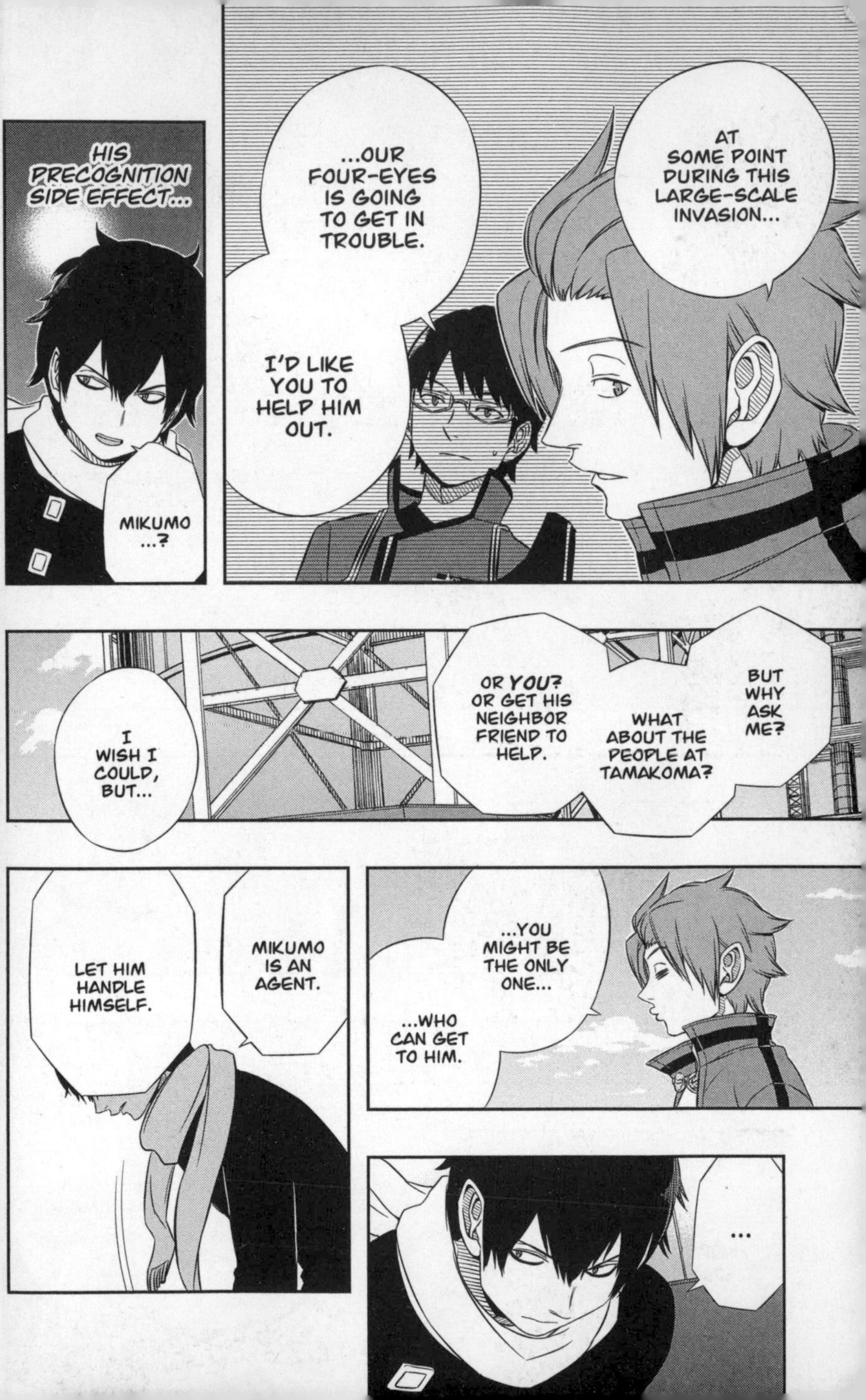
AT SOME POINT DURING THIS LARGE-SCALE INVASION...
...OUR FOUR-EYES IS GOING TO GET IN TROUBLE.
I'D LIKE YOU TO HELP HIM OUT.
HIS PRECOGNITION SIDE EFFECT...
MIKUMO ...?
BUT WHY ASK ME?
WHAT ABOUT THE PEOPLE AT TAMAKOMA?
OR *YOU*? OR GET HIS NEIGHBOR FRIEND TO HELP.
I WISH I COULD, BUT...
...YOU MIGHT BE THE ONLY ONE...
...WHO CAN GET TO HIM.
...
MIKUMO IS AN AGENT.
LET HIM HANDLE HIMSELF.

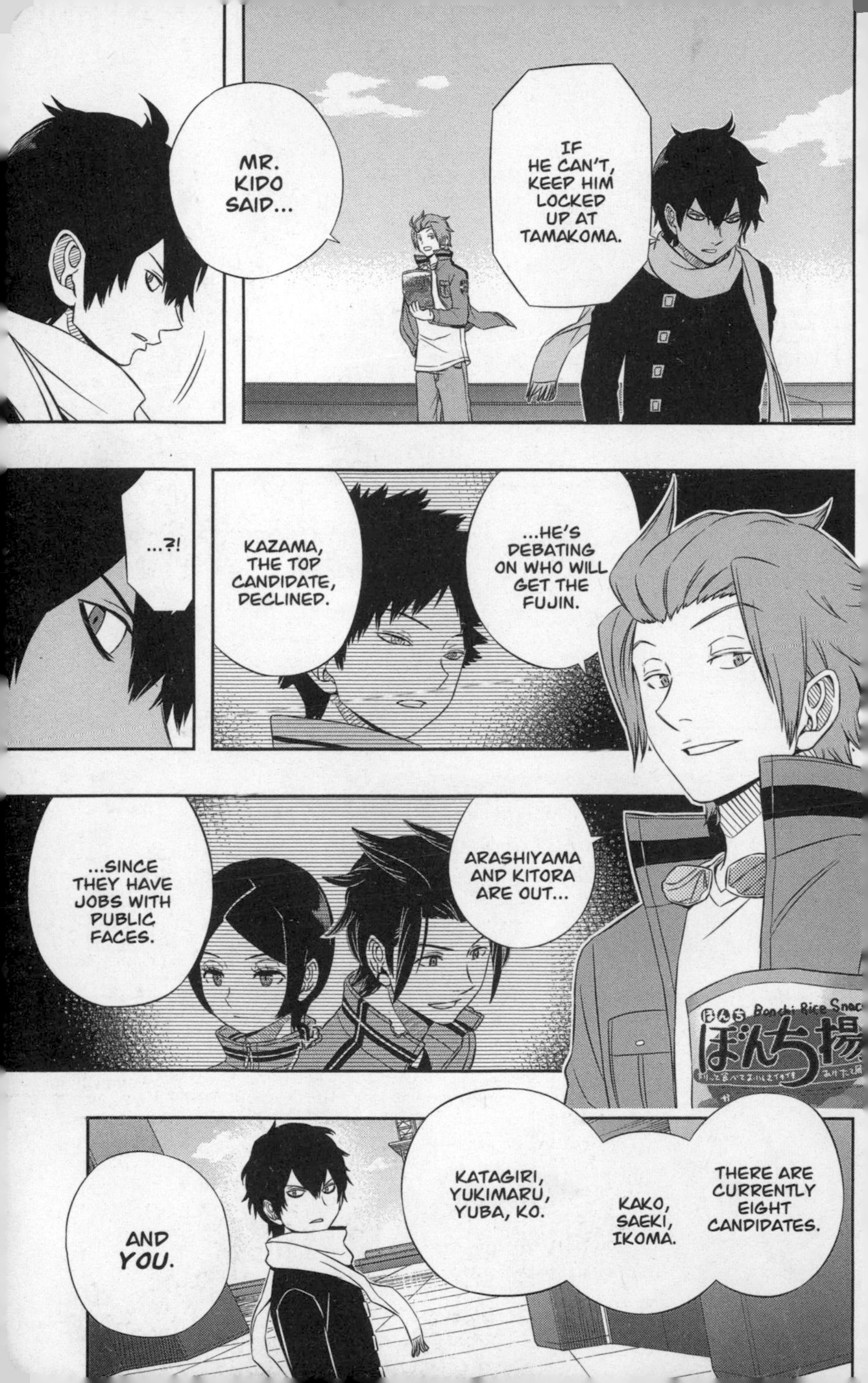
IF HE CAN'T, KEEP HIM LOCKED UP AT TAMAKOMA.
MR. KIDO SAID...
...HE'S DEBATING ON WHO WILL GET THE FUJIN.
Bonchi Rice Snac
ぼんち揚
KAZAMA, THE TOP CANDIDATE, DECLINED.
...?!
ARASHIYAMA AND KITORA ARE OUT...
...SINCE THEY HAVE JOBS WITH PUBLIC FACES.
THERE ARE CURRENTLY EIGHT CANDIDATES.
KAKO, SAEKI, IKOMA.
KATAGIRI, YUKIMARU, YUBA, KO.
AND *YOU*.

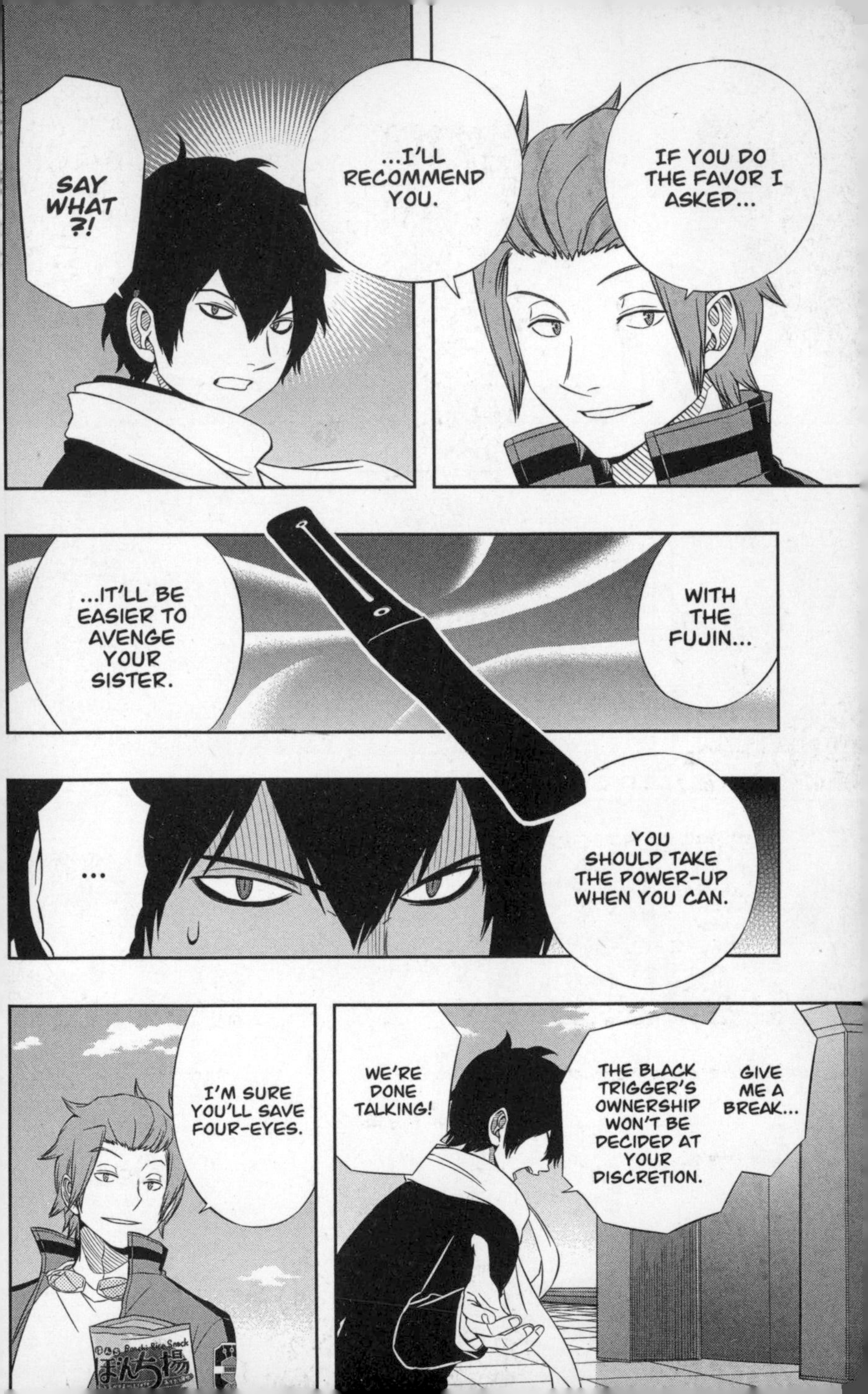
IF YOU DO THE FAVOR I ASKED...
...I'LL RECOMMEND YOU.
SAY WHAT?!
WITH THE FUJIN...
...IT'LL BE EASIER TO AVENGE YOUR SISTER.
YOU SHOULD TAKE THE POWER-UP WHEN YOU CAN.
...
GIVE ME A BREAK...
THE BLACK TRIGGER'S OWNERSHIP WON'T BE DECIDED AT YOUR DISCRETION.
WE'RE DONE TALKING!
I'M SURE YOU'LL SAVE FOUR-EYES.

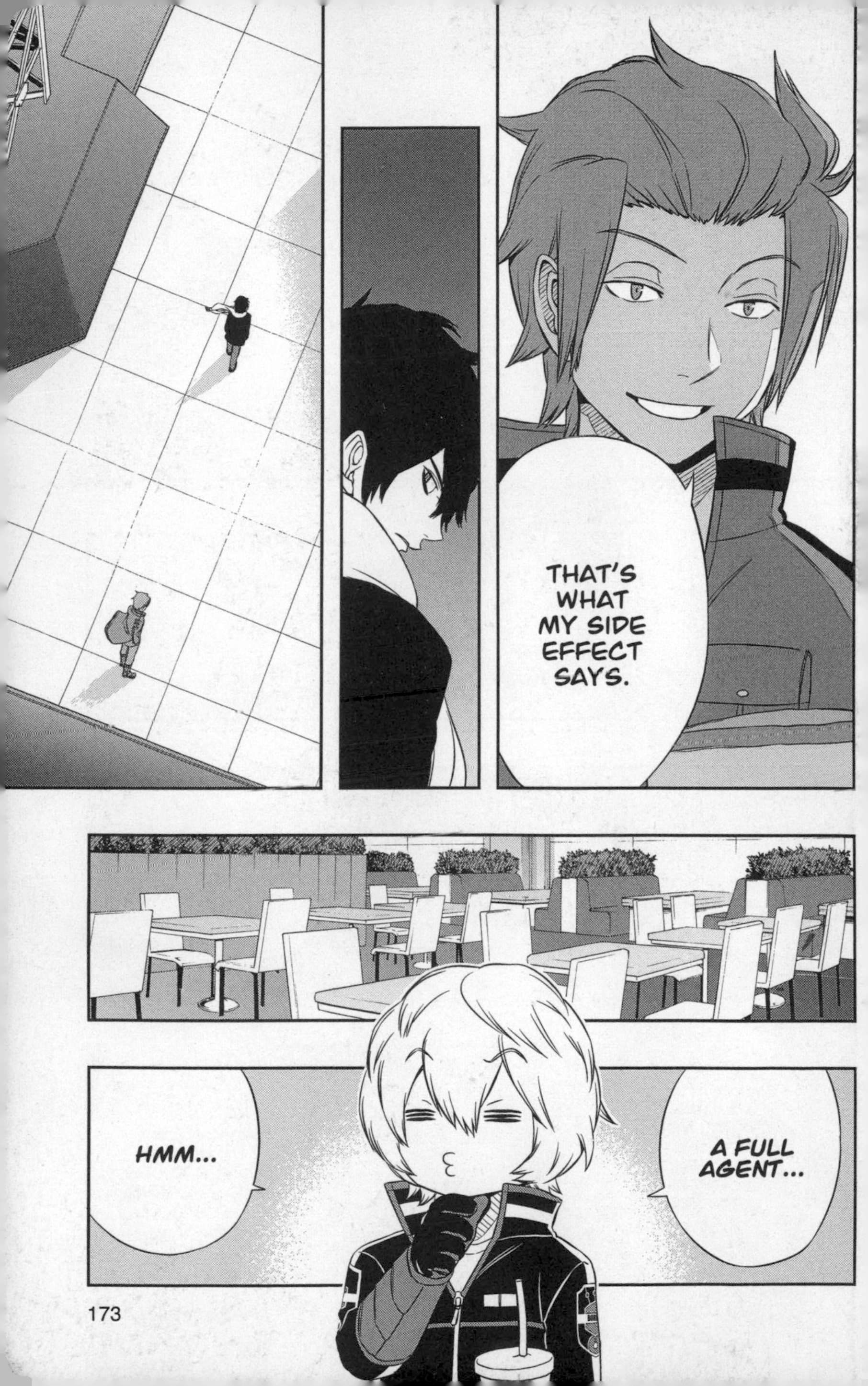
THAT'S WHAT MY SIDE EFFECT SAYS.
A FULL AGENT...
HMM...

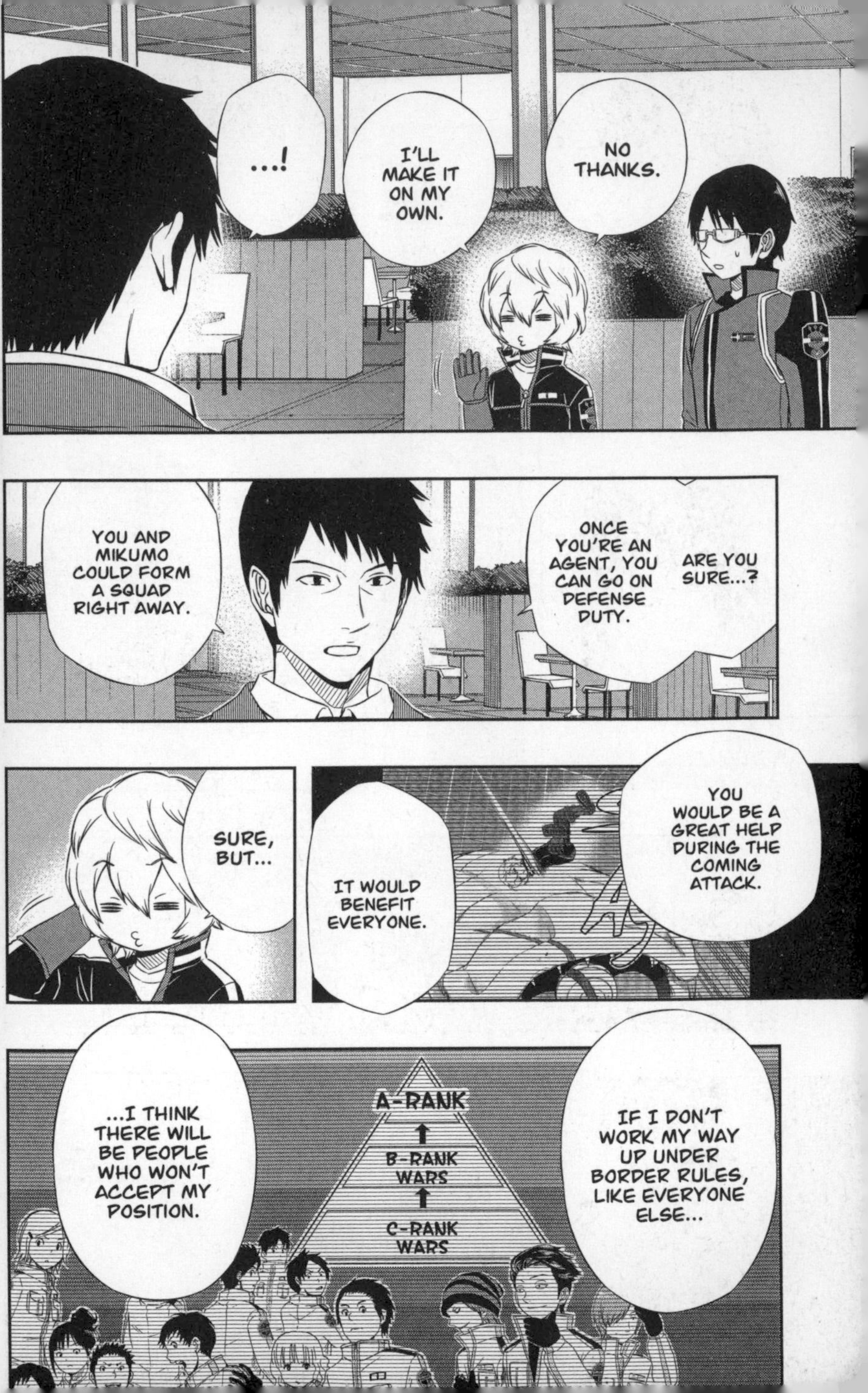
NO THANKS.
I'LL MAKE IT ON MY OWN.
...!
ARE YOU SURE...?
ONCE YOU'RE AN AGENT, YOU CAN GO ON DEFENSE DUTY.
YOU AND MIKUMO COULD FORM A SQUAD RIGHT AWAY.
YOU WOULD BE A GREAT HELP DURING THE COMING ATTACK.
IT WOULD BENEFIT EVERYONE.
SURE, BUT...
IF I DON'T WORK MY WAY UP UNDER BORDER RULES, LIKE EVERYONE ELSE...
A-RANK
B-RANK WARS
C-RANK WARS
...I THINK THERE WILL BE PEOPLE WHO WON'T ACCEPT MY POSITION.

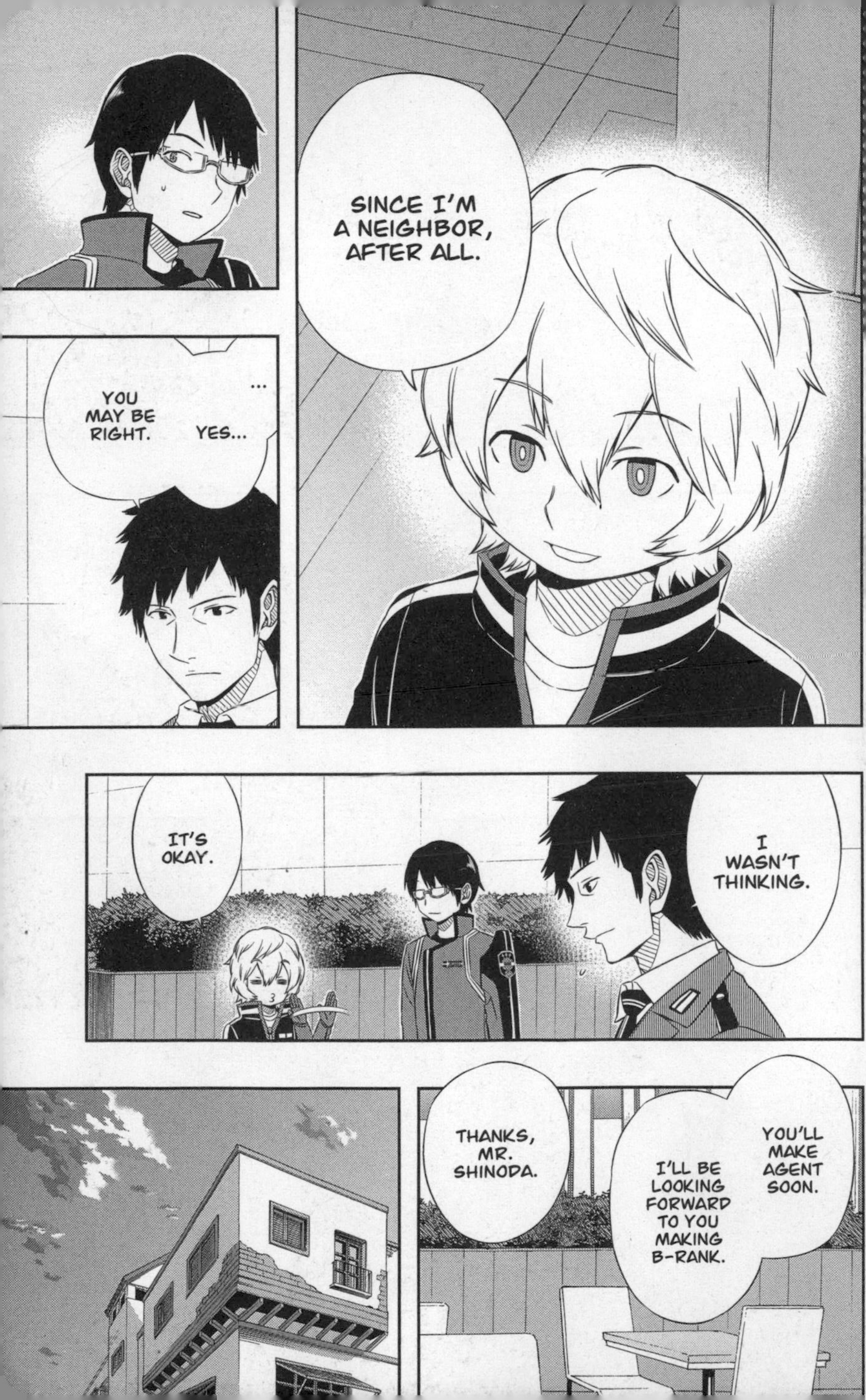
SINCE I'M A NEIGHBOR, AFTER ALL.
...
YES...
YOU MAY BE RIGHT.
I WASN'T THINKING.
IT'S OKAY.
YOU'LL MAKE AGENT SOON.
I'LL BE LOOKING FORWARD TO YOU MAKING B-RANK.
THANKS, MR. SHINODA.

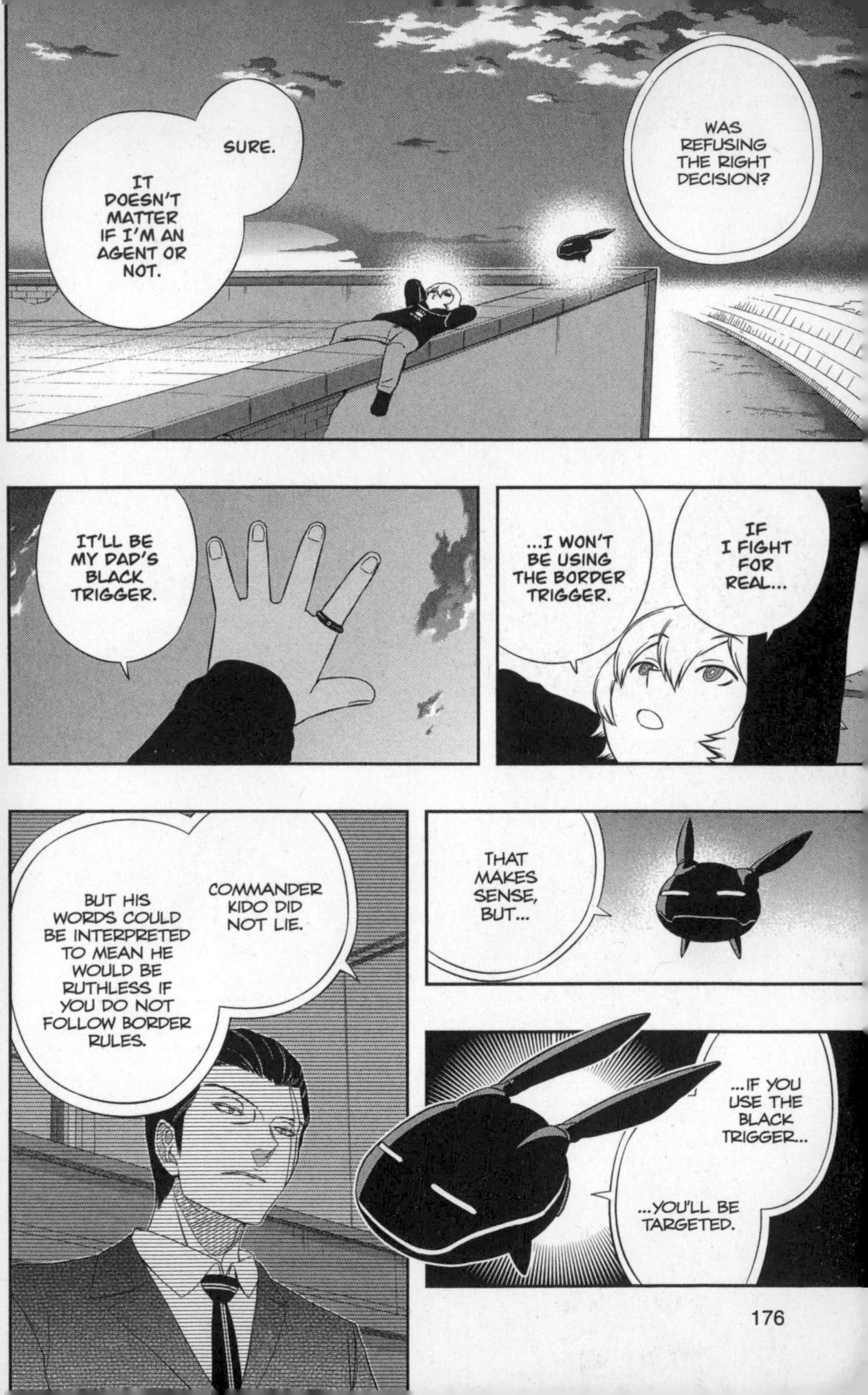
WAS REFUSING THE RIGHT DECISION?
SURE.
IT DOESN'T MATTER IF I'M AN AGENT OR NOT.
IF I FIGHT FOR REAL...
...I WON'T BE USING THE BORDER TRIGGER.
IT'LL BE MY DAD'S BLACK TRIGGER.
THAT MAKES SENSE, BUT...
...IF YOU USE THE BLACK TRIGGER...
...YOU'LL BE TARGETED.
COMMANDER KIDO DID NOT LIE.
BUT HIS WORDS COULD BE INTERPRETED TO MEAN HE WOULD BE RUTHLESS IF YOU DO NOT FOLLOW BORDER RULES.

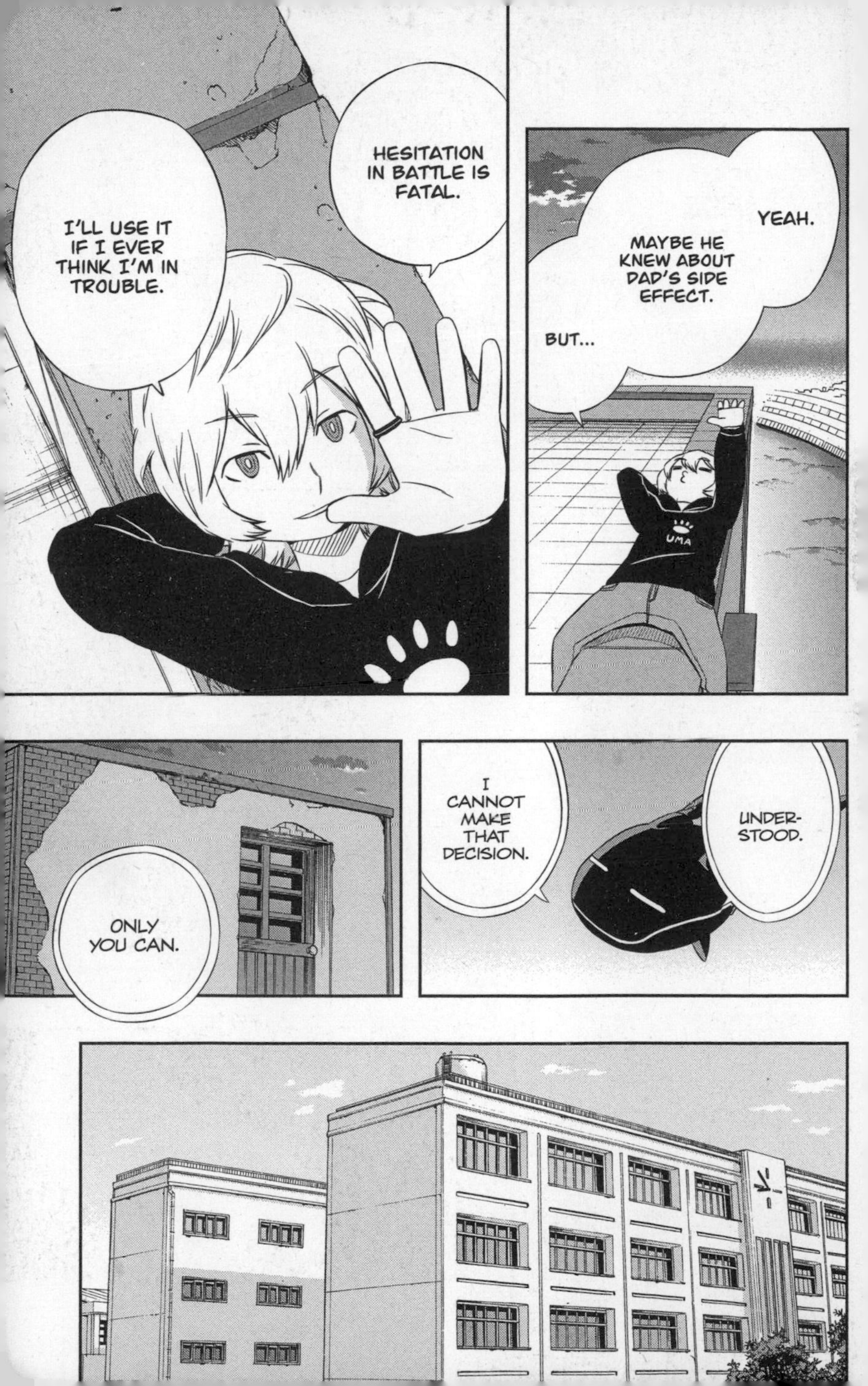
YEAH.
MAYBE HE KNEW ABOUT DAD'S SIDE EFFECT.
BUT...
HESITATION IN BATTLE IS FATAL.
I'LL USE IT IF I EVER THINK I'M IN TROUBLE.
UNDER-STOOD.
I CANNOT MAKE THAT DECISION.
ONLY YOU CAN.

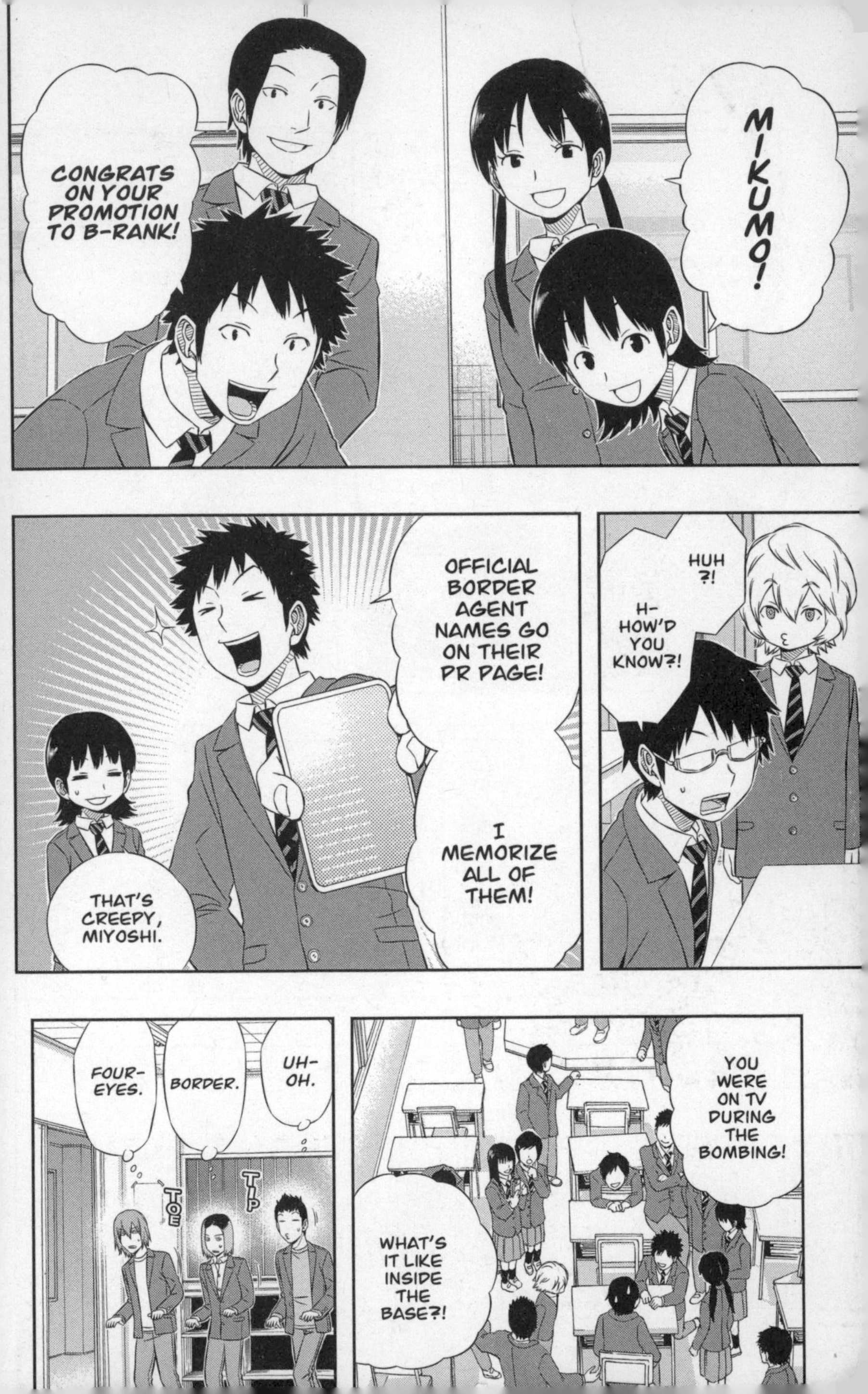
MIKUMO!
CONGRATS ON YOUR PROMOTION TO B-RANK!
HUH?!
H-HOW'D YOU KNOW?!
OFFICIAL BORDER AGENT NAMES GO ON THEIR PR PAGE!
I MEMORIZE ALL OF THEM!
THAT'S CREEPY, MIYOSHI.
YOU WERE ON TV DURING THE BOMBING!
WHAT'S IT LIKE INSIDE THE BASE?!
UH-OH.
BORDER.
FOUR-EYES.
TIP
TOE

READ THIS WAY

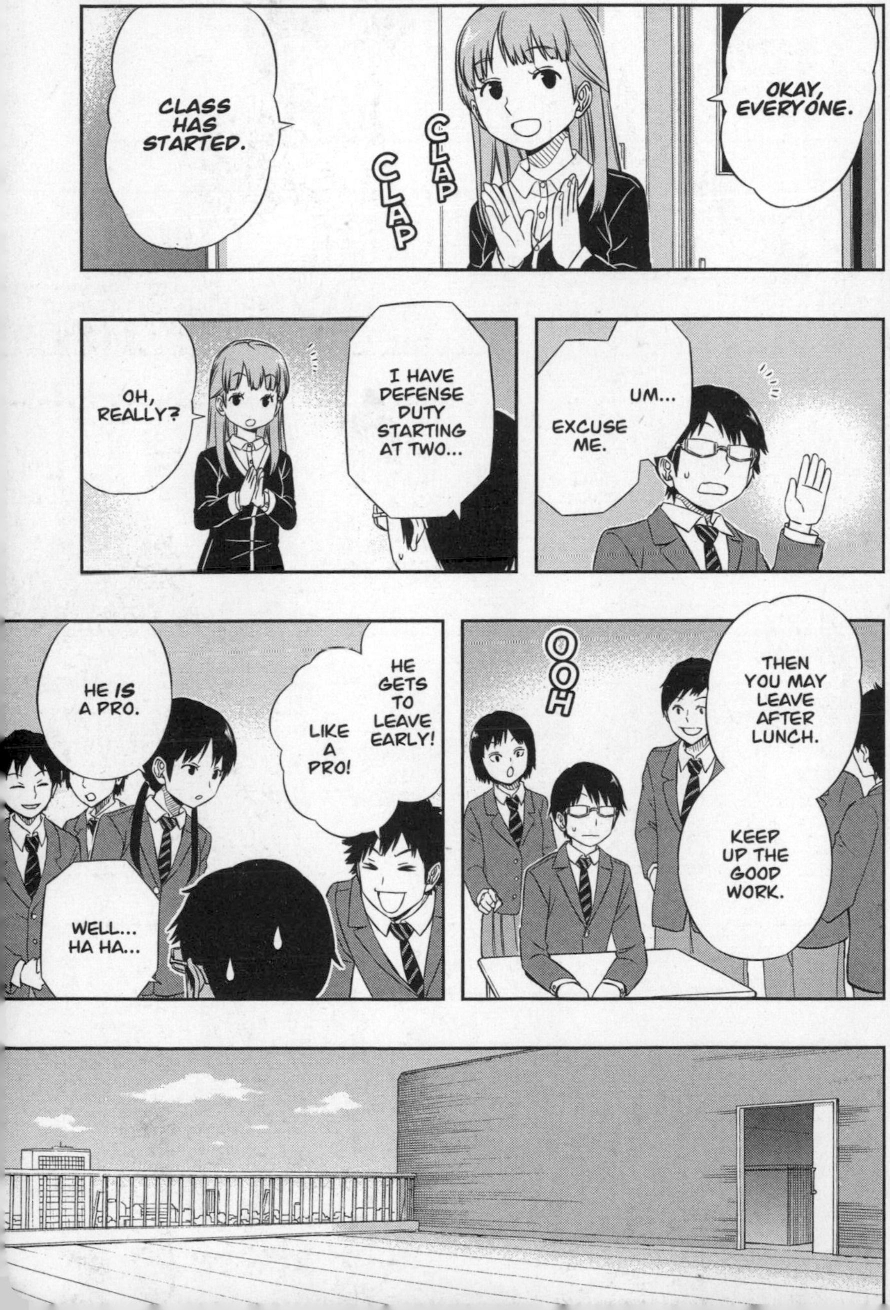
OKAY, EVERYONE.
CLAP CLAP
CLASS HAS STARTED.
UM... EXCUSE ME.
I HAVE DEFENSE DUTY STARTING AT TWO...
OH, REALLY?
OOH
THEN YOU MAY LEAVE AFTER LUNCH.
KEEP UP THE GOOD WORK.
HE GETS TO LEAVE EARLY!
LIKE A PRO!
HE IS A PRO.
WELL... HA HA...

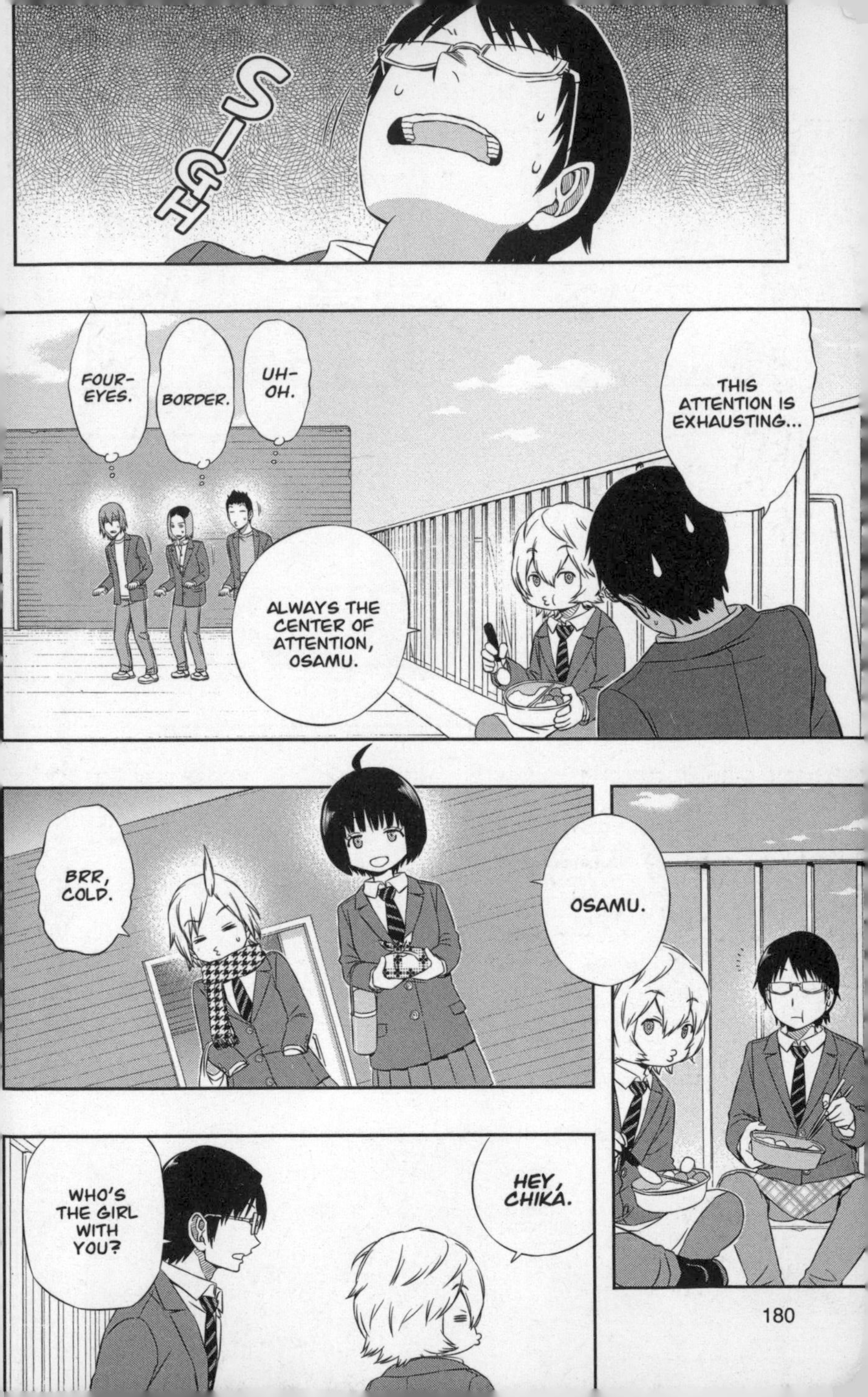
SIGH
THIS ATTENTION IS EXHAUSTING...
UH-OH.
BORDER.
FOUR-EYES.
ALWAYS THE CENTER OF ATTENTION, OSAMU.
OSAMU.
BRR, COLD.
HEY, CHIKA.
WHO'S THE GIRL WITH YOU?

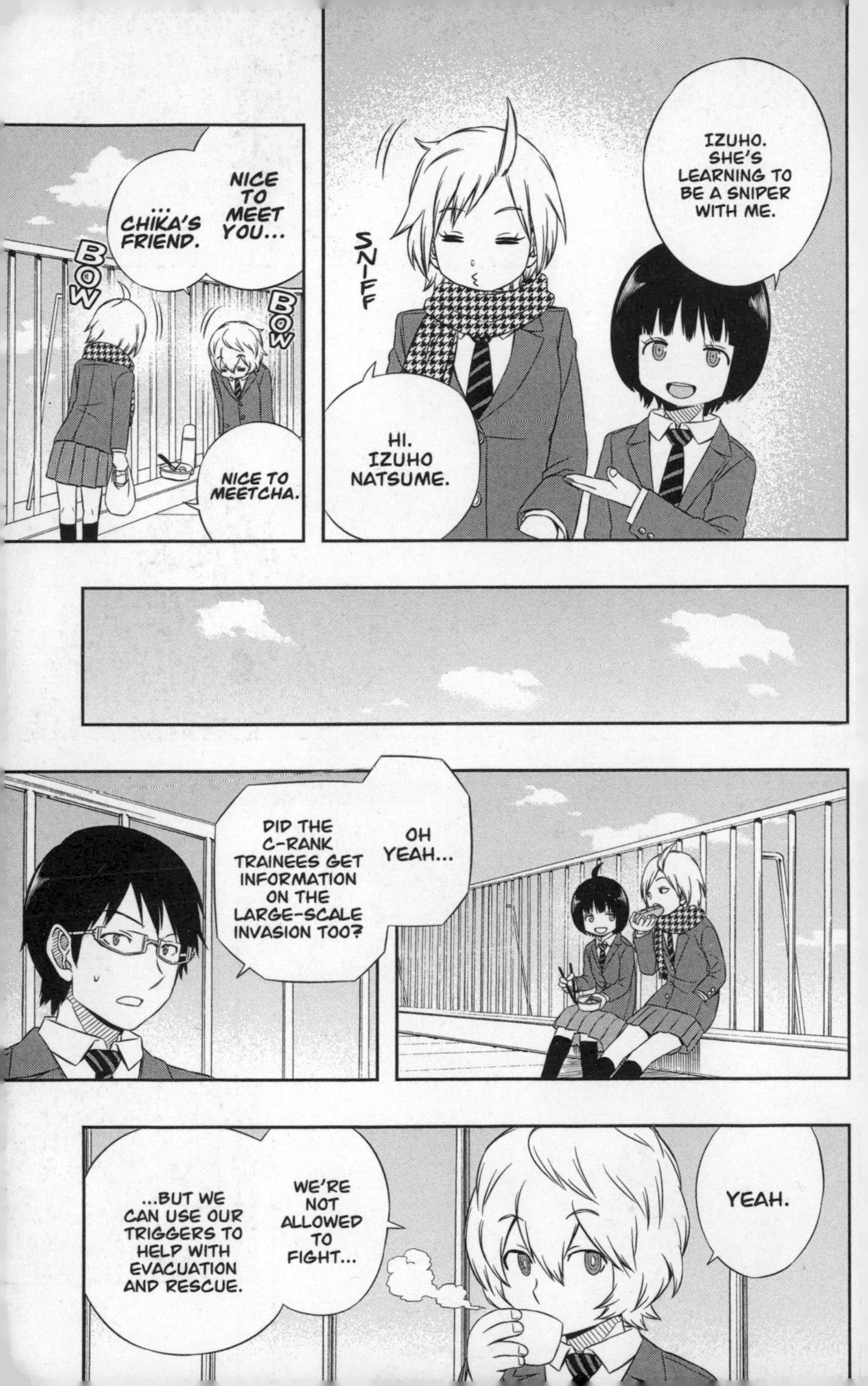
IZUHO. SHE'S LEARNING TO BE A SNIPER WITH ME.
SNIFF
HI. IZUHO NATSUME.
NICE TO MEET YOU...
...CHIKA'S FRIEND.
BOW
BOW
NICE TO MEETCHA.
OH YEAH...
DID THE C-RANK TRAINEES GET INFORMATION ON THE LARGE-SCALE INVASION TOO?
YEAH.
WE'RE NOT ALLOWED TO FIGHT...
...BUT WE CAN USE OUR TRIGGERS TO HELP WITH EVACUATION AND RESCUE.

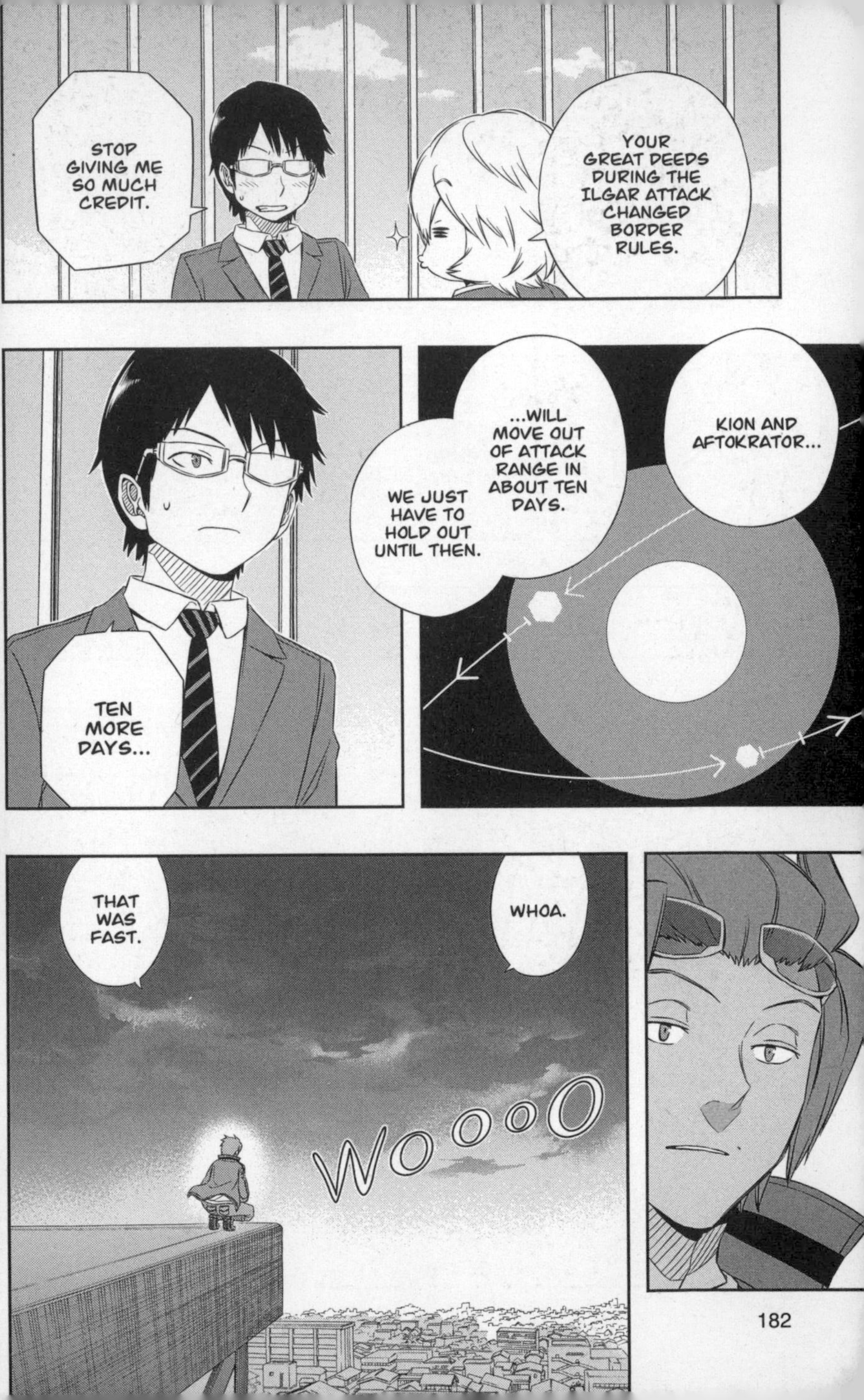
YOUR GREAT DEEDS DURING THE ILGAR ATTACK CHANGED BORDER RULES.
STOP GIVING ME SO MUCH CREDIT.
KION AND AFTOKRATOR...
...WILL MOVE OUT OF ATTACK RANGE IN ABOUT TEN DAYS.
WE JUST HAVE TO HOLD OUT UNTIL THEN.
TEN MORE DAYS...
WHOA.
THAT WAS FAST.
WOoooO

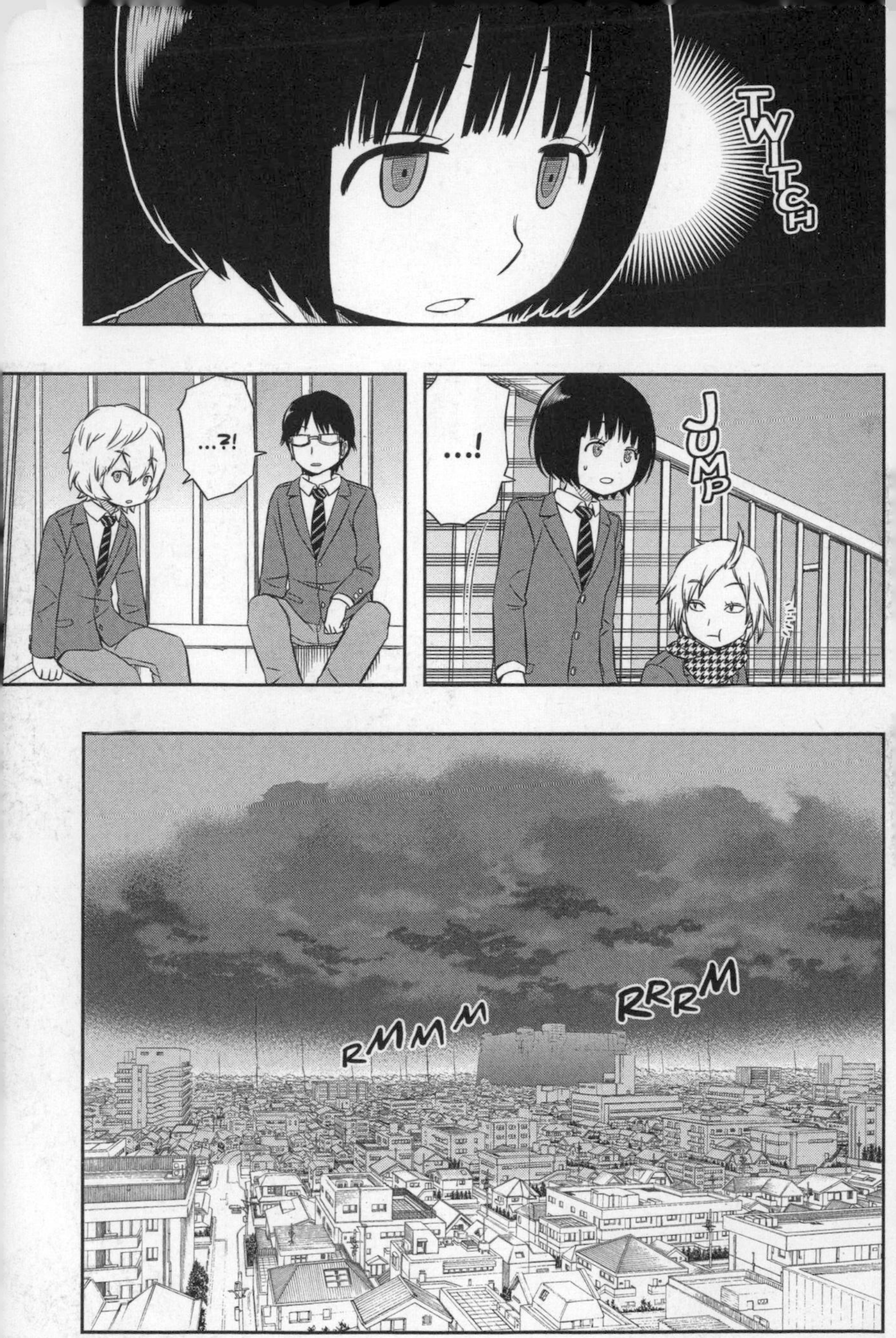
TWITCH
...!
JUMP
...?!
RRRM
RMMM

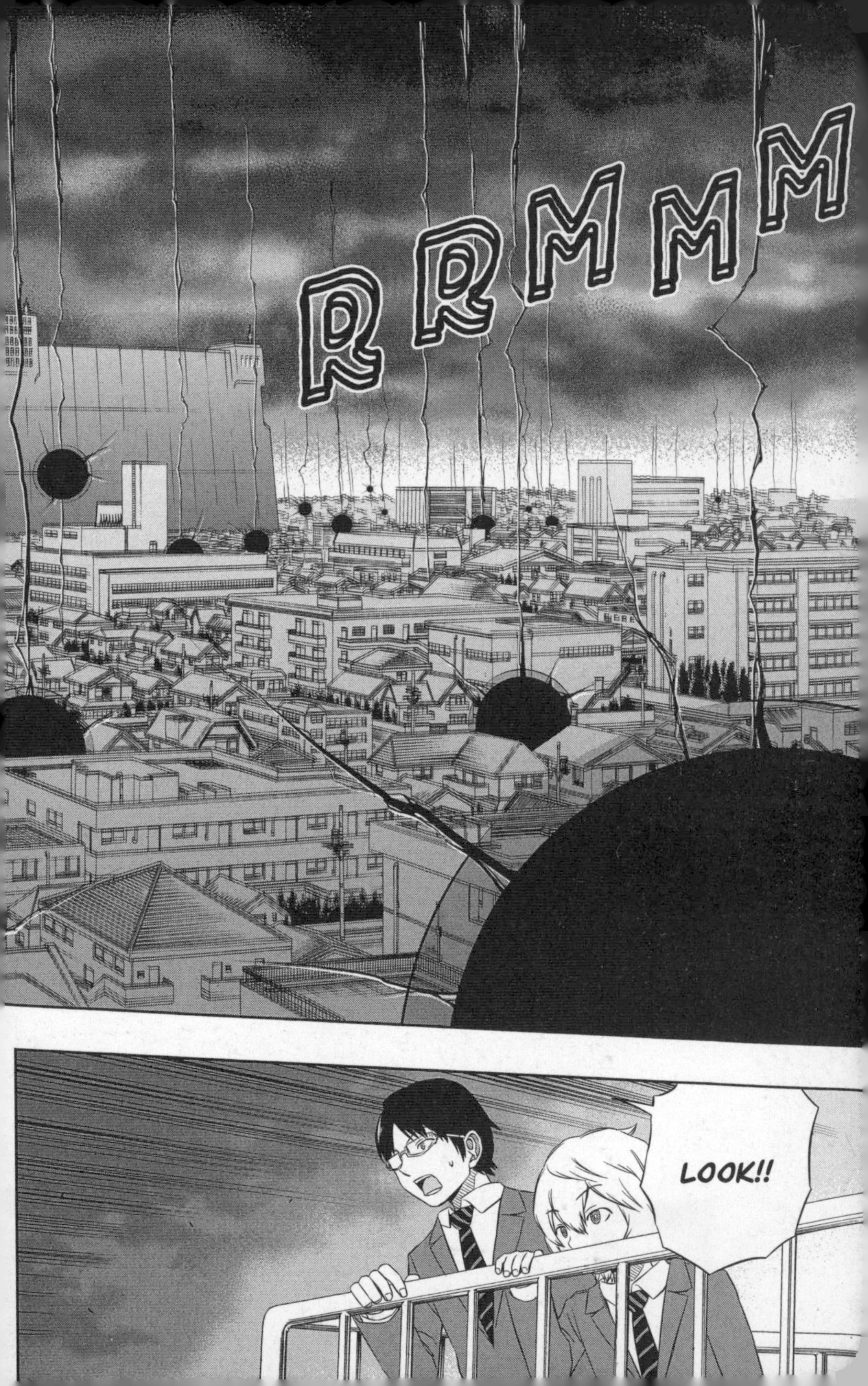
RRRMMMM
LOOK!!

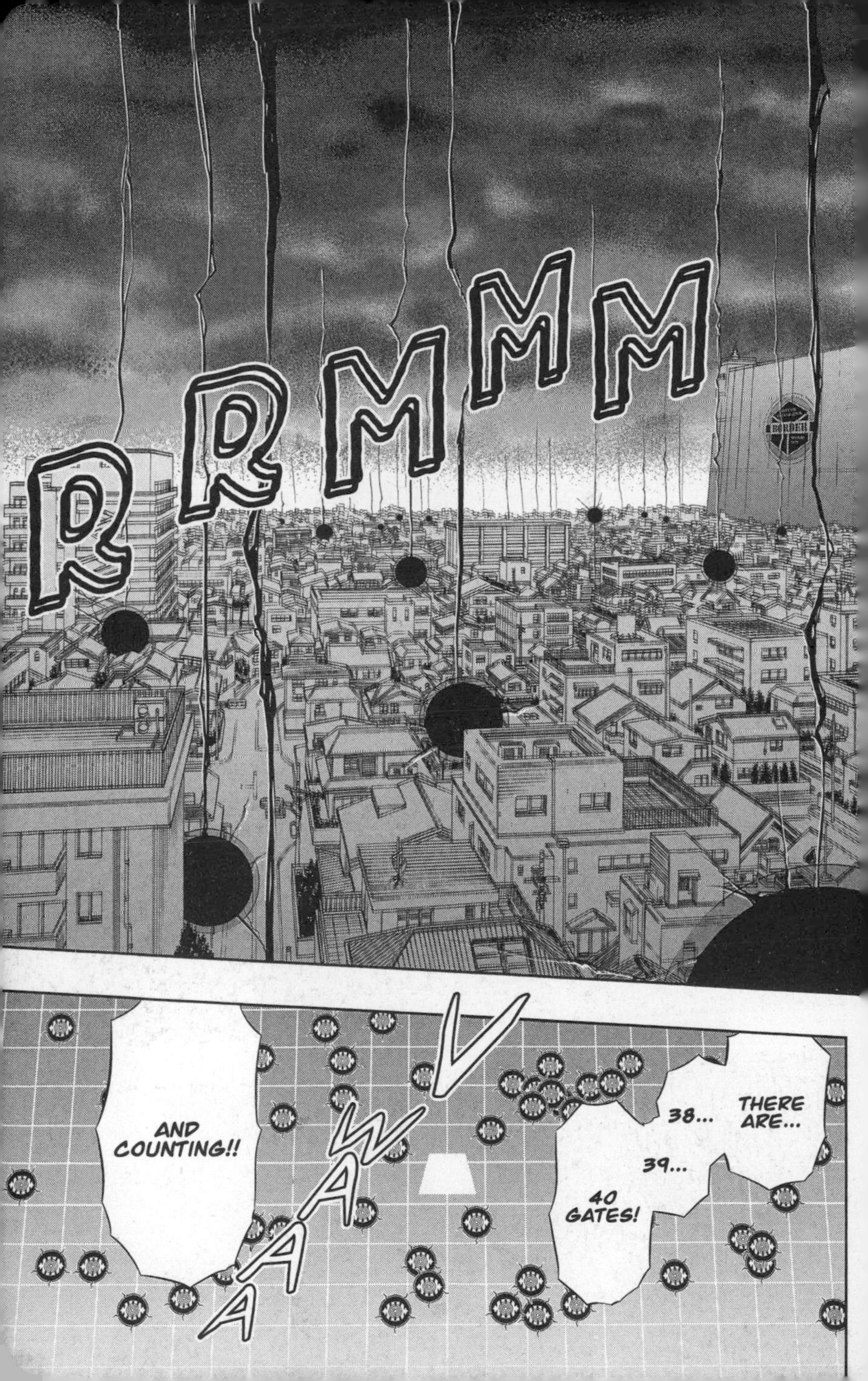
RRMMM
THERE ARE...
38...
39...
40 GATES!
VWAAA
AND COUNTING!!

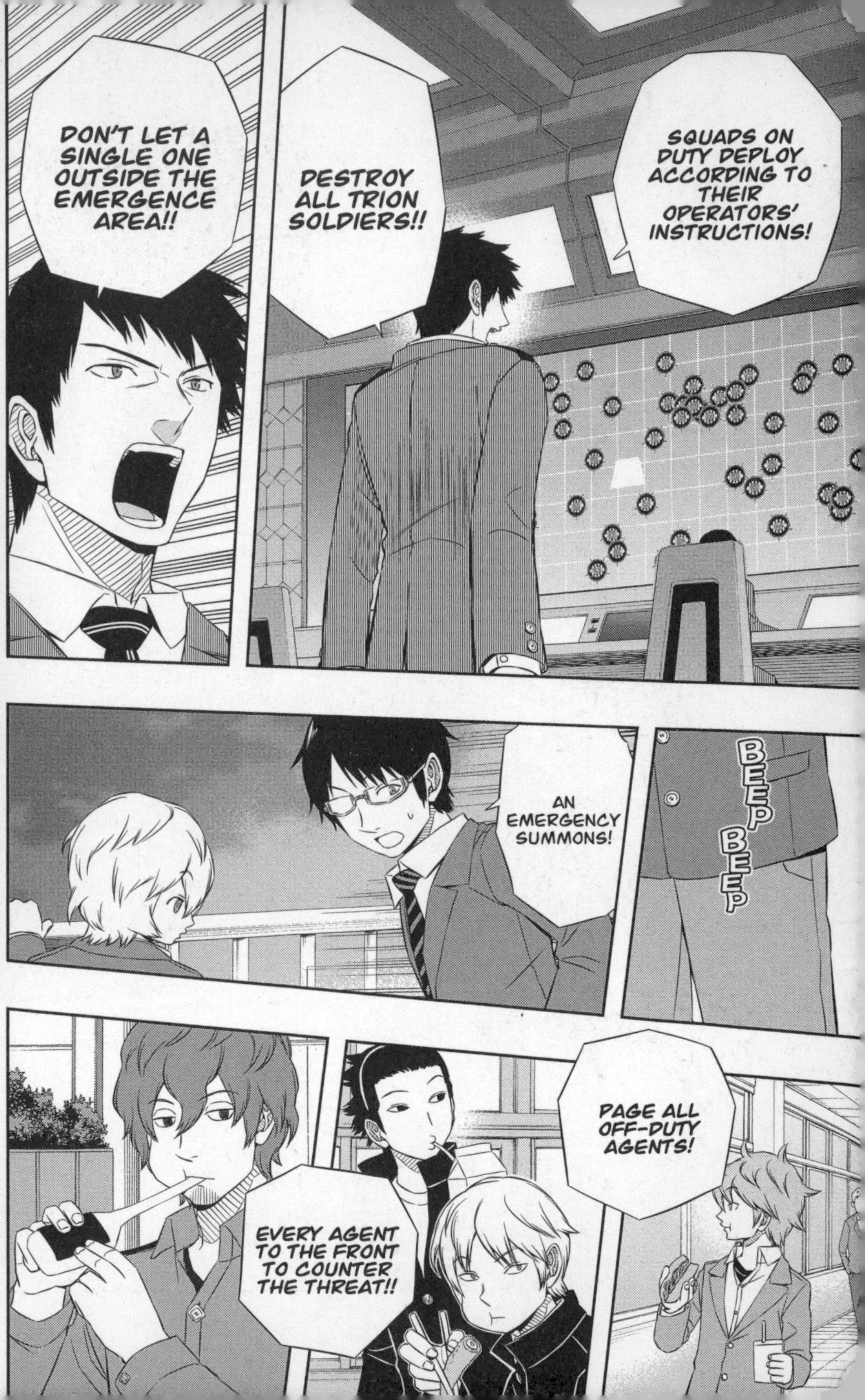
SQUADS ON DUTY DEPLOY ACCORDING TO THEIR OPERATORS' INSTRUCTIONS!
DESTROY ALL TRION SOLDIERS!!
DON'T LET A SINGLE ONE OUTSIDE THE EMERGENCE AREA!!
BEEP BEEP BEEP
AN EMERGENCY SUMMONS!
PAGE ALL OFF-DUTY AGENTS!
EVERY AGENT TO THE FRONT TO COUNTER THE THREAT!!

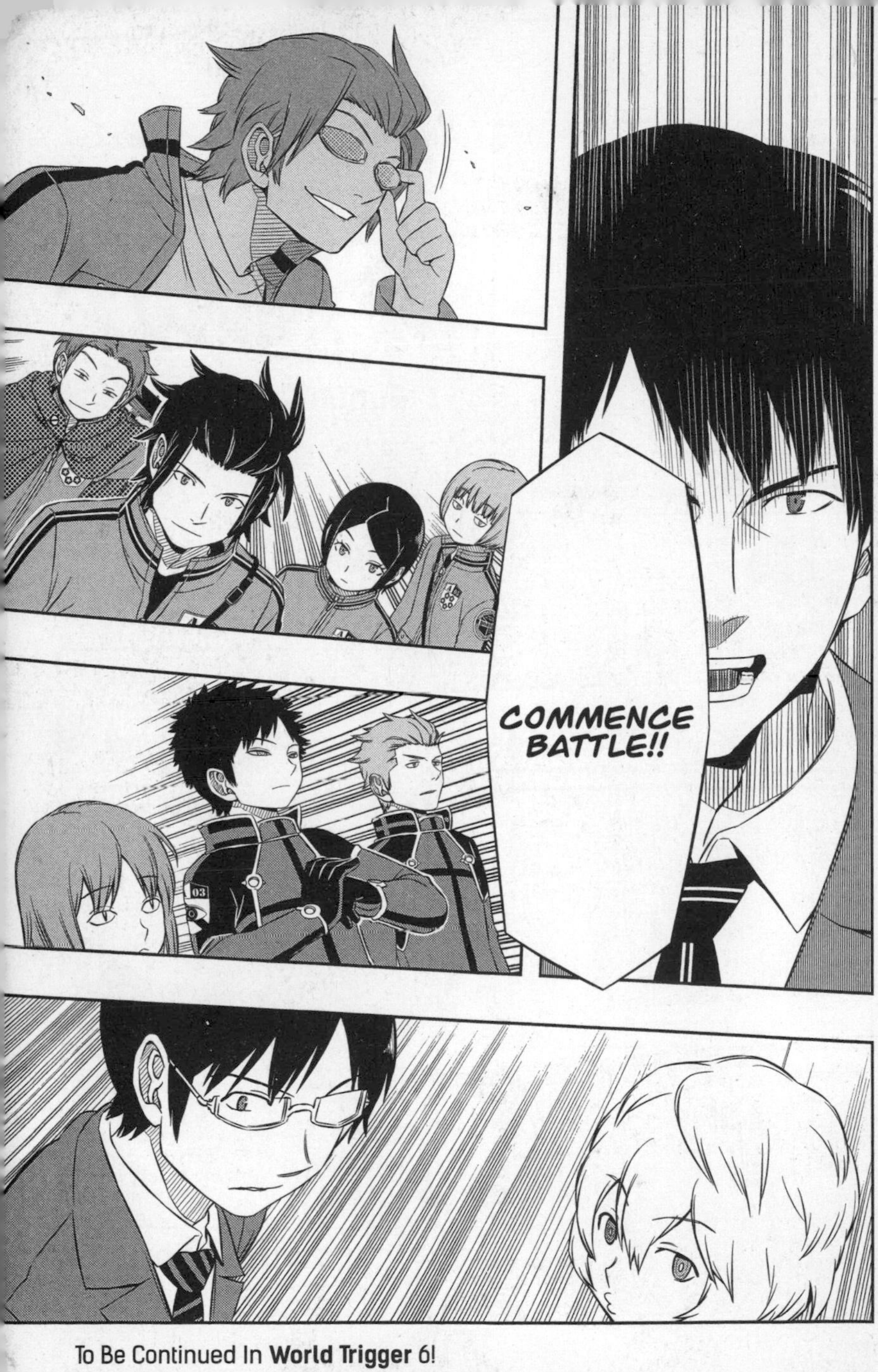
COMMENCE BATTLE!!

To Be Continued In **World Trigger** 6!

Jump NEXT! 2014 Issue 1

WORLD TRIGGER

Bonus Comic Strips

If Osamu

said to someone eating pasta with a spoon:

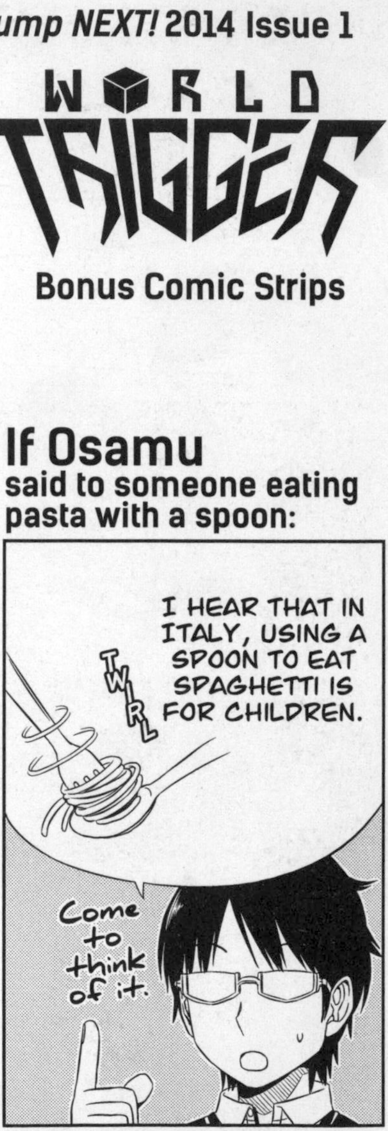
I HEAR THAT IN ITALY, USING A SPOON TO EAT SPAGHETTI IS FOR CHILDREN.
TWIRL
Come to think of it.

What would happen?

Konami's Case

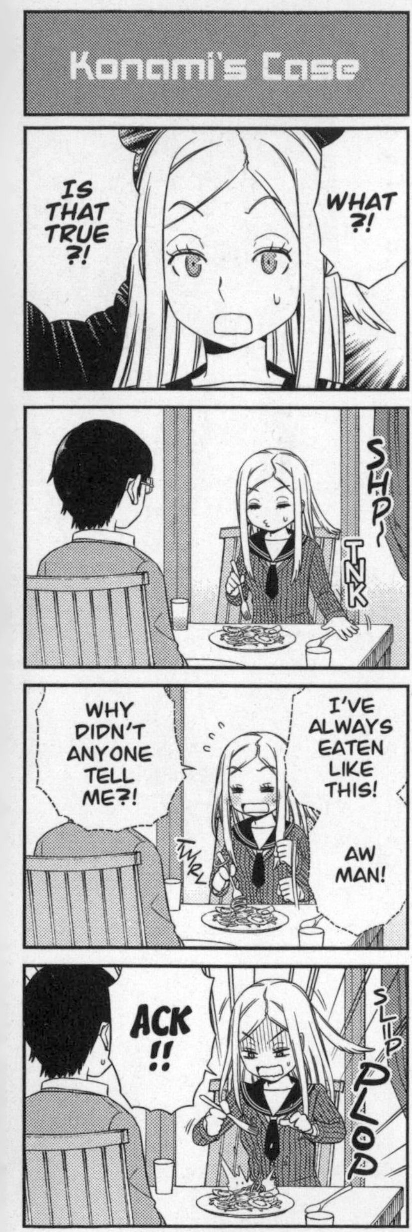
WHAT ?!
IS THAT TRUE ?!
SHP~
TNK
I'VE ALWAYS EATEN LIKE THIS!
WHY DIDN'T ANYONE TELL ME?!
AW MAN!
TWRL
SLIP
PLOP
ACK !!

Shiori's Case

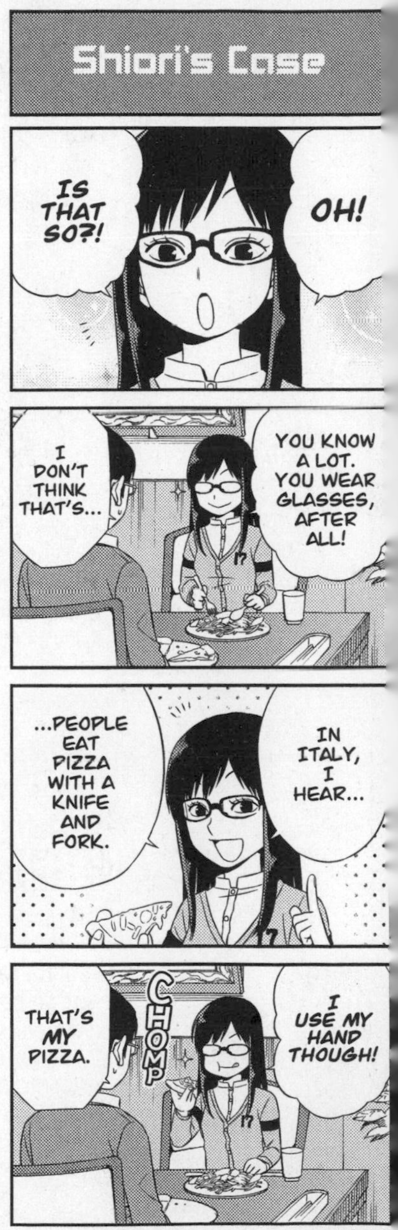
OH!
IS THAT SO?!
YOU KNOW A LOT. YOU WEAR GLASSES, AFTER ALL!
I DON'T THINK THAT'S...
IN ITALY, I HEAR...
...PEOPLE EAT PIZZA WITH A KNIFE AND FORK.
I USE MY HAND THOUGH!
CHOMP
THAT'S MY PIZZA.

Kazama's Case

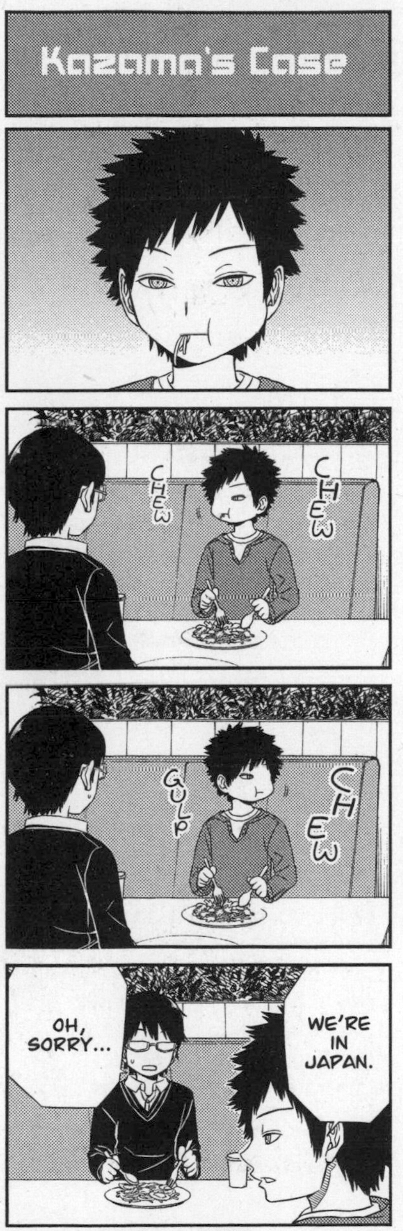
CHEW
CHEW
CHEW
GULP
WE'RE IN JAPAN.
OH, SORRY...

Bonus strips: END

WORLD TRIGGER

Bonus Character Pages

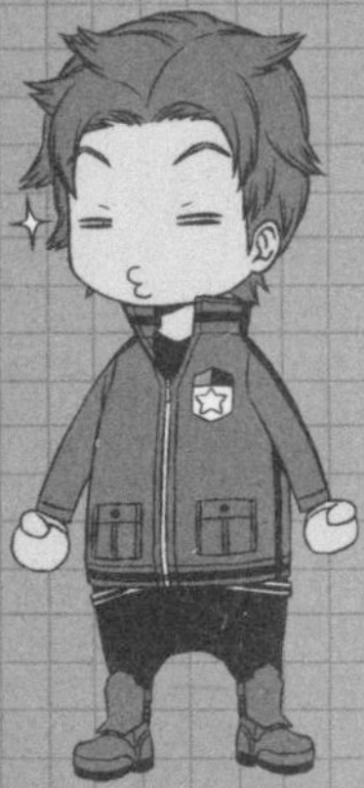

SATO-KEN

Didja See My Lightning Kowtow

My plan was to make him one of Border's foremost playboys, with Arashiyama Squad fangirls screaming for him, but he turned into the kowtowing comic relief. I'll state here that it was through no fault of Satori's, but because girls were already screaming for Arashiyama. I wanted to avoid overlap.

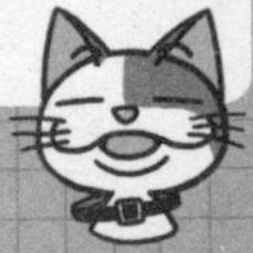

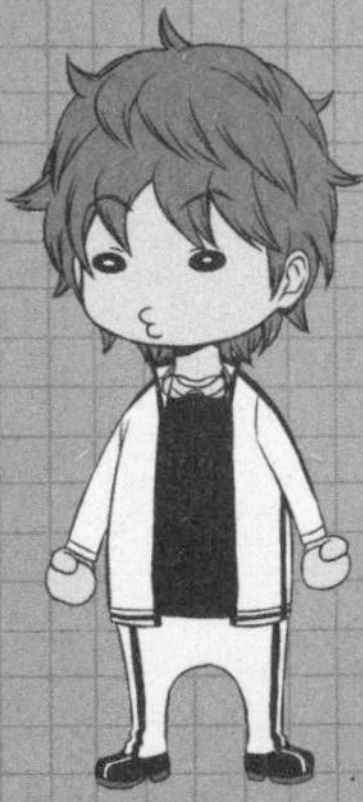

MIDORIKAWA

A-Rank Jin Fan

First mentioned in volume 2 (chapter 10). He was going to be one of *World Trigger*'s rare jerk characters, but he matured during battle, and as if in orbit, circled back to dancing around Jin. A valuable younger character, the same age as Chika. Might be a juicy role.

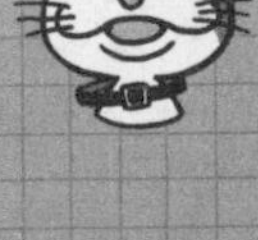

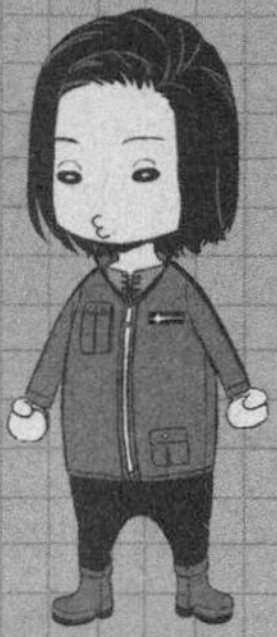

AZUMA

Low-tension, Long-range, Long-hair

Border's first Sniper, a dyed-in-the-wool, long-range, long-hair guy. He taught sniping to Reiji, Toma and Narasaka. He also has the smarts to use Satori as an icebreaker. He probably blames Satori for a lot of things too. And he still gets a lot of respect.

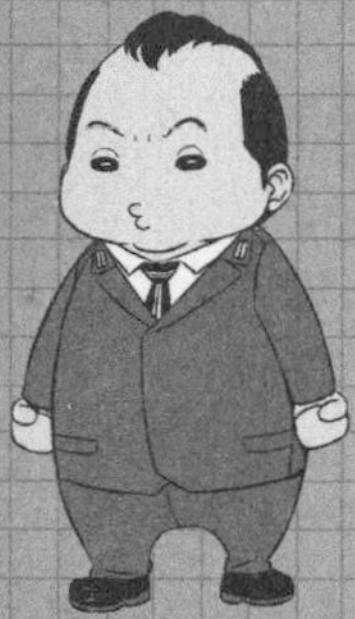

MR. KINUTA

Talented Tanuki

He made a deal with the devil: he became an R&D genius in exchange for giving up human form. His cheeks get bigger with every chapter, engaging in a silent battle with gravity. The spell will be broken in the final chapter. Probably while seeing a vision of himself becoming handsome again and reuniting with his wife and daughter, he'll die at work.

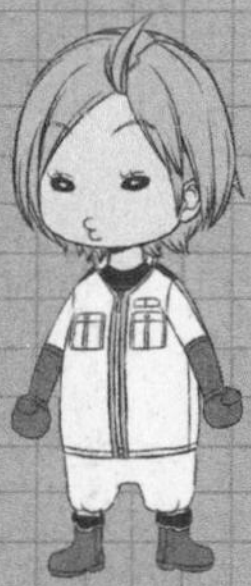

IZUHO

Probably Stronger than Sato-ken in a Fistfight

She hates kids, but she's the type that kids gravitate to. I imagined her as a B-Rank Sniper, but she got demoted to interact with Chika. Now she has more screen time. She's one of my favorite among the current bit players. She's easy to draw and easy to move, which is ideal for that type of character. I may have nothing but praise, but that's okay once in a while, isn't it?

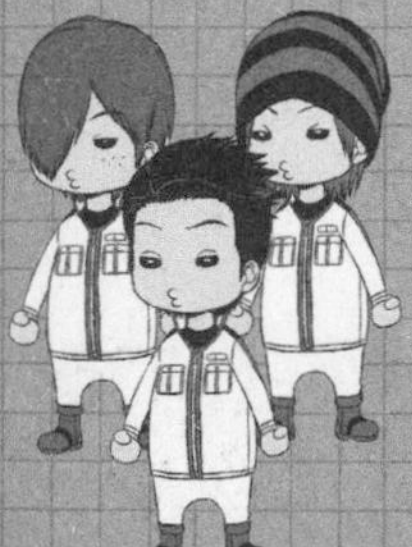

THE NEW "THREE IDIOTS"

Shimmering Youth

Consummate expendable trio of Know-it-all, Vanity and Instant Kill (killed, not killer). They're probably enjoying life at Border more than any other characters. They were insta-killed by Yuma, but otherwise they're promising new recruits, so they're actually more talented than Osamu. There may be some usurping in the future...

YOU'RE READING THE WRONG WAY!

World Trigger reads from right to left, starting in the upper-right corner. Japanese is read from right to left, meaning that action, sound effects, and word-balloon order are completely reversed from the English order.

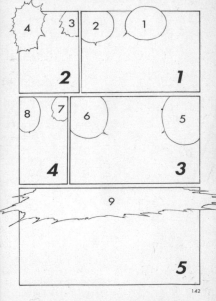